THE AFRIC
ORIGINS

BOOK I
THE AFRICAN ORIGINS
OF
AFRICAN CIVILIZATION, RELIGION, YOGA MYSTICISM
ETHICS PHILOSOPHY
AND
A HISTORY OF EGYPTIAN YOGA

Dr. Muata Abhaya Ashby
Edited by Dr. Karen Vijaya Ashby

Plates
(for color plates see the Hard Cover First Edition)

Color Plate 1: Below left – late 20th century Nubian man. Below right-Nubian Prisoners of Rameses II - Image at the Abu Simbel Temple

Color Plate 2: Bottom left-Ancient Egyptians (musicians) and Nubians (dancers) depicted in the Tombs of the Nobles with the same hue and features. Bottom right- Nubian King Taharka and the Queen offering to Amun (blue) and Mut (yellow) depicted as a red Egyptians. 7th cent BCE

Color Plate 3: Below-left, Egyptian man and woman-(tomb of Payry) 18th Dynasty displaying the naturalistic style (as people really appeared in ancient times). Below right- Egyptian man and woman-Theban tomb – displaying the colors red and yellow.

Color Plate 4: Below-left, Stele of Niptah - end of Middle Kingdom (man in red, woman in white with breasts exposed). Below right- Minoan man in red and Minoan woman in white with breasts exposed. (1400 B.C.E.).

Color Plate 5: Nubians (three figures prostrating) and Egyptians (standing figures) are depicted with the same colors of their skin of alternating black and brown -Tomb of Huy

Color Plate 6: Black and Red Pottery, Below left (A)- Painted Pottery from Mohenjodaro –Indus Valley, India[1]: Below right (B & C)- Painted Pottery from the Pre-Dynastic Period – Egypt Africa.[2]

(A)   (B)   (C)

Color Plate 7: Below left- Pottery Black and Red - from north and south India- c. 500 B.C.E. tomb at Manla Ali, Hyderabad (British Museum) – Below right- Black and Red pottery from Pre-Dynastic Egyptian burial now at Metropolitan Museum New York.
Photos by M. Ashby.

Color Plate 8 above right - Nubian depictions from Akhnaton period (1352 B.C.E-1347 B.C.E)

Color Plate 9: Ancient Egyptians and Nubians depicted in the Tomb of Rameses III

The Tomb of Seti I (1306-1290 B.C.E.-below) which comes earlier than that of Rameses III (above) shows a different depiction. Note that the same labels are used to describe the Egyptians and Nubians in the pictures of both tombs.

Color Plate 10: Ancient Egyptians and Nubians depicted in the Tomb of Seti I

Rtji Ancient Egyptian   *Ahsu* Ancient Nubian

Philip Arrhidaeus, successor of Alexander, a Greek, in depicted in Red (From the Napoleonic Expedition)

Cruzian Mystic Books / Sema Institute of Yoga

P. O. Box 570459
Miami, Florida, 33257
(305) 378-6253 Fax: (305) 378-6253

The author is available for group lectures and individual counseling. For further information contact the publisher.

Ashby, Muata
The African Origins of African Civilization, Mystic Religion, Yoga Mystical Spirituality and Ethics Philosophy ISBN: 1-884564-55-0

Library of Congress Cataloging in Publication Data

1 Comparative Religion 2 History 3 Culture, 4 Egyptian Philosophy.

Sema Institute

Website
www.Egyptianyoga.com

The Book

AFRICAN ORIGINS
OF CIVILIZATION, RELIGION AND YOGA SPIRITUALITY

is inspired by the Original Research Which Was presented in the Book

Egyptian Yoga Vol.1: The Philosophy of Enlightenment
By
Dr. Muata Ashby

1st Edition Published in 1995

With gratitude

To

Cheikh Anta Diop

An African Genius

"Today, what interests me most is to see the formation of teams, not of passive readers, but of honest, bold search workers, allergic to complacency and busy substantiating a exploring ideas expressed in our work, such as…"

"Ancient Egypt was a Negro civilization. The history of Black Africa will remain suspended in air and cannot be written correct until African historians dare to connect it with the history of Egypt In particular, the study of languages, institutions, and so forth, cannot be treated properly; in a word, it will be impossible to build African humanities, a body of African human sciences, so long as that relationship does not appear legitimate. The African historian who evades the problem of Egypt is neither modest nor objective, nor unruffled; he is ignorant, cowardly, and neurotic. Imagine, if you can, the uncomfortable position of a western historian who was to write the history of Europe without referring to Greco-Latin Antiquity and try to pass that off as a scientific approach."

"I should like to conclude by urging young American scholars of good will, both Blacks and Whites, to form university teams and to become involved, like Professor Lawrence, in the effort to confirm various ideas that I have advanced, instead of limiting themselves to a negative, sterile skepticism. They would soon be dazzled, if not blinded, by the bright light of their future discoveries. In fact, our conception of African history, as exposed here, has practically triumphed, and those who write on African history now, whether willingly or not, base themselves upon it. But the American contribution to this final phase could be decisive."

"It is evident that if starting from Nubia and Egypt, we had followed a continental geographical direction, such as Nubia-Gulf of Benin, Nubia-Congo, Nubia-Mozambique, the course of African history would still have appeared to be uninterrupted.
This is the perspective in which the African past should be viewed. So long as it is avoided, the most learned speculations will be headed for lamentable failure, for there are no fruitful speculations outside of reality. Inversely, Egyptology will stand on solid ground only when it unequivocally officially recognizes its Negro-African foundation. On the strength of the above facts and those which are to follow, we can affirm with assurance that so long as Egyptology avoids that Negro foundation, so long as it is content merely to flirt with it, as if to prove its own honesty, so long will the stability of its foundations be comparable to that of a pyramid resting on its summit; at the end of those scholarly speculations, it will still be headed down a blind alley."

-Cheikh Anta Diop July 1973
African Origins of Civilization: Myth or Reality
(Edited by Mercer Cook)

DEDICATION

To the *Shepsu* (departed venerated ancestors) and opener of the road upon which this work treads.

Chancellor Williams,
Cheikh Anta Diop,
John Henrik Clarke,
Joseph Campbell
Swami Sivananda Radha,

This book is also dedicated to all who have assisted me in the journey of life to disseminate the wisdom of the past which is so desperately needed in our times. While the list is too numerous to place here in its entirety, the following deserve special mention.

My Parents Reginald Ashby Sr. and Carmen Nieves Ashby

To my students, and all the practitioners and teachers of Indian and Kamitan Yoga around the world.

To my spiritual partner and editor as well as colleague and best friend, Dja (Karen Vijaya Ashby) without whom this project would not have reached the height of quality and concordance. She is a proficient editor but even more valuable than her editorial qualities are her sagely wisdom and knowledge of the teachings, which allow her to fill a position that no one else can. She understands and can therefore facilitate my words and thus this work has truly been a collaborative effort not unlike the creation of a new life. Such works produced by such partnerships are few in history and are therefore special and precious. May God bless her with the glory of long life with health and unobstructed happiness.

May you find this book enlightening and may it strengthen your ability to teach the wisdom of the ancients and the glorious path of life!

Table of Contents

Table of Figures

Table of Plates

List of Tables

About the Author

Who is Sebai Muata Abhaya Ashby D.D. Ph. D.?

Priest, Author, lecturer, poet, philosopher, musician, publisher, counselor and spiritual preceptor and founder of the Sema Institute-Temple of Aset, Muata Ashby was born in Brooklyn, New York City, and grew up in the Caribbean. His family is from Puerto Rico and Barbados. Displaying an interest in ancient civilizations and the Humanities, Sebai Maa began studies in the area of religion and philosophy and achieved doctorates in these areas while at the same time he began to collect his research into what would later become several books on the subject of the origins of Yoga Philosophy and practice in ancient Africa (Ancient Egypt) and also the origins of Christian Mysticism in Ancient Egypt.

Sebai Maa (Muata Abhaya Ashby) holds a Doctor of Philosophy Degree in Religion, and a Doctor of Divinity Degree in Holistic Health. He is also a Pastoral Counselor and Teacher of Yoga Philosophy and Discipline. Dr. Ashby received his Doctor of Divinity Degree from and is an adjunct faculty member of the American Institute of Holistic Theology. Dr. Ashby is a certified as a PREP Relationship Counselor. Dr. Ashby has been an independent researcher and practitioner of Egyptian Yoga, Indian Yoga, Chinese Yoga, Buddhism and mystical psychology as well as Christian Mysticism. Dr. Ashby has engaged in Post Graduate research in advanced Jnana, Bhakti and Kundalini Yogas at the Yoga Research Foundation. He has extensively studied mystical religious traditions from around the world and is an accomplished lecturer, musician, artist, poet, screenwriter, playwright and author of over 25 books on Kamitan yoga and spiritual philosophy. He is an Ordained Minister and Spiritual Counselor and also the founder the Sema Institute, a non-profit organization dedicated to spreading the wisdom of Yoga and the Ancient Egyptian mystical traditions. Further, he is the spiritual leader and head priest of the Per Aset or Temple of Aset, based in Miami, Florida. Thus, as a scholar, Dr. Muata Ashby is a teacher, lecturer and researcher. However, as a spiritual leader, his title is *Sebai,* which means Spiritual Preceptor.
Sebai Dr. Ashby began his research into the spiritual philosophy of Ancient Africa (Egypt) and India and noticed correlations in the culture and arts of the two countries. This was the catalyst for a successful book series on the subject called "Egyptian Yoga". Now he has created a series of musical compositions which explore this unique area of music from ancient Egypt and its connection to world music.

Who is Hemt Neter Dr. Karen Vijaya Clarke-Ashby?

Karen Clarke-Ashby (Seba Dja) is a Kamitan (Kamitan) priestess, and an independent researcher, practitioner and teacher of Sema (Smai) Tawi (Kamitan) and Indian Integral Yoga Systems, a Doctor of Veterinary Medicine, a Pastoral Spiritual Counselor, a Pastoral Health and Nutrition Counselor, and a Sema (Smai) Tawi Life-style Consultant." Dr. Ashby has engaged in post-graduate research in advanced Jnana, Bhakti, Karma, Raja and Kundalini Yogas at the Sema Institute of Yoga and Yoga Research Foundation, and has also worked extensively with her husband and spiritual partner, Dr. Muata Ashby, author of the Egyptian Yoga Book Series, editing many of these books, as well as studying, writing and lecturing in the area of Kamitan Yoga and Spirituality. She is a certified Tjef Neteru Sema Paut (Kamitan Yoga Exercise system) and Indian Hatha Yoga Exercise instructor, the Coordinator and Instructor for the Level 1 Teacher Certification Tjef Neteru Sema Training programs, and a teacher of health and stress management applications of the Yoga / Sema Tawi systems for modern society, based on the Kamitan and/or Indian yogic principles. Also, she is the co-author of "The Egyptian Yoga Exercise Workout Book," a contributing author for "The Kamitan Diet, Food for Body, Mind and Soul," author of the soon to be released, "Yoga Mystic Metaphors for Enlightenment."

Hotep -Peace be with you!
Seba Muata Ashby & Karen Ashby

NOTE on the use of encyclopedic and dictionary references.

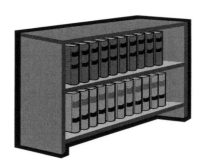

The use of encyclopedias in this book will not be for the purpose of providing proofs or to verify specific correspondences between cultures. Rather, the encyclopedia references will be provided to show the reader what the current state of established knowledge is. The sum total of modern cultural knowledge is based on the amassing of information. This information is collected into volumes. As time passes and the knowledge base changes, so too does the knowledge collection (encyclopedia). So the encyclopedic and dictionary references are provided (wherever used) to establish what the currently accepted norms of culture are, and also to provide a reference point for the reader for the study of history, culture, religion, and even philosophy. Even though a knowledge source may be faulty or incomplete, it is still necessary to begin somewhere. This reference point, tempered by our own understanding and scholarship, allows us to take on distance in our exploration and then *sankofa,* or turn back to see where we were and determine indeed where we have been and where we truly are so that we may begin to know where we are heading.

Preface

The Impetus For This Work

Over the past several years I have been asked to put together, in one volume, the most important evidences showing the ancient origins of civilization and religion in Africa, and the correlations and common teachings between Kamitan (Ancient Egyptian) culture and religion and that of India. The history of Ancient Egypt, especially in the light of the most recent archeological evidences documenting civilization and culture in Ancient Egypt and its spread to other countries, has intrigued many scholars, as well as mystics, over the years. Also, the possibility that Ancient Egyptian Priests and Priestesses and sages migrated to Greece, India and other countries to carry on the traditions of the Ancient Egyptian Mysteries has been speculated over the years as well.

In Chapter 1 of the book *Egyptian Yoga: The Philosophy of Enlightenment* (first edition 1995), I first introduced the basic comparisons between Ancient Egypt and India that had been brought forth up to that time. Now, in the year 2002, this new book, *THE AFRICAN ORIGINS of Civilization, Religion and Yoga Spirituality*, more fully explores the motifs, symbols and philosophical correlations between Ancient Egyptian and Indian mysticism and clearly shows not only that Ancient Egypt and India were connected culturally, but also spiritually. It shows that the mysteries of Ancient Egypt were essentially a yoga tradition which did not die, but rather, developed into the modern day systems of Yoga technology and mysticism of India, thus, India has a longer history and heritage than was previously understood. It further shows that African culture developed Yoga Mysticism earlier than any other civilization in history. All of this expands our understanding of the unity of culture and the deep legacy of Yoga, which stretches into the distant past, beyond the Indus Valley civilization, the earliest known high culture in India, as well as the Vedic tradition of Aryan culture. Therefore, Ancient Egyptian Yoga culture and mysticism are the oldest known traditions of spiritual development, and Indian mysticism an extension of the Ancient Egyptian tradition. By understanding the legacy which Ancient Egypt passed on to India, the mysticism of India is better understood, and also, by comprehending the heritage of Indian Yoga, rooted in Ancient Egyptian Mysticism, Ancient Egypt is also better understood. This expanded understanding allows us to prove the underlying kinship of humanity, through the common symbols, motifs and philosophies which are not disparate and confusing teachings, but in reality expressions of the same study of truth through metaphysics and mystical realization of Self. This has great importance for the Yogis and mystics who follow the philosophy of Ancient Egypt and the mysticism of India.

The origins and influences that the Ancient Egyptian religion had on world religion and philosophy is another important theme explored in this volume. We will also explore the basis of Christianity, Hinduism, Buddhism, Ancient Greek religion and Nubian religion in Ancient Egyptian religion.

The Goals of This Book and How to use This Book

This book was created to assist in the study of comparative mythology and yoga mysticism, specifically related to the Kamitan culture and spiritual systems (Neterianism) and their relationship to Indian culture and spiritual traditions coming down to modern times.

This book follows along with a 2-hour video Introduction to the Ancient Egyptian Origins of Yoga and a 12-hour video presentation entitled *African Origins of Civilization, Religion and Yoga Spirituality*, and the course *African Origins of Civilization, Religion and Philosophy* conducted at Florida International University by Dr. Muata Ashby. Also, it follows the video recording of the class conducted at Florida International University in the Spring Term 2002: Introduction to African Civilization, Religion and Philosophy. Since this book is fully referenced, it can also be used as a stand-alone text book for the study of the historical-cultural-spiritual connections between Ancient Egypt (Africa) and India as well the origins of Kamitan and Hindu religion, mythology and Yoga philosophy. The suggested method of study is to first become well grounded in the understanding of the purpose of religion, mythology and history, and the nature of culture and its manifestations. Then the items of comparison may be approached and their significance better understood in the context of this study. References for each item of comparison are provided in each section. In order to understand how the following scriptural, iconographic and archeological evidences discovered by myself or others demonstrate a connection between the seemingly different spiritual traditions, it is necessary to establish a basis for the study and comparison of religions and philosophies. This book is in no way complete, since the flow of more and more points of comparison continue to be discovered. However, the sheer magnitude of the present compilation should provide a good, broad picture of the interaction between Ancient Egypt and India. It is anticipated that there will be expanded versions of this volume in the coming years.

The purpose of this book is in many ways to build upon the work of other scholars in the area of Ancient African civilization and culture. However, these subjects are very relevant to us today because the heritage of a people plays an important role in directing those people in their present endeavors. Therefore, these studies are not entered into for the purpose of denigrating other cultures or to impose an Africentric ideal on people while excluding their achievements and struggles in the Diaspora as if any and all answers for today's problems could be found by, for example, reviving Ancient Egyptian Culture. Rather, it is enjoined for the purpose of providing a basis, a foundation for modern culture, because it has been determined that humanity is operating in accordance with an incorrect basis, a notion about history that has led it astray from the possibility of achieving a real harmony and prosperity for all human beings. In seeking a destination it is important to start a journey with the proper direction and this direction leads to the eventual discovery of the destination that was sought. A peoples direction comes from their culture and all of its elements. If the culture is damaged, as the Kenyan Social and Political Sciences researcher Ali Mazrui[1] would say, then that direction will be faulty. If the directive is erroneous the destination will elude the seeker. Likewise, without a proper basis, a proper foundation, people of African descent and all humanity will be forever searching and missing the path to peace, prosperity and enlightenment.

---

[1] *The Africans* by Ali Mazrui

Foreword

New Terms

This volume introduces new concepts for understanding the culture and philosophy of the civilization today known as "Ancient Egypt." In order to understand this subject most effectively a proper terminology more closely based on the language of Ancient Egypt has been adopted in order to more fully convey the feeling and essence of Ancient Egyptian society and tradition. The detailed explanation for the use of these terms and their origin based in the culture and tradition of Ancient Egypt will be explained throughout the book.

"Kamit"

Firstly, the term Kamit, as a name for Ancient Egypt, has received wide attention. This term rightly uses the consonant elements of the word (Kmt) since the Ancient Egyptians did not record the vowels in a way that is easy to discern. This term will be used interchangeably with the term "Ancient Egypt."

"Kamitan"

This volume will adopt the term Kamitan when referring to the country itself. This term will be used interchangeably with the term "Ancient Egyptian." The term "Kamitan" therefore replaces the term Kamitan.

"Neterianism"

When referring to the religion of Ancient Egypt itself the term "Neterianism" will be used. So this term will substitute for or be used interchangeably with the term "Ancient Egyptian Religion" or Kamitan Religion.

"Neterian"

When referring to anything related to the religion of Ancient Egypt, the term Neterian will be used interchangeably with the terms Shetaut Neter, as it relates to the Kamitan term for religion, "Shetaut Neter."

Outline of the African Origins Book Series and How to Use this present Volume

The present Volume is one in a set of three books. Each one treats one of the major aspects in the study of African history and culture. It is highly recommended that all volumes be acquired and studied although they may be approached individually especially if the reader has a particular interest in the specific subject matter of the individual volume. However, the other volumes augment and expound on the subjects of the others and together they project a wholistic understanding of each subject in relation to the others. This promotes a broader understanding of African history and culture in the context of world history and culture. The titles of the three books are:

Volume 1:

1 AFRICAN ORIGINS-BOOK The African Origins of African Civilization, Religion, Yoga Mysticism and Ethics Philosophy

Volume 2:

1 AFRICAN ORIGINS-BOOK The African Origins of Western Civilization, Religion, Yoga Mysticism and Philosophy

Volume 3:

1 AFRICAN ORIGINS-BOOK The African Origins of Eastern Civilization, Religion, Yoga Mysticism, Hinduism, Buddhism and Ethics Philosophy

Note that the three volumes of African Origins are actually parts of a massive 700 page hardbound book designed as a university text book. Each volume has the same introduction since this section is relevant to every individual volume. The table of contents of all of the volumes is included below so that the reader may have an idea of the varied sections that are treated in all of the volumes and how they interrelate with each other.

TAB OF CONTENTS FOR ALL THREE VOLUMES

BOOK 1 – PART 1
PART I: THE AFRICAN ORIGINS OF AFRICAN CIVILIZATION, RELIGION, YOGA MYSTICISM AND PHILOSOPHY

BOOK 2 – PART 2
PART II: THE AFRICAN ORIGINS OF WESTERN CIVILIZATION, RELIGION, AND PHILOSOPHY

BOOK 3 – PART 3
PART III: THE AFRICAN ORIGINS OF EASTERN CIVILIZATION, RELIGION, YOGA MYSTICISM AND ETHICS PHILOSOPHY

Book 1, Part 1	Book 2, Part 2	Book 3, Part 3
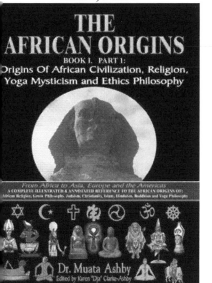	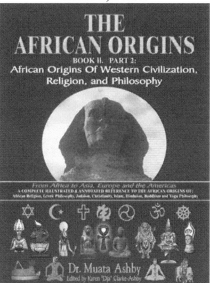	
$24.95	$24.95	$29.95

Introduction to The Study of African Origins of Civilization And Religion and Comparative Cultural and Mythological Studies

My hope is that a comparative elucidation may contribute to the perhaps not-quite desperate cause of those forces that are working in the present world for unification, not in the name of some ecclesiastical or political empire, but in the sense of human mutual understanding. As we are told in the Vedas: "Truth is one, the sages speak of it by many names."

—Joseph Campbell
June 10, 1948

As one can ascend to the top of a house by means of a ladder or a tree or a staircase or a rope, so diverse is the ways and means to approach God, and every religion in the world shows one of these ways.

—Paramahamsa Ramakrishna (1836-1886)
(Indian Sage)

There is no more important knowledge to a people than their history and culture. If they do not know this they are lost in the world.

—Cicero, Roman Philosopher (106-43 BC)

The Basis for the Study of Comparative Religions and Mythologies

This first section deals with the most important questions that will shape the context as well as the manner in which we will explore the themes presented. Therefore, it is prudent to establish, as it were, a common basis for our study, and present the parameters which we will use to conduct our study and look at evidences to determine social interrelationships and the interconnectedness of certain cultures. The following questions are vital to our study. The implications of the answers will be a prominent aspect of this first section, but will also be a central theme throughout the entire book.

Question: What is Humanity and how is the origin and history of humanity classified by scholars?

Question: What is "Culture"? What are the characteristics of culture? How important is culture in studying a people, their customs and traditions?

Question: What is "Civilization"?

Question: Where did Civilization begin?

Questions: Can the common basis of cultural expressions, concepts and doctrines between cultures be determined? If so, what are the criteria or factors to be examined and compared for such a study, and what is the methodology to be applied to those criteria to reveal their similarity or disparity? Can a scientific procedure be applied to those criteria in order to systematically arrive at a conclusive determination and thereby allow a researcher to ascertain the existence or non-existence of a relationship between the cultures, and possibly also the nature of such a relationship?

Question: If it is possible to answer the questions above might it also be possible to rediscover and perhaps even reconstruct and authentic history and description of ancient African Culture so as to repair or reconstruct African civilization, Religion and Philosophy?

The Origins of Civilization and the Classifications of Human Social Evolution

The Ancient Origins of the Human Species

Generally, human beings are regarded by science as a species of beings who evolved from primitive forms to the more advanced form, known today as *Homo Sapiens*. Homo Sapiens means "the modern species of human beings, the only extant species of the primate family Hominidae."[3] Species means "a fundamental category of taxonomic classification, ranking below a genus or subgenus and consisting of related organisms capable of interbreeding."[4] Webster's encyclopedia describes the scholarly consensus on "the origins of human species" as follows:

> Evolution of humans from ancestral primates. The African apes (gorilla and chimpanzee) are shown by anatomical and molecular comparisons to be the closest living relatives of humans. Humans are distinguished from apes by the size of their brain and jaw, their bipedalism, and their elaborate culture. Molecular studies put the date of the split between the human and African ape lines at 5–10 million years ago. There are only fragmentary remains of ape and hominid (of the human group) fossils from this period. Bones of the earliest known human ancestor, a hominid named Australopithecus ramidus 1994, were found in Ethiopia and dated as 4.4 million years old.[5]

The Stone Age period of history is that span of time regarded as being early in the development of human cultures. The Stone Age refers to the period before the use of metals. The artifacts used by people as tools and weapons were made of stone. In the discipline of archaeology, the Stone Age has been divided into the following main periods: Eolithic, Paleolithic, Mesolithic and Neolithic. The ages were experienced at different times in different geographical areas of the world in accordance with the particular culture's capacity for technological ingenuity or contact with other technologically advanced groups.

Following the Stone Age is the Metal Age. Three important ages follow which are marked by the use of metals. These are the Copper Age, Iron Age and the Bronze Age.

> **Copper Age**, or Chalcolithic Age, is the time period in which man discovered how to extract copper by heating its ore with charcoal. This art was known in the Middle East before 3500 BC. A subsequent important development was the alloying of copper with tin to produce bronze.[6]

> **Bronze Age,** period from the early fourth millennium BC onward, in which man learned to make bronze artifacts and to use the wheel and the ox-drawn plow which allowed agriculture to support a larger population. The resulting growth of technology and trade occasioned the rise of the first civilizations in Sumer and Egypt.[7] In the Bronze Age, copper and bronze became the first metals worked extensively and used for tools and weapons. It developed out of the Stone Age, preceded the Iron Age, and may be dated 5000–1200 BC in the Middle East and about 2000–500 BC in Europe. Recent discoveries in Thailand suggest that the Far East, rather than the Middle East, was the cradle of the Bronze Age.[8]

> **Iron Age,** period succeeding the Bronze Age in which man learned to smelt iron. The Hittites probably developed the first important iron industry in Armenia soon after 2000 BC. Iron's superior strength and the widespread availability of its ore caused it gradually to supersede bronze.[9]

The theories about the origins of humanity are not firm because much of the evidence of the evolutionary development of human beings has been swept away by the active nature of the planet. Volcanoes, storms, floods, etc., eventually wipe away all remnants of everything that happens on the surface of the earth as they recycle matter to bring forth life sustaining conditions again. For example, the city of Rome was buried in several feet of dust, ash and other natural particles, which eventually claimed the surface of the earth through the action of wind and other natural phenomena of planetary weather. The encroaching sands of North East Africa tend to erode and encroach on the monuments in Egypt. For example, the Sphinx enclosure can fill up and cover the Sphinx with sand due to winds and sandstorms in just 20 years. Complicating these factors is the modern urbanizing of archeological areas. People move in and actually live over important archeological sites, preventing their discovery. Also, there is the confirmed fact that entire cultures have been lost over time, leaving little more than a scarce trace of their existence. Further, new scientific evidence compels scientists to revise their estimates to account for the new findings. One important example in this subject relates to the Ancient Egyptian Sphinx, located in the area today known as Giza, in Egypt. The Great Sphinx was once known as *Horemakhet* or "Heru in the Horizon." It was later known by the Greeks as Harmachis. New discoveries show the Ancient Egyptian Sphinx to be much older than previously thought. The importance of this discovery is that it places advanced civilization first in northeast Africa (Ancient Egypt), at the time when Europe, Mesopotamia[10] and the rest of Asia were just coming out of the Paleolithic Age.

Thus, when Ancient Egyptians had already created the Sphinx monument, and its attendant massive temple and other structures that would have required multitudes of workers, food, organization, etc., the rest of the world was just beginning to learn how to practice farming and to use sleds, boats and other elementary instruments which were just being invented there. The new findings related to the Sphinx, which are supported by many ancient writings, are leading us to realize the true depths of human origins and the starting point for civilization.

Principles of Cultural Expression

What is Culture?

The concept of culture will be an extremely important if not the most important aspect of humanity to our study and so it will be a developing theme throughout our study. The following principles are offered as a standard for understanding what culture is, how it manifests in the world, and how that manifestation affects other cultures.

> **cul·ture** (kŭl′chər) *n.* **1.a.** The totality of socially transmitted behavior
>
> patterns, arts, beliefs, institutions, and all other products of human work
>
> and thought.
>
> > -American Heritage Dictionary

Purpose of Culture:

- Culture is a people's window on whatever they perceive as reality (to understand the world around them) and their concept of self.

- Culture is a conditioning process, necessary for the early development of a human being.

- Culture defines the agenda of a society (government, economics, religion). Religion is the most powerful force driving culture.

The Study of Culture

Cultural Anthropology is the study concerned with depicting the character of various cultures, and the similarities and differences between them. This branch of anthropology is concerned with all cultures whether simple or complex and its methodology entails a holistic view, field work, comparative analysis (both within the society and cross-culturally), and a tendency to base theoretical models on empirical data rather than vice versa.[11]

Ethnology, is the comparative study of cultures. Using ethnographic material from two or more societies, ethnology can attempt to cover their whole cultural range or concentrate on a single cultural trait. Ethnology was originally a term covering the whole of anthropology, toward the end of the 19th century historical ethnology was developed in an attempt to trace cultural diffusion. Now ethnologists concentrate on cross-cultural studies, using statistical methods of analysis.[12]

While this work may be considered as a form of cultural anthropology and ethnology, it will also serve as an overview of the theological principles espoused by the cultures in question. The techniques used in this book to compare cultures will lay heavy emphasis on iconographical and philosophical factors as well as historical evidences, as opposed to statistical methods of analysis. It is possible to focus on the apparent differences between cultures and religious philosophies. This has been the predominant form of philosophical discourse and study of Western scholarship. The seeming differences between religions have led to innumerable conflicts between the groups throughout history, all because of the outer expression of religion. However, throughout this work I will attempt to focus on the synchretic aspects of the philosophies and religions in question because it is in the similarities wherein harmony is to be found; harmony in the form of concurrence in ideas and meaning. In light of this idea of harmony, it is possible to look at the folklore of cultural traditions throughout the world and see the same psycho-mythological message being espoused through the various cultural masks. They are all referring to the same Supreme Being. While giving commentary and adding notes, which I feel will be helpful to the understanding of the texts which I will compare, I have endeavored to use the actual texts wherever possible so that you, the reader, may see for yourself and make your own judgment.

Culture is everything a human being learns from living in a society including language, history, values and religion, etc. However, the outer learning masks an inner experience. Spirituality is that movement to transcend culture and discover the essence of humanity. This Ultimate Truth, known by many names, such as God, Goddess, Supreme Being, and their varied names in all of the world's cultures, is revered by all peoples, though culture and folk differences color the expression of that reverence. This is what is called the *folk expression of religion based on culture and local traditions.* For example, the same Ultimate Reality is expressed by Christians based on European culture and traditions, as God. The same Ultimate Reality is expressed by Muslims based on Arab culture and traditions as Allah. The same Ultimate and Transcendental Reality is worshipped by Jews based on Hebrew culture and traditions. The same Ultimate and Transcendental Reality is worshipped by the Chinese based on Chinese culture and traditions, etc. If people who practice religion stay at the outer levels (basing their religious practice and wisdom on their culture, myths and traditions), they will always see differences between faiths. Religion has three aspects, myth, ritual and mysticism. Myth and ritual relate to the folk expression of religion, whereas mysticism relates to that movement of self-discovery that transcends all worldly concepts. Mysticism allows any person in any religion to discover that the same Supreme Being is being worshipped by all under different names and forms, and by different means. It is the worship itself and the object of that worship that underlies the human movement. Therefore, the task of all true mystics (spiritual seekers) is to go beyond the veil of the outer forms of religion, including the symbols, but more importantly, the doctrines, rituals and traditions (see model below).

Figure 1: Below: The Culture-Myth Model, showing how the folk expression of religion is based on culture and local traditions.

Figure 2: Below: The Culture-Myth Models of two world spiritual systems, showing how the folk expression of each religion is based on culture and local traditions.

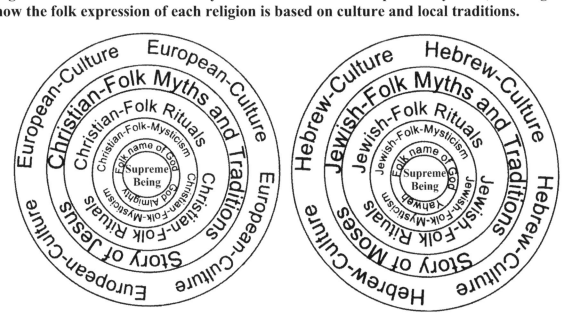

In studying and comparing diverse groups of peoples, we are essentially comparing their cultures. Culture includes all activities and manners of manifestation, which a group of peoples have developed over the period of their existence. Cultural expressions may fall under the following categories. An important theme to understand throughout this study is that the underlying principle purpose or function of culture in a given society may be equal to that of another culture, but the mode of manifestation will invariably be unique. The exception to this is when there is contact between the cultures. Some coincidental similarities may be found between two cultures that have never been in contact with each other, but the frequency and quality of those correlations belies the superficiality of the contact or random nature of the correlation. Similarities and commonalties pointing to a strong interrelationship between the cultures can be expected when comparing two apparently different cultures if the cultures in question have sustained some form of contact or emerged from a common origin. The degree of parallelism and harmony between varied cultures can be measured by the nature and frequency of synchronicity or concordance of the factors from each culture being compared.

In the study of the theology[13] of the varied religious traditions of the world (comparative religious studies), it is very possible to encounter similar general points of philosophical conceptualization in reference to the institutions for the worship of a spiritual being or divinities. In other words, religion itself is a point of commonality in all cultures and all historical periods. The basic common ideas manifested by cultures in and of themselves cannot be used as justification for concluding that there is a common origin or common cultural concept being expressed by two different religions. So just because two religions espouse the idea that there is a Supreme Being or that Supreme Being is one, a scholar cannot conclude that the religions have a common origin or that their concept in reference to the entity being worshipped is compatible. The factor of theology is there in both cultures, but the mode of expression may be different, and even if it is not different, it may have been arrived at by different means. That is, the myth-plot system of the religion may contain various episodes which are not synchronous, thus expressing a divergent theological idea even though it may ultimately lead to the same philosophical realization. The forms of iconography may show depictions of the divinities in different situations and engaged in different activities. The rituals and traditions related to the myths of the religions may be carried out in different ways and at different times. These deviating factors point to a different origin for the two cultures in question. On the other hand it is possible to have a common origin and later observe some divergence from the original expression while the theme and plot of myth within the religion stays essentially the same. This finding may not only point to a common origin, but also to a divergent practice in later times. If two traditions are shown to have been in contact, and they are found to have common elements in the basis of their espoused philosophy, as well as the manifestation of that philosophy through iconography, artifacts, rituals, traditions, myth-plots, etc., then this determination suggests a strong correlation in the origin, and or contact throughout the development of the cultures in question. In order to make such a judgment, it is necessary to identify and match several essential specific criteria or factors confirming the commonality or convergence indicating a communal[14] origin and or common cultural factor.

Table 1: Categories of Cultural Expression and Factors of Cultural Expression

Categories of Cultural Expression

1. Art: design (lay out), composition-style, and pattern
2. Artifacts - tools
3. Customs and Traditions - secular
4. Ethnicity
5. Folklore - legend
6. Form –Architecture
7. Language
8. Music and Performing arts – Theater
9. Philosophy
   a. Social
      i. Economics
      ii. Legal system
      iii. Government
10. Religion-Spirituality
    a. Myth and Mythological motif
    b. Customs and Traditions - Ritual
    c. Mystical philosophy

Factors of Cultural Expression

These categories can be correlated by matches in the following features:

Myth and Religion Related Correlation Methods

1. Gender concordance[2]
2. Iconography
   a. Conventional
   b. Naturalistic
   c. Stylized
3. Myth-
   a. Plot
   b. Motif[3]
   c. Theme
4. Rituals and or Traditions
   a. Function
   b. Actions performed
5. Scriptural Synchronicity

General Correlation Methods

1. Evidence of Contact
   a. Concurrent – cultures develop at the same time - equal exchanges relationship
   b. Dependent – one culture depends on the other for technology, instruction - Donor – recipient relationship
   c. Common Origins- Cultures originate from the same point with the same primary categories and then branch off and develop independently.
   d. Eye witness accounts
   e. Self descriptions – Their own writings acknowledge the contact.
   f. Pacts – treaties, etc.
2. Form
   a. Architecture
   b. Artifacts
3. Function – usage -purpose
   a. Architecture
   b. Artifacts
4. Grammar
   a. Phonetics
   b. Linguistics
5. Historical Events
   c. Common origins of the Genesis of the Cultures
   d. Concurrent events throughout the history of the cultures
6. Genetics
7. Nationality

---

[2] Gender of characters in the myth
[3] Myth and Mythological motif (subject matter)

Definitions of the Categories of Cultural Expression and Factors of Cultural Expression system of Cultural Anthropology

The following are general designations to describe the dominand cultures or world views being expored in this volume. These do not include all the cultures of the world.

Definition: *Western Culture* = For the purpose of this study, "Western Culture" constitutes the traditions, beliefs and productions of those people who have developed societies in the western part of the continent of Asia (Europe), and who see this part of the world as their homeland or view the world from the perspective of the traditions (including religion) and norms of that region (Eurocentric). This includes the United States of America, Canada, as well as other countries which have societies that are descendants from the European colonial rulers, and which control the governments of the former colonies (including Australia, New Zealand, etc.). Also included are countries where the political order is supported or enforced (neocolonialism or capitalistic globalism) by the Western countries. In a broad sense, Western Culture is a way of thinking that has spread far a field and now includes all who adopt the philosophies, norms and customs of that region, including secularism and religions that are predominantly Christian, followed by the Jewish and Islamic.

Definition: *Arab Culture* = For the purpose of this study, "Arab Culture" constitutes the traditions, beliefs and productions of those people who have developed societies in the south-western part of the continent of Asia (Arabia, Mesopotamia and now also north Africa), and who see this part of the world as their homeland or view the world from the perspective of the traditions (including religion) and norms of that region. In a broad sense, Arab Culture is a way of thinking that has spread far a field and now includes all who adopt the philosophies, norms and customs of that region.

Definition: *Eastern Culture* = For the purpose of this study, "Eastern Culture" constitutes the traditions, beliefs and productions of those people who have developed societies in the Eastern part of the continent of Asia (India, China) and who see this part of the world as their homeland or view the world from the perspective of the traditions (including religion) and norms of that region (Indocentric). In a broad sense, Eastern Culture is a way of thinking that includes all who adopt the philosophies, norms and customs of that region.

Definition: *African Culture* = For the purpose of this study, "African Culture" or "Southern Culture" constitutes the traditions, beliefs and productions of those people who have developed societies in the continent of Africa (Sub-Saharan countries) and who see this part of the world as their homeland or view the world from the perspective of the native traditions (including religion) and norms of that region (Africentric {Afrocentric}). In a broad sense, African Culture is a way of thinking that includes all who adopt the philosophies, norms and customs of that region.

The following definitions are the two simple keys to understanding the Categories of Cultural Expression and Factors of Cultural Expression system of Cultural Anthropology.

Definition: *Categories of Cultural Expression* = Broad areas whereby a culture expresses itself in the world. Exp. Religion is a broad category of cultural expression. All cultures may have a religion, however, those religions are not necessarily the same. What are the differences? How can these differences be classified and compared?

Definition: *Factors of Cultural Expression* = methods or means by which a culture expresses its categories. Exp. Myth is a factor of religion by which a religion is expressed in a unique way by a particular culture. In determining the common elements of different religions, there are several factors which can be used as criteria to determine whether or not cultures had common origins. If cultures are related, they will use common stories or other common factors or patterns to express the main doctrines of the religion or spiritual path, social philosophy, etc. These are listed below.

The following section introduces the categories of cultural expression as well as factors or aspects of the Categories which reflect the unique forms of manifestation within a given culture.

Linguistics

Linguistics – Spelling, grammar and script symbols
linguistics (**a.** Of or relating to the synchronic[15] typological[16] comparison of languages)

Phonetics – Sound of the words
phonetics (**2.** *The system of sounds of a particular language.*)[17]

In using linguistics as a factor for determining the common elements between two religions, the following should be noted. The existence or lack thereof of commonality in the use of language spelling or script symbols to describe objects, deities and or spiritual philosophy of a culture in and of itself cannot be used to conclude that there is or is not a common basis, origin or concept between the cultures in question. It is possible that these (language, spelling or script symbols to describe objects and deities) may have developed independently over a period of time after the initial contact; the meaning may be the same while the language developed independently.

The comparison of the phonetics as opposed to linguistics, for example, the names used to describe deities or philosophies is a better factor to compare since in ancient times, before the movements to standardize spellings and script symbols, script forms tended to change while name sounds remained more constant. The impetus in society to standardize and stabilize language only began in the 18th to the 19th centuries.[18] Therefore, it is possible to find name sounds and uses for the name that are alike in two different cultures, while their spellings or script forms may be different. Therefore, the requirement of the presence of a logical sequence of grammatical relationships between the languages of the two cultures need not be present in order to establish a relationship. The common basis in this case can be confirmed by the evidence of contact and the usage of the name and can be further confirmed by the form or gender related to the name.

Many people have been led to believe that the Kamitan language pronunciations are not certain. Modern Egyptological and linguistic scholarship has reconstituted hundreds of words by means of extrapolation from the last major manifestation of the Ancient Egyptian language, the Coptic language, as well as the Ancient Greek translations of Ancient Egyptian words. However, there has been a reluctance to look at other sources for comparison and extrapolation. The language could be even further reconstituted if even more comparative work was undertaken to study the Kamitan language in light of other African languages where there is documented evidence of contact, including those of the Dogon ethnic group of Mali, the Wolof[19] ethnic group of Senegal, and as we will see, also the Indian Bengali language. A few scholars have taken up this work in the past 44 years, but still to date there is no comprehensive work which takes all the factors into account, making them available to all Egyptologists and Indologists.

Further, the Kamitan language is special in many ways because it reflects many universal cosmic principles of sound. An example of this is the Ancient Egyptian word "*mut.*" Mut means mother and it is reflected in "mata" of the Hindu language, "madre" of Spanish, "mother" in English, etc. The "m" sound is a universal "seed sound" principle of motherhood. However, this is not an absolute rule because other words can and are used in other languages as well. The use of names in the Kamitan language is important because they act as keys to unlocking the mysteries of life, but this is true only for those initiated into the philosophy. In Kamitan philosophy, words are seen as abstract representatives of phenomenal reality. Since the mind is the only reality, and the external world only reflects a conceptualized form based on an idea in the mind of the Supreme Being, words are a higher reality when compared to the physical world. All Kamitan words are names for objects and/or concepts. In fact, in Kamitan and other mystical philosophies, Creation is viewed as a concept given a name and not an absolute, abiding reality in and of itself.

Thus, by studying the phonetic and pictorial (Kamitan language is not only phonetic, but also illustrative) etymology (the origin and development of a linguistic form) and etiology (the study of causes or origins) of names and applying the initiatic science, it is possible to decipher the mysteries of Creation by discovering the teachings embedded in the language by the Sages of Ancient Egypt.

Moreover, in the Kamitan language as in others such as the ancient Greek, Hebrew, and Sanskrit, where the pronunciations and meanings of some words are not known with certainty or at all, the meaning of many more words and terms are known with exactness. So, while a time traveler who has studied the Kamitan language in modern times might have some difficulty speaking to an Ancient Egyptian person, they would have less trouble communicating in the written form of the language. This means that the philosophy and myth can be understood even if the pronunciation of some words is uncertain. Therefore, comparisons can be made between the philosophy of the Kamitan culture and that of others. This also means that philosophy is a legitimate and viable means to compare mythologies as a factor in determining the contact and communication between cultures and their relationship, if any.

Form

> **form** *(fôrm) n. 1.a. The shape and structure of an object. b. The body or outward appearance of a person or an animal considered separately from the face or head; figure.)* [20]

The form of an object is related to its name and function. Thus, correlations based on form will often be noted in conjunction with the other related factors. As we saw earlier, language (name) is merely a symbol of concept, which is itself a representation of truth. However, the concept of something which exists at the level of the unconscious mind will be compatible even if at the conscious level of mind of people who speak different languages. Aspects of human activity such as concept, intent, desire, etc., can be alike, while the manifestation is variable. Again, if the concepts, intents, desires, etc., are alike, but there is an absence of manifestations (language, artifacts, myths, etc.) that can be compared in order to confirm this likeness at the conscious level, the case is hard to make that there is a commonality or contact between the two cultures. The specificity of form in ritual objects, architecture, artifacts, myths, etc. makes them excellent factors to compare between cultures in order to determine their synchronism or nonconformity. However, the unconscious psychological principles being conveyed through the medium of the forms of the objects, iconographies, rituals, etc. are to be compared along with the external forms used to symbolize those principles.

Architecture

ar·chi·tec·ture (är'kĭ-tĕk'chər) *n. Abbr.* **archit.**, **arch. 1.** The art and science of designing and erecting buildings. **2.** Buildings and other large structures. **3.** A style and method of design and construction.

Architecture is the conscious creation of buildings and dwellings which the culture may use to promote its existence. The implementation of architecture signifies the existence of organized culture because architecture requires the orderly and systematic application of mathematics, geometry, the organization of labor, resources, etc. Architecture invariably reflects the philosophical and/or spiritual outlook of a culture, and thus is distinctive. Some cultures have created architecture that supports war (castles, fortresses, etc.), others have created architecture that supports commerce, while others have created architecture that seeks to reflect spiritual principles. For example, Islamic architecture reflects Islamic culture and beliefs. Modern American architecture reflects modern American culture and beliefs. In the same manner, Ancient Egyptian architecture reflects Ancient Egyptian culture and beliefs, and includes art and iconography which give insights into the values and beliefs of the Ancient Egyptians that may be compared to the values and beliefs of other cultures.

Kamitan architecture exhibits one additional aspect which is not found in most cultures. In Ancient Egypt, architecture was used to express a concretized coming into being of the spiritual myth and to reflect the nature of the cosmos. This is to say, the architecture was created in such a way as to express the religious philosophy in a concrete form. For example, the placing of a winged sundisk above the Temple entrances follows the decree given by the God Djehuti in the myth of the Asarian Resurrection to do so. This factor of mythological expression in architecture is also found in other spiritual traditions.

Function – Usage

(**1.a.** *The act, manner, or amount of using; use.*)[21]

The usage of an artifact, particularly a ritual object, is important when considering their origins. There are some important artifacts which are central to the rituals of the religions and they, therefore, constitute "mythological anchors" or focal points for the practice of the religion or spiritual tradition. These objects remain constant throughout the history of the culture while items of lesser importance may come into and out of existence over periods of time, being created with the same general form and having the same ritual function. This constitutes an important key in determining the congruence of the religious traditions in question, as it may support other forms of congruent factors such as the symmetry between the myths and or plots in religious stories being compared.

Rituals and Traditions

rit·u·al (rĭch′o͞o-əl) *n.* **1.a.** The prescribed order of a religious ceremony. **b.** The body of ceremonies or rites used in a place of worship. [22]

tra·di·tion (trə-dĭsh′ən) *n.* **1.** The passing down of elements of a culture from generation to generation, especially by oral communication. **2.a.** A mode of thought or behavior followed by a people continuously from generation to generation; a custom or usage. **b.** A set of such customs and usages viewed as a coherent body of precedents influencing the present. **3.** A body of unwritten religious precepts. **4.** A time-honored practice or set of such practices.[23]

Rituals, ritual objects and traditions (implying observances, festivals, holidays, etc., related to the myths) are used as tangible symbols of the myth. Traditions, in this context, may be understood as a legacy of rituals performed at an earlier point in history and handed down to the descendants of a mythological-religious-spiritual heritage to which a particular culture adheres. As such they are instruments to facilitate the remembrance, practice and identification with the key elements of a myth. This function of rituals and traditions is more significant than just being a social link to the past generations of a culture. When the identification is advanced, the practitioner of the rituals and traditions of the myth partakes in the myth and thus becomes one with the passion of the deity of the myth and in so doing, attains a communion with that divinity. This advanced practice of rituals and traditions constitutes the third level of religion, the metaphysics or mystical level, which will be explained in the following section.

Myth and its Origins, Psychology, Spirituality, Metaphor, Language, Plot, and Theme

Since the study of myth and mythic symbolism in ancient scriptures, iconography, etc., will form an integral part of the comparison of cultures, we must first begin by gaining a deeper understanding of what myth is, and its purpose. With this understanding, we may then undertake the study of the Asarian myth, or any other mystical story, and be able to understand the psycho-spiritual implications which are being imparted.

The American Heritage Dictionary defines *Myth* as follows:

1. A traditional story presenting supernatural beings, ancestors, or heroes that serve as primordial types in a primitive view of the world.
2. A fictitious or imaginary story, person, or thing.
3. A false belief.

The American Heritage Dictionary defines *Myth* as follows:

1. A body of myths about the origin and history of a people.
2. The study of myths.

The Random House Encyclopedia defines *Myth* as follows:

Myth, a body of myths or traditional stories dealing with gods and legendary heroes. The myths of a people serves to present their world view, their explanations of natural phenomena, their religious and other beliefs. Mythological literature includes the Greek *Iliad* and *Odyssey*, the Scandinavian *Edda*, the Indian *Ramayana*, and the Babylonian *Gilgamesh*, among others. Various interpretations of myth have been made by anthropologists such as Sir James Frazer and Claude Lévi-Strauss. In literature, myth has been used as the basis for poetry, stories, plays, and other writings.

Excerpted from *Compton's Interactive Encyclopedia*:

MYTHOLOGY. The origin of the universe can be explained by modern astronomers and astrophysicists, while archaeologists and historians try to clarify the origin of human societies. In the distant past, however, before any sciences existed, the beginnings of the world and of society were explained by mythology.

The word myth is often mistakenly understood to mean fiction something that never happened, a made-up story or fanciful tale. Myth is really a way of thinking about the past. Mircea Eliade, a historian of religions, once stated: "Myths tell only of that which really happened." This does not mean that myths correctly explain what literally happened. It does suggest, however, that behind the explanation there is a reality that cannot be seen and examined.

Myth-ology is the study or science (ology) of myths and their deeper implications. In relation to mythology, the term epic is also used. The American Heritage Dictionary defines an *Epic* as:

1. A long narrative poem that celebrates episodes of a people's heroic tradition.

The Encarta/Funk & Wagnall's Encyclopedia defines an Epic as:

"A long narrative poem, majestic both in theme and style. Epics deal with legendary or historical events of national or universal significance, involving action of broad sweep and grandeur. Most epics deal with the exploits of a single individual, thereby giving unity to the composition. Typically, an epic involves the introduction of supernatural forces that shape the action, conflict in the form of battles or other physical combat, and certain stylistic conventions: an invocation to the Muse, a formal statement of the theme, long lists of the protagonists involved, and set speeches couched in elevated language. Commonplace details of everyday life may appear, but they serve as background for the story, and are described in the same lofty style as the rest of the poem."

These definitions have been included here to give a reference as to what society at large, especially in the West, has accepted as the definition and purpose of mythological and epic literature. Now we will explore the initiatic-yogic-mystical meaning of *Myth*. First however, one more definition is required. We need to understand what is a *Metaphor*. The American Heritage Dictionary defines *Metaphor* as follows:

"A figure of speech in which a term that ordinarily designates an object or idea is used to designate a dissimilar object or idea in order to suggest comparison or analogy, as in the phrase *evening of life*."

The Universal Vision of Comparative Mythology

In the book *Comparative Mythology,* the author, Jaan Puhvel, traces the term "myth" to the writings of Homer (900 B.C.E.), with the usage *épos kai muthos* 'word and speech.' In the writings of Homer and the ancient Greek writers of tragic plays, Jaan Puhvel also sees that the term can mean "tale, story, narrative," and that this story or tale can be without reference to truth content.[24] Truth content here implies a historical or real relationship to time and space events or realities. In the writings of the later Greek authors such as Herodotus, Puhvel sees a different meaning in the term Mûthos, that of fictive "narrative," "tall tale," and "legend." It is felt that Herodotus spoke of Mûthos as those items he himself found incredulous, and used the term *logos* for that information which he felt was more or less based on truth or facts. Further, with the writings of Plato, a new interpretation of the terms emerge, as Mûthos takes on a different character in relation to logos. Mûthos (myth) is more of a non-rational basis for understanding existence while logos is seen as the rational basis. In Western Culture, the term logos has come to be associated with absolute knowledge and logical thinking and analysis. In terms of mysticism, it is understood as the Divine intelligence, consciousness, which permeates and enlivens matter, time and space. In later times logos came to be known as 'the Word' or inner, esoteric spiritual knowledge, and in early Christianity, Jesus became 'the word (logos) made flesh.' From these origins and many deprecating arguments from the church and western scientists, through the middle and dark ages and into the renaissance period of Western Culture, the meaning of the word, myth, in modern times, has come to be understood primarily in Western Culture as a colloquialism to refer to anything devoid of a basis in truth or reality. Saying "it's a myth" has come to be understood by most people as a reference to something that does not contain even a fragment of truth. Myth has come to be thought of in terms of being neurotic expressions of ancient religions, movie ideas spinning out of Hollywood, governments telling myths (lies) or Madison Avenue advertising (the "myth-makers"), etc., in other words, something without any truth or factual basis. In ancient times, Plato referred to the term 'mythologia' as meaning "myth-telling," as opposed to storytelling. Modern scholars refer to this term as mythology (the study of myth), which, until recently, primarily meant Greek Mythology. The body of ancient Greek narratives relating to the legends and traditions connected to the gods and goddesses of Greece are referred to as the mythological narratives.

Mythology is the study of myths. Myths (mythos) are stories which relate human consciousness to the transcendental essence of reality. This work is essentially a study in comparative mythology. It seeks to discover the common elements in two or more systems of mythos in order to understand their deeper meaning and develop the larger picture as they are fitted into the overall patchwork of traditions throughout history. In effect, this work attempts to show a connection and continuity between traditions that will enable the comprehension of them as a flow of the one primordial and recurrent theme of self-discovery. In such a study, there are always some who object, maintaining that differences are the overriding defining factors in any aspect of life. But this way of thinking is incongruous in the face of all the scientific evidence pointing to a common origin for all humanity as well as of Creation itself. Therefore, it seems that the movement to understand our common bonds as human beings should as well move into to the arena of the mythology and psychology. In this manner we may discover that what binds us is greater than that which tears us apart, for when we examine the arguments and concepts used to separate, they are inevitably derived from emotion, politics, misconception or superficialities based on ignorance. These lead to major controversies, debates, refutations and egoistic opinions founded on nothing but faith in rumors, conjectures and speculation, and not on first hand examination of the traditions from the point of view of a practitioner. Joseph Campbell summed up this issue as follows.

"Perhaps it will be objected that in bringing out the correspondences I have overlooked the differences between the various Oriental and Occidental, modern, ancient, and primitive traditions. The same objection might be brought, however, against any textbook or chart of anatomy, where the physiological variations of race are disregarded in the interest of a basic general understanding of the human physique. There are of course differences between the numerous mythologies and religions of mankind, but this is a book about the similarities; and once these are understood the differences will be found to be much less great than is popularly (and politically) supposed. My hope is that a comparative elucidation may contribute to the perhaps not-quite desperate cause of those forces that are working in the present world for unification, not in the name of some ecclesiastical or political empire, but in the sense of human mutual understanding. As we are told in the Vedas: "Truth is one, the sages speak of it by many names."

J.C.
New York City
June 10, 1948

In *Comparative Mythology,* Puhvel underscored the importance of myth and the operation of myth as an integral, organic component of human existence. It is a defining aspect of social order in which human existence is guided to discover the "sacred" and "timeless" nature of self and Creation. He also discusses how the "historical landscape" becomes "littered with the husks of desiccated myths" even as "societies pass and religious systems change," remaining submerged in the traditions and epics of modern times.

"Myth in the technical sense is a serious object of study, because true myth is by definition deadly serious to its originating environment. In myth are expressed the thought patterns by which a group formulates self-cognition and self-realization, attains self-knowledge and self-confidence, explains its own source and being and that of its surroundings, and sometimes tries to chart its destinies. By myth man has lived, died, and-all too often-killed. Myth operates by bringing a sacred (and hence essentially and paradoxically "timeless") past to bear preemptively on the present and inferentially on the future ("as it was in the beginning, is now, and ever shall be"). Yet in the course of human events societies pass and religious systems change; the historical landscape gets littered with the husks of desiccated myths. These are valuable nonmaterial fossils of mankind's recorded history, especially if still embedded in layers of embalmed religion, as part of a stratum of tradition complete with cult, liturgy, and ritual. Yet equally important is the next level of transmission, in which the sacred narrative has already been secularized, myth has been turned into saga, sacred time into heroic past, gods into heroes, and mythical action into "historical" plot. Many genuine "national epics" constitute repositories of tradition where the mythical underpinnings have been submerged via such literary transposition. Old chronicles can turn out to be "prose epics" where the probing modem mythologist can uncover otherwise lost mythical traditions. Such survival is quite apart from, or wholly incidental to, the conscious exploitative use of myth in literature, as raw material of fiction, something that Western civilization has practiced since artful verbal creativity began."[25]

The key element in myth is its metaphorical purpose in that its stories and characters are designed to provide a reference towards an etiological, moral or spiritual message that transcends the story itself. This means that there is an exoteric meaning which refers to the events and circumstances in the story, which may or may not have a basis in fact, and also an esoteric or mystical meaning which refers to a deeper teaching or message which transcends the boundaries of the events in the story. This message is spiritual in nature when the myth is religious. Through the myth many ideas which are not easily explained in rational, logical terms can be freely explored and elucidated in imaginative and colorful ways. Mystical myths are particularly important because their purpose is to point to where the answers to the most important questions of every individual may be found. Everyone is searching for answers to questions like "Who am I really?" "Is this all that I am?" "Where do I come from?" "What is death?" and "What is my purpose in life?" Through myths, the teachings of Sages and Saints can take full flight, free of the constraints of normal grammatical or thematic boundaries. Therefore, myths are an ideal way to impart spiritual truths which transcend ordinary human experiences and ordinary human concepts of rationality.

The question of the similarities between myths, rituals and traditions has been explored in the book *"The Mythic Image,"* where the late world renowned mythologist, Joseph Campbell explained the concepts surrounding the treatment of equivalent elements and symbols that can be seen in myths from apparently separate cultures.

One explanation that has been proposed to account for the appearance of homologous structures and often even identical motifs in the myths and rites of widely separate cultures is psychological: namely, to cite a formula of James G. Frazer in *The Golden Bough,* that such occurrences are most likely *"the effect of similar causes acting alike on the similar constitution of the human mind in different countries and under different skies."*

There are, however, instances that cannot be accounted for in this way, and then suggest the need for another interpretation: for example, in India the number of years assigned to an eon[26] is 4,320,000; whereas in the Icelandic *Poetic Edda* it is declared that in Othin's warrior hall, Valhall, there are 540 doors, through each of which, on the "day of the war of the wolf,"[27] 800 battle-ready warriors will pass to engage the antigods in combat.' But 540 times 800 equals 432,000!

Moreover, a Chaldean[28] priest, Berossos, writing in Greek ca. 289 B.C., reported that according to Mesopotamian belief 432,000 years elapsed between the crowning of the first earthly king and the coming of the deluge.

No one, I should think, would wish to argue that these figures could have arisen independently in India, Iceland, and Babylon.[29]

Campbell explains that there is a view that the commonalties observed in myth, symbolism, etc., are a factor of psychological forces that are common to all human beings. One example of this concept is that every human being on earth feels the desire for happiness. Therefore, when we see people from different places (*"different countries and under different skies"*), who have never met each other, pursuing happiness in similar ways, we should not be surprised. However, Campbell makes the point that some coincidences go beyond the nature of conformity due to a primal urge. Those concurrences can only be explained by a closer relationship, because the uniformity of "structure" or configuration of the myths as well as the usage of the exact same symbols and rites could only occur when there is an intimate relationship between the cultures. In other words, the two pursuers of happiness can be explained by the theory of common urges, however, the pursuit of happiness using the same procedures (rites or rituals), the same way of defining happiness, the same philosophy of how to go about looking for happiness, idealizing happiness in the same way (myth), representing happiness the same way (symbolism), etc., are signs that the cultures have had a common origin, upbringing, socialization, indoctrination, contact, etc. This occurs when a culture "diffuses" some new technology, philosophy or cultural element to another culture. Campbell continues:

A second approach to interpretation has therefore been proposed, based on the observation that at certain identifiable times, in identifiable places, epochal transformations of culture have occurred, the effects of which have been diffused to the quarters of the earth; and that along with these there have traveled constellations of associated mythological systems and motifs.[30]

Thus, Campbell introduces another way to understand the commonalties observed in separate cultures that cannot be explained by the theory of similar forces operating on the minds of separate individuals. There are milestones in history wherein major social events or advancements in culture affect humanity as if like a ripple of water caused by a stone being dropped into a calm lake. The resulting undulations of powerful concepts, and technologies move along the trade and communication routs, the arteries of human communication and interaction, spreading (diffusing) the advanced knowledge in waves across the cultural ocean of humanity throughout the world. Like a surfer, being carried along with the force of the wave, so too the concepts and symbols move across the human landscape being empowered by the innate human desire to achieve higher understanding and the intellectual capacity to recognize something better or a new way to express the same treasured truths. This important principle related to the transference of ideas and symbols between cultures was seminal to Campbell's groundbreaking work as a teacher of comparative mythology in the West.

Psychomythology

Mystical teaching holds that the essence of Creation and therefore, of each individual human being, is transcendental; it transcends the ordinary bounds of mental perception and understanding. However, all human experiences occur in and through the mind. Therefore, the heart of all human experiences, be they painful or pleasurable, is rooted in the mind. The purpose of myth is to bridge the gap between the limited human mind and its conscious, worldly level and that which transcends all physicality as well as the mind and senses. Thus, religious myths, which will be our primary focus in this volume, must be understood in the light of their psychological and mystical (transcending body, mind and senses) implications. We will refer to this concept by a new term: *"Psycho-Mythology."*

So the term *"psycho,"* as it is used here, must be understood as far more than simply that which refers to the mind in the worldly sense. The term "psycho" must be understood to mean everything that constitutes human consciousness in all of its stages and states, but most importantly, the subconscious and unconscious levels of mind. *"Mythology"* here refers to the study of the codes, messages, ideas, directives, stories, culture, beliefs, etc., that affect the personality through the conscious, subconscious and unconscious aspects of the mind of an individual, specifically those effects which result in psycho-spiritual transformation, that is, a transpersonal or transcendental change in the personality of an individual which leads to the discovery of the transcendental reality behind all existence.

A myth should never be understood literally even though some of its origins may involve actual events or actions, otherwise one will miss the transcendental message being related through the metaphor. This would be like going to a theater to see a fictional movie or reading a fantasy novel, and believing it to be real. However, as a movie or novel may be based on unreal events and yet carry an important message which is imparted through the medium of actors, a plot and so on, mystical myths are not to be understood as being completely baseless nor as having been put together purely for entertainment or as "primitive mumbo-jumbo." Myths constitute a symbolic language that speaks to people in psycho-symbolic ways, satisfying their conscious need for entertainment, but also affecting the subconscious and unconscious mind and its need for spiritual evolution. This psychological language of myths can lead people to understand and experience the transcendental truths of existence, which cannot be easily expressed in words.

Myth is the first stage of religion and the reenactment of the myth constitutes the second level religion: Ritual.[31] Myths constitute the heart and soul of rituals. Myth is a mystical language for transmitting and teaching the principles of life and creation. Rituals are the medium through which the myths are practiced, lived and realized.

The study of religious mythical stories is important to gain insight into the *"Psycho-Mythology"* or psychological implications of myth for the spiritual transformation of the individual which leads to the attainment of Enlightenment. Enlightenment implies the attainment of an expanded state of consciousness, termed as *"awet ab,"* dilation (expansion) of the heart in Ancient Egyptian Mystical Philosophy, in which there is a full and perfect awareness of one's existence beyond the mind and body. Thus, when you delve into a myth, you must expect more than just entertainment. You should be equipped with the knowledge which will allow you to decipher the hidden meanings in the story so that you may also begin to experience and benefit from them on a personal level, i.e. live the myth and on a spiritual level, i.e. attain enlightenment. Only then will a person be able to engender a real transformation in their life which will lead you to true fulfillment and happiness as well as contentment. This is the third level of religious practice, the mystical or metaphysical level.

The Keys to Reading and Understanding a Myth

> *Religion without myth not only fails to work, it also fails to offer man the promise of unity with the transpersonal and eternal.*
>
> —C. G. Jung (1875-1961)

Key #1: Myths (Religious/Mystical) are relevant to our lives in the present.

The first and most important key to understanding a myth is comprehending that the myth is not talking about some ancient personality or story which occurred a long time ago and which has no relevance to the present. In fact, the myth is speaking about you. It is a story about human life, its origins, its destiny, its plight and the correct action, in the present, which is based on the same principles of the past, for leading a truly successful life which paves the way to Enlightenment and true happiness.

Key #2: Myth is a journey of spiritual transformation.

The second key to understanding a myth is comprehending that it is usually written in the form of a journey in which the subject must learn about himself or herself and transcend the ordinary human consciousness, thereby discovering a greater essence of self. In this movement there are experiences of happiness, sorrow, struggle and learning. It is a movement from ignorance and darkness towards light, wisdom and ultimately, to spiritual Enlightenment.

Key #3: Myths are to be lived in order to understand their true meaning.

The third key to understanding a myth is that comprehension comes from living the myth. Living a myth does not mean simply reading a myth, being able to recount the events with perfect memory or simply practicing the rituals of a myth without a deeper understanding of their implications and purpose. It means making the essence of the teaching being conveyed through the myth an integral part of your life. If this practice is not implemented, the teachings remain at the intellectual level and the deeper truths of the myth are not revealed. One lives with dry intellectualism or blind faith, the former leading to a superficial and therefore frustrated spiritual life, and the latter leading to dogmatism and emotional frustration. Therefore, you must resolve to discover the myth in every facet of your life, and in so doing, you will be triumphant as the hero(ine) of the myth.

Key #4: Myth points the way to victory in life.

Myths show us our heritage as a culture as well as the legacy we are to receive. They give human beings a place in the scheme of things as well as a purpose in life and the means to achieve the fulfillment of that purpose. The ultimate purpose is to achieve victory in the battle of life, to defeat the forces of ignorance within oneself which lead to adversity and frustration and thereby become masters of life here and hereafter, discovering undifferentiated peace, love and joy...Enlightenment.

> "God is a metaphor for a mystery that transcends all human categories of thought...It depends on how much you want to think about it, whether or not it's doing you any good, whether it's putting you in touch with the mystery which is the ground of your own being."
>
> —Joseph Campbell

Thus, when comparing the myths of different cultures for the purpose of religious studies, it is necessary to understand their respective metaphorical aspects as well as their attendant underlying philosophies along with their apparent iconographical form and artistic intent (naturalistic[4] or stylized[5]).

Other Aspects of Myth

Plot refers to the plan of events or main story in a narrative or drama.[32] The synchronicity in the situations presented in myths can be used as a factor in discerning the communal nature of two myths. This congruence must be specific, involving characters of similar age group, gender and genealogy or provenance, experiencing similar situations in the same or similar ways.

In comparing myths, there are several important concerns. The purpose of myth, the language of myth and the levels of myth must be understood prior to making a comparison. *Myth is a language*[33] by which sages and saints transmit the basic elements of culture through a "common story" for all within the culture to believe in as well as draw answers to the basic questions of life such as, Where do I come from?, To which group do I belong? What is the purpose of life? and How do I fulfill that purpose? This is all conveyed through the story, plot and theme of the myth and their inherent teachings of social order as well as their spiritual morals.

Most religions and spiritual philosophies tend to be *deistic* at the elementary levels. **Deism**, as a religious belief or form of theism (belief in the existence of a Supreme Being or gods) holds that the Supreme Being's action was restricted to an initial act of creation, after which He/She retired (separated) to contemplate the majesty of His/Her work. Deists hold that the natural creation is regulated by laws put in place by the Supreme Being at the time of creation which are inscribed with perfect moral principles. Therefore, deism is closely related to the exoteric or personal but also outer (phenomenal) and dogmatic and conventional understanding of the Divinity.

> Two approaches to myth dominate the intellectual landscape during the first half of the twentieth century: the ritualistic and the psychoanalytic. The former, epitomized by the "myth and ritual" or Cambridge school beholden to the Oxonian E. B. Tylor's *Primitive Culture* (1871) and with James G. Frazer's *Golden Bough* as its central talisman, owes its theoretical underpinnings to Jane E. Harrison's *Prolegomena to the Study of Greek Religion* (1903) and *Themis* (1912). Harrison provided a strikingly simple and exclusionary definition of myth: myth is nothing but the verbalization of ritual, "the spoken correlative of the acted rite" *(Themis,* P. 328), *ta legomena* 'what is said'

---

[4] Imitating or producing the effect or appearance of nature.

[5] To restrict or make conform to a particular style. **2.** To represent conventionally; conventionalize.

accompanying *ta dromena* 'what is being done', myth and ritual being accordingly but two sides of the same religious coin; thus in principle there can be no myth without ritual, although time may have obliterated the act and left the narrative free to survive as myth or its debased subspecies (saga, legend, folktale, etc.). [34]

An assumption adopted by many comparative mythology scholars is the idea that myth is a means of explaining ritual. This idea is often predicated upon the concept that "primitive" cultures developed myth as a means of coping with the mysteries of life and Creation due to the lack of "scientific" knowledge. In the absence of science, ritual and superstition were substituted in order to allay the fears caused by the unknown. Further, this theory therefore holds that myth developed as an emanation of the actions of the practitioners of the rituals to justify those rituals. While this point of view is accurate with respect to certain cultures whose practitioners who are ignorant as to the reason behind the rituals of their religion, it is wholly incorrect when considering cultures possessing mystical philosophy. In those cultures the sacred writings of their religions present models of rituals as expressions of myth, and myth as expressions of philosophy or mysticism. Ritual is therefore a means to understand myth, and the realization of myth is a means to attain spiritual enlightenment. The erroneous concept is evident not only in modern scholarship, but also in ancient cultures which adopted symbols and myths from other cultures without fully understanding their purpose or the philosophy behind them. The following example given by Count Goblet D' Alviella provides an insight into the process called "iconological mythology."

> Sometimes, in similar cases, the new owners of the image will endeavor to explain it by a more or less ingenious interpretation, and in this manner they will restore to it a symbolical import, though applied to a new conception.
>
> The rising sun has often been compared to a new-born child. Amongst the Egyptians, this comparison led to Horus being represented as an infant sucking its finger. The Greeks imagined that he placed his finger on his lips to enjoin secrecy on the initiated, and they made him the image of Harpocrates, the god of silence. [35]
>
> This is what M. Clermont-Ganneau has very happily termed *iconological mythology*; it is here no longer the myth which gives rise to the image, but the image which gives rise to the myth.
>
> We may further quote, as an interpretation of the same kind, the legend related by Hygin, which made the Caduceus originate in Hermes throwing his wand between two serpents fighting. It is evident that, here also, this hypothesis, soon to be transformed into a myth by the popular imagination, was due to a desire, unconscious perhaps, to explain the Caduceus.
>
> Most frequently it is a conception pre-existent in the local traditions which we think we find amongst the products of foreign imagery. [36]

Another case in point is the relationship between Ancient Egypt and Greece. The Greeks adopted what they could understand of Ancient Egyptian philosophy, but did not adopt the culture or social philosophy. The Greeks made some changes in what they learned. Therefore, Greek culture cannot be claimed as an African (Ancient Egyptian) heritage. The problem was so severe that the Sages of Ancient Egypt felt the need to reprimand and denounce the Greek distortions. They indicted Greek culture as the culprit leading to the way of speech (communication and relation) which was of a "loose," "disdainful" and "confusing" character.

"The Greek tongue is a noise of words, a language of argument and confusion."

"Keep this teaching from translation in order that such mighty Mysteries might not come to the Greeks and to the disdainful speech of Greece, with all its looseness and its surface beauty, taking all the strength out of the solemn and the strong - the energetic speech of Names."

"Unto those who come across these words, their composition will seem most simple and clear; but on the contrary, as this is unclear, and has the true meaning of its words concealed, it will be still unclear, when, afterwards, the Greeks will want to turn our tongue into their own - for this will be a very great distorting and obscuring of even what has heretofore been written. Turned into our own native tongue, the teachings keepeth clear the meaning of the words. For that its very quality of sound, the very power of Kamitan names, have in themselves the bringing into act of what is said."

Myth in Orthodox Religion

Myth ⇢ Ritual ⇢ Mysticism

As previously discussed, in its complete form, religion is composed of three aspects, *mythological, ritual* and *metaphysical* or the *mystical experience* (mysticism - mystical philosophy). Mystical philosophy is the basis of myth. It is expressed in ritual and experienced in the metaphysics (spiritual disciplines, yoga) of the given religion. While many religions contain rituals, traditions, metaphors and myths, there are few professionals trained in understanding their deeper aspects and psychological implications (metaphysics and mystical). Thus, there is disappointment, frustration and disillusionment among many followers as well as leaders within many religions, particularly in the Western Hemisphere, because it is difficult to evolve spiritually without the proper spiritual guidance. Through introspection and spiritual research, it is possible to discover mythological vistas within religion which can rekindle the light of spirituality and at the same time increase the possibility of gaining a fuller experience of life. The exoteric (outer, ritualistic) forms of religion with which most people are familiar is only the tip of an iceberg so to speak; it is only a beginning, an invitation or prompting to seek a deeper (esoteric) discovery of the transcendental truths of existence.

While on the surface it seems that there are many differences between the philosophies, upon closer reflection there is only one major division, that of belief (theist) or non-belief (atheist). Among the believers there are differences of opinion as to how to believe. This is the source of all the trouble between religions and spiritual groups. One reason for this is because ordinary religion is deistic, based on traditions and customs which are themselves based on culture. Since culture varies from place to place and from one time in history to another, there will always be some variation in spiritual traditions. These differences will occur not only between cultures but also even within the same culture. An example of this is orthodox Christianity with its myriad of denominations and fundamental changes over the period of its existence.

Doctrine	Early church doctrine	Later church doctrine
Who is Jesus Christ?	Savior	Son of God
When is Christ returning?	any day now	nobody knows for certain
What is the Christian church?	group of those who are preparing for Christs return	those receiving the message of Christianity
Who can be part of the church?	only Jews	Gentiles as well as Jews
What is the proper way of Christian worship?	in Synagogues and Jewish temple services	the Christian church and the Christian rituals

Later we will see the changes within Indian religion, which are in many ways even more startling. Therefore, those who cling to the idea that religion has to be related to a particular culture and its specific practices or rituals will always have some difference with someone else's conception. This point of view may be considered as "dogmatic" [37] or "orthodox." [38] In the three stages of religion, Myth, Ritual and Mysticism, culture belongs to the myth and ritual stages of religious practice, the most elementary levels.

An important theme, which will be developed throughout this volume, is the understanding of complete religion, that is, in its three aspects, *mythological, ritual* and *metaphysical* or the *mystical experience*. At the first level, a human being learns the stories and traditions of the religion. At the second level, rituals are learned and practiced. At the third level the practitioner, now called a spiritual aspirant, is led to actually go beyond myths and rituals and to attain the ultimate goal of religion. This is an important principle, because many religions present different aspects of philosophy at different levels, and an uninformed onlooker may label it as primitive or idolatrous, etc., without understanding what is going on.

For example, Hinduism[39] and Ancient Egyptian religion present polytheism and duality at the first two levels of religious practice. However, at the third level, mysticism, the practitioner is made to understand that all of the gods and goddesses being worshipped do not exist in fact, but are in reality aspects of the single, transcendental Supreme Self. This means that at the mystical level of religious practice the concept of religion and its attendant symbols must also be left behind, that is to say, transcended. The mystical disciplines constitute the technology or means by which the myth and ritual of religion, and the spiritual philosophy can be developed to its highest level.

In contrast, orthodox religions present images as if they are in fact mundane realities as well as transcendental reality. By definition, idolatry is the presentation of an image of the divine as if it is a reality. Therefore, orthodox traditions are the true idolaters and mystical religions, since they do not ascribe absolute or abiding qualities to their images, are not idolatrous.

Myth: The Fluid Language of the Unconscious Mind

Myth is a fluid language. It is the language of concepts, which are represented through the symbols, themes, legends, traditions, heritage and philosophy contained in the myth. Myths are representations of the higher transcendental spiritual experience. These representations are manifestations of intuitional truths that are mirrored in the unconscious mind as the transcendent spirit projects into time and space. As it relates to something otherworldly, the language of myth is necessarily free from the encumbrance of historicity, race, politics, economics, gender, or even culture. Thus, the cultural manifestation of spiritual concepts are not the meaning or essence of the myth, but rather its mode of manifestation within that particular culture. Accordingly, myth is highly interchangeable in a way that the written word is not. This is why concepts are more easily communicated between people who speak a different language than translated words; concept is closer to reality than words. The more a concept is concretized, codified, interpreted as historical events or made into dogmatic teachings and imposed on culture, their power to communicate the transcendental nature of self is subverted. Then myth becomes a whipping tool to use against political, religious or social enemies. At this level, true religion cannot be practiced. The myth degrades to the level of dogmatism which expresses as narrow-mindedness, social pride, nationalism, sexism, prejudice, intolerance, and racism. Consequently, it is important and at times, a matter of life (peace) and death (war), to understand the deeper psychological and spiritual nature and purpose of myth.

The philosophy of spiritual transcendence and Enlightenment through mythic living did not begin with the dawn of the Dynastic Period in Ancient Egyptian history. The evidence from ancient texts and the History of Manetho show that the Ancient Egyptian history which is known and written about in modern times is only the descendent of a much more ancient era of Kamitan civilization which began many thousands of years before the dynastic era. The Ancient Egyptian sages recognized that the concept of a Supreme Being cannot be circumscribed by one image or symbol and thus, many were used, but also the symbols of other peoples were recognized and respected as manifestations of that same reality.

Cultural Interactions, Their Effect on the Emergence of New Religions and The Adoption of Myths, Symbols and Traditions from one Culture to Another

How Do Cultures Interact?

How do people from different cultures interact? How do religions borrow and or adopt myths, symbols, philosophies or traditions from each other? Several examples from history will be used here to show how spirituality, as an aspect of one culture, was influenced by other cultures. The following essays relate documented historical accounts of cultural interactions of the past between two or more civilizations. They are included to illustrate how the process of cultural interaction leads to cultural exchanges, adoptions, inculturations, etc., as well as the emergence of new religions and philosophies out of teachings received from other cultures. They will also serve to provide insight into the manner in which ancient African history has diffused into present day cultures by introducing various basic principles of cultural interaction and how these interactions are to be recognized and studied.

Cultural Interactions Between Christianity and Neterian Religion and Mysticism

In the case of Christianity it has been amply shown that several factors present in Ancient Egyptian Religion were adopted directly as the Christian religion developed in Egypt and the land of Canaan (now known as Palestine). In fact the church itself admits this as the late mythologist Joseph Campbell relates in an interview with Bill Moyers.[40] (Note: Highlighted portions are by Ashby)

M O Y E R S: If we go back into antiquity, do we find images of the Madonna as the mother of the savior child?

CAMPBELL: The antique model for the Madonna, actually, is Isis with Horus at her breast.

MOYERS: Isis?

CAMPBELL: In Egyptian iconography, Isis represents the throne. The Pharaoh sits on the throne, which is Isis, as a child on its mother's lap.[41] And so, when you stand before the cathedral of Chartres, you will see over one of the portals of the western front an image of the Madonna as the throne upon which the child Jesus sits and blesses the world as its emperor. That is precisely the image that has come down to us from most ancient Egypt. *The early fathers and the early artists took over these images intentionally.*

MOYERS: The Christian fathers took the image of Isis?

CAMPBELL: Definitely. They say so themselves. Read the text where it is declared that *"those forms which were merely mythological forms in the past are now actual and incarnate in our Savior."* The mythologies here referred to were of the dead and resurrected god: Attis, Adonis, Gilgamesh, Osiris,[42] one after the other. The death and resurrection of the god is everywhere associated with the moon, which dies and is resurrected every month. It is for two nights, or three days dark, and we have Christ for two nights, or three days in the tomb.

No one knows what the actual date of the birth of Jesus might have been, but it has been put on what used to be the date of the winter solstice, December 25,[43] when the nights begin to be shorter and the days longer. That is the moment of the rebirth of light. That was exactly the date of the birth of the Persian God of light, Mithra, Sol, the Sun.

Along with the iconographies, symbols and rituals mentioned above, Christianity adopted many other aspects of the Neterian Religion such as the Ankh-cross symbol, the anointing, the resurrection, the mutilation of the savior, the triune nature of the spirit (The Trinity), the Eucharist, as well as other symbols, motifs and teachings. [44] When the Roman Emperor Justinian closed the Neo-Platonic academies in 529 A.C.E. along with other spiritual and religious institutions which were considered by him to be cult or pagan systems, such as that of the Ancient Egyptian goddess Aset (Isis), Orthodox Christianity was closing its doors on the last links to the mystical philosophy of the traditions from which they had adopted so much. This led to a situation wherein the esoteric meanings of many symbols and metaphysical teachings were lost. Still, their subtle influences on Christianity persisted through medieval times and continued into the present because in order to be accepted, the Orthodox Church had to adopt many customs and symbols of other religions. The remnants of the Ancient Egyptian and other traditions of the past are still inherent in modern Orthodox Christianity as it is practiced today. The Christian church co-opted the customs and traditions of other religions in order to be able to convince the followers of the other religions that Christianity had those symbols and customs previous to their "pagan" religions, and therefore, they should abandon their religions in favor of the only "true" and "original" religion, Orthodox Christianity.

The evidence given by the Christian tradition and its documents suggests that many icons such as the images of the Madonna and child (Mary and Jesus) were taken as is during the early years of Christianity, renamed (rededicated as it were) and used in Christian worship. This practice may be described as *inculturation*,[45] also known as *co-optation*.[46] These terms relate to the process of adopting symbols, traditions and rituals from other religions and calling them Christian, which were officially confirmed and endorsed as church policy. It is a practice that continues to be a means by which the church, as well as other groups, seek to expand their beliefs internationally. This process was instituted in the time of the early development of the Christian church. A prime example of inculturation is seen in the actions of Pope St Gregory the Great, who in a letter given to priests written in 601 A.C.E. endorsed this strategy as a means to attract followers from other spiritual traditions. He writes:

> "It is said that the men of this nation are accustomed to sacrificing oxen. It is necessary that this custom be converted into a Christian rite. On the day of the dedication of the [pagan] temples thus changed into churches, and similarly for the festivals of the saints, whose relics will be placed there, you should allow them, as in the past, to build structures of foliage around these same churches. They shall bring to the churches their animals, and kill them, no longer as offerings to the devil, but for Christian banquets in name and honor of God, to whom after satiating themselves, they will give thanks. Only thus, by preserving for men some of the worldly joys, will you lead them thus more easily to relish the joys of the spirit."

When the Roman Empire took control of Egypt, the Egyptian religion spread throughout the Roman Empire. However, later on, when Christianity took hold in Rome, the Ancient Egyptian religion and other mystical religions became an obstacle to the Christian Church which had developed divergent ideas about spirituality, and also to the Roman government which sought to consolidate the empire under Rome. Also, the plagiarism of the Ancient Egyptian symbols, traditions and holidays could not be effective if there were living Ancient Egyptian Priests and Priestesses to tell and show the truth about the origins of those symbols, traditions and holidays. Further, Ancient Egyptian religion served to refer people to Egypt as well as to mystical spiritual practice. In short, Christianity could not survive as a cult among many other more ancient religions, so it was necessary to dispose of the competition. The most politically expedient way to do this was to close all mystical religious temples.

At the end of the fourth century A.C.E., the Roman emperor Theodosius decreed that all religions except Christianity were to be stopped, and that all forms of Christianity besides that of the "Byzantine throne" would also cease to exist. During this time The Temple of Isis (Aset) at Philae in Upper Egypt (deep south of Egypt) temporarily escaped the enforcement of the decree. Consequently, the hieroglyphic inscriptions of this Temple, dated at 394 A.C.E., are the last known Kamitan hieroglyphics to be recorded. Also, the last demotic inscriptions there date to 452 A.C.E. It was not until the sixth century A.C.E. that Emperor Justinian entered a second decree that effectively stopped all mystical religious practices in the Roman Empire. This means that not only were the Mystery-Yoga schools and temples to be closed, but also all forms of mystical Christianity which did not agree with the style of Christianity espoused in Rome were to be abolished. Therefore, the Gnostic Christians (Christians who practiced mystical Christianity), were persecuted and their churches rededicated to Roman Catholicism. Much of their writings were destroyed. Thus, it is evident that the Ancient Egyptian teachings were being practiced and taught well into the Christian era.

What is Civilization, What is the Difference Between Civilization and Culture and What Causes the Rise and Fall of Civilizations?

In order to continue our journey of discovery into the origins of civilization, religion and yoga philosophy, we will need a reference point. Science offers, not an absolute, but a useful reference point to understand the progress towards human civilization and human evolution. It is important to understand the classifications of ancient societies as they are used in modern scholarship in order to better understand their meaning in context.

In anthropology, civilization is defined as an advanced socio-political stage of cultural evolution, whereby a centralized government (over a city, ceremonial center, or larger region called a state) is supported by the taxation of surplus production, and rules the agricultural, and often mercantile base. Those who do not produce food become specialists who govern, lead religious ritual, impose and collect taxes, record the past and present, plan and have executed monumental public works (irrigation systems, roads, bridges, buildings, tombs), and elaborate and formalize the style and traditions of the society. These institutions are based on the use of leisure time to develop writing, mathematics, the sciences, engineering, architecture, philosophy, and the arts. Archeological remains of cities and ceremonial centers are evaluated to determine the degree of civilization of that culture, based on the trappings of both style and content.[47] The American Heritage Dictionary defines civilization as:

> **civ·i·li·za·tion** *n.* **1.** An advanced state of intellectual, cultural, and material development in human society, marked by progress in the arts and sciences, the extensive use of writing, and the appearance of complex political and social institutions.

Strictly speaking, civilization is defined as a highly developed human society with structured division of labor,[48] an advanced state of intellectual, cultural, and material development, marked by progress in the arts and sciences, the extensive use of writing, and the appearance of complex political and social institutions.[49] In simple terms, civilization means acting in a civil manner towards other people, which implies cooperation in the furtherance of community goals and the upliftment of the individuals within the civilization. The earliest "highly developed human societies" developed in ancient times out of Neolithic farming societies. These in turn developed out of Mesolithic societies, and these out of Paleolithic societies. Thus, civilization or the lack thereof, can be considered in many ways. Prior to the existence of farming, human beings were considered to be "hunter gatherers," primitive groups fending for food, territory and the right to mate, with little conception of what lies beyond the basic survival activities of life. Since time is constantly spent in competition for food and warding off potential danger, there is little opportunity for the higher aspects of life such as art, religion or philosophy. At most these factors will not progress beyond a primitive level under such conditions. It is thought that the development of pottery, which follows agriculture, signifies a major step towards the establishment of a civilized society. The invention of writing is regarded as a very high development of civilization. For many years it was thought to have been first invented by the Sumerians, but the recent evidence shows that the invention of Ancient Egyptian writing and Ancient Egyptian architecture predate Sumerian civilization. The following report by the British team excavating the Ancient Egyptian city of Abdu (modern Abydos) dispels the misconceptions related to the first origins of writing in history.

> "Until recently it was thought that the earliest writing system was invented by the Sumerians in Mesopotamia towards the end of the fourth millennium BC and that the idea was borrowed by the Egyptians at the beginning of the First Dynasty (c.3100 BC). However, recent discoveries at Abydos have shown that the Egyptians had an advanced system of writing even earlier than the Mesopotamians, some 150 years before Narmer. Remarkably, there is no evidence that this writing developed from a more primitive pictographic stage. Already, at the very beginning, it incorporated signs for sounds.
>
> Unlike Mesopotamian writing, which can be shown to have gradually evolved through a number of stages, beginning as an accounting system, Egyptian writing appears to have been deliberately invented in a more-or-less finished form, its underlying principles fully in place right from the outset. A parallel for such a process is known from more recent times: in AD 1444 the Korean script (still widely regarded as one of the world's most efficient) was invented by order of the king, who assembled a group of scholars for the purpose.

In Egypt this invention corresponds with the birth of the Egyptian state, and its growing administrative and bureaucratic needs."[50]

However, the aforementioned criteria denoting the presence or absence of "civilization" relate mostly to technological developments and increased sociopolitical complexity. Complexity in society and highly advanced technology cannot in themselves be used to determine the presence of civilization, because many cultures have had these in the past and they have fallen into oblivion (forgetfulness, unconsciousness) nevertheless. Some examples of these are the Greek Empire, the Roman Empire, the Ottoman Empire, the British Empire, etc. And yes, what happened to the Ancient Egyptian civilization? If civilization is an advancement in society, then it would follow that the advanced civilization must be doing something better, more efficient, that would promote not only prosperity, but also its own longevity. So what were these "civilizations" missing that allowed them to fall? Where did they go wrong?

Albert Schweitzer (1875-1965), the German-born theologian, philosopher, musicologist, medical missionary, and Nobel laureate, was one of the first Western scholars to examine the issue of civilization and the causes for its downfall as well as the means for its maintenance. As a missionary doctor in Africa, prior to and after the First World War, he gained valuable experiences while treating the sick there. He would doubtless have had occasion to experience the misery imposed on Africans due to the colonial system, and also he would have experienced the African concept of Ubuntu (humanity) and caring for family.

From 1917-1918 Schweitzer, who was a German national, was incarcerated in France, which was at war with Germany. During this period he wrote two volumes which became a projected philosophical study of civilization called *The Decay and the Restoration of Civilization* and *Civilization and Ethics* (both 1923). These volumes were concerned with ethical thought in history. Schweitzer maintained that modern civilization is in decay because it lacks the will to love. As a solution to this problem he suggested that society should develop a philosophy based on what he termed "reverence for life," embracing with compassion all forms of life.[6] It is interesting to note that Schweitzer's solution, a return to love, is the primary concept behind the African philosophies of *Ubuntu* (caring for humanity) and Maat (righteousness in society and caring for humanity). He was also exposed to Eastern mysticism which also exhorts the necessity to develop the capacity for compassion and love in order to attain spiritual enlightenment. He attempted to discover the mystical love upon which Christianity is founded and to raise the awareness of this aspect of Christianity, as he saw the lack of such awareness in the Western practice of the Christian religion as contributing to Western Culture's inability to love humanity. His other works include the theological studies *Indian Thought and Its Development* (1935; trans. 1936), *The Kingdom of God and Primitive Christianity* (1967; trans. 1968), *The Mysticism of Paul the Apostle* (1930; trans. 1931) and the autobiographical *Out of My Life and Thought* (1931; trans. 1933).

The problem of inability to love and care in a civilization develops when it is not managed or ceases to be managed by leaders with the capacity to care for others, to be compassionate to others. It is often not realized that the concept of the word civilization includes the term *Civility* which means 1. Courteous behavior; politeness. 2. A courteous act or utterance. -*American Heritage Dictionary*. Caring and compassion are expressions of a spiritual consciousness, an awareness of the Divinity in all. Therefore, mystical studies (spiritual perspective encompassing all humanity transcending religion) are imperative for any true leader of a society, and any society who does not have such leaders will be bent on greed, power and pleasure seeking as opposed to human and ethical issues. Such a society will be eventually doomed to self-destruction because this way of life promotes degraded culture and selfishness instead of respect for life. Consequently, under these conditions, people develop the capacity to hurt each other to achieve their own material goals, perpetuating a cycle of vice, violence, mistrust and hatred, leading to war, disease, poverty and suffering. This of course cannot be called "civilization." It is a form of culture which is struggling to discover itself, and in the process, like a child playing with matches, it burns itself and others in the process of its learning experience.

---

[6]"Schweitzer, Albert," *Microsoft® Encarta® Encyclopedia 2000.* © 1993-1999 Microsoft Corporation. All rights reserved.

So civilization means the coming together of a group of people to organize themselves and promote the general good. This they do by using technology to facilitate their activities, promote health and the perpetuation of life. What sustains civilization is an ethical social conscience. The ethical social conscience comes from an underlying spiritual basis that recognizes all life a sacred. The philosophical insight which allows a human being to realize that all life is sacred is the fact that the universe promotes the continuation of life in all respects, animal, vegetable and mineral. The spiritual consciousness is predicated upon the idea that even death is not the final reality. This can be proven through the experience of spiritual enlightenment. The process of spiritual enlightenment is achieved when a human being discovers what lies beyond their physical mortal existence. As we will see, African Religion was the first to proclaim this discovery and the means for any human being to achieve its realization. This (spiritual enlightenment) is the authentic basis for civilization. Until a society achieves this general awareness so that it is promoted in its policies, inventions, technologies and activities, (its institutions) it cannot be considered to have achieved the status of "civilized." Philosophy is the most important factor influencing the development of a culture. The way of thinking (belief system) dictates whether a culture will develop civilized institutions (promote life) or institutions that promote destruction, slavery, greed and other vices (Barbarism). Thus, "Civilization" is an outgrowth of a well ordered and spiritually based culture. A culture without a philosophy that affirms universal divinity cannot develop into a "civilization." Just as a mother expresses love for a child by taking care of the child the culture that takes care of people's social needs is a loving culture. See Appendix B for full Criteria of what constitutes a "Civilization."

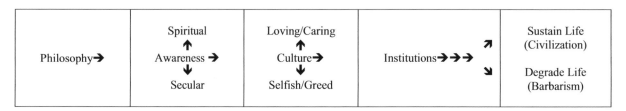

The Standard of What Constitutes Civilization

As we have seen, civilization cannot be considered just as a society possessing intellectual capacity, technology, social organization, etc. These aspects are merely the basis for civilization. Civilization is an expression of a mature culture which allows it to build social structures that perpetuate its existence. Promoting existence means promoting life. Promoting life means protecting life and the quality of life for all members of the civilization, as well as the capacity to carry on life, which means also protecting nature. Since no society or culture in the world exists in a vacuum or on an island, separate from other societies or cultures, it is erroneous to believe that a civilization can advance in the absence of the general advancement of all humanity. Therefore, a society or culture's level of civilization is judged as much by its advancement as well as its compassion and assistance to other societies or cultures. Thus, a selfish or greedy society cannot be considered by these criteria as a civilization, but rather as a degraded culture. This means that civilization is an aspect of culture. It is based on the cultural beliefs and traditions of a people and underlying this culture is a way of thinking about the world and that is based on a peoples philosophy of live, as to its meaning and purpose.

The following Standard is therefore set for the determination of a society or culture's level of civilization. In order to be considered as a civilization, the society must possess and practice the following elements of civilized culture:

1. **Mystical Philosophy** – to allow the advanced members of the society to seek for the answers to the transcendental questions of life, to Know Self.
2. **Myth** – is the means by which the ethics and spiritual consciousness are transferred from generation to generation and acts as a self-definition of culture, conveying the mythic history (folklore and legends), cultural identity and common traditions of the society.
3. **Spiritual consciousness** – religion and spirituality that affirms the universal divine essence of Creation.
4. **Ethics** – philosophy of social justice to promote equality, order, peace and harmony in the absence of which a civilization cannot function efficiently.
5. **Organization** - The society or culture must display social organization- a group of people coming together for promoting a common goal.

6. **Agriculture** - The society or culture must conduct agriculture to sustain the society and allow the members of the society to develop regular routines so as to engage in contemplative endeavors.
7. **Writing, language** or set (agreed upon) means of communication.
8. **Mathematics** – used as the foundation of distribution of resources, architecture, etc.
9. **Art** – is the means by which the ethics, spiritual consciousness and myth become visual icons for a society and through which a society views and understands the world around them. Therefore, the art of a civilization conveys its highest ethics and spiritual conscience.

The Rediscovery of Ancient Egyptian Culture, Philosophy and Religion

Many scholars and world renowned spiritual masters have recognized the strong connections between India and Ancient Africa, namely Joseph Campbell, R.A. Schwaller de Lubicz, Omraam Mikhael Aivanhov, and Swami Sivananda Radha. However, what they stated amounted to a few pieces of a larger puzzle, which until now had not been pursued in an extensive manner.

All of this comes down to the following. Mystical spiritual culture is not the exclusive property of any culture. Further, mystical philosophy operates through culture and is not culture itself. Culture relates to the mannerisms, customs, icons, language and traditions that are specific to a particular group of people. These may be related, adopted or influenced by other peoples. However, mysticism transcends cultural conventions; it is universal. Therefore, if one understands mystical philosophy, one can understand the expression of mystical philosophy through any culture. This means that if a mystic of India were to examine the mysteries of China, that mystic would understand those mysteries. Likewise, by understanding one form of mysticism, another may be recognized. Thus, by collecting the pieces of Kamitan mysticism which have survived in various cultures, the mysticism of Kamit may be fully understood and rediscovered.

Since Judaism, Christianity, Hinduism, Buddhism, Islam, Dogon and Yoruba spirituality are based on Ancient Egyptian Religion and philosophy, the basic principles of Kamitan Mysticism can be traced through those religions back to Ancient Egypt. Besides these there are other less known and less numerous groups of people who follow the Kamitan tradition and who claim to be descendants of the Ancient Egyptian living in present day Asia Minor. Their traditions also correlate with the evidences gathered from the other systems. However, in the case of Ancient Egypt and Ancient India, there is sufficient evidence to show that there was a cultural and social connection between the two cultures so close that it is possible to say that Indian spirituality is a development of Ancient Egyptian religion and mystical philosophy.

Thus, by tracing the historical connection between the two countries and tracing the evolution of culture, it is possible to see the living manifestations of Ancient Egyptian religion which are match in the major mystical principles. So even though the modern Indians may not uphold the exact disciplines or even acknowledge the Kamitan origins of their systems of spirituality, nevertheless the living Kamitan tradition can be discerned in the Indian traditions, customs and symbols.

Therefore, not only is it possible to recreate Kamitan religion and mysticism through studies based on present forms of mysticism, but it may be said that the Kamitan tradition never ceased and only transformed. So this work is more along the lines of outlining the essential elements of Kamitan religion and culture as they survive in present day cultures rather than recreating or deducing based on modern unrelated systems of spirituality. The key to the rediscovery of Ancient Egyptian spirituality was due to the understanding that is a yogic mystical system of spirituality whose goal is to promote spiritual enlightenment. This is why past attempts at reconstructing Ancient Egyptian religion were frustrated.

Thus it has been possible to understand the mysteries of Ancient Egypt as an original source for many of the most fundamental teachings surviving not just in Hinduism but also Ancient Greek Philosophy, Judaism and Christianity. So, the research that led to the Egyptian Yoga book series and the revival of Kamitan culture was like tracing back to the source, like discovering the seed from which a plant has grown. Also, in knowing the seed it is possible to know the plant (spirituality) and its branches (the religions) better and vise versa, thereby illuminating them in modern times with the depth of their own deeper history which leads back to the place where all life and civilization was born.

The Methods to Rediscover and Reconstruct a Culture and its Civilization

The fundamental aspects of a culture (its categories of cultural expression) can be rediscovered through the following methods of cultural anthropology[7].

1. Studying the writings left by the ancient "extinct" culture itself (if any).
2. Studying the traditions albeit with diluted knowledge that are carried on by the descendants (if any).
3. Studying the other cultures (if any) carry on some of the customs of the "extinct" culture in the form of traditions and or legends of the "extinct" culture.
4. Studying other religions (if any) that have adopted symbols, tenets (philosophies) or rituals of the "extinct" culture.
5. Studying the other cultures (if any) that have had contact with the "extinct" culture and which have described the "extinct" culture.

Figure 3: The African Family Tree of Cultural Interactions

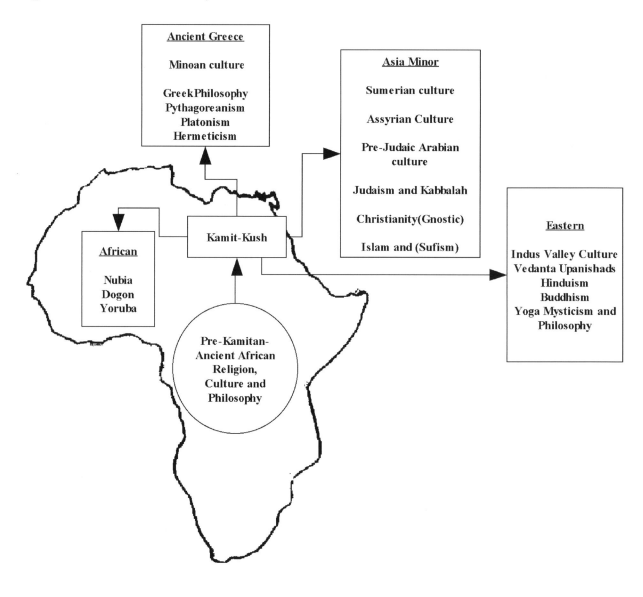

---

[7] The scientific study of the origin, the behavior, and the physical, social, and cultural development of human beings.

Linguists and others who study "dead" languages are always on the look out for a "Rosetta Stone" that will allow them to decipher the language they are studying. The Rosetta Stone is a slap upon which an edict was written on behalf of the King of Egypt. The special thing about it is that it was written in three different languages, Hieroglyphic, Demotic and Greek. Since the closing of the Ancient Egyptian temples at about 450 A.C.E. had forced the hieroglyphic text into disuse it has become forgotten by the world. Even if the letters of a word are understood a language may not be understood because there is no context to understand the meaning of each world and then to relate them to each other in order to formulate rational sentences in order to derive ideas and thoughts. Such an example of the Meroitic language. Its letters have been deciphered but the language remains a mystery. Since Greek was still understood and since the texts are a translation of the same message. It was possible to discover the "context" of the images (words) upon the slab. This led to the decipherment of the Ancient Egyptian Hieroglyphic language.

In like fashion, mythologists search for "Factors of Cultural Expression" the methods in which the "Categories of Cultural Expression" such as symbols, artifacts, myths, architecture, traditions, customs, etc., are used. The Categories are the fundamental aspects of all cultures but these may have different forms of manifestation and thus may not relate to each other. If the factors match then this provides a context in which to understand the Categories of the no longer "dead" culture. Taking this a step further, when the previously "Dead" culture has left a language it is possible to verify the findings of the Cultural Anthropology studies. That is, the context that has been established can be verified by the ideas and thoughts contained in the language of the "previously dead culture." Ancient Egypt is such a case. These studies have yielded a framework through which to understand and bring back to life the culture of Ancient Africa. Having decoded the language of myth, a mythologist can understand when the fundamental principles of myth are being espoused and {she/he} can also determine the nature of those expositions in order to see if the methods used coincide with others and thereby establish relationships between myths of different peoples. Joseph Campbell and others accomplished this work successfully in their areas of study. The same success can be achieved in other Categories of Cultural Expression besides Myth. When the Factors of varied Categories are studied a quite complete picture can emerge of what the previously dead culture was all about, and this of course can lead to a revival of that culture.

So the objective of this kind of study is to discover which factors of Cultural Expression correlate (match) between the "extinct" culture and the "living" culture. Those matching Factors of Cultural Expression (aspects of culture that are proven as borrowings from one culture to another) constitute practices in common between the ancient culture and the modern culture. A partial match such as adoption of a symbol but not the meaning of a symbol denotes a possible initial adoption of the symbol and a loss of the interpretation over time due to cultural changes. Thus, an "extinct" culture whose customs, traditions, teachings and symbols have been transferred to writings, descendants, other cultures religions or philosophies cannot be said to be "dead" or "extinct" since these aspects of culture "live" on albeit in a dormant state in the present day "living" culture.

The methods of cultural anthropology outlined above are very difficult to apply in the study of most ancient cultures. This is because their impact was not felt to the degree of leaving those traces of traditions, symbols etc. with descendants of other cultures. Sometimes they have no writings about themselves for researchers to go on. The writings are the primary source material for discovering a people. Archeology is an inexact profession and cannot be relied upon completely for such determinations. There need to be language studies, cultural anthropology studies and if possible hard science evidences such as geological evidences in order to confirm the findings of archeology. Fortunately, in the case of Ancient Egypt, unlike the case of the Sumerians, we are in the position to engage in all of the methods of study outlined above and this gives us the opportunity to reconstruct Kamitan culture and thereby also discover the source of many modern cultures and religions. So in order to proceed with our study we will need to outline what the fundamental aspects of cultural expression are and how do judge cultural interactions.

Cultural Category - Factor Correlation System Application

Theoretical Methodology for the Comparison of Cultures

A myth in its pristine state is by definition specific to a given human environment. How it fares from then on (its "life;' "afterlife'" survival, transposition, revival, rediscovery, or whatever) is a matter of historical accident. It follows that the study of any specific past body of myth has to be mainly a historical discipline employing written sources, whereas contemporary myth can be pursued by the methods of field anthropology.[51]

In the book *Comparative Mythology,* (quoted above), the author introduces certain formats for the study of comparative mythology, beginning with the premise that a myth is "specific to a given human environment." If human environment is taken to mean culture, then it follows that the study of myth needs to be carried out within the context of the culture, using the parameters of the culture. In other words, the myth needs to be studied from the perspective of someone living in the culture and not as an outsider. That is, a student of myth needs to practice and live the myth, to be part of the myth. Only in this way will the myth be fully understood. Otherwise, there will be a superimposition of outside cultural bias from the researcher or student on the myth being studied. This is one of the most difficult problems for any scientist to overcome, how to fully understand the object of study. The usual logic in Western scientific methodology is to strive for "objectivity."

Modern science has now accepted that research examining or studying "physical reality" cannot exist outside of the person conducting the experiments. An older theory held that the person conducting the experiment could be considered separate and apart from the phenomena being observed. Modern science now holds that nature and all phenomena occur because of an experimenter's ability to conceptualize the phenomena and to interpret it. Therefore, the observer is inevitably part of the phenomena being observed. Consequently, modern science now uses a new term for the experimenter. The new term is Participant. Thus, the experimenter is really a participant in the experiment because his or her consciousness conceives, determines, perceives, interprets and understands it. No experiment or observed phenomena in nature can occur without someone to conceive that something is happening, determine that something is happening, perceive that something is happening (through instruments or the senses), and finally to interpret what has happened and to understand that interpretation.

Since everything in the universe is connected at some underlying level and since human existence and human consciousness is dependent upon relationships in order to function, then it follows that objectivity is not a realistic attitude for most human beings, including scientists. The only way to achieve objectivity is to transcend "human" consciousness. That is, one must extricate one's egoistic vision of life, which based on the limitations of the mind and senses, by discovering one's "transcendental" nature. This grants one the experience of knowing the true, unchanging and unaffected nature and essence of existence beyond the limited capacities of the mind and senses. In this capacity one can temporarily identify with the object, any object of study, and achieve a complete knowledge of the subject. This capacity has been the legacy of science and the mystical disciplines, for concentration on any subject is the key to discovering the nature of that subject. However, the mystical disciplines go a step beyond in allowing the scientists to discover their essential nature as one with the object of study. Therefore, mystical training is indispensable in the study of any subject and the acquisition of the knowledge of the essential nature of a subject or object. This form of philosophy is antithetical to the orthodox practice of the "scientific method" but until the scientific method is adjusted to incorporate the training of the mystical disciplines, the knowledge gained from the sciences will be limited to the capacities of the logical mind and senses as well as the technological instruments that may be devised to extend the range of those limited, and therefore illusory, human abilities. So the historical and field anthropology[52] disciplines of study must be guided by the mystical experience.

When comparing two given cultures, we are not only concerned with the superficial aspects of their cultural expression, but also the underlying foundations of these. The fundamental core of any culture is its outlook or philosophy on life. This underlying philosophy gives rise to the varied forms of cultural expression just as the many leaves and branches of a tree arise from a seed (common origin). The mystical philosophy of a given culture is translated by the sages and saints of that culture into an easily understandable and transmittable myth using the cultural factors available to them within that particular culture. Therefore, a sage in Kamitan culture may espouse a teaching using metaphors particular to

Kamitan culture while a Christian sage may espouse the same teaching while using a different cultural metaphor which is particular to Christian culture. The myth is supported and sustained by the plots and story-lines. Next, it is supported by the rituals and traditions associated with them. The rituals and traditions are supported by the combined factors of cultural expression including: architecture, iconography, artifacts and ritual objects (amulets, etc.), spiritual scriptures, language, form and function of objects produced by the culture, etc. Thus, when there is an overwhelming number and quality of synchronicities between the factors of expression in two cultures, a commonality in their underlying philosophies will also be discovered.

How the philosophy of a culture expresses through the cultural factors of that culture:

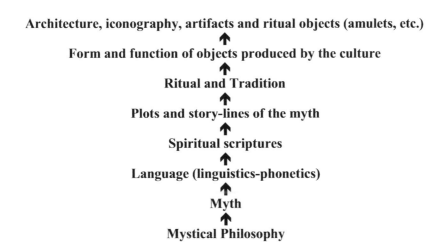

Architecture, iconography, artifacts and ritual objects (amulets, etc.)

↑

Form and function of objects produced by the culture

↑

Ritual and Tradition

↑

Plots and story-lines of the myth

↑

Spiritual scriptures

↑

Language (linguistics-phonetics)

↑

Myth

↑

Mystical Philosophy

Through studies based on the factors and parameters listed above, it has been possible to show that there are at least four main world religions that have a strong basis in a common origin which transcends the cursory or superficial levels of similarity. These traditions are the Kamitan, Ancient Greek, Hindu, and Judeo-Christian. I have already presented and in-depth exploration of the Kamitan/Greek connection in my book *From Egypt to Greece* and the Kamitan/Judeo-Christian connection in my book *The Mystical Journey From Jesus to Christ.* Through these kinds of study, it is possible to bring unity to disparaging and conflicting points of view which lead to dissent, disagreement and misunderstanding that are based on ignorance, adherence to dogma and cultural-theological pride[53] and orthodoxy, instead of the deeper nature and purpose of culture which is to lead human beings to spiritual enlightenment. By such studies it is possible to lead open-minded people to understand the purpose of religion and to discover the value of all traditions which are ultimately seeking to accomplish the same task, to bring harmony, peace and order to the world and to allow human beings of all cultures to discover the supreme and essential nature of existence.

The Standard for Determining Whether or Not a Correlation is Present

Determining an objective standard for any critical study is an enormously difficult task since the human mind is ultimately what must be satisfied in a particular judgment. That is, when we are trying to determine some kind of rule or guideline to follow which will lead to an unbiased conclusion, the mind of the observer, with his/her preconceived notions, desires, leanings, etc., comes into play, and what one person may consider reasonable, another may regard as groundless. For example, a person may think a color is especially suited for a particular room while another person may say that that color is exactly the opposite of what should be used. Who is right? Well, in this question there is an arbitrary, aesthetic factor which draws upon a person's particular upbringing, particular experiences, particular education, etc. Another example seen often in modern culture is a situation where one person sees a business opportunity as clear as day, while others do not. That person will later capitalize on that opportunity. Was the opportunity there all along or was it a coincidence? In addition, we recognize factors in life that cannot be objectively proven, and yet we "know" they exist. There is a transcendental reality about them that we recognize. When that businessperson, with their training and intuition, spots an opportunity, they perceive it and register it as a reality. In this manner, scientists using training, data collection and intuition in order to "discern" the underlying truth of myths, can discover the correlating factors between cultures.

Nonetheless, in the study of science, one would expect the process to be more "objective," being "either right or wrong," but even in the sciences, the ego and its prejudices can impinge on reason. So what kind of standard can be used to discern between coincidences and synchronous correlations between cultures? Any standard to be used must be based on verifiable evidence and logical analysis, but also on reason. However, if unreasonable people review the evidence, no amount of evidence will suffice, because their minds are already prejudiced.

There is often much confusion and conflict in the world due to disagreements and misunderstandings. Many have cited the lack of reason as a primary cause of human conflict. But what is reason? The following dictionary and encyclopedic definitions may provide some guidance.

> **reason: 1** to think logically about; think out systematically; analyze **2** to argue, conclude, or infer: now usually with a clause introduced by *that* as the object **3** to support, justify, etc. with reasons **4** to persuade or bring by reasoning.

> **reasoning:** (-i) *n.* **1** the drawing of inferences or conclusions from known or assumed facts; use of reason **2** the proofs or reasons resulting from this.

> **in reason**. With good sense or justification; reasonably. **Within reason**: Within the bounds of good sense or practicality.

In the context of the definitions above, reason is that faculty in human consciousness wherein two minds can arrive at a conclusion that is within the bounds of practical reality based on known or assumed facts which justify or support the conclusions drawn. But how is it possible for people to apply those standards and draw rational or reasonable conclusions? Certainly, maturity in life and qualitative experience in human interactions, (i.e. based on honesty, truth, righteousness, justice and universal love) scholarship and balance in life are prerequisites for promoting soundness of the intellect and an understanding of reality within the sphere of human interactions and social intercommunications. In order to promote social order and harmony, the ancient disciplines of righteousness, known as Maat in Kamit and Dharma in India, were devised. This shows that from ancient times, the necessity of promoting reason (ability to think and act by truth) as a mental faculty, in the philosophical disciplines as in government, was understood and appreciated.

Ancient Egyptian Hermetic Philosophy

> "Though all men suffer fated things, those led by reason (guided by the Higher Intellect), do not endure suffering with the rest; but since they've freed themselves from viciousness, not being bad, they do not suffer bad. Though having thought fornication or murder but not having committed these, the Mind-led man will suffer just as though he had committed fornication, and though he be no murderer, as though he had committed murder, because there was will to commit these things."[54]

Gita: Chapter 2: Samkhya Yogah--The Yoga of Knowledge

> "63. From anger there arises delusion, from delusion loss of memory, from loss of memory one loses the function of pure reason, and from the loss of reason one heads towards destruction."[55]

Reasoning involves objectivity and detachment. The parties must strive to pursue truth as opposed to proving a point for their own ends. The highest and best way to promote truth is to promote humility and effacement of the egoistic nature. Also, there should be a deference to evidence and reason as opposed to argument and supposition or emotion. These failings are the sources of partisanship, fanaticism and disagreement. Reasoning should follow logical thinking, and logical thinking should be based on evidence. Thereby the conclusions drawn from evidences and rational thinking about those evidences will receive the correct (reasonable) weight. In this way, the misconceived notions, misjudgments, biases and desires of the deeper aspects of the personality will not impinge on the faculty of reason. Then such a person will be able to reason with other reasonable persons and arrive at reasonable conclusions or courses of action. So while defining "reason" is an abstract endeavor, certainly mature persons can rationally understand that it is a reality in principle. Life, culture and civilization cannot exist in the absence of reason, for even when there is internal disagreement with a decision or course of action, reasonable people understand they must place their personal desires aside for the collective good, or they must simply realize that other people deserve equal consideration. That is, even in arguments where two individuals may disagree, there can be an objective resolution of the disagreement. One or both parties may choose to refrain from allowing animosity to develop and to remain patient until an answer emerges from the situation or question itself, while in the mean time assisting in the development of stronger arguments which are supportable over time until the validity or invalidity of a conclusion may no longer be avoided. The calmness of a mind unfettered by emotion and desire, a hallmark of a well-adjusted self-realized human being, allows a person to disagree with a conclusion while maintaining respect for the person advancing it. This allows people to live together and organize in order to work together.

So, for the purposes of this section, as throughout this book, the opinions of scholars will not be used in place of actual evidences or if the conclusions of scholars are used they will be supported by evidences, and "reasonable arguments" related to those evidences. In this manner, it is hoped that the discussion will be elevated to the determination of the evidences as opposed to debates over the bias of the scholars and their opinions. There are certain valid conclusions that can be drawn from the totality of evidences; these will be presented separately as summaries, conclusions or epilogues.

Methodology for the Comparisons Between Cultures in Order to Determine the Correlations Between Cultures

The methodology for understanding mythology and its purpose, which has been presented in the previous section as well as those which will follow, present myth and metaphor as abstract principles that manifest through cultural factors in the form of recurrent themes. While these are subject to some interpretation, the possibility for bias becomes reduced as the associated factors add up to support the original conjecture about the particular factor being compared. In other words, *single event proposed correlations* (correlations between cultural factors that are alleged but not yet proven or supported) between cultures can often be explained away as coincidences. However, when those correlations are supported by related factors or when those correlations are present in the framework of other correlations, then the position of bias or simple disbelief is less tenable. The basis for the objective standard will be set forth in the following logical principles which indicate congruence between the two cultures. In order to study and compare the Kamitan and Indian cultures, we will make use of the categories of cultural expression.

As explained earlier, in determining the common elements of different religions, there are several factors that can be used as criteria to determine whether or not cultures had common origins. If cultures are related, they will use common stories or other common factors or patterns to express the main doctrines of the religion or spiritual path, social philosophy, etc. These are listed below. Before proceeding to the items being compared, the criteria used to compare them must be understood. The following section introduces the categories of cultural expression factors and some subdivisions within them.

The Possible Standards for Use in Determining the Correlations Between Cultures

The Scientific Method for Studying Correlations Between Cultures

> "Scientific Method, general logic and procedures common to all the physical and social sciences, which may be outlined as a series of steps: (1) stating a problem or question; (2) forming a hypothesis (possible solution to the problem) based on a theory or rationale; (3) experimentation (gathering empirical data bearing on the hypothesis); (4) interpretation of the data and drawing conclusions; and (5) revising the theory or deriving further hypotheses for testing. Putting the hypothesis in a form that can be empirically tested is one of the chief challenges to the scientist. In addition, all of the sciences try to express their theories and conclusions in some quantitative form and to use standardized testing procedures that other scientists could repeat."[56]

Many Western scholars adhere to the "Scientific Method" of research. This concept originated in Western Culture for the study of nature, to determine the criteria for what can be accepted as truth. The definition above provides the step by step procedures accepted in the Western conception of a scientific method. It is further defined and contrasted from philosophy by the Encarta Encyclopedia as *(highlighted portions by Dr. Ashby)*:

> "Scientific Method, term denoting the principles that guide scientific research and experimentation, and also the philosophic bases of those principles. Whereas philosophy in general is concerned with the why as well as the how of things, science occupies itself with the latter question only. Definitions of scientific method use such concepts as objectivity of approach to and acceptability of the results of scientific study. Objectivity indicates the attempt to observe things as they are, without falsifying observations to accord with some preconceived worldview. Acceptability is judged in terms of the degree to which observations and experimentations can be reproduced. *Such agreement of a conclusion with an actual observation does not itself prove the correctness of the hypothesis from which the conclusion is derived.* It simply renders the premise that much more plausible. The ultimate test of the validity of a scientific hypothesis is its consistency with the totality of other aspects of the scientific framework. This inner consistency constitutes the basis for the concept of causality in science, according to which every effect is assumed to be linked with a cause."[57]

Refutation of Conclusions arrived at through the Scientific Method

Conversely, if one attempts to show that a scientific conclusion is wrong, it is necessary to:

(1) show a misconception or wrongly stated a problem or question;
(2) show that the hypothesis (possible solution to the problem) based on a theory or rationale is incorrect;
(3) show that the experimentation (gathering empirical data bearing on the hypothesis) is biased or being carried out in an incorrect way;
(4) show that the process for interpreting the data and drawing conclusions has not followed a logical procedure or is biased;
(5) show that the revising process of the theory or deriving further hypotheses for testing is needed.
(6) show that the experiment is not consistent with the totality of other aspects of the scientific framework.
(7) show evidences that contradict the conclusion.
(8) show more evidences to prove other conclusions than what have been presented to advance the other unreasonable conclusion.

The Limitations of the Scientific Method

The scientific method is an attempt to remove ambiguity from the body of human knowledge and the means by which knowledge is added to the storehouse of human learning. The problem with this method of gathering knowledge is that it necessarily receives information only from empirical evidence. However, as the great scientist Einstein and the modern day quantum physicists have proven, Creation is not absolute or empirical. Creation is composed of variables wherein some aspects operate in different ways under different circumstances. This is why the concept of cause and effect is also flawed. Ignorance of the mystical law of cause and effect known as the law of *Ari* in Kamitan philosophy and Karma in Indian philosophy, leads scientists to seek for causes or reasons for what they see in nature, somewhere within the confines of the time and space of the event in question. In reference to Yoga and mystical religion, as concerns people and their actions, mostly, what is occurring today could be a result of what happened in a previous lifetime (philosophy of reincarnation-already proven in parapsychology experiments).[58] As concerns nature, what occurs today is sustained by the Transcendental Essence, i.e. Supreme Being. Further, the observers, the scientists themselves, and the very perception of these experiments are factors in the experiments and are therefore, factors in the results. This is where the problem of skewing of the results and interpretations of results based on conscious or unconscious prejudices or misconceptions comes in, that is, the problem of "falsifying observations to accord with some preconceived worldview."

As the modern discipline of Quantum Physics has shown, nature itself is not what it appears. It is not solid and distinct but rather interrelated energies in varied forms of expression. Physics experiments have shown that matter is not solid as it appears but that it is rather, energy in different forms of manifestation. So the instruments used to discern reality, the logical conditioned mind, and the limited senses, are inadequate for discriminating between what is real and what is unreal. The fallacy of believing in the absolute authority of science is evident in the inability of science to discover anything that is absolute. Something absolute is unchangeable in the beginning, middle and end. Every decade medical science makes "new breakthroughs." This means that they are discovering something "new" which supersedes their previous knowledge. This necessarily means that the previous knowledge was conditional and imperfect and therefore, illusory. Thus, science has its value, but it is not to be considered a reliable source for truth or as a substitute for the disciplines of self-knowledge. So, only a mind that has been trained in transcendental thinking and intuitional realization can discover "truth." Yoga and mystical religion are spiritual sciences that promote the cultivation of the higher faculties of the mind. The mystics of Yoga the world over have for thousands of years proclaimed that the mystical reality which is to be discovered through the disciplines of Yoga and Mystical religion is the same Absolute essence which has always sustained Creation and all existence, including human consciousness. It is the same essence that was discovered by Imhotep and other Sages of Kamit, the Upanishadic Sages of India, Buddha, Jesus, etc., and it is the same absolute reality that can be discovered by anyone today or in the future, who applies the teachings of Yoga and Mystical religion.

So, the idea of the objective observer or that only experimental results which can bring forth repeatable results or parameters that show "consistency with the totality of other aspects of the scientific framework" are valid is sometimes contradictory with respect to nature and logic. Nature is not a machine and even if it were to be treated as such it is not a machine for which the parts are all known and understood. There is an aspect of nature that transcends empirical observation; it must be intuited. This aspect of nature is ignored by the scientific method, by its own bindings, and therefore, the ability to use science as a tool to discover truth, is limited. Since the world is variable (relative), then it follows that any "scientific" data obtained from experiments will also be relative and variable. It is useful within the framework of science, but not beyond that framework. In other words, it cannot be used to ascertain anything about realities outside of its framework. This is why philosophy is an important tool of science. It allows the intuitive faculty of the mind to be cultivated and directed towards discovering the aspects of nature that no physical testing equipment can penetrate.

The world is not to be discerned through the intellect because the intellect is also limited. It cannot comprehend the totality of Creation. However, by intuitional (knowing that transcends the thought process) reasoning through transcendence of the relativity of nature, it is possible to discover that absolute reality which is common, and therefore uniform in its *"consistency with the totality"* of human and spiritual experience. The problem is that this aspect of existence can only be approached through a scientific application of philosophical principles and disciplines that can provide results only in the mind of an individual. The Western scientific community shuns this approach, likening it to primitive and unscientific speculations. By ignoring the "why" of things, as the definition of the scientific method above suggests, the scientific method is cutting itself off from the source of knowledge, and looking only at its effect, the "what," and then accepting this as a basis to discern reality. It is like experimenting on the sunrays, neglecting to notice the sun, but extrapolating from the limited experiments and making assertions about what the sun is. In like manner, science looks at nature and notices the relativity, but does not allow itself to explore the mystical-spiritual dimensions of cause. Rather, it seeks to ascribe factors within the realm of the flawed relative field of Creation itself, as the reason behind existence. In fact, for all the knowledge that Western Culture has amassed, in reality there is perhaps no more important knowledge than that which has been recently derived from Quantum Physics, because these clearly point to a transcendental essence of Creation.[59 / 60/61]

Western Culture's adherence to the "Scientific Method" has turned it away from the science of self-development (myth, religion and yoga mysticism) since it (spiritual evolution) cannot be proven empirically according to its current criteria as different people are at different stages of evolution and the process may require many lifetimes to complete. Here again, even the parameters set by Western Culture as the procedure of the "Scientific Method" are not being followed. The statement that there is no science beyond the existential aspect of Creation is in effect a violation of the "scientific" rule of objectivity to *"observe things as they are, without falsifying observations to accord with some preconceived world view."* The predilection to discount the transcendent as "un-provable" is a worldview which typifies Western Culture. Thus, the objectivity in the scientific method has at least two built in flaws. First, is the insistence on determining scientific fact based on evidence that can be observable to the physical senses with or without assistance from technology, and therefore can only exist in time and space. Secondly, the necessity for human standards in determining *"conclusions"* based on the data, for it has been shown that the same data can lend itself to different interpretations based on conflicting views, even within the scientific community. A true scientific method should require an objective standard which cannot be violated by the whims of the observers or scientists. Its conclusions must be accepted and not refuted by opinions or desires to uphold particular worldviews. However, again, all of the best standards will be useless if the scientists are biased.

A further connotation, prevalent in Western Culture arising from adherence to the "scientific method" is that what is transcendent is imagined, superstition and unfounded illusion, and only what the "Scientific Method" deems as provable is correct and acceptable. Hence, since myth and mysticism are in the realm of the transcendent, then by this type of Western logic it follows that they are also un-provable and unreal. This is a very powerful argument that further develops into the most dangerous concept, that Western Culture is the determiner of what is truth and that the art, culture, science and religion, etc., of other cultures, past or present, are inferior due to their primitive and "unscientific" manner of approaching nature.

Applying the Scientific Principles and Procedures to study Mysticism

The application of scientific principles and procedures in mystical philosophy can and should be accomplished in the following manner. A theory that the Supreme Being exists, for instance, can be developed. Now the experiment is to practice certain myths, rituals and mystical exercises (technologies). Then the practitioner must insightfully look within and see if there are any changes in the personality, and if there is anything transcending the personality. The premise that observable and repeatable results can be obtained is to be understood as an intuitional realization or recognition of truth. So, while it is possible to show many illustrations and iconographical correlations in the scientific comparison of two forms of myth, the ultimate realization of the truth behind these is to be achieved in the understanding of the observer. The mystical scriptures have long held that if this procedure is followed, any person can discover the transcendental essence of Self. This is the scientific formula for Enlightened Sagehood or Sainthood, which mystical philosophy holds to be the only goal in and purpose of life. Thus, from ancient times, the Yogic and other authentic Mystical systems have defined themselves as sciences, since the proper application of the correct philosophy, disciplines and principles of living leads to the same results of spiritual awakening in all human beings who apply them.

Due to the uniqueness of each person when dealing with human beings, there are variables in the degree of understanding and practice. Thus, in evaluating students of the Yogic and other Mystical sciences (spiritual aspirants or initiates), the results of spiritual practices cannot be assessed in terms of an all or nothing equation or within a given time frame or situation, since evolution is occurring even when outwardly there appears to be a backward movement. Also, spiritual evolution occurs over a long period of time encompassing many lifetimes. So these results cannot necessarily be seen in the form of data, but other criteria may be used to evaluate them: a calmer personality, a human being who is expanding in consciousness, discovering the inner depths of consciousness and the universality of life, increasing contentment and fearlessness, a stronger will, and magnanimousness, wisdom and inner fulfillment. Some of these evidences cannot be put on paper, and yet they can be experienced just as the message of a painting or the love of a relative can be intuited and felt, but not explained or proven to others. From time immemorial, the sages and saints of all world traditions have maintained the initiatic principles and technologies, the mystical philosophy and art of spiritual culture, that has been handed down through time. It has been found that when human beings are properly instructed and when they engage in certain disciplines of Yoga and mystical culture, they develop expanded consciousness and spiritual awareness, as well as intuitional realization of the divine presence in a predictable manner.

The correct practice of myth and mystical philosophy in yoga requires a scientific approach, using the personality as the subject, and the mind as the instrument for proving the existence of the transcendent. It is necessary to apply philosophy scientifically, incorporating intuition and spiritual culture when engaging in any study of religion, myth, mysticism, etc.

The following is a standard for our exploration into comparative mythology, which will be used to discover the validity of the hypothesis that Ancient Egyptian and Ancient Indian culture and civilization were related and share common cultural manifestations. This analysis will be accomplished by establishing what culture is and what factors within it can be identified and compared. Then the procedure to be followed in comparing them will be determined.

In a scientific investigation, opinions have no place beyond the stating of the hypothesis. Also, the constraints of social propriety do not apply. It is perfectly scientific to state a theory that the Ancient Egyptians were not black Africans, but rather Asiatics, or that Indian Vedic culture and not Kamitan culture gave rise to civilization. There is nothing wrong in making those statements. However, if the person stating these ideas wants to put them forth as "facts" or "reality" or consider these ideas as "proven," then a more rigorous process of supporting those ideas must be undertaken. The evidence must be accurate, available to all investigators, and it should be primary and not second-hand conjectures. Therefore, the opinions of other scholars, no matter how reputable they may be, must be based on primary evidence, and that evidence cannot be substituted by the scholars conclusions or opinions about it. Therefore, scholarly dictums[8] are worthless if the scholar cannot or does not support them with evidence. Other terms, often used synonymously in scientific discussions are "postulate" or "axiom."

An **axiom** is a self-evident or universally recognized truth; a maxim.

A **dictum** is an authoritative, often formal, pronouncement.

A **postulate** is a *statement or proposition that is to be assumed to be true without proof and that forms a framework for the derivation of theorems.*[62]

Many times scientists or others relying on them treat corollaries as proofs.

A **corollary** is a *proposition that follows with little or no proof required from one already proven, A deduction or an inference.*[63]

So corollaries, postulates, etc., are also useless in a presentation of scientific findings. They should not even be discussed because they have no merit. Sometimes merit is placed on dictums or corollaries due to the reputation of a scientist, or for political, social or economic reasons but these have no place in a scientific discussion. Thus, if a scientist is not dispassionate, an unconscious or conscious alternative agenda will be put forth. Further, if no evidence is produced to support a contention, then a scientist might be in danger of appearing biased, promoting a political or social point of view or expressing personal beliefs and sentiments about a particular issue. Over time, they themselves begin to believe in those opinions. This is the power and danger of the human mind.

---

[8] American Heritage Dictionary

The Factors That Make Cultures Distinct and the Methodology for Comparing Them

In the book *Comparative Mythology,* the author introduces two formats or models for the study of comparative mythology, based on the concepts of abstraction and generalization.

> Comparative mythology of separately localized and attested traditions can be practiced on different levels of abstraction and generalization.

> "Universal mythology" is essentially reduced to explaining accordances (and, if relevant, differences or contrasts) by appeal to human universals or at least common denominators based on similarities of psychological patterning, environment, or levels of culture. Needless to say, it has to pursue the typical and usual at the expense of the specific and unique.

> "Diffusionary mythology" studies how traditions travel, charting the spread and transmission of myth. The trouble is precisely that myth does not "travel" very well and, when it does travel, frequently moves from its specific historical and geographical fulcrum into the international realm of legend, folktale, fairy tale, and other debased forms of originally mythical narrative.[64]

While the above author speaks primarily of mythological studies, the ideas are relevant to our study since mythology is an integral if not central aspect of culture. In our study, we will strive to raise the methodology for the comparative cultural study to a high standard that goes beyond the universalistic aspects of culture, that is, those factors that are innate to all human beings.

The author quoted above also works with the premise that mythology becomes "debased" or degrades due to the changes and additions it experiences over time. While this model occurs and may even be considered as the norm, it is also possible to see a sustained practice of myth and other aspects of culture from one group to the next. We will also strive to determine if there is a degradation that can be discerned. The criteria here is the determination of the function and metaphorical significance of the cultural factors over time. That is, if the function and metaphorical significance of the cultural factors is lost over time, the model above is correct. However, if the function and metaphorical significance of the cultural factors are sustained over time, this indicates a closer connection between the two cultures, and the model is one of initiatic continuity (culture A has taught culture B directly) as opposed to blind diffusion of ideas without their full understanding. The closer bond can be expected in the contiguous relationship of a culture with its own legacy. That is, a modern culture can be expected to exhibit a lesser degree of deterioration of indigenous fundamental cultural factors as opposed to those that have been imported. The model presented in ordinary comparative mythology studies is that myth may retain its form but degrade in content. If a sustained (un-degraded) correlation can be shown between two cultures over time (one emerging after the other), then it is possible to maintain that the cultures are not separate and disparate but actually elements of a continuous manifestation of cultural expression. In other words, the two cultures are actually part of one evolving culture. Another factor to be considered is the concept of a study that works within the framework of different levels of abstraction and generalization. The principles under which this current study of Kamitan and Indian culture will be conducted is based on the contention that when several cultural factors can be correlated or matched, then the study becomes more concrete and specific as opposed to abstract and general. This of course raises the validity of the arguments and the conclusions drawn from them.

> "The twentieth-century search for universally applicable "patterns" that so clearly marks the ritualist and psychoanalytic approaches to myth is also characteristic of the trends that remain to be mentioned, the sociological and the structuralist. Whereas ritualism had its roots in England and psychoanalysis in the German cultural orbit, the French contribution is important here, starting with the sociological school of Emile Durkheim and Marcel Mauss. Durkheim's "collective representations," Mauss's seminal studies on gift giving and sacrifice, and Bronislaw Malinowski's views on myths as social "charters" all recognized the paramount role of myths as catalysts in cementing structured human coexistence. The structural study of myth, with Claude Levi-Strauss as its most flamboyant paladin, also stresses the role of myth as a mechanism of conflict resolution and mediation between opposites in the fabric of human culture and society, not least in

the great dichotomy of nature versus culture itself. But Levi-Strauss's analytic method is one of binary oppositions influenced by structural linguistics (especially the work of Roman Jakobson) and folklore (starting with Vladimir Propp's *Morphology of the Folktale* [1928], which themselves are but manifestations of the vast structuralist movement in science and scholarship."[65]

The view that myth is a manifestation of ritual or of a psychological state is a barrier between scholarship and myth. This is because the very premise for the study is flawed. Created by sages, saints, seers, etc., mystical mythology is an "explanation" of something that is transcendental, something that exists in a form that cannot be communicated by rational thinking or linear logical conceptualizations. When mystical mythology is reduced by scholars to a support for rituals, manifestations of the psyche or a tool to "glue" or bind members of a culture to a common concept, the original intent of myth is displaced and the resulting conclusions about myths, their import and pervasiveness, will be elusive. These models may be grouped together and referred to as logical models since they neglect to take into account the transcendental aspects of myth and indeed, also the human experience. The models that take into account the mystical nature and purpose of myth along with the disciplines of anthropology, archeology, philology and historical linguistics, phonetics and phonology, may be referred to as mystic or intuitional models. In another section, the author continues to outline the previous approaches taken by other mythologists in an attempt to determine the benefits or pitfalls of their concepts and methodologies.

"While Levi-Strauss himself, after starting with the Oedipus myth, has for the most part resolutely ranged from Alaska to the Amazon, structuralist ideas have begun to seep into the study of classical myth and "historical" mythology in general. The obvious danger is that the approach is by nature generalist, universalizing, and ahistorical, thus the very opposite of text oriented, philological, and time conscious. Overlaying known data with binaristic gimmickry in the name of greater "understanding" is no substitute for a deeper probing of the records themselves as documents of a specific synchronic culture on the one hand and as outcomes of diachronic evolutionary processes on the other. In mythology, as in any other scholarly or scientific activity, it is important to recall that the datum itself is more important than any theory that may be applied to it. Hence historical and comparative mythology, as practiced in this book, is in the last resort not beholden to any one theory on the "nature" of myth or even its ultimate "function" or "purpose." But it is fully cognizant that myth operates in men's minds and societies alike, that it is involved in both self-image and worldview on an individual and a collective level (being thus tied to religion and its manifestations such as ritual and prayer, and to societal ideology as well), and that it creates potent tensions of language and history (speaking of timeless happening, narrating eternal events in the grammatical frame of tense forms for [usually]) past or [rarely] future occurrences [as in the case of prophecy], never in the generalizing present)."[66]

While there have been a wide range of scholars and writers who have taken note of and even asserted the similarities of the myths of widely varying cultures by citing simple similarities, there have been relatively few serious, rigorous, scholarly researches and documentations. Mostly, there have been many anecdotal and or unsubstantiated claims that do not reconcile history with the events that are being artificially connected. Further, there is little accounting for the discrepancies and inconsistencies that arise. While it is true that all humanity emerged from the same source, it is not necessarily correct to say that all cultures are related since people, having moved away from their original ancestral home (Africa) when humanity first appeared on earth, developed varying ways of life and cultural expression. So making the standard too tight or too loose leaves us with either biased conclusions or unsubstantiated conjecture respectively. The author ends his introduction to comparative mythology with a caveat for entering into those studies.

"Thus the twentieth-century lessons of ritualism, psychoanalysis, sociology, and structural anthropology alike deserve to be heeded by the historical and comparative student of myth and religion, but only to the extent that they offer viable insights into a study that is by definition historical, and more specifically philological, rooted in the minute and sensitive probing and comparison of primary written records."[67]

If the categories of cultural expression are found to match in several areas, the mythic principles will have survived the passage of time even as cultures interact with others and adopt new factors into their culture. The factors of cultural expression will remain embedded in the culture as layers upon which new traditions, names and idiosyncrasies[68] have been acquired. This layering of symbol, myth and metaphor is starkly evident in several examples that will be presented in this section. This pattern of diffusion was noticed early on in the study of the correlations between the myths of varied cultures. The writings of Count Goblet D' Alviella present a typical example, referring to the Sacred Tree symbolism.

> "Each race, each religion has its independent type, which it preserves and develops in accordance with the spirit of its own traditions, approximating it, however, by the addition of extraneous details and accessories, to the equivalent image adopted in the plastic art of its neighbors. Thus the current which makes the Lotus of Egypt blossom on the Paradisaic Tree of India has its counter-current which causes the *Asclepias acida* of the Hindu Kush to climb upon the Sacred Tree of Assyria. Art and mythology comply, in this respect, with the usual processes of civilization, which is not the fruit of a single tree, but has always been developed by grafts and cuttings between the most favoured branches of the human race."[69]

The models (principles) presented in this book adopt the mystic understanding of myths and cultures in the determination of their compatibility. While this study will make use of such disciplines as anthropology, archeology, philology and historical linguistics, phonetics and phonology, it will lay heavy emphasis not so much on the historicity of the factors of cultural expression, although this forms an important aspect of the evidences related to prior contact, but rather on the substance or symbolic, philosophical and metaphoric significance of the items in question. Written records do constitute an essential aspect of the study but this definition needs to be broadened to include iconography, as symbol, metaphor, and iconography are also forms of language, as we will see. The following principles will be used in this comparative cultural study.

Principle 1: Single Event (one occurrence) Match Un-supported By Matches in Other Factors

Example: If one artifact looks the same (correlation of form) in two separate cultures, *this single event proposed correlation* may be explained as a coincidence. But if the primary factor upon which the conjecture is based, for example, *form,* is supported by correlations in other factors such as usage, philosophy, myth, etc., then the argument that it is only a coincidence becomes less tenable. That is, just because the *ontology*[70] of two cultures is expressed through mythology does not suggest a correlation between the two cultures. In order to be considered as a *proposed correlation* for the purpose of determining the congruence of the two cultures, the simple correlation must be supported by at least one or more matching elements of cultural expression. So if there is no other match beyond the initial apparent match this proposed correlation will be considered as being "unsupported."

A- Example of a *Unsupported single event proposed correlation:*

Primary Category proposed as a correlation between two cultures ➔ *Myth* ⬅ Supported by *Iconography*

In this example, one category, the myths of the two cultures match wholly or partially in iconography only.

Typically, the common forms of evidence used to support the theory of cultural connections is a Single Event (one occurrence) Unsupported Match in One Cultural Category which may or may not occur in the presence of other unrelated single event matches in the same or in related but separate cultural categories.

If the *single event proposed correlation* is devoid of additional supports (ex. correlation is of form only) but is found to be part of a group (occurring within the same culture) of several other *single event proposed unsupported correlations* in the same category or other cultural expression categories, then the conclusion that the correlating factors are simple coincidences is less supportable because the frequency of correlations rises beyond the threshold of chance as would be determined by statistical analysis of the normal probability of the existence of such correlations.[71] The correlations here are basic and superficial, usually of appearance, and yet they are suggestive of a deeper connection.

Table 2: **Example of Single Event (one occurrence) Unsupported Matches in One Cultural Category Occurring in the Presence of Other Unrelated Single Event Matches in the Same Cultural Categories**

Single Event Unsupported Match	Culture A	Culture B	Culture A	Culture B	Culture A	Culture B	Supported Matches
The primary matching Categories	*Mythic Character 1*	*Mythic Character 1*	*Mythic ritual*	*Mythic ritual*	*Mythic ritual*	*Mythic ritual*	← Matches
The primary supporting factor →	*Iconography*	*Iconography*	*Iconography*	*Iconography*	*Iconography*	*Iconography*	← Matches

Table 3: Example of Single Event (occurrence) Unsupported Match in One Cultural Category Occurring in the Presence of Other Unrelated Single Event Matches in Related but Separate Cultural Categories

Single Event Unsupported Match	Culture A	Culture B	Culture A	Culture B	Culture A	Culture B	Supported Matches
The primary matching Categories	*Mythic Character 1*	*Mythic Character 1*	*Architecture*	*Architecture*	*Ritual*	*Ritual*	← Matches
The primary supporting factors →	*Iconography*	*Iconography*	*Style*	*Style*	*Tradition*	*Tradition*	← Matches

Additional criteria for Principle 1:

Single event proposed correlations that are unsupported by other factors and unrelated to other categories require a more rigorous standard of discernment in order to be included as evidence of congruence. A *single event proposed correlation* that is unsupported by other factors and unrelated to other categories will be accepted as evidence of congruence if it occurs in the presence of at least three or more other unrelated single event matches in the same or other cultural factor categories.

B- Example of a *Supported Single event proposed correlation:*

Primary factor proposed as a correlation between two cultures➔ ***Myth*** ← Supported by
Iconography

↑↑↑

Cultural elements that may support the primary factor ➔➔➔➔   Plot,
gender,
theme,
action,
etc.

In this example, the myths of the two cultures match wholly or partially in iconography, plot, gender, theme, action, etc. Therefore, the initial correlation is supported by more than one factor (iconography).

Table 4: Supported Matching Cultural Factors

Supported Matching Cultural Factors	Culture A	Culture B	Supported Matches
The primary matching category ➔	***Myth*** ↑↑↑ **Supporting Factors**	***Myth*** ↑↑↑ **Supporting Factors**	← **Matches**
The primary supporting factor ➔	***Iconography***	***Iconography***	← **Matches**
Secondary supporting factor ➔	Plot,	Plot,	← **Matches**
Tertiary supporting factor ➔	gender,	gender,	← **Matches**
Quaternary supporting factor ➔	theme,	theme,	← **Matches**
Quinternary supporting factor ➔	action, etc.	action, etc.	← **Matches**

Additional criteria for Principle 1:

A *supported single event proposed correlation* between the categories being compared within the two cultures will be accepted as evidence of congruence if that *single event proposed correlation* is supported by at least one or more (secondary, tertiary, quaternary, etc.) cultural factors that match exactly in the two cultures (see table above).

Principle 2: Pattern-Multiple Correlations Occur Within the Same Cultural Category or Across the Landscape of Cultural Categories

Single event proposed supported correlations between two cultures that occur as a part of a pattern comprised of several *single event proposed supported correlations* will be accepted as evidence of congruence between the categories being compared among the two cultures. Pattern here implies consistency in the appearance of the number of correlating factors in the same or different categories.

Depth (deepness-vertical) *pattern of correlations*

If two or more independent factor matches within one category appear, they will be considered as a part of a pattern denoting congruence between the two cultures. These correlations will be considered as equivalencies within a particular category of expressions such as, art, architecture, myth, etc. This pattern is referred to as a *depth* (deepness-vertical) *pattern of correlations* and the category will be accepted as evidence in the determination of congruence between two cultures.

Table 5: Example-Supported Matching Cultural Factors within the Cultural Factor/Category: Myth

Depth pattern of correlations	Culture A	Culture B	Culture A	Culture B	Culture A	Culture B	Supported Matches
The primary matching categories	*Myth*	*Myth*	*Mythic Character 1*	*Mythic Character 1*	*Mythic Theme*	*Mythic Theme*	← Matches
The primary supporting factor →	↑↑↑ Supporting Factors	↑↑↑ Supporting Factors	↑↑↑ Supporting Factors	↑↑↑ Supporting Factors	↑↑↑ Supporting Factors	↑↑↑ Supporting Factors	
	Iconography Plot, gender, theme, action, etc.	*Iconography* Plot, gender, theme, action, etc.	*Iconography* Plot, gender, theme, action, etc.	*Iconography* Plot, gender, theme, action, etc.	*Iconography* Plot, gender, theme, action, etc.	*Iconography* Plot, gender, theme, action, etc.	← Matches ← Matches ← Matches ← Matches ← Matches

Breadth (wideness-horizontal) *pattern of correlations*

The pattern may appear as a consistent number of single event correlations discovered in different cultural categories. For example, several correlations in a study of comparative culture may be found in any of the cultural categories discussed earlier. If two or more instances of matching factors arise then this pattern is referred to as a *breadth* (wideness-horizontal) *pattern of correlations* and the category will be accepted as evidence of congruence.

Table 6: Example-Supported Matching Cultural Factors within the wide range of Cultural Factor/Categories

Breadth pattern of correlations Factors	Culture A	Culture B	Culture A	Culture B	Culture A	Culture B	Supported Matches
The primary matching Categories	*Mythic Character 1*	*Mythic Character 1*	*Architecture*	*Architecture*	*Ritual*	*Ritual*	← Matches
	↑↑↑ Supporting Factors	↑↑↑ Supporting Factors	↑↑↑ Supporting Factors	↑↑↑ Supporting Factors	↑↑↑ Supporting Factors	↑↑↑ Supporting Factors	
The primary supporting factor →	*Iconography* Plot, gender, theme, action, etc.	*Iconography* Plot, gender, theme, action, etc.	*Iconography* Plot, gender, theme, action, etc.	*Iconography* Plot, gender, theme, action, etc.	*Iconography* Plot, gender, theme, action, etc.	*Iconography* Plot, gender, theme, action, etc.	← Matches ← Matches ← Matches ← Matches ← Matches

Principle 3: Cross-Cultural Correlations

Principle #1 represents the most common form of evidence that can be presented as proof of congruence between two cultures. Therefore, this is the principle within which most simple correlations between cultures are to be found. However, the nature and exactness of the correlations of the factors between the two cultures may be deserving of greater weight. An example of this is the correlation between the relationship of the numbers used in Indian, Icelandic and Chaldean myth, presented in this text. Cross-cultural correlations (correlations between three or more cultures) may be observed in the unsupported or supported state. They may most likely be found in the breadth pattern of distribution. This pattern of correlation suggests a *diffusion* of the expressions of the cultural factors from one original source and / or a relationship between the cultures being studied.

Table 7: Single Event Unsupported Cross Cultural Correlations

Cross-Cultural Correlations	Culture A	Culture B	Culture C	Culture D	Culture E	Culture F	Supported Matches
The primary matching category	*Mythic Character 1*	*Mythic Character 1*	*Mythic Character 1*	*Mythic Character 1*	*Mythic Character 1*	*Mythic Character 1*	← Matches
The primary supporting factor →	*Iconography*	*Iconography*	*Iconography*	*Iconography*	*Iconography*	*Iconography*	← Matches

In order for these principles to carry weight and to be considered a substantive arguments for theorizing that the given cultures are related and or that they adopted cultural factors from the other cultures, it is advisable to establish evidence of contact and a correlation of at least one additional factor of correlation. In this regard, once a factor has been preliminarily established to match, say as a mythic character appearing to possess the same iconography, if it can be determined that the mythic characters, for instance, perform the same function or if a mythic artifact or symbol carries the same usage in the mythic system, then it is possible to assert with greater confidence that there is a connection between the two cultures. The particular example used in this principle is one of the main patterns of cultural congruence discovered by mythologist Joseph Campbell, which he presented in his groundbreaking work *The Hero of A Thousand Faces*. The mythic, heroic character exhibits particular patterns in myths from various cultures which can be readily discerned. The myth of the Asarian Resurrection of Ancient Egypt, in which a prince is born, his father is killed by the uncle, the child flees into exile to be brought up by sages so that he/she may return and face the evil tyrant and reestablish order and justice, can be seen in the myth of Krishna of India, the story of Jesus, the story of Hamlet, and even in modern times with the story of the movie "Star Wars" and the even more recent "Lion King." The table gives an example of a single event supported cross-cultural correlation. Examples of multiple event supported cross-cultural correlations can be seen in the connections between Ancient Egyptian mythology, Indian mythology, Sumerian mythology, Greek mythology and Christian mythology.

Table 8: Single Event Supported Cross Cultural Correlations

Cross-Cultural Correlations	Culture A	Culture B	Culture C	Culture D	Culture E	Culture F	Supported Matches
The primary matching category	*Mythic Character 1*	*Mythic Character 1*	*Mythic Character 1*	*Mythic Character 1*	*Mythic Character 1*	*Mythic Character 1*	**← Matches**
The primary supporting factor ➔	*Iconography*	*Iconography*	*Iconography*	*Iconography*	*Iconography*	*Iconography*	**← Matches**
Other possible additional supporting factors ➔➔ ↘ ↘ ↘ ↘ ↘	Function	Function	Function	Function	Function	Function	**← Matches**
	Actions	Actions	Actions	Actions	Actions	Actions	**← Matches**
	Gender	Gender	Gender	Gender	Gender	Gender	**← Matches**
	Age	Age	Age	Age	Age	Age	**← Matches**
	Metaphoric significance	Metaphoric significance	Metaphoric significance	Metaphoric significance	Metaphoric significance	Metaphoric significance	**← Matches**

Final Standard

A. CULTURAL INFLUENCE- In order to establish the influence of one culture on another it must be possible to show concordances in any categories, including Evidence of Contact, but not necessarily including Ethnicity.

  a. Each category of cultural expression match must be supported by at least one Method of Correlation –

B. COMMON CULTURAL ORIGINS- In order to establish the common origins of two given cultures it must be possible to show a pattern of concordances in any of 6 or more categories including Evidence of Contact and Ethnicity.

  a. Each category of cultural expression match must be supported by at least two Methods of Correlation – Breadth Proof

and/or

  b. Each category of cultural expression match must be supported by at least two Methods of Correlation – Depth Proof

C. CULTURAL PRIMACY- In order to demonstrate that culture has come first in history and that the later (secondary) culture has drawn cultural factors from the primary culture, it is necessary to first establish Evidence of Contact, the exchange of cultural factors from the primary to the secondary culture, and next, it is necessary to show a chronology in which the primary culture is shown to have developed previous to the secondary culture.

The Fundamental Cultural Factors

What is it that distinguishes one culture from another? What factors determine whether or not a cultural factor is borrowed by one group from another, and what criteria determines that a culture is not simply influenced, but is actually part of another culture. As stated earlier, the principles under which this current study of Kamitan and Indian culture will be conducted is based on the contention that when several cultural factors can be correlated or matched, and when these matches can be supported by varied aspects within the two cultures, then the study becomes more concrete and specific as opposed to abstract and general. This of course raises the validity of the arguments and the conclusions drawn from them. But where is the threshold wherein it becomes obvious that a group of peoples is related to another? The following cultural principles are offered as criterion for such a determination. The latter four (Ethnicity, Myth, Philosophy and Rituals and Tradition) may be considered as the basic qualities which define a culture and which it carries forth over time. These cultural factors may be thought of as the core fundamental elements of culture which makes it unique from the standpoint of the determination of its kinship to another culture. Contact is considered here because interactions with other cultures can have a profound effect on the direction of a society and its cultural development.

> **Contact – evidence of prior contact (relationships)**
> **Ethnicity – both groups matching in their ethnic background**
> **Myth synchronism**
> **Philosophical synchronism**
> **Rituals and traditions synchronism**

So under this model, even if people born in Kamit were to be found in India, if their lives and activities did not match in the other areas, they would not be considered as members of the same culture for the purposes of this study. Accordingly, it must be understood here that the term "ethnicity" does not relate to race. The word "ethnic" may have originated from the Biblical term "ethnos" meaning "of or pertaining to a group of people recognized as a class on the basis of certain distinctive characteristics, such as religion, language, ancestry, culture, or national origin."[124]

Ethnicity, Race as Culture Factors

Modern scientists and scholars say that race distinctions based on genetics is unscientific and wrong. The animosity and hatred of modern times, caused by distortion of religious scriptures when being rewritten or reinterpreted by various groups or ignorance of the true intent of the teachings of the religious holy books, has led to a situation where social problems have rendered practitioners of religion incapable of reaching a higher level of spiritual understanding. Many people in modern society are caught up in the degraded level of disputes and wars in an attempt to support ideas, which are in reality absurd and destructive in reference to the authentic doctrines of religion. Ironically, the inability of leaders in the church, synagogue or secular society to accept the truth about the origins of humanity comes from their desire to gain and maintain control and fear of losing control over their followers. Now that modern science is showing that all human beings originated from the same source, in Africa, and that racial distinctions are at least questionable and misleading and at worst, malicious lies and race baiting, it means that those who have perpetrated and sustained racism can no longer use science or religious teachings to support their iniquity and ignorant designs. They have no leg to stand on. The following excerpt was taken from Encarta Encyclopedia, and is typical of the modern scientific understanding of the question of human genetics and race issues.

> "The concept of race has often been misapplied. One of the most telling arguments against classifying people into races is that persons in various cultures have often mistakenly acted as if one race were superior to another. Although, with social disadvantages eliminated, it is possible that one human group or another might have some genetic advantages in response to such factors as climate, altitude, and specific food availability, these differences are small. There are no differences in native intelligence or mental capacity that cannot be explained by environmental circumstances. Rather than using racial classifications to study human variability, anthropologists today define geographic or social groups by geographic or social criteria. They then study the nature of the genetic attributes of these groups and seek to understand the causes of changes in their genetic makeup. Contributed by: Gabriel W. Laser "Races, Classification of," Encarta." Copyright (c) 1994

It should be noted here that there is no evidence that racial classifications for the purpose of supporting racist views existed in Ancient Egypt. However, the concept of ethnicity, which is often erroneously confused with the modern concept of race, was acknowledged in ancient times. That is to say, the Ancient Egyptians recognized that some of the physical features and characteristics of the Asiatics, Europeans, and other groups were different from themselves and the Nubians. They recognized themselves as looking like the Nubians, but as possessing differences in culture. The Ancient Egyptian's depictions of themselves and their neighbors shows us beyond reasonable doubt, that they were dark skinned people like all other Africans, before the influx of Asiatics and Europeans to the country. Since genetics is increasingly being recognized as a false method of differentiating people the concept of phenotype has progressively more been used.

> **phe·no·type** (fē′nə-tīp′) *n.* **1.a.** The observable physical or biochemical characteristics of an organism, as determined by both genetic makeup and environmental influences. **b.** The expression of a specific trait, such as stature or blood type, based on genetic and environmental influences. **2.** An individual or group of organisms exhibiting a particular phenotype.[9]

It has been shown that climactic conditions, geography, solar exposure, vegetation, etc., have the effect of changing the appearance of people. This means that while people (human beings) remain equally human internally, their physiognomy and shade of skin adapt to the conditions where they live. This means that the external differences in people have little to do with their internal humanity and therefore are illusory. The concept of social typing is therefore based on ignorance about the race issue and its misconceptions, and cannot be supported by the scientific evidences. Further, an advancing society cannot hold such erroneous notions without engendering strife, and confusion, within the society. An advancing society will not be able to attain the status of "civilization" while holding on to such spurious concepts.

One of the major problems for society and non-secular groups is that the teachings and scientific evidence presented here has not been taught to the world population at large as part of the public or private education system. Even if it were, it would take time for people to adjust to their new understanding. Most people grow up accepting the ignorance of their parents who received the erroneous information from their own parents, and so on. Racism, sexism and other scourges of society are not genetically transmitted. They are transmitted by ignorant family members who pass on their ignorance, prejudices and bigotries to their children, and so on down through the generations.

The only fair and accurate standard to classify people is by means of education and ethics. Here education refers not just to trades or technical endeavors but to the origins of humanity and the contributions of all members (especially the Africans) of humanity to the evolution of world culture and the advancement towards civilization. This knowledge directly impacts a person's ethics, as once the common origins of humanity and the falseness of the race issue are understood and affirmed in a person's life, their ethics, and relations this will have an impact on how people view each other and consequently this will improve how people treat each other.

Below is a listing of the world's major cultures and a timeline of their rise and fall for the purpose of comparative study.

---

[9] American Heritage Dictionary

Examples of Cultural Interactions Throughout History

Timeline of World Cultures

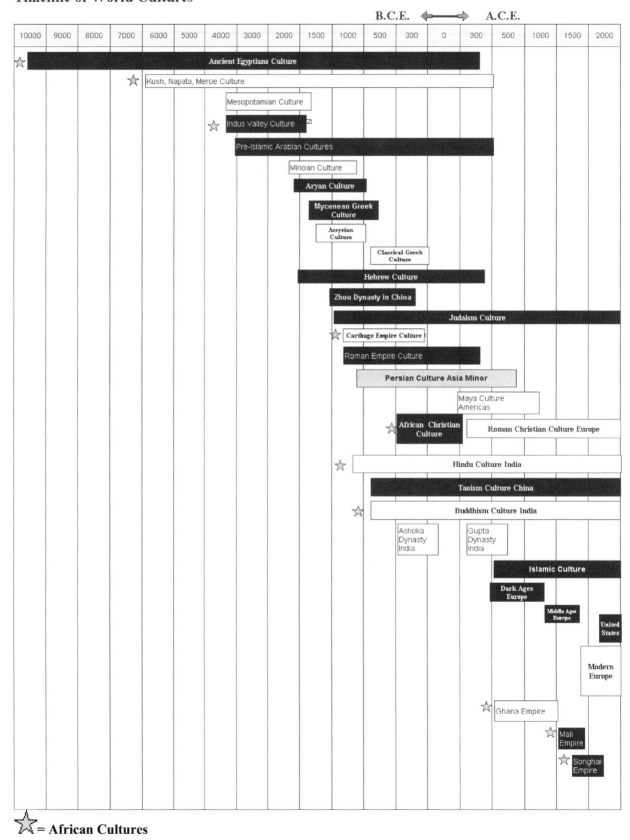

☆ = **African Cultures**

The Ancient Egyptian Creation Myths and Their Relationship to Christianity and Gnosticism

> Bible - Genesis 1
> 2 And the earth was without form, and void; and darkness [was] upon the face of the
> deep. And the Spirit of God moved upon the face of the waters.

The idea of the primeval waters, and the original primeval Spirit that engendered life in it, occurs in several myths from around the world. It occurs both in the Jewish Bible as well as in Hindu mythology. However, the earliest record of the idea of the primeval waters occurs in the Pre-Dynastic culture of Ancient Egyptian religion. This Pre-Dynastic (10,000-5,500 B.C.E.) myth spoke of a God who was unborn and undying, and who was the origin of all things. This Deity was described as un-namable, unfathomable, gender-less and without form, although encompassing all forms and being transcendental. This being was the *God of Light* which illumines all things, and thus was later associated (in Dynastic times) with the Sun in the form of the deities, *Ra* or *Tem, Heru* (Horus) who represents *that which is up there* and *the light,* and finally *Aton.* Tem or Temu were Ancient Egyptian names for the ocean that is full of life giving potential. This ocean is likened to the deep and boundless abyss of consciousness of the Supreme Deity from which the phenomenal universe emerged. Tem was analogous in nature to later deities such as the Babylonian *Tiamat,* the Chaldean *Thamte,* the Hebrew *Tehorn,* and the Greek *Themis.*

Cultural Interactions Between Judaism and Ancient Egypt

The next prominent example of adoption of religious culture comes from the relationship between Judaism and Ancient Egypt. Many times in the emergence of new mythologies throughout history, the founders or followers of the new system of religion will create stories to show how the new system surpasses the old. The story of Exodus is such an example. Moses went to Mount Sinai to talk to God and brought back Ten Commandments. At the time that Moses was supposed to have lived (1,200?-1,000? B.C.E.), Ancient Egypt was the most powerful culture in the ancient world. However, at the time when the bible was written (900 B.C.E.-100 B.C.E.), Egypt was on a social and cultural decline from its previous height as the foremost culture in religious practice, art, science, social order, etc. So it became necessary for the Jews, a small group of Ancient Egyptians (according to the Bible, the early Jews were ethnic Ancient Egyptians),[72] to legitimize the inception of their new theology by claiming to have triumphed over the mighty Egyptian gods with the help of their new "true god" who defeated the "weak" gods of Egypt. This triumphant story would surely bring people to convert to the new faith, since up to that time, the Ancient Egyptian gods and goddesses had been seen not only as the most powerful divinities, but also, according to the Greeks, as the source of other deities in other religions. So in effect, by saying that the Jewish God "defeated" the Ancient Egyptian God by freeing the Jews, it is the same as saying that a new, more powerful religion is to be followed. This form of commencement for a spiritual tradition is not uncommon. As an example of inculturation, the similarity between the story of Moses of the Jews and Sargon I from Assyria (reigned about 2,335-2,279 B.C.E.) is instructive. Sargon also was placed in a basket and floated down a river to be picked up by the royal household. So part of the story of Moses is borrowed from Assyrian history.

In almost the exact same expression as one of the Ancient Egyptian creation myths, the original Jewish Bible and related texts also describe the Creation in terms of an act of sexual union. *Elohim* (Ancient Hebrew for gods/goddesses) impregnates the primeval waters with *ruach,* a Hebrew word which means *spirit*, *wind* or the verb *to hover*. The same word means *to brood* in Syriac. Elohim, also called El, was a name used for God in some Hebrew scriptures. It was also used in the Old Testament for heathen gods. Thus, as the Book of Genesis explains, Creation began as the spirit of God "moved over the waters" and agitated those waters into a state of movement. In Western traditions the active role of Divinity has been assigned to the male gender, while the passive (receiving) role has been assigned to the female gender. This is in contrast to the Southern and Eastern philosophical views where the passive role is assigned to the male gender, and the active role to the female.

Cultural Interactions Between Judaism and Babylonia

In this area of study, an important figure from Mesopotamia is Hammurabi. Hammurabi is believed to have lived around 1,792-1,750 B.C.E. He was king of Babylonia in the first dynasty. He expanded his rule over Mesopotamia and organized the empire by building wheat granaries, canals and classified the law into the famous "Code of Hammurabi." The divine origin ascribed to the Code is of particular interest to our study. Hammurabi can be seen receiving the Code in a bas-relief in which he is depicted as receiving the Code from the sun-god, Shamash, in much the same way that Moses would later receive the Ten Commandments from God, who had appeared as the burning bush (fire is a solar motif). This mode of introducing a teaching or new order, by claiming it to be divinely ordained, is in reality an attempt to impress on the masses of people the authenticity, importance and force with which the new teaching was received and must therefore be followed. Like Moses, Hammurabi created the laws himself, or in conjunction with others, wishing to institute a new order for society. Whether or not they were divinely inspired relates to the degree of communion they were able to achieve with the Divine Self, God. This they could only ascertain for themselves. Spiritually immature people tend to follow a teaching when they believe that it was inspired by God, even if they cannot know for certain intellectually. They feel they somehow "know" in their hearts as they are urged by passionate preachers to have faith. However, if people are fanatical instead of introspective and sober in their religious practice, they may follow the teachings of those who are not authentic spiritual leaders and be led blindly, even to their death.

Cultural Interactions Between Ancient Egypt and Ancient Greece

Greek Myth is a conglomeration of stories related to certain divine personalities and their interactions with each other and with human beings. The main stories about the Greek divinities (gods and goddesses) are contained in the epics, *The Iliad* and *The Odyssey,* written by Homer (900 B.C.E.). The main functions of the gods and goddesses and their mingling with human beings was outlined in these early Greek mythologies. The early Greeks also spoke of the origins of their gods and goddesses. It must be clearly understood that at the time when the early Greeks organized themselves sufficiently enough in order to take up the task of learning art, culture and civilization, they had very little in the way of culture, and what they did have was primitive by Ancient Egyptian and Indus Valley standards thousands years earlier. The force of the Ancient Egyptian culture created perhaps the strongest impression, but it was not the only impression, since the Greeks traveled to other lands and attempted to assimilate the teachings of others as well. This, coupled with their own ideas, caused a situation wherein they created a synthesis of religious philosophies. The expression of Greek culture and philosophy in later periods is reflective of this synthesis. In short, what is regarded as Greek myth was in reality a patchwork of differing ideas that had their basis in Ancient Egyptian philosophy, but which did not follow its precepts entirely as the following statement from Herodotus suggests. *(Bold portions are by Ashby)*

> 35. **"Almost all the names of the gods came into Greece from Egypt. My inquiries prove that they were all derived from a foreign source, and my opinion is that Egypt furnished the greater number**. For with the exception of Neptune and the Dioscuri, whom I mentioned above, and Juno, Vesta, Themis, the Graces, and the Nereids, **the other gods have been known from time immemorial in Egypt**. This I assert on the authority of the Egyptians themselves."
>
> - Herodotus

> **"Solon, Thales, Plato, Eudoxus** and **Pythagoras** went to Egypt and consorted with the priests. **Eudoxus** they say, received instruction from Chonuphis of Memphis,* **Solon** from Sonchis of Sais,* and **Pythagoras** from Oeniphis of Heliopolis."*
> –Plutarch (Greek historian c. 46-120 A.C.E.)
> *(Greek names for cities in Ancient Egypt)

Greek Philosophy has been equated with the origin of Western civilization. Ancient Greek philosophers such as Thales (c. 634-546 B.C.E.) and Pythagoras (582?-500? B.C.E.) are thought to have originated and innovated the sciences of mathematics, medicine, astronomy, philosophy of metaphysics, etc. These disciplines of the early Greek philosophers had a major impact on the development of Christianity since the version of Christianity which was practiced in the Western (Roman) and Eastern (Byzantine) empires was developed in Greece, alongside Greek culture and the Greek language.[73] However, upon closer review, the ancient writings of contemporary historians of those times (early Christianity) also point to sources other than Greek Philosophy, and hence we are led to discover similarities in philosophy by tracing their origins to a common source.

As stated earlier, there is evidence that shows how Ancient Egypt supported not only the education of the early Greek philosophers who came to study in Ancient Egypt itself, but Egypt also supported the Ancient Egyptian Mystery Temples that were established in Greece. Some Egyptian pharaohs sponsored and financed temples abroad which taught mystical philosophy as well as other disciplines. One such effort was put forth by the Ancient Egyptian king, Amasis, who financed the reconstruction of the famous Temple of Delphi in Greece, which was burnt down in 548 B.C.E.[74] This is the Temple which made the saying "Know Thyself" famous.[75] The Ancient Egyptian philosophy of self-knowledge was well known throughout the ancient world. The oracle of Zeus at Dodona was the oldest; and the one at Delphi, the most famous. Herodotus records a Greek tradition which held that Dodona was founded by the Priesthood in Egyptian Thebes. Further, he asserts that the oracle at Delos was founded by an Egyptian who became the king of Athens in 1558 B.C.E. This would be one of the earliest suggested dates for the existence of civilization in Greece, and it is being attributed to an Ancient Egyptian origin by the Greeks themselves, in their own myth and folklore. The connection to and dependence on Ancient Egypt for the creation of Greek culture is unmistakable and far-reaching. Along with this is the association between the Greek city of Athens and the Ancient Egyptian city of Sais. These two were known as "sister cities" in ancient times. Also, the Greeks and Egyptians regarded the goddesses of those cities as being one and the same, i.e. Athena of Greece and Net (Neith) of Egypt.

Thales was the first Greek philosopher of whom there is any knowledge, and therefore he is sometimes called the "Father of Greek Philosophy." After studying in Egypt with the Sages of the Ancient Egyptian temples, he founded the Ionian school of natural philosophy which held that a single elementary matter, water, is the basis of all the transformations of nature. The similarity between this teaching, the Ancient Egyptian Primeval Waters and the creation story in Genesis may be noted here. The ancient writings of the Greeks state that Thales visited Egypt and was initiated by the Egyptian priests into the Egyptian Mystery System, and that he learned astronomy, surveying, engineering, and Egyptian Theology during his time in Egypt. This would have certainly included the theologies related to Asar, Amun and Ptah. Pythagoras was a native of Samos who traveled often to Egypt on the advice of Thales and received education there. He was introduced to each of the Egyptian priests of the major theologies which comprised the whole of the Egyptian religious system based on the Trinity principle (*Amen-Ra-Ptah*). Each of these legs of the Trinity were based in three Egyptian cities. These were Heliopolis (Priesthood of Ra), Memphis (Priesthood of Ptah) and in Thebes (Priesthood of Amen {Amun}) in Egypt.

In reference to the Ionian school that Thales founded after his studies in Egypt, a student from that school, Socrates, became one of the most famous sage-philosophers. Socrates (470? -399? B.C.E.) was regarded as one of the most important philosophers of ancient Greece. He ended up spending most of his life in Athens, however, he was known to have studied under the Ionian philosophers. This establishes a direct link between Socrates and his teaching with Ancient Egypt. Socrates had a tremendous influence on many disciples. One of the most popular of these was Plato. Plato in turn taught others, including Aristotle (384-322 B.C.E.) who was Plato's disciple for 19 years. After Plato's death, Aristotle opened a school of philosophy in Asia Minor. Aristotle educated Philip of Macedon's son, Alexander (Alexander the Great), between the years 343 and 334 B.C.E. Aristotle then returned to Athens and opened a school in the Lyceum, near Athens; here Aristotle lectured to his students. He urged Alexander onto his conquests since in the process, he, Aristotle, was able to gain in knowledge from the ancient writings of the conquered countries. After Alexander's conquest of Egypt, Aristotle became the author of over 1,000 books on philosophy. Building on Plato's *Theory of the Forms*, Aristotle developed the theory of *The Unmoved Mover*, which is a direct teaching from Memphite Theology in Ancient Egypt. Among his works are *De Anima, Nicomachean Ethics and Metaphysics*.[76]

Cultural Interactions Between Greece, Rome, Egypt and Ethiopia, and the Indian, Egyptian and Ethiopian relationship.

As Rome emerged as a powerful military force in the period just prior to the birth of Christ (200 B.C.E.-30 B.C.E.), they adopted Greek customs, religion and art, seeing these as their legacy. Just as the Greeks adopted *The Illiad* and *The Odyssey*, the Romans enthusiastically embraced *The Aeneid* as their national epic. Vergil or Virgil (70-19 B.C.E.) was a Roman poet who wrote *The Aeneid* in the Latin language.[77] *The Aeneid* is actually a story that was written in the same form as *The Odyssey* and *The Illiad* of the Greek writer Homer. It was widely distributed and read throughout the Roman Empire. Thus, *The Aeneid* is considered to be a classical Latin masterpiece of ancient world literature, which had enormous influence on later European writers.[78] Some portions of these texts have important implications to understand the relationship between the Egyptians, the Ethiopians and the Indians in ancient times. *(italicized portions are by Ashby)*

> Mixed in the bloody battle on the plain;
> *And swarthy Memnon in his arms he knew,*
> *His pompous ensigns, and his Indian crew.*
> — *The Aeneid*, Book I, Vergil or Virgil (70-19 BC)[79]

In Greek myth, Memnon was a king from Ethiopia, and was openly referred to as being "burnt of skin", i.e. "black."[10] He was the son of Tithonus, a Troyan (Trojan) prince, and Eos, a Greek goddess of the dawn. Tithonus and Eos represent the sky and romantic love, respectively. During the Troyan war, Memnon assisted Troy[80] with his army. Even though he fought valiantly, he was killed by Achilles. In order to comfort Memnon's mother, Zeus, the king of the Greek gods and goddesses, made Memnon immortal.[81] The Greeks revered a colossal statue of the Ancient Egyptian king Amenhotep III as an image of Memnon. During the times of Greek (332 B.C.E.-30 B.C.E.) and Roman (30 B.C.E.-450 A.C.E.) conquest of Egypt, it became fashionable for Greek and Roman royalty, nobles and those of means from all over the ancient world, especially Greece, to take sightseeing trips to Egypt. The "Colossi of Memnon" were big attractions. The Colossi of Memnon are two massive statues that were built under Amenhotep III, 1,417-1,379 B.C.E.[82] The statues fronted a large temple[83] which is now in ruin, mostly depleted of its stonework by nearby Arab inhabitants who used them to build houses.

This passage is very important because it establishes a connection between Ethiopia, Egypt and India. Further, it establishes that the Indians made up the army of Memnon, that is to say, Ethiopia. Thus, in the time of Virgil, the cultural relationship between north-east Africa and India was so well known that it was mythically carried back in time to the reign of Pharaoh Amenhotep III, the father of the famous king Akhnaton. Pharaoh Amenhotep III was one of the most successful kings of Ancient Egypt. He ruled the area from northern Sudan (Nubia) to the Euphrates river. The Euphrates river is formed by the confluence of the Murat Nehri and the Kara Su Rivers. It flows from East Turkey across Syria into central modern day Iraq where it joins the Tigris River. The land referred to as Mesopotamia, along the lower Euphrates, was the birthplace of the ancient civilizations of Babylonia and Assyria, and the site of the ancient cities of Sippar, Babylon, Erech, Larsa, and Ur. The length of the river is 2,235mi (3.598km).[84] So again we have support for the writings of Herodotus and Diodorus who related the makeup of the ethnic groups in Mesopotamia as belonging to the Ancient Egyptian-Nubian culture.

At first inspection, this relationship appears to be perhaps an allusion to Virgil's times when it is well known and accepted that there was trade and cultural exchange, not only between India and Egypt, as we and other scholars have shown, but also between India and Greece.

Also, in contrast to present day society, there is no racist concept detected or being either implied or inferred, in the Greek writings. Also, there is no apparent aversion to having a personage of African descent (someone from a different ethnic group) in the Greek religion as a member of the family of Greek Gods and Goddesses. There is a remarkable feeling in reading the Greek texts that they had no compunction about admitting their association with Africa and Africans. The Greeks received much in terms of civilization and culture from Africa, in particular, Ethiopia and Ancient Egypt. This may be likened to modern college graduates who are proud to boast of their successful attendance at prestigious schools. There seems to be an eagerness to admit traveling to Egypt, as if it were a stamp of approval for

---

[10] Recall that the term Ethiopians means "land of the burnt (black) faces."

their entry into society as professionals in their fields. There are other passages of interest in *The Aeneid,* which support the cultural connection similar to the previous verse.

Figure 4: The Pharaoh Amenhotep III

Figure 5: The Colossi of Memnon- built under Amenhotep III, 1,417 B.C.E. -1,379 B.C.E. 59 feet tall

(italicized portions are by Ashby)

Ceasar himself, exalted in his line;
Augustus, promised oft, and long foretold,
Sent to the realm that Saturn ruled of old;
Born to restore a better age of gold.
Africa and India shall his power obey;
- The Aeneid, Book VI, Vergil or Virgil (70-19 BC)[85]

This seen, Apollo, from his Actian height,
Pours down his arrows; at whose winged flight
The trembling Indians and Egyptians yield,
- The Aeneid, Book VIII, Vergil or Virgil (70-19 BC)[86]

In the first passage above, Africa and India are being linked as two countries that will be controlled by the Roman emperors (Ceasar, Augustus). Also, this statement implies that Egypt is an African country and not an Asiatic country. The time when this text was written is the period just prior to the Roman conquest of Ancient Egypt (30 B.C.E.). Therefore, it follows that the intent of the Romans, based on this passage, was to expand their empire to encompass north-east Africa and India. This repeated reference to India in conjunction with Africa and Egypt seems to imply a connection between the two countries, relating to a vast empire with two major geographic locales (Kamit and India).

Cultural Interactions Between Hinduism and Vedic Culture In India

In India, the emergence of Hinduism saw a similar situation as with the one that occurred between the Jewish and Ancient Egyptian Religion. In a later period (c. 800 B.C.E.-600 B.C.E.), the earlier Vedic-Aryan religious teachings related to the God Indra (c. 1,000 B.C.E.) were supplanted by the teachings related to the Upanishadic and Vaishnava tradition. The Vaishnava tradition includes the worship of the god Vishnu, as well as his avatars (divine incarnations), in the form of Rama and Krishna. The Vaishnava tradition was developed by the indigenous Indian peoples to counter, surpass and evolve beyond the Vedic religious teachings. In the epic stories known as the Ramayana and the Mahabharata[87], Vishnu incarnates as Rama and Krishna, respectively, and throughout these and other stories it is related how Vishnu's incarnations are more powerful than Indra's, who is portrayed as being feeble and weak. Some of the writings of the Upanishadic Tradition,[88] the writings which succeed the Vedic tradition, contain specific verses which seem to profess that the wisdom of the Vedas is lesser than that of the Upanishads, and that they therefore supersede the Vedas. One such statement can be found in the *Mundaka Upanishad*. The following segment details the view of the two sets of scriptures in relation to each other and the two forms of knowledge. (italicized portions are by Ashby)

> Those who know Brahman (God)... say that there are two kinds of knowledge, the higher and the lower. *The lower is knowledge of the Vedas* (the Rik, the Sama, the Yajur, and the Atharva), and also of phonetics, grammar, etymology, meter, and astronomy. *The higher is the knowledge of that by which one knows the changeless reality.*

Cultural Interactions Between Hinduism and Buddhism

A similar situation that transpired with Kamitan religion with respect to Judaism, and with Hinduism with respect to Vedic religion, as discussed above, occurred between Hinduism and Buddhism with the advent of Buddhism. The story of Buddha's struggle to attain enlightenment, the inceptive and most influential work of Buddhist myth, relates how he strove to practice the austere paths of Hinduism (Upanishadic wisdom, Vedanta, Brahmanism, austerity, yoga, etc.). He practiced renunciation of the world and all sorts of penances and asceticism, even to the point of almost starving himself to death. Then he "discovered" a "new" path, "The Middle Path," and for a long time it was held to be superior to Hinduism by many. It found a great following in China and Tibet, as well as other countries of Indo-China.[89] Currently in the west, Buddhism is rarely related to its roots in Hinduism and Yoga philosophy. Upon close examination, the roots of the teaching of the middle path, along with the other major tenets of Buddhism such as the philosophy of *Karma* (action), *Maya* (cosmic illusion) and *Samsara* (philosophy of worldly suffering) can be traced to the Upanishadic Tradition,[90] especially in the Isha Upanishad. Thus, the early Buddhist teachers found it necessary to disparage the other practices in order to highlight the Buddhist faith, and yet what developed is a reworking of the same teaching that was there previously, not only in Indian mystical philosophy, but also in the mystical and yogic teachings of Ancient Egypt.

Buddha emphasized attaining salvation rather than asking so many questions. He likened people who asked too many intellectual questions to a person whose house (lifetime) is burning down while they ask, "How did the fire get started?" instead of first worrying about getting out of the house. Further, Buddha saw that renouncing attachment to worldly objects was not primarily a physical discipline, but more importantly, it was a psychological one. Therefore, he constructed a philosophical discipline, based on already existing philosophical tenets that explained the psychology behind human suffering and how to end that suffering. The Middle Path emphasized balance rather than extremes. He recognized that extremes cause mental upsets because one extreme leads to another, and the mind loses the capacity for rational thought and intuitional awareness which transcends thought itself. Therefore, mental balance is the way to achieve mental peace and serenity, which will allow the transcendental vision of the Self to emerge in the mind. The following segment from the *Isha Upanishad* shows that having a balanced approach and proceeding according to the *"middle path"* with respect to the practice of spiritual disciplines was already addressed as being desirable for spiritual growth prior to the emergence of Buddhism. Buddhism later represented an accent or emphasis on this feature of the doctrine so it is clear that Buddhism "adopted" many pre-existing philosophical principles from Hinduism.

> "To darkness are they doomed who devote themselves only to life in the world, and to a greater darkness they who devote themselves only to meditation.
> Life in the world alone leads to one result, meditation alone leads to another. So we have heard from the wise. They who devote themselves both to life in the world and to meditation, by life in the world overcome death, and by meditation achieve immortality. To darkness are they doomed who worship only the body, and to greater darkness they who worship only the spirit."

This Buddhist Yogic psychological discipline became known as the Noble Eight-fold Path, the disciplines of Buddhist Yoga which lead to spiritual enlightenment. The "Middle Path," is also the central feature of Maat Philosophy from Ancient Egypt. It was referred to as "Keeping the Balance."[91]

In India, five to six hundred years before Christianity, Buddhism had caused a renaissance of sorts. The Brahmanic system (based on the Vedic Tradition) of ritual, asceticism and elaborate myth began to lose favor with many aspirants who were seeking a more psychologically based approach to the pursuit of spiritual enlightenment that did not include the use of deities or elaborate symbolism. The ideas inherent in Buddhism such as Karma, (the law of cause and effect and reincarnation), *Maya,* (Cosmic Illusion) and *Buddhi* (Intellect) existed in the Vedantic and Yogic scriptures of India prior to the formulation of the Buddhist religion. However, the spiritual system developed in the sixth century B.C.E. by Gautama, the Buddha, represented in a way a reform as well as a refinement of the older teachings which were already widely accepted. Especially emphasized was that God, the ultimate reality, alone exists and that everyone is equally able to achieve oneness with that reality. However, the concept of God in Buddhism is that God is not to be considered as a deity, but as an abstract state of consciousness which is achieved when the mind is free of desires and consequently free of the fruits of action. Buddhism also placed important emphasis on non-violence which certainly became a central part of the Christian doctrine as well, in philosophy if not in practice. In the same sense that Buddhism proclaims everyone can have *Buddha Consciousness* (or *Buddha Nature*) and thus become a Buddha, Gnostic Christianity affirms that everyone can achieve *Christ Consciousness* and thus become a *Christ.*

As explained earlier, the Buddha or *"The Enlightened One"* developed a philosophy based on ideas that existed previously in the Upanishads. In much the same way as the term Christ refers to anyone who has attained "Christhood," the term Buddha refers to any one who has attained the "Buddha Consciousness," the state of Enlightenment. In this context there have been many male and female Christs and Buddhas throughout history, since the earliest practice of mystical spirituality in Kamit.

Prior to Buddha, other teachings such as those of the "Brahmins," (followers of the teachings related to Brahman of the Upanishads) the *Samnyasa* or renunciates, and the Jains promoted the idea that one was supposed to renounce the apparent reality of the world as an illusion by detachment, privation and austerity. The Buddhists as well as the Jains[92] deny the divine origin and authority of the Vedas. The Buddhists revere Buddha and the Jains revere certain saints who espoused the Jain philosophy in ancient times. Buddha recognized that many people took the teachings to extreme and saw this as the cause of failure in attaining progress in spirituality. Teachings such as reducing one's Karma by reducing one's worldly involvements were misunderstood by many to mean escaping the world by running away to some remote forest or mountain area. Also, the teachings of non-violence which stressed not harming any creatures were taken to the extreme by some in the Jain religion, to the point that they would not physically move so as not to step on insects, or not breathe without covering the mouth and nostrils, so as not to kill microorganisms. Others felt that they should not talk to anyone or interact with others in any way. These teachings were taken to such extremes that some aspirants would remain silent so long as to lose their capacity to speak at all. Others starved themselves while others practiced severe austerities such as meditating in the cold rivers or not sleeping. Others became deeply involved with the intellectual aspects of philosophy, endlessly questioning, "Where did I come from? Who put me here? How long will I need to do spiritual practice? Where did Brahman (God) come from?" etc. These questions were entertained ad-infinitum, without leading to answers that promote the attainment of enlightenment. Buddha saw the error of the way in which the teaching was understood and practiced. He therefore set out to reform religion.

NOTES TO INTRODUCTION

---

[1] Photo by Gakuji Tanaka

[2] Petrie Museum, London England.

[3] American Heritage Dictionary

[4] ibid.

[5] Copyright © 1995 Helicon Publishing Ltd Encyclopedia

[6] Copyright © 1995 Helicon Publishing Ltd Encyclopedia, Random House Encyclopedia Copyright (C) 1983,1990, Microsoft (R) Encarta Encyclopedia. Copyright (c) 1994

[7] Random House Encyclopedia Copyright (C) 1983,1990

[8] Copyright © 1995 Helicon Publishing Ltd Encyclopedia

[9] Copyright © 1995 Helicon Publishing Ltd Encyclopedia, Random House Encyclopedia Copyright (C) 1983,1990, Microsoft (R) Encarta Encyclopedia. Copyright (c) 1994

[10] Mesopotamia (from a Greek term meaning "between rivers") lies between the Tigris and Euphrates rivers, a region that is part of modern Iraq.

[11] Random House Encyclopedia Copyright (C) 1983,1990

[12] ibid.

[13] **the·ol·o·gy** (thē-ŏl′ə-jē) *n., pl.* **the·ol·o·gies**. *Abbr.* **theol. 1.** The study of the nature of God and religious truth; rational inquiry into religious questions. (American Heritage Dictionary)

[14] *com·mu·nal* (kə-myōō′nəl, kŏm′yə-) *adj.* **1.** *Of or relating to a commune.* **2.** *Of or relating to a community.* **3.a.** *Of, belonging to, or shared by the people of a community; public.* **b.** *Marked by collective ownership and control of goods and property.* (American Heritage Dictionary)

[15] **syn·chro·ny** (sĭng′krə-nē, sĭn′-) *n., pl.* **syn·chro·nies**. Simultaneous occurrence; synchronism. (American Heritage Dictionary)

[16] **ty·pog·ra·phy** (tĭ-pŏg′rə-fē) *n., pl.* **ty·pog·ra·phies**. *Abbr.* **typ.**, **typo.** *Printing* **2.** The arrangement and appearance of printed matter. (American Heritage Dictionary)

[17] American Heritage Dictionary

[18] Random House Encyclopedia Copyright (C) 1983,1990

[19] *The African Origin of Civilization*, *Civilization or Barbarism,* Cheikh Anta Diop

[20] American Heritage Dictionary

[21] American Heritage Dictionary

[22] American Heritage Dictionary

[23] American Heritage Dictionary

[24] *Comparative Mythology,* Jaan Puhvel

[25] *Comparative Mythology,* Jaan Puhvel

[26] A "Great Cycle" *(Mahayuga)* of cosmic time.

[27] i.e., at the ending of the cosmic eon, Wagner's *Götterdämmerung.*

[28] According to the Egyptians, Diodorus reports, the Chaldaens were *"a colony of their priests that Belus had transported on the Euphrates and organized on the model of the mother-caste, and this colony continues to cultivate the knowledge of the stars, knowledge that it brought from the homeland."*

[29] *The Mythic Image*, Joseph Campbell

[30] *The Mythic Image*, Joseph Campbell

[31] *Resurrecting Osiris ,* Muata Ashby, 1997

[32] American Heritage Dictionary

[33] *The Power of Myth,* Joseph Campbell

[34] *Comparative Mythology,* Jaan Puhvel

[35] G. Lafaye. *Historie des divinités d'Alexandrie hors de l' Egypte.* Paris, 18984, p.259

[36] *The Migration of Symbols,* Count Goblet D' Alviella, 1894

[37] **dog·ma** (dôg′mə, dŏg′-) *n., pl.* **dog·mas** or **dog·ma·ta** (-mə-tə). **1.** *Theology.* A doctrine or a corpus of doctrines relating to matters such as morality and faith, set forth in an authoritative manner by a church.

[38] **or·tho·dox** (ôr′thə-dŏks′) *adj.* **1.** Adhering to the accepted or traditional and established faith, especially in religion.

[39] The word "Hinduism" is a Western term. The religion called Hinduism is actually referred to by the Hindus themselves as "Sanatana-Dharma," which means "the eternal law" or "the path or righteous actions or way of life." The major religion of the Indian subcontinent is Hinduism. The word derives from an ancient Sanskrit term meaning "dwellers by the Indus River," a reference to the location of India's earliest known civilization in what is now Pakistan. (*Feuerstein, Georg, The Shambhala Encyclopedia of Yoga* 1997 and *Compton's Interactive Encyclopedia.* Copyright (c) 1994, 1995 Compton's NewMedia, Inc. All Rights Reserved) .

[40] *The Power of Myth,* Bill Moyers, 1989.

[41] In Ancient Egyptian mythology, the son of Isis (Aset), Heru, represents rulership and the upholding of righteousness, truth and order. Thus, the Pharaoh is Heru incarnate and when that person dies, he/she becomes Asar (Osiris), the resurrected (Enlightened) spirit.

[42] The Asar from Ancient Egypt.

[43] December 25th is also the birthday of the Ancient Egyptian god Heru.

[44] For more details see the book *Christian Yoga: The Journey from Jesus to Christ* by Muata Ashby

[45] Adopting cultural expressions of other cultures and making them part of one's own culture thereby subsuming the cultural factors from other cultures within the larger one and consequently dissolving the adopted culture into the larger one. Over a period of time, the original source of the tradition becomes blurred or forgotten because the original tradition is no longer presented as such. Examples: Moslem and Christian church practice of destroying indigenous temples and placing Mosques or churches, respectively, on the same sites. Christian adoption of the Ancient Egyptian cross, eucharist, resurrection, birthday of Heru, Madonna, etc.

[46] To neutralize or win over (an independent minority, for example) through assimilation into an established group or culture. (American Heritage Dictionary)

[47] Copyright © 1995 Helicon Publishing Ltd Encyclopedia

[48] Copyright © 1995 Helicon Publishing Ltd Encyclopedia

[49] American Heritage Dictionary

[50] *Egypt Uncovered*, Vivian Davies and Renée Friedman

[51] *Comparative Mythology*, Jaan Puhvel

[52] The scientific study of the origin, the behavior, and the physical, social, and cultural development of human beings.

[53] The belief that one's own culture is primary and superior to other cultures.

[54] *Egyptian Proverbs* by Dr. Muata Ashby

[55] Bhagavad Gita by Swami Jyotirmayananda

[56] Random House Encyclopedia Copyright (C) 1983,1990

[57] "Scientific Method," Microsoft (R) Encarta. Copyright (c) 1994

[58] for evidences see the book *The Conscious Universe: The Scientific truth of Psychic Phenomena* By Dean Radin, Ph. D.

[59] *Memphite Theology*, Muata Ashby

[60] *The Tao of Physics*, Fritjof Capra

[61] *Dancing Wu Li Masters* by Gary Zukov

[62] American Heritage Dictionary

[63] American Heritage Dictionary

[64] *Comparative Mythology*, Jaan Puhvel

[65] Ibid

[66] Ibid

[67] Ibid

[68] A structural or behavioral characteristic peculiar to an individual or a group.

[69] *The Migration of Symbols,* Count Goblet D' Alviella, 1894

[70] Ontology, in philosophy, the branch of metaphysics that studies the basic nature of things, the essence of "being" itself.

[71] *Statistics-probability-* A number expressing the likelihood that a specific event will occur, expressed as the ratio of the number of actual occurrences to the number of possible occurrences. (American Heritage Dictionary)

[72] From more details see the book *Christian Yoga: The Journey from Jesus to Christ* by Muata Ashby

[73] ibid

[74] Stolen Legacy, George G.M. James

[75] Inscription at the Delphic Oracle. From Plutarch, Morals, *Familiar Quotations,* John Bartlett

[76] For more details on the interaction between Ancient Egypt and Greece see the book *From Egypt to Greece* by Muata Ashby.

[77] Random House Encyclopedia Copyright (C) 1983,1990

[78] "Vergil," Microsoft (R) Encarta. Copyright (c) 1994

[79] *The Aeneid By Virgil*, Translated by John Dryden

[80] Troy (Asia Minor), also Ilium (ancient Ilion), famous city of Greek legend, on the northwestern corner of Asia Minor, in present-day Turkey. "Troy (Asia Minor)," Microsoft (R) Encarta. Copyright (c) 1994

[81] "Memnon," Microsoft (R) Encarta. Copyright (c) 1994

[82] Random House Encyclopedia Copyright (C) 1983,1990

[83] *The Complete Temples of Ancient Egypt*, Richard Wilkinson, (C) 2000

[84] Random House Encyclopedia Copyright (C) 1983,1990

[85] *The Aeneid By Virgil*, Translated by John Dryden

[86] *The Aeneid By Virgil*, Translated by John Dryden

[87] *Mahabharata* (Sanskrit, *Great Story*), longer of the two great epic poems of ancient India; the other is the *Ramayana*. The *Mahabharata* was composed beginning about 300B.C.E. and received numerous additions until about 300 A.C.E.. "Mahabharata," *Microsoft® Encarta® Encyclopedia 2000.* © 1993-1999 Microsoft Corporation. All rights reserved.

[88] Any of a group of philosophical treatises contributing to the theology of ancient Hinduism-Vedanta Philosophy, elaborating on and superseding the earlier Vedas.

[89] The Indochinese peninsula includes a small part of Bangladesh, most of Myanmar (Burma), Thailand, Cambodia, and parts of Malaysia, Laos, and Vietnam.

[90] Spiritual tradition in India based on the scriptures known as the Upanishads. It is also referred to as Vedanta Philosophy, the culmination or summary of the Vedic Tradition whish is itself based on the scriptures known as the Vedas.

[91] *"The Wisdom of Maati,"* Dr. Muata Ashby. *"The Egyptian Book of the Dead,"* Dr. Muata Ashby.

[92] Religion founded by Mahavira, a contemporary of Buddha. "Jainism," Microsoft (R) Encarta. Copyright (c) 1994

PART I: THE AFRICAN ORIGINS OF AFRICAN CIVILIZATION, RELIGION, YOGA MYSTICISM AND ETHICS PHILOSOPHY

Chapter 1: The People and History of Ancient Egypt and Nubia

Rtji Ancient Egyptian

Ahsu Ancient Nubian

"From Ethiopia, he (Osiris) passed through Arabia, bordering upon the Red Sea to as far as India, and the remotest inhabited coasts; he built likewise many cities in India, one of which he called Nysa, willing to have remembrance of that (Nysa) in Egypt where he was brought up. At this Nysa in India he planted Ivy, which continues to grow there, but nowhere else in India or around it. He left likewise many other marks of his being in those parts, by which the latter inhabitants are induced, and do affirm, that this God was born in India. He likewise addicted himself to the hunting of elephants, and took care to have statues of himself in every place, as lasting monuments of his expedition."

-Recorded by Diodorus (Greek historian 100 B.C.)

Chapter 1-Section 1: Introduction

This chapter has three parts. First we will present an introduction to the Ancient Egyptians and an overview of their place in history. Secondly, we will explore the Nubian origins and history of Ancient Egypt, which will give a depth to our knowledge of the Ancient Egyptians. It is important for us to have this understanding of their origins in Nubia and their relationship to the Nubians (Ethiopians), because by doing so, we will become cognizant of and gain deeper insight into the African origins of Kamitan culture as well as the extent of its impact and influence on the rest of Africa beginning with the Nubian kingdoms, and through their influence, extending into the other countries in the interior of Africa. Then we will explore the different periods of Ancient Egyptian history in detail.

Who Were the Ancient Egyptians and why Should we Learn About Them?

The Ancient Egyptian religion (*Shetaut Neter*), language and symbols provide the first "historical" record of Mystical Philosophy and Religious literature. Egyptian Mysticism is what has been commonly referred to by Egyptologists as Egyptian "Religion" or "Myth," but to think of it as just another set of stories or allegories about a long lost civilization is to completely miss the greater teaching it has to offer. Mystical spirituality, in all of its forms and disciplines of spiritual development, was practiced in Ancient Egypt (Kamit) earlier than anywhere else in history. This unique perspective from the highest philosophical system which developed in Africa over seven thousand years ago provides a new way to look at life, religion, the discipline of psychology and the way to spiritual development leading to spiritual Enlightenment. Ancient Egyptian myth, when understood as a system of *Sema (Smai) Tawi* (Egyptian Yoga), that is, a system which promotes the union of the individual soul with the Universal Soul or Supreme Consciousness, gives every individual insight into their own divine nature, and also a deeper insight into all religions, mystical and Yoga systems.

Next, let us answer the question of "Why should we learn about the Ancient Egyptians? Of what benefit will it be to us today, in the here and now?" Ancient Egyptian culture and philosophy is crucial to the understanding of world history and spirituality. One of the misconceptions which is still promoted and prevalent in modern times is that Egypt is not a part of, or located on, the continent of Africa. Rather, it is espoused that Egypt is in the Middle East. This information is incorrect, as Egypt is where it has always been located, though in history it extended beyond its current margins, in the northeast corner of the African Continent. Further, it is widely believed by others that even though Egypt may be in Africa, that it was not an African country, and still others may agree that it was an African country, but not originally founded and populated by "black" African people (like present day Algeria, which is in Africa but populated by Middle Easterners -Arabs). These errors must be redressed in order for humanity to move forward. Truth must be promoted and in this case, it is crucial that this particular truth be brought forth into our human sphere of knowledge, as it offers a chance to humanity for achieving some level of peace and harmony as a world community. Also it will promote the redemption of African culture and thereby uplift African society and thereby the world. Africa provides a common ground, literally and figuratively, for humanity to come together, if we so choose, as both the physical origins of modern day humans is rooted in African soil, and also the spiritual roots of all religions and spiritual traditions can be traced there as well. Most of the wars that have occurred in human history after the close of Ancient Egyptian history have been due to religious differences, especially between orthodox aspects of the three major world religions, Christianity, Islam and Judaism, and the various subgroups of religions to which they each have given rise. Yet, all of these religions, and as we shall see, all spiritual traditions of the world, have their birthplace in Kamit. They are as if children and grandchildren of the Kamitan tradition. Imagine what happens in a simple human family when the children and grandchildren enter into conflicts and feuds. In the history of the U.S.A., there is a well-established example of the effects of this in the story of the Hatfields and the McCoys, a family feud that lasted for generations. Also, consider the United States' civil war. From this viewpoint, it is easy to understand why the world is in the shape it is in today. In the case of the world religions, they are not directly fighting to claim the cultural inheritance and prestige of their Kamitan ancestors, although their traditions utilize many of the symbols or concepts of the Kamitan tradition in limited ways. Rather, for the most part they have shunned their ancestry and the history of their "roots" in favor of each trying to legitimize themselves as the only "true" religion, without regards to the culture and land of origin which forms the very nucleus (core, nidus) of all current traditions. Not only have they shunned their ancestry, but in many ways also disparage it. Consequently, although they all claim to have some aspects of commonality (Muslims accept Jesus, but only as a prophet, and Jews and Christians have the Old Testament in common, etc.), they are inherently unable to unite, as ultimately, each tradition believes and espouses that it is the only one true religion and has the only one true God.

The current state of human relations in the world has been likened to a family of dysfunctional people. One of the causes cited for this disfunctionality is the misunderstanding of human origins and relationships which leads to the adoption of bogus concepts such as racism, religious sectarianism, superiority complexes, inhumanity, violence and war. The world community needs to have the knowledge of its African human and spiritual origins so that Africa can take its rightful place as the "parent" of all humanity. In this way the error by which most people live will be resolved in the understanding that we are all of one family, one "race". It is also important for people who identify themselves as being of African descent to know and understand their deepest "roots" beyond the most current history of enslavement and all the negative racist ramifications it spawned (i.e. Africans are inferior, stupid, etc.). Most people of African ancestry have had to live with, and to some degree accept, denigrating and deprecating conditions, in order to survive. Thus, those who identify themselves as being ethnically of African origins can, through espousing and accepting the truth with respect to world history, become esteemed members of the world community.

The study of Kamitan Spirituality is also of particular importance for people of Indian descent, as they too share directly in the Kamitan legacy. This knowledge will allow them to understand the depth of their own culture and spiritual tradition, as well as aid in the restoration of positive interactions with people of African descent in India, the Diaspora, and Africa itself.

Where is Egypt?

Figure 6: Egypt is located in the north-eastern corner of the African Continent.

Figure 7: Below left: A map of North East Africa showing the location of the land of *Ta-Meri* or *Kamit,* also known as Ancient Egypt and South of it is located the land which in modern times is called Sudan.

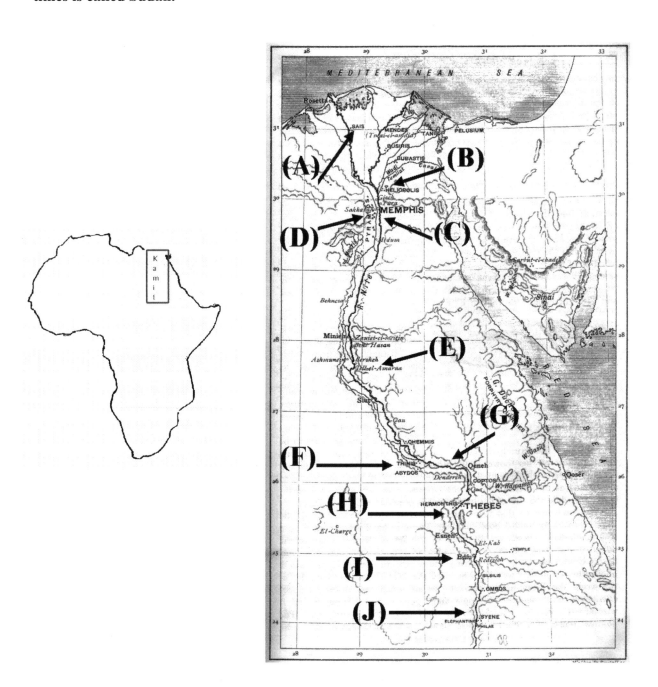

Figure 8: Above right- The Land of Ancient Egypt-Nile Valley

The cities wherein the theology of the Trinity of Amun-Ra-Ptah was developed were: A- Sais (temple of Net), B- Anu (Heliopolis- temple of Ra), C-Men-nefer or Hetkaptah (Memphis, temple of Ptah), and D-Sakkara (Pyramid Texts), E- Akhet-Aton (City of Akhnaton, temple of Aton), F- Abdu (temple of Asar), G-Denderah (temple of Hetheru), H- Waset (Thebes, temple of Amun), I- Edfu (temple of Heru), J- Philae (temple of Aset). The cities wherein the theology of the Trinity of Asar-Aset-Heru was developed were Anu, Abydos, Philae, Denderah and Edfu.

The Two Lands of Egypt

In Chapter 4[93] and Chapter 17[94] of the Ancient Egyptian mystical text, the *Prt m Hru, The Ancient Egyptian Book of Enlightenment*, more commonly known as the *Book of the Dead,* the term "Sema (Smai) Tawi" is used. It means "Union of the two lands of Egypt." The two lands refers to the two main districts of the country, North and South, and, in a mystical sense they refer to the gods Heru (the north) and Set (the south land), who are elsewhere referred to as the spiritual Higher Self and lower self of a human being, respectively. Thus, the term Sema Tawi is compatible with the Indian Sanskrit term "Yoga," which also means union of the Higher Self and lower self as well as other terms used by other systems of mystical spirituality (Enlightenment, Kingdom of Heaven, Liberation, etc.).

Diodorus Siculus (Greek Historian) writes in the time of Augustus (first century B.C.):

"Now the Ethiopians, as historians relate, were the first of all men and the proofs of this statement, they say, are manifest. For that they did not come into their land as immigrants from abroad, but were the natives of it and so justly bear the name of autochthones (sprung from the soil itself) is, they maintain, conceded by practically all men..."

"They also say that the Egyptians are colonists sent out by the Ethiopians, Asar having been the leader of the colony. For, speaking generally, what is now Egypt, they maintain, was not land, but sea, when in the beginning the universe was being formed; afterwards, however, as the Nile during the times of its inundation carried down the mud from Ethiopia, land was gradually built up from the deposit...And the larger parts of the customs of the Egyptians are, they hold, Ethiopian, the colonists still preserving their ancient manners. For instance, the belief that their kings are Gods, the very special attention which they pay to their burials, and many other matters of a similar nature, are Ethiopian practices, while the shapes of their statues and the forms of their letters are Ethiopian; for of the two kinds of writing which the Egyptians have, that which is known as popular (demotic) is learned by everyone, while that which is called sacred (hieratic), is understood only by the priests of the Egyptians, who learnt it from their Fathers as one of the things which are not divulged, but among the Ethiopians, everyone uses these forms of letters. Furthermore, the orders of the priests, they maintain, have much the same position among both peoples; for all are clean who are engaged in the service of the gods, keeping themselves shaven, like the Ethiopian priests, and having the same dress and form of staff, which is shaped like a plough and is carried by their kings who wear high felt hats which end in a knob in the top and are circled by the serpents which they call asps; and this symbol appears to carry the thought that it will be the lot who shall dare to attack the king to encounter death-carrying stings. Many other things are told by them concerning their own antiquity and the colony which they sent out that became the Egyptians, but about this there is no special need of our writing anything."

Figure 9: Below- the Ancient Egyptian Hor-m-Akhet (Sphinx).

The archeological and geological evidence surrounding the great Sphinx in Giza, Egypt, Africa, shows that it was created no later than 10,000 B.C.E. to 7,000 B.C.E. This gives us the understanding that Kamit, Ancient Egypt, produced the earliest known artifacts, which denotes civilization. Thus, the Kamitan or Ancient Egyptian civilization is the oldest known civilization in our history.

How Some Western and Arab Scholars Distort Evidence Pointing to the Older Age of Ancient Egyptian Culture

After examining the writings of many Western scholars, the feeling of many Africentrists and Africologists (researchers into African culture) of African descent and some non-African Western scholars is that traditional Egyptologists, a group comprised almost entirely of people of European descent or who have been trained by Western scholars, have over the years sought to bring down the estimated date for the commencement of the Dynastic Period in Egypt in order to show that Ancient Egyptian culture emerged after Mesopotamian culture. Presumably, this was done because Mesopotamia is held by many Western scholars to be their (Western Culture's) own, if not genetic, cultural ancestral homeland. The reader should understand the context of this issue that goes to the heart of cultural relations between Western Culture and Eastern and African cultures. From the perspective of many people of non-European descent, Western Culture has sought to establish its socio-economic supremacy by suppressing and undermining the capacity of indigenous peoples worldwide, to govern themselves and control their own resources. This is verified by the documented evidence of the African slave trade,[95] military and covert intervention to destabilize governments, distortion of history,[96\97] colonial and neocolonial systems,[98] etc., either set up or supported by Western countries in the past 500 years. In order to perpetuate this control, the image of superiority demands that Western Culture should be able to project an ancestral right, as it were, to control other countries. Therefore, twisting evidence in order to make Western Culture appear ancient, wise, beneficial, etc., necessitates a denial that there is any civilization that is older or possibly better than Western civilization, or that there could be any genetic or cultural relation with the non-Western Cultures which are being subjugated, or a common ancestry with the rest of humanity. An example of this twisting of history by Western scholars is the well known and documented deliberate misinterpretation of the Biblical story of Noah, so as to make it appear that the Bible advocated and condones the enslavement of the children (descendants) of Ham (all Hamitic peoples- people of African descent) by the children (descendants) of Japheth (all peoples of Germanic {European} descent).

Along with the natural stubbornness of ordinary human beings to accept change due to the their identification with prestige of their culture and heritage as a source of self-worth instead of truth and virtue, two methods of discrediting the early achievements of Ancient Egypt have been used.

The desire of Western Culture to envision their own history as a civilized culture stretching back into antiquity, having realized that Greek culture is too late in history to establish this claim, and not wanting to acknowledge that Ancient Greece essentially owes[99] its civilization to Ancient Egypt,[100] have promoted a process of downplaying the importance of Ancient Egypt in history, by means of reducing the chronology in which history took place. How could this obfuscation of the record occur?

In addition to the resistance by some in Western scholars to accept information, which they fear, will change the prestige of their culture and heritage with which they identify as a source of their self-worth, instead of defining themselves by the standards of truth and virtue, other methods of discrediting the early achievements of Ancient Egypt have been used. Two ways of invalidating Ancient Egyptian history are prominent: 1- misunderstanding or 2- supporting erroneous theories.

One method used by Western Egyptologists to contradict Kamitan history was to examine surviving[11] Ancient Egyptian mummies and apply undetermined forensic techniques in order to assign "causes of death" to the entire Ancient Egyptian culture. From this they concluded that the Ancient Egyptians had a short life span due to "primitive living conditions," and that the average life expectancy of a Pharaoh being no more than 20 years or so. However, since the cause of death can often not be determined even in modern times, how can the results derived from any technique(s) being applied to a 3,000 + years old mummified body be conclusive? When such rationales are not considered, and the erroneous pronouncements repeated over and over again, they become "accepted" as truth by scholars and lay persons for a variety of reasons, some of which we have already touched on above. The problem becomes compounded because many scholars and lay people alike do not do their own research or look at the evidence themselves and draw their own conclusions. Rather, they are comfortable accepting the information being provided, without questioning its validity. Some don't want to know, because they do not want to risk their positions by disrupting the status quo. Others may be unwilling, or unable due to blind faith and mental weakness, to examine the evidences. In addition, there are other factors to be considered such as socio-economic obstacles, physical barriers preventing access to information, training, etc.

Another method used to revise the history of the Dynastic Period in Kamit is to say that the kings or queens were ruling concurrently in certain periods as opposed to subsequently. In certain periods such as the invasion of the Hyksos and the Assyrians, Persians, etc. who conquered part of the country, Egyptian leaders ruled in their part of the country while the conquerors temporarily ruled the conquered territory that they captured. Also, this is possible in the Intermediate period when there was a partial breakdown of social order. Further, due to the destruction of records, there are many Ancient Egyptian rulers (kings and queens) mentioned whose names are no longer recorded. (See the Ancient Egyptian King and Queen List in Appendix A)

Since we have lists of the Pharaohs of the Dynastic Period, we can easily count the number of Pharaohs and use this figure to estimate what the average life span of each Pharaoh would have to be to cover the time span of the Dynastic Period, which lasted approximately 3,000 + years. Doing the math by multiplying this number by the life expectancy proposed by scholars (20 years), one arrives at a figure that is less than 3,000 years, the duration of the Dynastic period. Also, the conclusion drawn from the above methodology used to estimate the life span of the Kamitan peoples from mummified bodies (of the average life span of 20 years), even if it were accurate, does not make sense if we consider the ample documentation showing that Ancient Egypt was reputed to have the "best doctors" in the ancient world. Further, even if it were true that ordinary people existed in "primitive living conditions," does it make sense that the kings and queens would get the worst health care out of the entire population? Thus, as a scholar, is it prudent to apply this number to the royalty? Also, there is documented evidence to show that kings and queens, as well as other members of the society, lived normal healthy lives by modern standards. There are surviving records and statues, as well as illustrations, of kings, mummies and other royalty who lived well into their 80's and 90's such as Amunhotep Son of Hapu and Rameses II and others. One might also envision the wretchedness of such a life where members of a society die at such an early age. No sooner does one realize the potential of life, than one dies, as a mere child. Life would hardly be worth living. Also, since spiritual evolution requires maturity in ordinary human terms, that is, sufficient time to grow up and discover the meaning of life, a short life-span would make the vast number of extant Kamitan texts treating the subject of spiritual enlightenment impossible to create, and useless because there would not be sufficient time to take advantage of them.

Another method used to discredit the Kamitan history is to arbitrarily claim that when the Ancient Egyptians spoke of "years," they were actually referring to "months".[101] This practice is predicated on baseless supposition, and is therefore, patently false and demeaning since there is no precedent for this practice in Ancient Egyptian culture. It is an imaginary notion introduced by some Egyptologists who prefer to fantasize

---

[11] Many mummies have been destroyed throughout history by the early Christians and Muslims who wanted to eradicate all records of religions existing prior to their own, and also early European explorers who sold the mummies for experimentation as well as other Europeans who created a fad of pulverizing the mummies and using them in potions as medicinal supplements.

rather than face the magnitude of their discoveries. Thus, the corrupt nature of the historians, scholars and those who perpetuate such iniquitous misrepresentations is evident.

Still another motivation has been to try to synchronize the events such as those described in Ancient Egyptian texts or the Greek histories with those of the Bible. An example of this kind of writing can be found in a book by W. G. Waddell, called *Manetho*. Some historians feel this kind of distortion was done to establish the prestige of the Judeo-Christian tradition, the reasoning being similar to that discussed above. They believe that Judeo-Christian view was that having other traditions that are recognized as older and having more honor, heritage and prominence would undermine the perception that the Bible is ancient and infallible.

Others feel the reason was out of an effort to prove that Ancient Egyptian culture existed within the timeframe that the Bible has posed for the Creation of the world. The Creation was dated by the 17th-century[12] Irish archbishop James Ussher to have occurred in the year 4004 B.C.E.[102] If the world is approximately 6,005[13] years old, as postulated by the archbishop, this would support the teaching presented in the church and invalidate the existence of culture, philosophy, and most of all, religion, prior to the emergence of Christianity.

The work of Darwin (theory of evolution) and other scientists caused major controversies in western society. A case in point is the attempt to correlate the events of the Biblical story of Exodus with those of Ancient Egyptian Pharaoh, Rameses II. First, there are no accounts of any conflict between the Jews and the Egyptians in any Ancient Egyptian records yet discovered, beyond an inscription at the Karnak temple in Egypt stating that the Jews were one of the tribes under Egyptian rule in Palestine. Secondly, there are no corroborating records of the events chronicled in the Bible in any of the contemporary writings from countries that had contact with the Jews and the Ancient Egyptians. Thirdly, there were at least eleven kings who went by the title Rameses (Rameses I, II, III, III, etc.), spanning a period dated by traditional Egyptologists from 1,307 B.C.E. to 1,070 B.C.E. Further, some localities were also referred to as Rameses.

The oldest scholarly dating for the existence of Moses, if he did exist, is c. 1,200 B.C.E. However, most Bible scholars agree that the earliest texts of the Bible were composed around 1,000 B.C.E or later, and were developed over the next millennia. Also, most scholars are now beginning to accept the Ancient Egyptian and therefore, African ethnicity of the original Jewish peoples. An example of modern scholarship on the question of the origins of the Jews occurs in the book *Bible Myth: The African Origins of the Jewish People*. In a section entitled "Contradictory Biblical Evidence," the author, Gary Greenberg states:

> Dating the Exodus is problematic because evidence of its occurrence appears exclusively in the Bible, and what little it tells is contradictory. Exodus 12:40-41, for example, places the Exodus 430 years after the start of Israel's sojourn in Egypt (i.e., beginning with Jacob's arrival), whereas Genesis 15:13-14 indicates that four hundred years transpired from the birth of Isaac to the end of the bondage. Both claims cannot be true. Jacob was born in Isaac's 60th year,[103] and he didn't arrive in Egypt until his 130th year.[104] If the sojourn lasted 430 years, then the Exodus would have to have occurred 620 years after Isaac's birth.[105] On the other hand, if the Exodus occurred 400 years after Isaac was born, then the sojourn could only have been 210 years long.[106] Other biblical passages raise additional problems.[107]

The story of Sargon I points to another source and purpose for the Moses story, in our present context. According to the Biblical tradition, at about 1200? B.C.E., the Hebrews were in Egypt, serving as slaves. A Jewish woman placed her son in a basket and allowed it to float downstream where the Egyptian queen found it, and then adopted the child. The child was Moses, the chosen one of God, who would lead the Jews out of bondage in Egypt. Moses was taken in by the royal family and taught the wisdom related to rulership of the nation as well as to the Egyptian religion and the Egyptian Temples (Bible: Acts 7:22). He was being groomed to be king and high priest of Egypt. This is why the Bible says he was knowledgeable in the wisdom of the Egyptians (Bible: Acts 7:22 and Koran C.144: Verses 37 to 76).

A story similar to the birth of Moses, about a child being placed in a basket and put in a stream which was later found by a queen, can be found in Zoroastrian mythology as well.[58] Also, recall the Semitic ruler, Sargon I, was rescued in the same manner after he was placed in a basket and sent floating down a river. Sargon I

---

[12] 17th century refers to the time period from 1,600-1,699 A.C.E.
[13] 4,004 + 1,600 to1,699 gives a range of time span from 4,604-5,703; this has been conservatively rounded to 6,000.

reined about 2,335-2,279 B.C.E. He was called "Sargon, The Great." He was one of the first known major Semitic conquerors in history. He was successful in conquering the entire country of Sumer, an ancient country of southwestern Asia, which corresponds approximately to the biblical land known as Babylonia (Babylon). Babylon was an ancient city of Mesopotamia, which was located on the Euphrates River about 55mi (89km) South of present-day Baghdad. Sargon I created an empire stretching from the Mediterranean to the Persian Gulf in c.2,350 B.C.E. The adoption of the child into royalty and rulership motif was apparently a popular theme in ancient times for those who wanted to legitimize their ascendancy to power by creating the perception that it was divinely ordained.[108]

Despite the myriad of ongoing excavations that have been conducted, many sponsored by Christian or Jewish groups, no substantial evidence has been unearthed that supports the historicity of the Bible. However, new discoveries have been brought forth that corroborate Herodotus' statements and the histories relating to the fact that the land that is now called Palestine, was once part of Ancient Egypt.

An approximately 5,000-year-old settlement discovered in southern Israel was built and ruled by Egyptians during the formative period of Egyptian civilization, a team of archaeologists announced last week.

The new find, which includes the first Egyptian-style tomb known to have existed in Israel at that time, suggests that ancient Egypt exerted more control over neighboring regions than investigators have often assumed, contends project director Thomas E. Levy of the University of California, San Diego.

Source: Science News, Oct 5, 1996 v150 n14 p215(1).
Title: Ancient Egyptian outpost found in Israel.
(Halif Terrace site in southern Israel upsets
previous estimates of Egyptian imperialism) Author: Bruce Bower

Speaking out against the stronghold, which modern European and American Egyptologists have created, the Egyptologist, scholar and author, John Anthony West, detailed his experiences and those of others attempting to study the Ancient Egyptian monuments and artifacts who are not part of the "accepted" Egyptological clique. He describes the situation as a kind of "Fortress Egypt." He describes the manner in which, not only are the Ancient Egyptian artifacts closely protected from the examination of anyone outside this group, but also the interpretation of them as well. It is as if there is a propaganda machine, which, like the orthodox medical establishment, has set itself up as sole purveyors of the "correct" knowledge in the field, and thereby invalidates the findings of other scholars or scientists. In discussing the way in which mistakes made by scholars are treated, Mister West says the following:

In academia, the rules vis-à-vis mistakes change according to location. Only those within the establishment are allowed to 'make mistakes.' Everyone else is a 'crank' 'crackpot' or 'charlatan,' and entire lifetimes of work are discredited or dismissed on the basis of minor errors.

Also, the treatment of any scholar who reads metaphysical import in the teachings, literature or iconography of Ancient Egypt is generally ridiculed by orthodox Egyptologists. For instance, anyone suggesting that the Great pyramids were not used as burial chambers (mummies or remnants of mummies have never been discovered in them), but rather as temples, is openly called a "Pyramidiot,"[109] West describes the ominous power that orthodox Egyptologists have taken to themselves and the danger this power poses to humanity:

A tacit territorial agreement prevails throughout all Academia. Biochemists steer clear of sociology; Shakespearean scholars do not disparage radio astronomy. It's taken for granted that each discipline, scientific, scholarly or humanistic, has its own valid self-policing system, and that academic credentials ensure expertise in a given field.

With its jealous monopoly on the impenetrable hieroglyphs,± its closed ranks, restricted membership, landlocked philosophical vistas, empty coffers, and its lack of impact upon virtually every other academic, scientific or humanistic field, Egyptology has prepared a near-impregnable strategic position for itself - an academic Switzerland but without chocolate, cuckoo clocks, scenery or ski slopes, and cannily concealing its banks. Not only is it indescribably boring and difficult to attack, who'd want to?

But if Swiss financiers suddenly decided to jam the world's banking system, Swiss neutrality and impregnability might suddenly be at risk. That is partially analogous to the situation of Egyptology. The gold is there, but its existence is denied, and no one is allowed to inspect the vaults except those whose credentials make them privy to the conspiracy and guarantee their silence. To date, only a handful of astute but powerless outsiders have recognized that the situation poses real danger. But it's not easy to generate a widespread awareness or appreciation of that danger.

If you think of Egyptologists at all, the chances are you conjure up a bunch of harmless pedants, supervising remote desert digs or sequestered away in libraries, up to their elbows in old papyrus. You don't think of them as sinister, or dangerous. The illuminati responsible for the hydrogen bomb, nerve gas and Agent Orange are dangerous; if you reflect upon it you see that the advanced beings who have given us striped toothpaste and disposable diapers are also dangerous ... but Egyptologists?

Possibly they are the most dangerous of all; dangerous because false ideas are dangerous. At any rate *some* false ideas are dangerous. Belief in the flat earth never hurt anyone though it made navigation problematic. Belief in a geocentric universe held back advances in astronomy but otherwise had certain metaphysical advantages. Academic Egyptology is dangerous because it maintains, in spite of Schwaller de Lubicz's documented scholarly evidence, and the obvious evidence of our own eyes and hearts when we go there, that the race responsible for the pyramids and the temples of Karnak and Luxor was less, 'advanced' than ourselves. As long as academic Egyptology prevails, children will be brought up with a totally distorted view of our human past, and by extension, of our human present. And millions of tourists will continue to visit Egypt every year, and have the experience of a lifetime vitiated and subverted by a banal explanation that the greatest art and architecture in the world to superstitious primitives.

So the fabulous metaphysical gold of Egypt remains hidden; it's existence stridently denied. For orthodox Egyptology is really little more than a covert operation within the Church of Progress. Its unspoken agenda is to maintain the faith; not to study or debate the truth about Egypt.[14]

±NOTE (by West): Who will claim authority to challenge the accepted translations of the texts, even when these read as nonsense? Actually, a number of independent scholars have learned the hieroglyphs for themselves and produced alternative less insulting translations of some of the texts. But since these are either ignored or dismissed out of hand by orthodox Egyptologists, there is no way to know if these translations come closer to the real thinking of the ancients or if they are themselves no more than figments of the translators' imaginations, and in consequence no more representative and satisfactory than the standard translations.

Noting further difficulties of sustaining independent or "alternative" Egyptology studies, West remains hopeful that the pressure to revise their unsupportable findings, not just from alternative Egyptologists, but also from geologists who bring to bear an irrefutable and exacting science to the dating of Ancient Egyptian monuments as opposed to the methods which other reputable sociologists and historians have found to be unreliable. Of the major methods accepted for establishing a chronology to understand the origins of civilization and the history of the world such as Astronomical Time, Geological Time, Archaeological Time and Political or Historical Time, the use of Scriptural chronology is recognized as being "extremely uncertain because various local chronologies were used at different times by scriptural writers, and different systems were used by contemporaneous writers."[15]

An alternative Egyptology is less easily managed. Almost no one can earn a living from it. Serious research is difficult to accomplish on a spare-time basis, and research requires access to the few major Egyptological libraries scattered around the world. In Egypt itself, excavation and all work on or in the pyramids, temples and tombs are controlled by the Egyptian Antiquities Organizations. No one without academic credentials can expect to obtain permission to carry out original work[16] Infiltration from within is also peculiarly

---

[14] *Serpent in the Sky,* John Anthony West, p. 239
[15] "Chronology," Microsoft (R) Encarta Encyclopedia. Copyright (c) 1994
[16] West adds the following footnote: Prior to the development of modern day Egyptology by the western nations, native Egyptians showed little regard or respect for their distant dynastic ancestors; the temples were quarried for stone, anything movable was cheerfully sold to antiquities dealers. Islam, along with Christianity and Judaism, tended to regard ancient Egypt as pagan and idolatrous. But today, at least in private, Egyptian Egyptologists often display a much higher degree of understanding and sensitivity toward the Pharaonic achievement than their European and American colleagues. It would not surprise me to find some closet symbolists among them. Egyptian licensed tour guides (a much coveted job) must have degrees in academic Egyptology and pass an exacting test to

difficult. At least a few people I know personally have set out to acquire degrees in Egyptology, hoping to devote themselves full time to Egypt and ultimately to legitimize the symbolist interpretation. So far, none have been able to stick out the boredom or dutifully parrot the party line for the years necessary to get the diploma, knowing better from the onset.

It seems unlikely that symbolist Egypt will ever establish itself from within its own ranks. But pressure from outside Egyptology but within academia could force a change. Academics with an interest but no personal stake in the matter must sooner or later realize that the support of highly qualified geologists (of a fundamentally geological theory) must overrule either the clamor or the silence of the Egyptological/archeological establishment. At some point they must express those views.[17]

Having read the preceding excerpts published in 1993 by West, one might think that orthodox Egyptology has never been successfully challenged. African, African American and other African Egyptologists in the Diaspora faced the same problem when they brought forth evidences, which proved that the Ancient Egyptian civilization was originally created by African people, and that people of African descent played a crucial role in the development of Ancient Egyptian culture and its interactions with other world cultures. This engendered a major storm of repudiation and ridicule beginning in the 1970's. African, African American and other African scholars and Egyptologists in the Diaspora such as Chancellor Williams, George G. M. James, John H. Clarke, Yosef A. A. ben-jochannan[110] and Cheikh Anta Diop[111] were denigrated, and their struggle to be heard even in their own communities was hampered by the constant rhetoric and derision from orthodox Egyptologists. Catching orthodox Egyptology by surprise, however, Cheikh Anta Diop not only challenged their opinion about the African origins of Ancient Egyptian culture, religion and philosophy, but offered overwhelming proof to support his contentions at the 1974 Unesco conference in which he faced 18 of the (at that time) leaders of the orthodox Egyptological community. Describing the evidence presented at the Unesco conference, scholar Asa G. Hilliard, described the proceedings as recorded by a news media reporter.[18]

In a scientific forum such opinions are unlikely to be expressed, they will be unable to compete with data-based arguments for, example, Dr. Diop presented eleven categories of evidence to support his argument for a native black African KMT[19], including eye witness testimony of classical writers, melanin levels in the skin of mummies, Bible history, linguistic and cultural comparisons with the rest of Africa, Kamitan self descriptions, Kamitan historical references, physical anthropology data, blood type studies, carvings and paintings, etc.[20] That is why the reporter at the Cairo Symposium wrote the following in the minutes of the meeting:

"Although the preparatory working paper ... sent out by UNESCO gave particulars of what was desired, not all participants had prepared communications comparable with the painstakingly researched contributions of Professors Cheikh Anta Diop and Obenga. There was consequently a real lack of balance in the discussions."[21]

At this conference, there was either expressed or implied consensus on the following points. (No objections were raised to them.)

qualify. Over the course of years of research and leading tours myself, at least a few dozen have approached me, eager to learn more about symbolist Egypt. But within the closed ranks of practicing, professional Egyptology, academic prestige (such as it is) is still wielded by the major European and American Universities. So even though all ancient Egyptian sites are now entirely under Egyptian control, an Egyptian Egyptologist would be as unlikely to try to break the "common front of silence" as anyone else, whatever his or her private convictions."

[17] *Serpent in the Sky,* John Anthony West, p. 241

[18] *Egypt Child of Africa* Edited by Ivan Van Sertima, *Bringing Maat, Destroying Isfet: The African and African Diasporan Presence in the Study of Ancient KMT* by Asa G. Hilliard III

[19] Kamit (Ancient Egypt)

[20] Diop, Cheikh Anta (1981) "Origin of the ancient Egyptians" In Moktar, G. *(Ed.) General history of Africa: volume II, Ancient Civilizations of Africa.* Berkeley, California: University of California Press, pp. 27-57

[21] UNESCO, (1978) *The peopling of ancient Egypt and the deciphering of Meroitic script: The general history of Africa, studies and documents I, Proceedings of the symposium held in Cairo from 28 January to 3 February, 1974.* Paris: United Nations Educational, Scientific and Cultural Organization, p. 102.

1. In ancient KMT the south and the north were always ethnically homogeneous.
2. Professor Vercoutter's suggestion that the population of KMT had been made up of "black skinned whites" was treated as trivia.
3. There were no data presented to show that Kamitan temperament and thought were related to Mesopotamia.
4. The old Kamitan tradition speaks of the Great Lakes region in inner equatorial Africa as being the home of the ancient Kamitans.
5. There was no evidence of large-scale migration between Kamit and Mesopotamia. There were no Mesopotamian loan words in Kamitan: (therefore the two cultures could have no genetic linguistic relationship or be populated by the same people.) For comparison purposes, mention was made of the fact that when documented contact with Kamit was made by Asian Hyksos around 1700 B.C.E., loan words were left in ancient Kamit.
6. No empirical data were presented at the conference to show that the ancient Kemites were white. (Generally, there is a tendency for some historians to *assume* that developed populations are white, but to require proof of blackness.)
7. Muslim Arabs conquered Kamit during the 7th century of the Common Era. Therefore, Arabic culture is not a part of Kamit during any part of the 3,000 years of dynastic Kamit.
8. Genetic linguistic relationships exist between the African languages of Kamitan, Cushitic (Ethiopian), Puanite (Punt or Somaliland), Berber, Chadic and Arabic. Arabic only covered territory off the continent of Africa, mainly in adjacent Saudi Arabia, an area in ancient times that was as much African as Asian.
9. Dr. Diop invented a melanin dosage test and applied it to royal mummies in the Museum of Man in Paris, mummies from the Marietta Excavations. All had melanin levels consistent with a "black" population. The symposium participants made a strong recommendation that all royal mummies be tested. To date there is no word that this has been done. Dr. Diop struggled for the remaining years of his life to have access to the Cairo museum for that purpose, but to no avail.

Hilliard Concludes:

Significantly, it was at the urging of African scholars, led by Dr. Cheikh Anta Diop, that this UNESCO sponsored scientific gathering was convened. Interestingly, the reporter's comments quoted above actually used one of the aspects of MAAT, "balance," to describe Diop and Obenga's work. Truly open dialogue brings MAAT and destroys ISFET[22]. We know this but have not required the open dialogue.

---

[22] unrighteousness

Figure 10: Pictorial Evidence of the African Origins of Ancient Egyptian Culture and Civilization.

From the Tomb of Rameses III: The four branches of mankind, according to the Egyptians: A- Egyptian as seen by himself, B- Indo-European, C- Other Africans, D- Semites (Middle Easterners) (1194-1163 B.C.E.). [112]

Careful to avoid any future such exchanges which might prove to be more injurious to the orthodox Egyptological dogma, Diop was refused further access to materials or monuments for detailed research. However, by that time the injury to the orthodox Egyptological position had been done. Since that time other evidences, such as those presented in this book and by other scholars, have steadily chipped away at the orthodox Egyptological dogmas. In this sense the struggle[23] over the "guardianship," or as some might consider "ownership," over the prestige that comes with being able to consider oneself as an Ancient Egyptian Scholar will continue, because this is apparently a war of information in which western countries have taken the lead.

All kinds of information are valued, but the information on the origins of humanity and the metaphysics of spiritual evolution are both feared and awed by most ordinary human beings, and perhaps particularly the orthodox Egyptologists, because this information truly changes everything, from the concept of human origins to what is life all about. It brings the whole Western paradigm under scrutiny. Reflect on what would happen if those people in positions of authority as well as lay people in religions, governments and schools were suddenly faced with the realization that their knowledge is deficient, and ordinary people begin to understand that they are higher beings who should not be taken advantage of. This is the power of understanding the glory and truth about Ancient Egypt. All humanity, not just Africans or Europeans, can be transformed through it, for the better, to bring about a world culture based on unity camaraderie. The illusion which orthodox Egyptologists have promoted, and with which they have self-hypnotized themselves, will gradually give way to the truth, or else they will be left behind just as the Model "T" left the horse drawn buggy behind and, electricity left oil lamps behind.

The renowned Africologist, Basil Davidson, presented Dr. Diop briefly in Davidson's documentary program "Africa." He commented on this ancient ethnography and remarked that it was "rare," dismissing it as an anomaly. However, the following picture of an Ancient Egyptian "ethnography" was discovered by Dr. Muata Ashby in the book *Arts and Crafts of Ancient Egypt,* by Flinders Petrie. However, it was not ascribed as an ethnography, which included Ancient Egyptians, but rather, unknown "Abyssinians."

---

[23] over the ownership of the prestige of being a scholar of Egyptology.

Plate 1: Ancient Egyptian Depiction of Ethnic Groups (New Kingdom Dynastic Period)[113] **(Originally in the tomb of *Ramose* – drawn by Prisse d' Avennes)**

The picture above is an Ancient Egyptian depiction of the four ethnic groups of the ancient world. Described by Petrie as "the Four Races" the picture is one of the ethnographies that have come down to us from Ancient Egypt. It should be noted that the formal ethnographies are rare but depictions showing the Nubians and Egyptians as having the same skin coloration are indeed quite abundant. Petrie describes the face to the far left as being a "Negro" (native African man). The next, from left to right, as a "Syrian" man, the third is described as an "Abyssinian," and the last as a "Libyan." In following along with this description by Petrie without having further insight into these classes of Ancient Egyptian art, it may go unnoticed that there is supposed to be an Ancient Egyptian person present. Having assigned the other "races," (i.e. Syrian, Libyan, Abyssinian), the Egyptian person has been omitted in the description of the group. This picture is a variation of the previous picture discovered by Dr. Diop. If the picture is rendered as the original, it would mean that the first man on the left that Petrie is referring to as a "Negro" is actually an Ancient Egyptian man, and the other person of African descent, labeled as an "Abyssinian" man, would be the Nubian (Ethiopian), since the practice of scarification, common to Nubia, is rare or unknown in Ancient Egypt.

The term "Abyssinian" refers to languages often distinguished as belonging to the subgroup of Hamitic languages. The words Semitic (Asia Minor) and Hamitic (African) are derived from the names of Noah's sons, Shem and Ham (Christian Bible-Gen. 10). Ethiopia, formerly Abyssinia, is a republic in eastern Africa, currently bounded on the northeast by Eritrea and Djibouti, on the east and southeast by Somalia, on the southwest by Kenya, and on the west and northwest by Sudan. In ancient times the country was bounded in the north by Ancient Egypt. In ancient times Ethiopia and Egypt were strongly related. In fact, Ethiopia was the birthplace of the early Egyptians and also, according to Herodotus, the Indians as well. They appeared the same to him at the time of his travels through those countries. Thus, the picture shows that the Ancient Egyptians looked no different from other Africans.

> *"And upon his return to Greece, they gathered around and asked, "tell us about this great land of the Blacks called Ethiopia." And Herodotus said, "There are two great Ethiopian nations, one in Sind (India) and the other in Egypt."*
>
> —Herodotus (c. 484-425 BC)

It is unfortunate that as a result of the mishandling of the monuments due to destruction and neglect by the Arab peoples, the harsh elements and chemicals in the environment, the dams on the Nile River, and the push for tourism, many of the images that he saw can no longer be seen today in their original form, except for a limited amount of originals, like the one discovered by Dr. Diop. Very few monuments and images retain their original color so the only other means currently available to view the images in their original forms are from drawings or pictures made by the early Egyptologists during their expeditions to Egypt. However, we have sufficient images and corroborating texts to say with certainty that the ethnicity of the original peoples who created the culture and civilization of the Nile Valley (Ancient Egypt) were the same in appearance as those people living in modern day Nubia, i.e. they were indeed "black" Africans.

Ancient Egyptian Depictions of Egyptians and Nubians

One reason for the confusion about the ethnicity of the Ancient Egyptians is the misunderstanding about their depictions of themselves. The men were represented in their art in two distinct forms, the red or reddish-brown and the black, both of which are used interchangeably. This is what the early Egyptologists such as Champollion witnessed before the colors on many depictions had been damaged or lost. In recent times, Western Egyptologists have mistakenly or intentionally characterized these images as evidence of ethnic or "racial" difference between the Ancient Egyptians and Nubians. However, the images from the Tomb of Seti I provide insight into this matter.

Assyrian Descriptions of the Ancient Egyptians and Nubians

LEFT: In the year 667 B.C.E. the Assyrians invaded Kamit, pushed out the Egyptian-Nubian army and captured the capital city of Waset (Thebes). On a relief in the palace of the Assyrian king Assurbanibal (669-635), there is depicted the battle in which the Assyrians defeated the army of Kamit. The Assyrians (men with long beards and conned hats) took prisoners which included Kamitans and Nubians as well as the spoils of the victory back to their homeland. In this relief the Nubian and Kamitan soldiers are pictured equally, meaning that they did not recognize a "racial" difference, only the ethnic difference. As far as the physical appearance of the Nubians and Kamitans the Assyrians pictured them as having the same completion. Thus, here we have independent corroboration from the ancient Assyrians as to the ethnic homogeny of the Nubians and Kamitans.

RIGHT: Philip Arrhidaeus, successor of Alexander, a Greek, in depicted in Red in accordance with Ancient Egyptian Iconographical standards to denote "Egyptian." Phillip was not an Egyptian by birth but by conquest and dictatorship. So he wanted the people to think of him as an Egyptian King and the practice was to depict Egyptians as red. However, otherwise we have seen Asiatics and others depicted as pale ("white). This means that the red color is not to denote a race or the color of the actual people but to demonstrate or differentiate one group of people from another for information purposes and not for segregation in the modern sense of Western Racism. (from the Napoleonic Expedition)

Figure 11: Ancient Egyptians and Nubians depicted in the Tomb of Rameses III

Rtji Ancient Egyptian   *Ahsu* Ancient Nubian

The Tomb of Seti I (1306-1290 B.C.E.-below) which comes earlier than that of Rameses III (above) shows a different depiction. Note that the same labels are used to describe the Egyptians and Nubians in the pictures of both tombs.

Figure 12: Ancient Egyptians and Nubians depicted in the Tomb of Seti I

Rtji Ancient Egyptian   *Ahsu* Ancient Nubian

There are two more depictions from Ancient Egypt, which shed light on the ethnological iconography of the Ancient Egyptians. First is an image from the temple of Rameses II at Abu Simbel. It provides us with the key to understanding the Kamitan depictions. At a time when Egypt and Nubia are competing with each other, Rameses symbolically brings tied up Nubian prisoners as offerings to Amun (See below).

Figure 13: Below left – late 20th century Nubian man. Below right-Nubian Prisoners of Rameses II -Image at the Abu Simbel Temple

Figure 14: Bottom left-Ancient Egyptians (musicians) and Nubians (dancers) depicted in the Tombs of the Nobles with the same hue and features. Bottom right- Nubian King Taharka and the Queen offering to Amun (blue) and Mut (colored in yellow) depicted as a red Egyptians. 7th cent BCE

Figure 15: Below-left, Egyptian man and woman-(tomb of Payry) 18th Dynasty displaying the naturalistic style (as people really appeared in ancient times). Below right- Egyptian man and woman-Theban tomb – depicted in the colors red and yellow, respectively.

Figure 16: Below-left, Stele of Niptah - end of Middle Kingdom (man in red, woman in white with breasts exposed).

Figure 17: Nubians (three figures prostrating) and Egyptians (standing figures) are depicted with the same colors of their skin of alternating black and brown -Tomb of Huy

Figure 18: Nubians and Egyptians are depicted with the same colors of alternating black and brown -Tomb of Huy (Full Scene)

The two pictures above are extremely important to our understanding of the ethnicity of the Ancient Egyptians, Nubians and Ethiopians. It is a rendition by French orientalist and architect *Prisse d' Avennes* (1807-1879 A.C.E.). It is understood by orthodox Egyptologists to be the procession of Nubians who are bringing gifts of gold to Huy, the viceroy of Kush, for the Egyptian king Tutankhamun (1333 B.C.E-1323 B.C.E). Note that the classic style of depicting Nubians with black or brown skin and the pronounced cheek line (scarification -see example right) as well as the feather on the head is maintained. In the same view, there are five figures standing behind the ones that are prostrating, who do not have the feathers or cheek lines, but do have the same skin tone and is represented in the classical style of depicting the Ancient Egyptians. Notice here that the depictions of the skin coloration of the Ancient Egyptians are the same as used for the Nubians (brown and black). While Ancient Egyptians and Nubians are depicted individually in brown and black color, the alternating pattern of brown and black is also used to more easily differentiate individuals when people are depicted in close proximity.

Figure 19: above right - Nubian depictions from Akhnaton period (1352 B.C.E-1347 B.C.E) Brooklyn Museum (Photo by M. Ashby)

The Controversy Over the "Race" of the Ancient Egyptians (Kamitans) in European Scholarship and the Move to Refute the Testimony of the Seventeenth- and Eighteenth-century European Travelers to Egypt

The move to deny the appearance of the Ancient Egyptians and promote the idea that they were not African at all has been put forth by many western writers, even in the face of the writings of the Ancient Egyptians themselves who attest that

1. They are ancestors of the Nubians, to the south, in Africa.
2. Their own depictions of themselves as dark or "black" skinned people.
3. The descriptions of them as "black" people, by the Greek classical writers.
4. The genealogies provided by the Ancient Egyptians themselves stating that their parents are Nubian (such as Amunmhat I).

Jean Fransçois Champollion (1790 A.C.E.-1832 A.C.E.), the main decipherer of the hieroglyphic text in the early 19th century, who is often referred to as the "Father of Egyptology", remarked at the art he saw, which at the time was fully colored since the tombs and many other structures had been closed since the Middle Ages (Dark Ages). He described images of the Ancient Egyptians, created by them, in which they made themselves look like the Ethiopians, and concluded that they were of the same "race" as the modern day Nubians, who are "black" skinned African peoples, saying in a letter to his brother that he wrote while in Egypt examining the reliefs and studying the hieroglyphs: *We find there Egyptians and Africans represented in the same way".*[114] Jean Fransçois Champollion later states that based on the images he saw it was clear that the Ancient Egyptians looked like the people presently living in Nubia, i.e. they were "black Africans."

In this same manner, Count Volney wrote after a trip to Egypt between 1783 and 1785:

> "Just think that this race of black men, today our slave and the object of our scorn, is the very race to which we owe our arts, sciences and even the use of speech! Just imagine, finally, that it is in the midst of people who call themselves the greatest friends of liberty and humanity that one has approved the most barbarous slavery and questioned whether black men have the same kind of intelligence as whites!"[115]

Some of the these travelers were being referred to were *Livingstone, Speke, Baker and Junker.* Documenting the observations of travelers such as Livingstone, and others J. A Rogers recorded the following statements by them in his book *Sex and Race Vol. I*:

> "Livingstone said that the Negro face as he saw it reminded him more of that on the monuments of ancient Assyria than that of the popular white fancy.[116] Sir Harry Johnston, foremost authority on the African Negro, said that "the Hamite," that Negroid stock which was the main stock of the ancient Egyptians, is best represented at the present day by the Somali, Galla, and the blood of Abyssinia and Nubia."[117] Sergi compares pictorially the features of Ramases II with that of Mtesa, noted Negro king of Uganda, and show the marked resemblance.[118] Sir M. W. Flinders Petrie, famed Egyptologist says that the Pharaohs of the Xth dynasty were of the Galla type, and the Gallas are clearly what are known in our day as Negroes. He tells further of seeing one day on a train a man whose features were "the exact living, type" of a statue of ancient Libya, and discovered that the man was a American mulatto.[119]"

The stir that the early descriptions of the Egyptians based on their own depictions, as described and reproduced by early explorers and artists, created in Europe in the early years of Egyptology after the translation of the hieroglyphic language by Champollion (1822 A.C.E.) was an unforeseen controversy that later Egyptologists tried desperately to refute. The following memoir recorded by Champollion-Figeac, the brother of Jean Fransçois Champollion in 1829 denotes the "problem," which the western researchers who recognized the importance of Ancient Egyptian civilization, were facing. It was obvious that the writings were beginning to reveal religion, philosophy and evolved culture, all of which contradict the basic tenets used to justify the denigration of the "Negro" race and their enslavement in Africa, Europe and the "New World" (the Americas). Therefore, it became necessary to refute and even attempt to explain away the reason for the findings. (underlined portions by Ashby)

> The opinion that the ancient population of Egypt belonged to the Negro African race, is an error long accepted as the truth. Since the Renaissance, travelers in the East, barely capable of fully appreciating the ideas provided by Egyptian monuments on this important question, have helped to spread that false notion and geographers have not failed to reproduce it, even in our day. A serious authority declared himself in favor of this view and popularized the error. Such was the effect of what the celebrated Volney published on the various races of men that he had observed in Egypt. In his *Voyage,* which is in all libraries, he reports that the Copts are descended from the ancient Egyptians; that the Copts have a bloated face, puffed up eyes, flat nose, and thick lips, like a mulatto; that they resemble the Sphinx of the Pyramids, a distinctly Negro head. He concludes that the ancient Egyptians were true Negroes of the same species as all indigenous Africans. To support his opinion, Volney invokes that of Herodotus who, apropos the Colchians, recalls that the Egyptians had black skin and woolly hair. Yet these two physical qualities do not suffice to characterize the Negro race and Volney's conclusion as to the Negro origin of the ancient Egyptian civilization is evidently forced and inadmissible.
>
> It is recognized today that the inhabitants of Africa belong to three races, quite distinct from each other for all time: 1. Negroes proper, in Central and West Africa; 2. Kaffirs on the east coast, who have a less obtuse facial angle than Blacks and a high nose, but thick lips and woolly hair; 3. Moors, similar in stature, physiognomy and hair to the *best-formed* nations of Europe and western Asia, and differing only in skin color which is tanned by the climate. The ancient population of Egypt belonged to this latter race, that is, to the white race. To be convinced of this, we need only examine the human figures representing Egyptians on the monuments and above all the great number of mummies that have been opened. Except for the color of the skin, blackened by the hot climate, they are the same men as those of Europe and western Asia: frizzy, woolly hair is the true characteristic of the Negro race; the Egyptians, however, had long hair, identical with that of the white race of the West.[120]

Firstly, Champollion-Figeac affirms that the ancient "Egyptians had black skin and woolly hair." However, he and then goes on to say that these are not sufficient to characterize the Negro race. He thus contradicts himself later by saying "frizzy, woolly hair is the true characteristic of the Negro race." Obviously this is a contradiction in terms that is inescapable. In an attempt to formulate a thesis that the Ancient Egyptians were essentially "white people," like "the best-formed" Europeans, "except for the color of the skin, blackened by the hot climate," he stumbles on his own argument which is unreasonable at the outset. At no time previous or since has there been recognized anywhere on earth, a "race" of white-black people. This argument is based on observing the so-called "three races" of Africa of his time, as if these were representative of the ancient ethnicity of Africa and could have any baring on the question of the "race" of the Ancient Egyptians. This argument is of course contradictory and unworkable such as it is, but even more so when it is kept in mind that the Ancient Egyptians mixed with Asiatics and Europeans (Greeks) and even still the descriptions of the classical Greek writers unanimously considered them as what in the present day would be called "Negros." Also, the present day Copts, descendants of the Ancient Egyptians, of Champollion-Figeac's time were even then recognized as having "Negroid" features. By Champollion-Figeac's reasoning it would be necessary to conclude that Africans are white Europeans. The Kaffirs (Muslim word for pagans) being referred to are those people whom the Muslim Arabs found in Africa as they entered Africa from the Sinai Peninsula, which is the bridge between Asia Minor and Africa. From there they captured the countries in North Africa from Egypt, to Libya, Tunisia, Algiers and Morocco as well as Spain. Through limited genealogies left by the Moors it has been determined that they were a mixture of Arab and African blood.

Thus, the comparisons used by Champollion-Figeac are wholly useless for determining the "race" of the Ancient Egyptians, but they can however be used for comparisons to the Copts, who like the Moors, appeared to "have a bloated face, puffed up eyes, flat nose, and thick lips, like a mulatto" like the Moors, and also like the present day peoples of African descent living in the Diaspora (African Americans, African Brazilians, Africans in Jamaica, etc.). When this kind of comparison is made it is clear that the "mulatto" arises from a combination of African and Semite (Arab) or European. This of course means that the African features, (color of the skin, thick lips and woolly hair) must have been present in the past if they are present in the current population of mixed peoples, that is to say, the population goes from "black" skin to "lighter" skin color and not the other way around. Except for the effects of climactic changes on populations over a long period of time (thousands of years), which have been shown to cause changes in physical appearance, there is no record of "Black" populations arising from "white" populations. Lastly, in the time of the Ancient Egyptians, before the coming of the Greeks, there were no Europeans in Africa at all. The only populations recognized by the Egyptians were themselves, the other Africans, the Libyans and the Asiatics, all of whom vary in skin tone from dark "black" to light "brown" coloration. So if there are any "white" people in present day Africa they are descendants of the documented influx of Greeks who came in as invading forces with Alexander the Great (330 B.C.E.) and or the documented influx of Arabs which came with the advent of the expansion of Islam (650 B.C.E.) and after. In any case, when discussing the Ancient Egyptians of the Old and Middle Kingdoms and the Pre-Dynastic Period, we are not discussing "mulattos" since the admixture with other ethnic groups had not occurred until the New Kingdom period, and even more so in the Late period, through contact with the conquering Asiatic and European forces. Therefore, to look at the images of the Egyptians during the mixture period and to say that these are representative of the Ancient Egyptian ethnic origins is the worst kind of scholarship. This is a tactic used by some Western and Arab scholars to escape the conclusion that the Ancient Egyptians were "black." How is this possible? In places such as the United States of America, the "rule" established by the "white" ruling class has always been that "one drop of black blood make one black." This means that everyone from dark black skin color to the light brown or swarthy complexion, are recognized as being descendants of the African slaves, and are subject to being segregated and discriminated against. But in this argument it is also possible to say that those mulattos are not 100% African since they are mixed with European, Arab, etc. So they are trying to say that the Ancient Egyptians were either a mixed race or better yet, an indigenous Asiatic group that developed independently of the "black Africans." In any case, even in the late period the Greek classical writers witnessed the population of Kamit as being overwhelmingly "black" (Nubian). So we are not talking about "light skinned black people" or "dark skinned white people" but "dark skinned black people," like those who can be met even today (2002 A.C.E.) in the city of Aswan (Upper (southern) Egypt – see picture above).

There were several prominent and respected Linguists and Egyptologists who affirmed that the Ancient Egyptians were "African" or "Negros." Sir Henry Rawlinson, prominent linguist and decipherer of the mideastern scripts and widely regarded as the "father of Middle-Eastern Studies," said *"Seti's face is thoroughly African, strong, fierce, prognathous, with depressed nose, thick lips and a heavy chin..."*[121] Showing that certain foremost Egyptologists accept the "Negro" composition of the Ancient Egyptian people, J. A Rogers recorded the following statements by the famous British Egyptologist Flinders Petrie, in his book *Sex and Race Vol.I*:

> "Egyptian civilization, from its beginning to the Christian era, lasted for more than seven thousand years, that is, about four times as long as from "the birth of Christ" to the present, therefore, most of the records have been lost, and the little that remains must be pieced together. There are often great gaps. Between the Bushman period of 9000 B.C. and the First Dynasty (4477-4514 B.C.) very little is known. Some of the faces of the rulers of this dynasty are clearly Negroid. The founder of the Third Dynasty, Sa-nekht, was a full-blooded Negro, a type commonly seen in the Egyptian army today. Petrie says of him, "It will be seen how strongly Ethiopian the characters of it (the portrait) is even more so than Shabaka, most marked of the Ethiopian dynasty. The type is one with which we are very familiar among the Sudanese of the Egyptian police and army; it goes with a dark-brown skin and a very truculent character."

In the late 19th century (A.C.E.) the French director general of the Egyptian Service of Antiquities and regarded as a foremost Egyptologist, Gaston Maspero (1846-1916 A.C.E.), wrote about the controversy about the origins and descriptions of the Ancient Egyptians as it stood in his times. (underlined portions by Ashby)

> "In our day the origin and ethnographic affinities of the population have inspired lengthy debate. First, the seventeenth- and eighteenth-century travelers, misled by the appearance of certain mongrelized Copts, certified that their predecessors in the Pharaonic age had a puffed

up face, bug eyes, flat nose, fleshy lips. And that they presented certain characteristic features of the Negro race. This error, common at the start of the century, vanished once and for all as soon as the French Commission had published its great work."[122]

One of the questions that arise here is why was the unanimous reaction of the seventeenth- and eighteenth-century European travelers in Egypt so upsetting to the late eighteenth and twentieth century western scholars? They were the first Europeans in modern times to see the Ancient Egyptian reliefs and paintings and their reaction was the same as the Greek classical writers when it came to describing the peoples of Kamit and the rest of the Nile Valley. In fact, they did not base their assessment of the Ancient Egyptian ethnicity just by examining their descendants, the Copts, but on images left behind by the Kamitans, some that had been buried under the encroaching dessert sands, which for this reasons were preserved in very good condition. It is interesting to note that the appearance of the Copts was acknowledged as presenting the "mongrelized" features (puffed up face, bug eyes, flat nose, fleshy lips) and that these are understood as being generally representative of the "Negro race." This observation has been widely accepted by all who agree with the concept of ethnic differentiations among human populations. Yet, when it comes to acknowledging these features in the images of Ancient Egypt they become somehow unrepresentative or unreliable or insufficient in assisting in the determination about where those people came from and to which population they are related.

This move to obfuscate the issue gained momentum in the 20th century and became widely accepted by society in general, despite all the evidence to the contrary. Even in the late 20th century there are anthropologists and Egyptologists staunchly supporting the baseless construct of an other than "Negro" origin of the Ancient Egyptians. What has changed is the willingness to say that they were Africans. What has not changed is the reluctance to accept their "blackness." Being unable to refute the pictorial evidences or the writings by the Egyptians themselves, many present day researches who seek to prove that the Ancient Egyptians were not "black" Africans attempt to use other means to discredit the findings which do not support their contentions.

The work of a western scholar by the name of Martin Bernal, author of _Black Athena : The Afroasiatic Roots of Classical Civilization (The Fabrication of Ancient Greece 1785-1985,_ (published in 1989), a scathing report on the western falsification of the evidences pointing to an African origin of Greek (i.e. Western civilization) received a storm of criticism from some researchers who propose that his treatment of the statements by the classical Greek writers as "eager credulity." Jacques Berlinerblan, the author of _Heresy in the University: The Black Athena Controversy and the Responsibilities of American Intellectuals_ (1999) examines the charge against Bernal.

> "With this generous reading now rendered I would like to note that Bernal has offered no viable alternative or corrective to the approaches which he believes are responsible for the fall of the Ancient Model. Nor does he distinguish among better or worse types of exegetical and hermeneutic approaches, leaving us with the impression that he believes all are equally corrupt. His methodological credo seems to be _The Ancients could very well be telling us the truth._ While this is plausible, it is incumbent upon the author to advance a method which might help us to determine how scholars might go about distinguishing truthful accounts from untruthful ones. As Egyptologist John D. Ray asked, "Where are the final criteria to lie?" To this point, Bernal has neglected to articulate such criteria, and this leaves him vulnerable to Mary Lefkowitz's charge of "eager credulity" toward the ancient sources."[123]

There is an interesting process of selective acceptance of certain evidences from the ancient writers and overlooking or minimizing certain other evidences when it is convenient to explain a particular point. This is noticeable in the work of some western scholars of Ancient Egypt, Greece as well as India. Bernal's book drew such criticism, not because the information was new, since other writers such as Cheikh Anta Diop had presented it in his book _African Origins of Civilization, Myth or Reality._ The problem was that Bernal is a "white" European scholar, part of the establishment, and the information he presented was perceived by some of his peers as precipitating the fall of the walls of western academia's characterization of African civilization, and consequently the history of western civilization, and their prestige as western scholars with it. The objective here also seems to call into question the veracity of the ancient writers, or to say that they were gullible, or to make it appear that their Egyptian "guides" or "informants" were trying to impress the Greeks by telling them wild stories that they wanted to hear. In the third chapter of *Not Out of Africa: How Afrocentrism Became an Excuse to Teach Myth As History* (August 1997), Mary Lefkowitz reviews the texts which Bernal used in order to build his Ancient and Revised Ancient Models. "The idea that Greek religion and philosophy has Egyptian origins," she asserts, "may appear at first sight to be more plausible, because it derives, at least in part, from the writings of ancient Greek historians." The scholar Jacques Berlinerblan explains Lefkowitz's position, which he himself admittedly shares. (Underlined portions by Ashby)

> "Lefkowitz advances an unyieldingly critical appraisal of the writings of Herodotus, Diodorus, Plato, Strabo, and the Church Fathers on the subject of Egypt. These figures cannot be counted on to offer us objective accounts due to their "respect for the antiquity of Egyptian religion and civilization, and a desire somehow to be connected with it." This admiration inclined them to overemphasize their dependency on, and contacts with, the land of the Pyramids. But the presence of a pro-Egyptian bias in Greek thought is not the only drawback which Lefkowitz discovers. In true Hard Modern fashion she enumerates the failings of the ancients qua historical researchers. The Greeks were not sufficiently skeptical or critical of their informants and sources. They did not speak Egyptian, nor did they draw upon Egyptian archives. They misunderstood the very Egyptian phenomena they studied. Their linguistic surmises were predicated on simplistic and erroneous assumptions. They looked at Egypt "through cultural blinkers," producing an image that was "astigmatic and deeply Hellenized."[124] Again and again Lefkowitz pounds the point home-how poorly the Greeks performed when compared to us:
>
> Unlike modern anthropologists, who approach new cultures so far as possible with an open mind, and with the aid of a developed set of methodologies, Herodotus tended to construe whatever he saw by analogy with Greek practice, as if it were impossible for him to comprehend it any other way.
>
> Lest there exist any remaining question as to the reliability of the ancients, Lefkowitz proceeds to pulverize the final link in the chain of historical transmission. Not only were the Greeks unreliable, but so were their Egyptian informants. Jewish and Christian Egyptians supplied the gullible Greeks with self-aggrandizing information as "a way of asserting the importance of their culture, especially in a time when they had little or no political powers."[125]

We must keep in mind that scholars such as Lefkowitz are trying to discredit the ancient authors but the arguments of such scholars are not based on rationality or on evidences to prove their contentions.

1. People from different periods in time, removed in some cased by several hundreds of years, which means that they did not have an opportunity to conspire with each other to fabricate the same "fantasies".

2. They did not speak to the same people upon visiting Egypt or in such cases as Pythagoras and Plato, becoming students of the Egyptian masters for several years.

3. They had no reason to lie about their experiences as do present day western scholars, who need to uphold a view of the past that support western superiority and independence from the very people whose oppression is rationalized by saying that they had no culture, religion, philosophy or civilization.

4. The Greek classical writers (Herodotus, Plutarch, Pythagoras, Plato, Aristotle, Diodorus, Strabo, and others) did not rely simply on what they were told by their "informants." They presented evidences and described what they saw with their own eyes and when these descriptions are compared they are in agreement with their statements and with the evidences that can be examined by any person who takes the time to visit a serious museum of Egyptian antiquities or the monuments and tombs of Ancient Egypt themselves.

5. The use of the term "informants" in itself reveals the demeaning attitude and prejudicial manner of dealing with the Greek Classical writers, presumably because there is no other area that these scholars can attack in order to prove their theory.

6. There are ample forms of evidence besides the writings of the Greek classical authors upon which to investigate the ethnicity of the Ancient Egyptians and their contributions to early Greek culture. These other evidences, such as the adoption of Ancient Egyptian customs, tradition and religion by the

Greeks are irrefutable and inescapable and therefore, not to be mentioned. By creating a stir in one area, the western researchers hope to cloud the issue and taint an objective observer's view of other evidences.

In any case, such attacks can be easily dismissed since they are entirely without basis. The problem arises in the fact that they speak from a self-serving pulpit, the "western scholarly establishment" that is supported by the western media, which accepts documentaries that are made for television by these scholars or approved by the "legitimate" schools that they represent, rather than from conclusive evidence. Anyone who has worked in the western university setting knows that there is a lot of politics involved with attaining the coveted status as tenured professor. Of course, anyone who does not agree with the established opinions will have a difficult time breaking through the invisible walls of the western "ivory towers." The Western academia, which controls the scholars through the process of selectively accepting those who support the pre-established doctrines and rejecting those who do not. Scholarly criticism is one thing, but dismissing something just because it does not agree with one's views is simply unscientific and evidence of an ulterior motive or hidden agenda. Having the most powerful voice to speak with and being supported by the government, the western scholarly establishment has the capacity to put out skewed images of reality, that when repeated again and again over a period of time, attains a status of being "truth" and "real," but when examined closely, are found to be nothing more that the cries of unhappy children who cannot accept the evidences before them. A fault that was noted in Lefkowitz's work not by the Africentrists or by Bernal but by her own colleague Jacques Berlinerblan, which reveals her duplicitous manner of handling the statements of the Greek classical writers.

> In my own work on the Hebrew Bible I have argued, with no less passion, that we simply cannot believe what this text reports. Accordingly, I concur with her objections, and I find Lefkowitz's overarching skepticism justified. Yet in her haste to skewer Bernal, Lefkowitz avoids considering the drawbacks or implications of her - I should say "our"-position. At one point in Not Out of Africa she speaks of the "important," "generally accurate," and "useful information" which Herodotus makes apropos of the Nile, Egyptian monuments, and individual pharaohs. The problem is that Lefkowitz never pauses to tell us why she considers these particular observations to be "generally accurate." Further, she and other critics of Bernal often evince their own "eager credulity" toward ancient texts, especially when it permits them to criticize Bernal. Lefkowitz, for instance, is not averse to citing and accepting Herodotus's testimony if it helps her to refute *Black Athena's* historical claims.[126]

Lefkowitz's double standard sabotages her own integrity and thus invalidates her statements and motives as a scholar. When the empty attempts to impugn the statements of the Greek classical writers fails there is no recourse but to engage in attempts to discredit the scholars who advance their positions using the "unacceptable" evidences by referring to them as "wild," "flaky," etc., and refer to their positions as based on "fantasies." A western writer by the name of Steven Howe characterized the work of noted Africentric scholars in this way in his book. Without providing any evidence to refute their positions, a practice that is widely regarded as the hallmark of the western scientific process, he presented the opinions of other scholars who agree with him, they also being devoid of evidences to back up their positions. This of course is no scholarship at all, but merely the addition of one more voice to the cacophony of western scholarly discontent over the undeniable and overwhelming evidences contradicting their positions. The absence of real evidence to support their opinions is substituted with forceful opinions and emotional appeals and these cannot be accepted as science, but as disgruntled and frustrated outbursts. Mr. Howe makes the following assertions without supporting these with any evidence either in Egyptology, anthropology, genetics, geology or any other recognized science.

1. The ancient Egyptians belonged to no race, they were neither black nor white but Egyptian.
2. The white race did not evolve from the black.
3. The race concept did not exist in Ancient Egypt.
4. Arabs did not overrun or destroy north Africa.

The obvious misconceptions or misinformation or errors in Mr. Howe's arguments can be easily and concisely proven to be false, since there is no real evidence being presented:

A. The first point is bogus on its face. Even in the present day, the spurious concept of "racism" recognizes no such race as "Egyptian." All human beings have been regarded by the western race concept as either "white," meaning European, or of some "Negroid" stock, meaning descendant or affiliated with African ancestry, or fitting into some range of color between "black" and "white."

B. All the evidences from anthropology and genetic sciences point to a common origin for all modern human beings as having originated in Africa. Therefore, Mr. Howe is either misinformed or deliberately misdirecting the public. Inherent in the treatment of Egyptology is the practice of ignoring the findings of scientific disciplines which are widely regarded as being empirical as opposed to theoretical. These are ignored because they contradict the orthodox dogmatic position. These other sciences support the "black" African origins of Ancient Egyptian culture.

C. Mr. Howe proposes the idea that the Ancient Egyptians did not indeed have a concept of race in order to support the idea that there was no difference between how they saw themselves and the other peoples of the world. The Ancient Egyptians were not racists and consequently no record of race classifications, or racial practices such as those of modern Western Culture have been discovered even after 200 years of Egyptological research. However, the concept of ethnic differentiation did exist. The Ancient Egyptians did recognize and acknowledge the concept of ethnicity which includes an awareness of the differences in physical features like skin color, etc. Several examples of these "ethnographies" survive to this day. So the Ancient Egyptians saw themselves as being the same in appearance to the Nubians and other Africans and different from the Asiatics and the later Greeks (Europeans). Thus, the Greeks (Europeans) could not be Egyptians since the Egyptians depicted themselves as "black" Africans. It is interesting that some scholars try to hold on to the idea that race is not important based on the genetic evidence which shows the race concept to be bogus, when it suits the ideal of asserting that the Egyptians had no race so as not to be forced to admit that they were "black Africans," but when it comes to accepting people of non-European descent into European countries, equality in economics, social settings and government, the practice of segregation and discrimination based on racial bias, remains enforced.

D. Ample records and evidences from African peoples as well as the Assyrian, Persian, Greek and Arab conquerors attest to the fact of the movement from Europe, imposing Roman Christianity, and from Asia Minor into North Africa, imposing Islam and the destruction of "Kaffir" (pagan) monuments, temples and cultures which were seen as contradictory with the formation of a world dominated by Christianity, and later Islam.

Thus, even at the end of the 20th century the world is still contending with the agenda of some duplicitous or ignorant western scholars and writers of characterizing African culture as primitive and insignificant, and to elevate Western Culture and western scholarship without any footing in science. This is why the work of those who study Ancient Egyptian culture, religion and philosophy needs to confront the issue of history and the means to present evidences with rigorous standards that will lead to reasonable and useful conclusions, as opposed to disparaging remarks and insults calling the work of their opponents "wild", "flaky", "fantasies", opinion and innuendo.

Finally, this author (Ashby), knows of no African American Africentric scholar or African Africentric scholar who would say that Western civilization, as we know it today, is based on African civilization, it does however owe its existence to Ancient Africa since what the European countries built cannot be said to be in keeping with either the principles or philosophy of civilization enjoined by the Ancient Egyptian sages, nor the tenets that were learned by the Greek philosophers who were students of the Kamitan sages, who attempted to enlighten the early Greeks with the knowledge of the Land of the Pyramids. When asked by a western reporter what he thought about western civilization, the Indian leader Mahatma Ghandi is said to have replied: *That is a good idea!* He responded in this way because western civilization remains an idea yet to be realized. Technological advancement and material wealth or military power do not in themselves constitute "civilization." Western Culture cannot be considered to be a civilization since civilization means to be "civilized" in one's actions, constructions, and views towards the world. Being civilized means being civil (Civility = **1.** *Courteous behavior; politeness.* **2.** *A courteous act or utterance.* –American Heritage Dictionary) to other people. Civility is one of the most important concepts of Ancient Egyptian Maat philosophy. Being civilized does not mean just being courteous in social situations, but then taking advantage of the same people in another or promoting the welfare of one's own group, but promoting the welfare of all people in general, otherwise one's civilization is biased and therefore duplicitous and hypocritical, which disqualifies it from being regarded as a "civilization" in any stretch of the concept. Civilization benefits the world community as it sees all human beings as citizens of humanity. Being civilized cannot be equated with the denigration of women in the culture, the concept of a male god and the exclusion of women in religion, the global domination of people through economic manipulation and hoarding of resources, the enslavement of entire populations, the murder of entire populations and stealing their land, etc. These are not values of the ancient African culture, which was based on the principle of Humanism (Ubuntu/Maat) and required the provision of resources to meet the needs of all members of the population as well as the balance between male and female, etc. So Africa cannot be claimed to be the source of such acts of inhumanity, selfishness and greed. So wherever these were learned, they developed independently, perhaps due to the inability of people in Europe to heed the teachings of the Ancient Egyptian sages and their early Greek students. Thus, even though the early Greek philosophers created a spark in their home country that provided an impetus for the later development of European culture, that culture cannot yet be considered to be a civilization in the contexts of what was accomplished in Ancient Egypt (Africa).

References to the Nubian Genealogy of Kamitans in Kamitan Texts and Monuments

In the didactic treatise known as *The Prophesies of Neferti,* it is stated that Amunmhat I was the "son of a woman of Ta-Seti, a child of Upper Egypt. The term "Ta-Seti" means "Land of the Bow." This is one of the names used by the Ancient Egyptians to describe Nubia. Thus we are to understand that contrary to the assertions of orthodox Egyptologists, there are several Ancient Egyptian kings that can be recognized as "Nubian" besides those of the 25th dynasty. The late period Greeks and Romans accepted Pharaoh Amunhotep III (Memnon -18th Dyn.) as a Nubian in appearance and as Pharaoh. Yet there is a consistent effort to deny the obvious. When their histories and genealogies are examined, along with their statuary, it becomes clear that the Ancient Egyptians and their rulers were not just Africans but "black" skinned and also possessed the same physical features as other Africans.

One issue that western and Arab scholars who want to characterize the appearance of "Nubian features" in Ancient Egyptian art is that these are either rare or that they appear almost exclusively in the period of the 25th Dynasty when it is universally accepted that the Nubians from the south took over the all of Egypt. However, a cursory study of the Ancient Egyptian statues and relief provides insights into the insufficiency of any arguments pretending to suggest that there are no records besides the Greek classical writers which show that the Ancient Egyptians saw and depicted themselves as "black Africans," not just during the 25th Dynasty, but throughout the history of Ancient Egypt to the Greek and Roman periods.

Plate 2: Left- Peraah (Pharaoh) Muntuhotep II (Muntuhotep)[127] – 11th Dynasty

Plate 3: Center- Peraah Senusert I statue – 12th Dynasty

Plate 4: Right- Peraah Senusert I relief – 12th Dynasty

(A)   (B)   (C)

The images above are representative of the reliefs and statuaries that the Greek classical writers and the seventeenth- and eighteenth-century European travelers in Egypt saw in full color. Notice the features of the first two (A-B) faces. They clearly exhibit the characteristic traits that have been described as "Black African", including the "puffed up face." Plate (C) is actually a relief representing the same personality as plate (B). Notice that the features in the statues are more pronounced than in the reliefs. This same pattern of iconography can be observed in the statuary and reliefs of King Akhnaton. What we are witnessing is an Ancient Egyptian artistic standard practice of representing the personality in a more naturalistic form in the statuary, and a more standardized manner in the reliefs.[24] In all cases however, the features denote the "bloated face, puffed up eyes, flat nose, and thick lips, and woolly hair as well as the brown-red or black skin tone painting.

Plate 5: Below left, Per-aah Akhnaton Statue (18 Dynasty) – Cairo Museum

Plate 6: Below right, Per-aah Akhnaton Relief (18 Dynasty)

Mysticism of Color in Ancient Egyptian Art

Many Egyptologists and others have tried to put forth the idea that the reddish-brown (males) and yellow or white (for females) colors, which the Ancient Egyptians used in the artistic renditions of themselves, represented the hue of their skin. This argument is bogus since it is well known that if two people of different skin colors (pigmentation) mate, they will produce offspring displaying a mixture of the two hues, as well as a range of skin pigmentation hues which may extend even beyond the ranges represented by the parents, if the grandparents or those of even earlier generations were of different skin hues. So even if the Ancient Egyptians had consisted of a population of red men and yellow or white women, they would quickly transform themselves into pink and gold since red and yellow produces gold and red and white produces pink. Further, these mixtures would further combine until eventually only one hue would remain.

The color spectrum ranges, in order, from violet, through blue, green, yellow, and orange, to red.[128] The colors red and white hold special mystical significance, and this is why we see so many Ancient Egyptian couples represented by them, with the men painted reddish-brown and the women painted yellow or fully white. In color therapy, an art practiced in modern times as well as in Ancient Egypt,[129] the color red is understood as being an agitating or exciting (stimulating) color to the mind. White, on the other hand was considered in Ancient Egypt as soothing,[130] as the red male Hippo was considered violent, mischievous and destructive while the female was considered calm and helpful. Blue is considered as being soothing and relaxing to the mind. Mystically, red and white complement each other, as red symbolizes sexual potency or

---

[24] *The projection of figures or forms from a flat background, as in sculpture, or such a projection that is apparent only, as in painting.* – American Heritage Dictionary

virility, and white, having the capacity to reflect all colors, [131] symbolizes pregnancy and potential. This is why the Kamitan Peraahs (Pharaohs)[25] wears the double crown, consisting of red and white elements. Note that when considering the colors from a scientific standpoint, and their effect on the human mind we obtain meanings that is not to be acribed to the modern concept of race and racism. The colors do not refer to races but to energies and behavior patterns.

Mystically, the color gold symbolizes the sun and the spirit, as well as eternity and immortality. The color black symbolizes "the source" of all things, as it represents the capacity to absorb all colors."[132] Everything in Creation has color, in order to be seen. Black does not reflect any color due to its subtlety, thus it is "colorless," that is, uncolored by time and space, the realm (of Creation, duality and conditioning) where color exists. Another way to understand this is that black absorbs all colors, and does not let their light escape and white is opaque and thereby reflects all colors off itself, which is why movies use a white screen instead of black. This is why in mystical mythological philosophies of Kamit and India, the gods Asar and Amun in Ancient Egypt and the gods Vishnu and Krishna in India are referred to as the "black" ones. Amun and Krishna are also represented as dark blue. They represent the transcendent, beyond ordinary consciousness. Asar also symbolizes "nothingness." This is an allusion to the mind when it is void of concepts or thoughts. This spiritual idea is akin to the term "Shunya" used to describe the void that an aspirant strives to achieve in Buddhism.

Red + White thus means: Spirit + Matter = Creation. Thus these colors lead to productions (creations) in time and space as well as perfection in the physical plane.

Red + Yellow = Orange-Gold thus means: Spirit + Sublimated Matter = Eternity. Therefore these colors make each other whole and transcendental, i.e. symbolizing the movement from duality to non-duality.

Gold = Spirit and Eternity

Blue ➔ moving towards Violet ➔ leads to Black

Black = Transcendent

The Mystical Symbolism of Nothingness

In mystical traditions, the root of human spiritual obstruction is said to be the sense of individualism. From this individualism emerges egoistic desire. Upon reflection, you will discover that everything you are or believe yourself to be is related to your mental ideas which all reference you to a specific time and place, your body, your relatives, your society, your country, etc. Mystical traditions such as Kamitan and Eastern philosophy and Gnostic Christianity view these elements as superficial garments of the soul, which the soul clings to, due to ignorance. When these elements are given up, the practitioner of mystical spiritual discipline goes beyond them and discovers the "nothingness" out of which the universe arises. This nothingness was erroneously assumed by some to be a kind of non-existence.

At another level of understanding, this nothingness is a state of consciousness wherein there is no mental movement caused by thoughts. In reality the void refers to the absence of concepts in the mind. This state renders the mind undifferentiated, uncolored and free, that is, "black."

The Philosophy of "Nothingness" was extensively espoused by the Buddhist philosophers of India. Their attempt to explain what the phenomenal universe is began with an attempt to explain how the universe developed. It was assumed that there was a source that produced the universe. This philosophy led to the belief that the entire universe came from a primeval, ultimate void called *Shunya.*[133] Therefore, Buddhist disciplines are directed toward emptying the human mind of that which prevents the perception of that ultimate reality which according to their system of mysticism, is the source of all creation. This Buddhist discipline is directed towards the eradication of the superficial elements of the human mind, which they maintain, block {her/his} perception of ultimate existence. In effect, the mind can be trained to let go of thinking and classifying objects. When this occurs there are no more concepts in the mind and therefore, it is said to be void of concepts. When all of the concepts, which have been learned by the mind over many lifetimes, and the egoistic desires based on

---

[25] The term "Pharaoh" is a biblical (Hebrew-Jewish) translation oh the original Ancient Egyptian word "Per-aah".

those concepts, are dropped, then there arises the awareness of the Absolute. There is supreme calm and peace. Since thoughts are created by desires, the main aim of Buddhist philosophy is to end desires so that the human being may be able to discover his/her true Self as being one with the source of creation. Further, all the planets, matter, living beings, and even the individual human ego is discovered to be an emanation from that source. Hence the term *Nirvana* (Nir-vana), *without-desire* (craving), is used to denote this ultimate state of oneness with the source of creation. (See Chapter on African Origins of Buddhism)

The Mystical Symbolism of Darkness in Kamitan Philosophy and Mythology.

In Kamitan mysticism, one of the philosophies of "nothingness" is expressed in the concept of the Duat. The Duat is the netherworld of Kamitan philosophy and within it is to be found the *nrutf* region, the place of darkness, and within that region is Asar, the lord of the Perfect Black."

This notion of nothingness (*nrutf*) is akin to the Buddhist notion of *Shunya* or the "void," which refers to the area of consciousness, which is devoid of mental concepts and thoughts. When there are no thoughts or forms in the mind, it is calm, expansive and peaceful. When there are thoughts in the mind, the mental awareness is narrowed and defined in terms of concepts. If the mind is confined to these concepts and narrow forms of thought, then it is confined to that which is limited and temporal. If it eradicates its desires, cravings and illusions, then it becomes aware of the innermost reality and it realizes its connection to the entire cosmos. Thus, the teaching of the Duat gives insight into the nature of the human mind and its deeper unconscious levels. It is a description of the mental landscape, its demons, gods and goddesses (fantasies, desires and everything else that is a result of or leads to ignorance and mental agitation) as well as the way to discover the abode of the innermost Self (everything that leads to peace, harmony and wisdom). Demons, gods and goddess refer to one's mental concepts of right (gods and goddesses) and wrong (demons), and not to entities such as ghosts, angels, evil spirits, etc., as is commonly understood by non-mystical traditions. Therefore, the task of a spiritual aspirant is to eradicate the concepts, agitations, desires and cravings in the mind and to discover the "hidden" innermost reality, which is Hetep (Supreme Peace), eternity and infinite expansiveness.

From a higher level of understanding, the Duat is the unconscious mind and Asar is that level which transcends the thinking processes... its deepest region. It is the level of consciousness that is experienced during deep dreamless sleep. Therefore, it is the "hidden" aspect of the human heart, and thus, it is also known as Amun, the "witnessing consciousness".

This deepest and most dark realm of the Duat (Netherworld in Kamitan spirituality) is Asar, himself, and this is why Asar is referred to as the "Lord of the Perfect Black" and is often depicted as being black or green of hue. It is also why the goddesses Nut, Aset (Isis), and Hetheru (Hathor) are also described as "dark-skinned."[26] They are emanations from this realm of blackness, which is described as a void, or "*nothingness*" in the hieroglyphic papyrus entitled *The Laments of Aset (Isis) and Nebethet (Nephthys).*[134]

---

[26] From an inscription in the temple of Denderah, Egypt.

CONCLUSION: About the Ancient Egyptian and Nubian depictions in Ancient Egypt

Firstly, the fact that the later depictions of the Ancient Egyptians show them as having traditional African features similar to Nubians, indicates that the Ancient Egyptians were black "African" peoples even up to that time and when the Greek classical writers made their observations (450 B.C.E.-100 A.C.E). Secondly, notice that the Nubian men at the temple of Rameses are depicted as brownish red as well as black. The Nubian dancing girls, are also painted brownish red. This means that the Ancient Egyptians painted themselves and the Nubians with the same colors, but differentiated due to particular reasons not related to racism, but to cultural distinction. Thus, they used this artistic convention of alternating coloration and scarification as a means to tell the two groups (Egyptians and Nubians) apart when they were being depicted together. The use of color has mystical implications, like almost all Kamitan inscriptions do, and there can be no validity to the concept that the Ancient Egyptians were white and red in skin color. Therefore, the use of color must be understood as a mystical symbol as opposed to an ethnic depiction.

Chapter 1 Section 2: The Nubian Origins of Ancient Egypt

In order to understand the Ancient Egyptians, we must also understand their origins in Nubia and their relationship to the Nubians (Ethiopians). In this manner we will have a full grasp of the African origins of Kamitan culture as well as fathom the full impact that it had on the rest of Africa through the Nubian kingdoms, which in turn influenced other countries in the interior of Africa. So next we will explore the Nubian origins and history of Ancient Egypt, and then we will explore in detail the different periods of Ancient Egyptian history.

The Nubian Origins of Ancient Egypt

"Our people originated at the base of the mountain of the Moon,
at the origin of the Nile river where the god Hapi dwells."

-The Ancient Egyptian tradition.

The Ancient Egyptians themselves said that their ancestors originated in the very interior of Africa, the place known as the source of the Nile. The land they were referring to is up-river, in the area of modern day Africa that is today occupied by the countries Uganda and southern Sudan. The Nile River, which flows down to the Mediterranean sea originates in a mountainous region from which several tributary rivers flow to make one main watercourse known as the Nile River. The mountains in this region have such an elevation that even though they are located close to the equator, one may experience not only extremely low temperatures, but extreme weather conditions as well. This topography is ideal for promoting rains at particular times of the year. The interaction between the mountains and the winds and the attendant atmospheric conditions which develop annually are the key to what causes the production of snow. Then the snow melts forming streams, which then coalesce into rivers, which in turn nourish the entire region. Thus it is not surprising that this region, which includes Tanzania, would have been the place where the remains of the oldest known human being were discovered.

Below: Map of Africa

The waters that go to compose the Nile River originate in the area that is today known as southern Sudan/Uganda and Ethiopia. There are two main tributaries to the Nile. They are known as the White Nile and the Blue Nile. The White Nile originates in Southern Sudan, from waters flowing into it from the Mountain Nile, which comes from even farther south in Uganda, from other tributaries known as Albert Nile and Victoria Nile (Named after the king and queen of England at the time of the colonization[27] of the area).

Below: Map of Uganda.

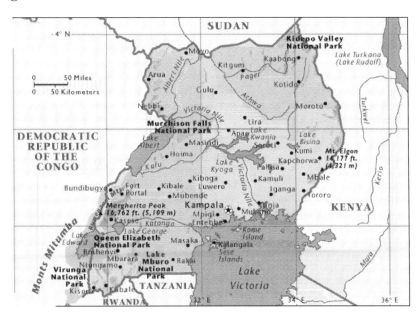

Below: Mountain Kiliminjaro – one of the mountains in the region at the source of the Nile

---

[27] Colonization, in the context of this book and as concerns the continent of Africa refers to the seizing of previously inhabited areas by force, and the enslavement of the people there, while at the same time confiscating and plundering the natural resources of the land and the wealth of the people of that land.

Images From The Early European Explorers of the Nile Valley

The following images from the early 19th century European explorers to the Nile Valley show the population that was found in Nubia and the lands to the south of Egypt as they moved in search of the sources of the Nile. Their search led them to Uganda. These images were produced to record the explorer's interactions with the Ugandans. Thus, the people who lived at the source of the Nile, the place where Ancient Egyptian legends say that the original Egyptian peoples originated, appear as with the Nubians, to be black Africans. Some of the pictures contain elements which demonstrate striking similarities with the earlier Ancient Egyptian symbolism, like the panther skin. The panther skin was a symbol of Ancient Egyptian Priests and Priestesses, teachers of the mysteries (mystical sciences).

Introducing the Bible to the native population. Note the panther skin used by the teacher. John Hanning Speke *Journal of Discovery of the Source of the Nile* (early 19th century explorations -published 1863)

Above left: Ancient Egyptian priest with the characteristic panther skin.
Above center: The King of Uganda. Above right: Nilotic dwarf man.

Descriptions of the Nubians (Ethiopians) by the Greeks

We are given to understand by the testimony of the Ancient Egyptians themselves that their ancestors came from Nubia. These were the people referred to by the Greeks as *Ethiopians*. The term Ethiopians means "land of the burnt (black) faces."

Herodotus called them ***"The tallest, most beautiful and long-lived of the human races."***

Homer referred to them as ***"The most just of men; the favorites of the gods."***

The Terms "Ethiopia," "Nubia," "Kush" and "Sudan"

The term "Ethiopian," "Nubian," and "Kushite" all relate to the same peoples who lived south of Egypt. In modern times, the land which was once known as Nubia ("Land of Gold"), is currently known as the Sudan, and the land even further south and east towards the coast of east Africa is referred to as Ethiopia (see map above).

Recent research has shown that the modern Nubian word *kiji* means "fertile land, dark gray mud, silt, or black land." Since the sound of this word is close to the Ancient Egyptian name Kish or Kush, referring to the land south of Egypt, it is believed that the name Kush also meant "the land of dark silt" or "the black land." Kush was the Ancient Egyptian name for Nubia. Nubia, the black land, is the Sudan of today. Sudan is an Arabic translation of *sûd* which is the plural form of *aswad*, which means "black," and *ân* which means "of the." So, Sudan means "of the blacks." In the modern Nubian language, *nugud* means "black." Also, *nuger*, *nugur*, and *nubi* mean "black" as well. All of this indicates that the words Kush, Nubia, and Sudan all mean the same thing — the "black land" and/or the "land of the blacks."[28] As we will see, the differences between the term Kush and the term Kam (Qamit, Kamit, Kemit - name for Ancient Egypt in the Ancient Egyptian language) relate more to the same meaning but different geographical locations.

The Term Kamit (Qamit, Kamit, Kamit) and Its Relation to Nubia and the term "Black"

As we have seen, the terms "Ethiopia," "Nubia," "Kush" and "Sudan" all refer to "black land" and/or the "land of the blacks." In the same manner we find that the name of Egypt which was used by the Ancient Egyptians also means "black land" and/or the "land of the blacks." The hieroglyphs below reveal the Ancient Egyptian meaning of the words related to the name of their land. It is clear that the meaning of the word Qamit is equivalent to the word Kush as far as they relate to "black land" and that they also refer to a differentiation in geographical location, i.e. Kush is the "black land of the south" and Qamit is the "black land of the north." Both terms denote the primary quality that defines Africa, "black" or "Blackness" (referring to the land and its people). The quality of blackness and the consonantal sound of K or Q as well as the reference to the land are all aspects of commonality between the Ancient Kushitic and Kamitan terms.

Qamit - Ancient Egypt

Qamit - blackness – black

Qamit - literature of Ancient Egypt – scriptures

Qamiu or variant - Ancient Egyptians-people of the black land.

---

[28]"Nubia," *Microsoft® Encarta® Africana.* © 1999 Microsoft Corporation. All rights reserved.

The ancient historian Stephanus of Byzantium said:

> "Ethiopia was the first established country on earth; and the Ethiopians were the first who introduced the worship of the gods, and who established laws."

The ancient historian Diodorus recorded the tradition of how the first Ethiopian/Nubian king Asar (Osiris) led a group of colonists up the Nile River and settled the area of the north-eastern corner of Africa which would later be known as "Kamit (Egypt)."

> *"From Ethiopia, he (Osiris) passed through Arabia, bordering upon the Red Sea to as far as India, and the remotest inhabited coasts; he built likewise many cities in India, one of which he called Nysa, willing to have remembrance of that (Nysa) in Egypt where he was brought up. At this Nysa in India he planted Ivy, which continues to grow there, but nowhere else in India or around it. He left likewise many other marks of his being in those parts, by which the latter inhabitants are induced, and do affirm, that this God was born in India. He likewise addicted himself to the hunting of elephants, and took care to have statues of himself in every place, as lasting monuments of his expedition."*
> -Recorded by *Diodorus* (Greek historian 100 B.C.)

Thus we are to understand that the ancient Nubians colonized (settled) the area north of the sources of the Nile River as they followed its flow, looking for more fertile lands. Further, we learn, from the legend of Asar[135], that after establishing civilization in Egypt, he proceeded to travel the ancient world and assisted those people in establishing civilizations outside of Africa, namely Asia Minor, India, China and southern Europe. Modern archeology has revealed that Asarian artifacts have been found in areas south of Uganda, specifically Zaire. Also, the Dogon peoples of West Africa hold that they are direct descendants of the Ancient Egyptians. So the influence of Asar (Ancient Egyptian civilization) was felt not only on the African continent, but far and wide. This is again supported by the ancient Greek and Roman historians.

> *"And upon his return to Greece, they gathered around and asked, "tell us about this great land of the Blacks called Ethiopia." And Herodotus said, "There are two great Ethiopian nations, one in Sind (India) and the other in Egypt."*
> —Diodorus quoting Herodotus (c. 484-425 B.C.E.)

> *"India taken as a whole, beginning from the north and embracing what of it is subject to Persia, is a continuation of Egypt and the Ethiopians."*
> -The Itinerarium Alexandri (A.C.E. 345)

Following the tradition as outlined above and taking into account the findings by geneticists and anthropologists which all show that human beings emerged from Africa through the Arabian desert and populated Asia, we are to understand that the Nubians gave rise to the Ancient Egyptians and the Ancient Egyptians gave rise to the peoples of Asia Minor and India.

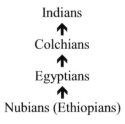

Indians
↑
Colchians
↑
Egyptians
↑
Nubians (Ethiopians)

The Ancient History of Nubia

Modern Western archeologists believe that the evidence shows that Nubian culture emerged by the year 3,800 B.C.E.,[29] with a monarchic system in place. They also consider that this monarchy emerged some generations prior to the Ancient Egyptian Pharaonic system. However, in light of the new evidence of the Sphinx, it is perhaps better to understand the monarchy of Nubia as an outgrowth of the flowering of its own child (Egypt). The Great Sphinx bears witness to the existence of the Pharaonic system as early as 10,000 B.C.E. So, the Nubians who moved to Egypt prior to 10,000 B.C.E. (now called the Kamitan people) were able to flourish there, and that prosperity affected Nubia, and there too, the same system of Pharaonic rule and culture developed.

Map of Ancient Kamit and Kush

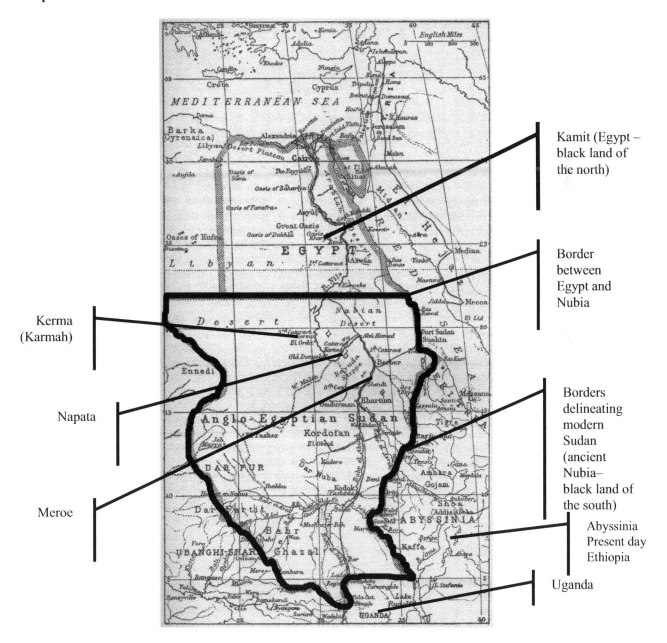

It was not until around 2000 B.C.E. that Nubia emerged from the shadow of Egypt as a strong nation, with the rise of the city-state of Kerma (see map above). Up to and during this period there was a harmonious

---

[29] Prior to that time, evidence indicates that the Nubian people had a rudimentary civilization.

relationship with Egypt, and trade boomed between the two countries. Later, during the reign of the kings Amenemhat I, Senusert I and Senusert III, Nubia was formally annexed to Egypt.

In the Late Period of Ancient Egyptian history, when it was invaded by the Assyrians, the Nubians regained control of Egypt and ruled Nubia and Egypt until the Assyrians retook Egypt and the Nubians were pushed down to Napata (see map above) . Nubia defended Egypt against the Assyrians and the Libyans during their tenure. They also led a resurgence in Ancient Egyptian art and culture as well as spiritual philosophy, as evinced by the patronage of the King Shabaka towards the restoration of Memphite Theology. The Nubians did not have to undergo any conflicts with respect to whether or not they should accept the Ancient Egyptian gods and goddesses, because these were always theirs as well. An Ancient Egyptian born prince by the name of Psametichus temporarily ousted the Assyrians. The Nubians moved their capital to the south, to Napata at around 667 B.C.E., and began trading with other African states in the interior of Africa. Note that the Egyptians did not oppose the Nubians, but did oppose the Assyrians and the Libyans. The Libyans later captured Napata, and the Nubians moved their capital to Meroe (see map above) in 593 B.C.E., and a new flourishing of trade and culture emerged again in Nubia.

The Ancient Egyptians referred to Nubia as *Ta Seti* ("Land of the Bow") presumably because of the skill of the Nubian archers who served in the Egyptian armies. The Ancient Egyptians also referred to Nubia as Wawat and Yam, which were capitals or centers of power in Nubia. Thus, these names were used at different periods. The term Yam is not used after the Old Kingdom Period. The term Kush (Cush) appears at about 2000 B.C.E., and at this time Kerma was the capital of the Nubian nation.

The Relationship between Nubia and Egypt

The situation between Ancient Egypt and Nubia may be likened to that of England and the United States. Far from being a racial issue, it so happened that the child, Egypt, grew to such stature and glory, that it surpassed the parent. Due to certain cultural differences that developed between the countries, there was a vying over control of trade just as two siblings quarrel over clothing or jewelry. The true state of affairs between the two countries became evident when Egypt was besieged and occupied by foreign conquerors. The Nubians lent their support as allies, if not as family members coming to the rescue of kin in trouble, to restore Egypt to her former glory.

At around 2000 B.C.E., the Kingdom of Kerma or Karmah grew in power and ambition, and became an economic competitor with Egypt. When Egypt experienced a period of social upheaval beginning around 1700 B.C.E., when the Hyksos (Asiatics most likely from present-day Syria) conquered lower (northern) Egypt, armies of upper or southern Egypt withdrew from lower Nubia and Karmah took over this region. However, soldiers from Karmah fought on both sides in the warfare between the Egyptians and the Hyksos, pointing to the fluidity of the situation in Nubia and the ambivalence of the Nubians in this period. The Egyptians began a national war of liberation by around 1570 B.C.E. They waged war first against Karmah, because during the war conflict with the Hyksos, the Egyptian Pharaoh Kamose intercepted a message from the Hyksos ruler to the new king of Karmah. This message invited Karmah to join forces with Hyksos to conquer Egypt, and they would share its spoils between them

Egypt moved to reconquer lower Nubia to prevent such an alliance, and then the Egyptians drove the Hyksos from Egypt. The ambivalence of the Kingdom of Karmah proved costly for them since Egypt then waged a series of attacks against Karmah until around 1450 B.C.E., when Egypt destroyed the kingdom and its capital. Egypt then occupied Nubia for approximately 500 years, and the Nubians (or Kushites) absorbed Egyptian culture.[136] This period also marked the beginning of the New Kingdom era in Ancient Egyptian history, a period marked by a flowering in Egyptian culture. In the New Kingdom and Late Periods of Ancient Egyptian history, the Nubians adopted the worship of Amun, particularly in his ram form, and also the architectural style of Kamit (pyramid with attached chapel in the characteristic form with two pylons . The Nubians also adopted the art of building pyramids, but most of these were for use as tombs, somewhat like the pyramid tombs of the Ancient Egyptian Old Kingdom Period. This building boom was especially marked during the Meroitic Period of Nubian history. Thus, there is a larger total number of pyramids in Nubia than in Egypt itself.

Above-left: Pyramid temple Nubian Meroitic (last Nubian capital 4th century B.C.E. to 3rd century A.C.E.). Above right: Pyramid tomb of Nubian King and Egyptian Pharaoh Taharka- Late Period 25 Dynasty –8th century B.C.E.

Below: Nubian Meroitic Period Temple complete with pylons.

Below: Typical Egyptian New Kingdom Period Temple.

Below: left- Nubian Meroitic Period Temple complete with pylons. Below: right- Typical Egyptian New Kingdom Period Temple.

The Nubian Gods and Goddesses in the Kamitan Paut[30]

Left: The God Amun in the form of the Ram headed man.

While the divinity Amun was popular in Nubia, this popularity was exemplified in the later periods of Nubian history which began with the New Kingdom Period in Kamit. The Nubian preference was the ram-headed man while the preference in Kamit was either the ram in a completely zoomorphic (animal) form or the divinity as a man with the body and head of a man (anthropomorphic).

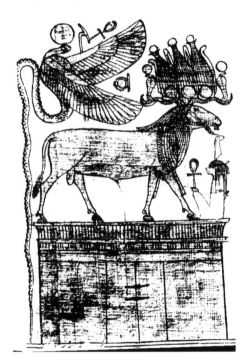

Figure 20: Above left, the God Amun-Ra from Ancient Egypt as a man. Above right- the god Amun-Ra from Ancient Egypt as a ram.

---

[30] Company of Ancient Egyptian Neteru (Gods and Goddesses) – similar in some ways to the term "Pantheon" meaning All the gods of a people. –American Heritage dictionary

If we look further back however, we will discover that the mythic association between the Kamitans and the Nubians in Pre-Dynastic times is supported by the earliest writings of Ancient Egypt. Firstly, the god Bas (Basu, Bes), who is usually referred to as a "Sudani" god, is also equated by the Ancient Egyptian scripture and iconography with the divinity Heru. The following panel shows this link most succinctly.

Figure 21- Above: left -Heru as a Divine child, master of nature, controller of beasts (evil, unrighteousness, the lower self), wearing mask of Basu. Above right – Basu as the dwarf with the characteristic Nubian plumes as headdress.

In anthropology, pigmies are known as members of any of various peoples, especially of equatorial Africa and parts of southeast Asia, having an average height less than 5 feet (127 centimeters).[138]   In the ancient period, the pigmies of Nubia were renowned for knowing "the dance of the God" and for being jovial but forthright people. In this vein they were renowned musicians and lovers of play and festivity, but also leaders in wars of righteousness and protectors of children. These are all attributes of Basu. Basu also appears in the Pyramid Texts along with the other gods and goddesses of Kamit. The Pyramid Texts are the earliest known extensive writings about the myth and philosophy of Kamit (Ancient Egypt). Therefore, any divinity which is mentioned in those texts, emerges with at least the same importance of the other Kamitan gods and goddesses depending on the interrelationships provided in the text itself. The system of Neteru (gods and goddesses) of Kamit may be divided into the following groups for easy understanding.

Transcendental
Divinities: Neberdjer, Heru – beyond the cosmos, beyond time and space
⇕
Cosmic
Divinities: Ex. Asar, Amun, Ra, Net, etc.—universal worship
⇕
Natural
Divinities: Geb, Nut, Shu, Tefnut, etc.— divinities symbolizing the cosmic forces of nature
⇕
Local (worldly)
Divinities: worshipped at the particular nome (city-town) but not nationally throughout Egypt
⇕
Legendary
Divinities: – original divinities of the ancient period that gave rise to the ones worshipped in the later forms

Figure 22- Above left: Kamitan depictions of the Kamitan/Nubian God Bas as the Harpist. Above right: The Kamitan/Nubian god Bas in the form of the all-encompassing divinity, Neberdjer.[139]

Bas and a host of other Nubian divinities can be seen as the legendary divinities which appear in the early Kamitan texts, but later take on new Kamitan forms, under which their worship continues. Bas, for example, continues to be worshipped as Heru. Bas also figures prominently as a part of the Kamitan concept of the transcendental divinity, Neberdjer. The iconography of Bas in the form of Neberdjer (above) closely follows that of the representation of Heru as the Divine Child (above) in the following respects. Both are regarded as the all-encompassing Divinity, masters of the animal forces. In the picture of Heru above, this is symbolized by Heru holding and standing on the animals; his nudity is a symbol of transcendentalism (unconditioned consciousness). The Bas mask he wears is a symbol of the wonderful and magnificent nature of the Divine, who manifests as a dwarf, and at the same time as a personality overflowing with joviality and life.

Neberdjer represents all of the forces of the other divinities including Ra, Amun and Heru thus representing (see picture above) non-duality and Supreme Divinity. This being is in control of the seven eternal animal forces (seven animals encircled by the serpent with its tail in its mouth-symbolizing eternity).

Other Nubian divinities which were mentioned in the Ancient Egyptian Pyramid Texts include:

Aahs

The Nubian divinity Aahs is referred to as the "Regent of the land of the south."

Ari Hems Nefer

The Nubian divinity Ari Hems Nefer is referred to as the "beautiful womb." *Ari Hems Nefer* was a divinity of the area 15 miles south of the modern Egyptian city of Aswan, where the temple of Aset is located. In ancient times it was known as Pilak or the limit or southern border of Egypt. Today it is called Philae.

or

The Nubian divinity **Meril** is referred to as the "beloved lion" divinity of the city of Kalabshah (city located 35 miles south of the modern Egyptian city Aswan), where the temple of Knum is located. In ancient times it was known as Elephantine by the Greeks or the first cataract of Egypt. Today it is called Aswan.

Symbol A   ,   Symbol B   ,   Symbol C

The symbols above for the Nubian divinity **Dudun** show the association with one of the oldest most worshipped and most powerful divinity of Kamit, Heru, whose symbol is the falcon (hawk). Symbol A shows the characteristic Heruian icon, the hawk, perched on the divine solar boat. Symbol B shows one of the full spellings of the name including the phonetic signs and again, including the hawk, this time perched on the standard, meaning *Dudun Sa Heru:* "Dudun the son of Heru." Symbol C shows one of the full spellings of the name including the phonetic signs and this time showing the symbol of the two lands, meaning *Dudun Sa Tawi* "Dudun the son of the two lands (i.e. Nubia and Egypt)." The divinity Dudun was important in Kamitan spirituality even into the late period. The evidence of this can be found in the fact that it was Dudun who symbolically burnt the special Nubian incense through which the royalty of Kamit was to be purified for induction to the high offices, including the throne of rulership. Pharaoh Djehutimes III built temples to Dudun in Nubia at *el-Lessya* and *Uronarti.* Below we see the symbols of Heru used in Kamit. Notice the correlation to the symbols of Dudun.

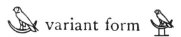 variant form

The symbols of Heru and those of Dudun are a perfect match. Therefore, Dudun was the name for the same divinity which was called Heru in Kamitan religion. Another strong correlation between Nubian and Kamitan religion is the dwarf figure. We have already been introduced to Basu. This quality of stature and Nubian features is also present in the figure of Asar in his aspect of Ptah-Seker-Asar.

Ptah-Seker-Asar (as Pigmy)

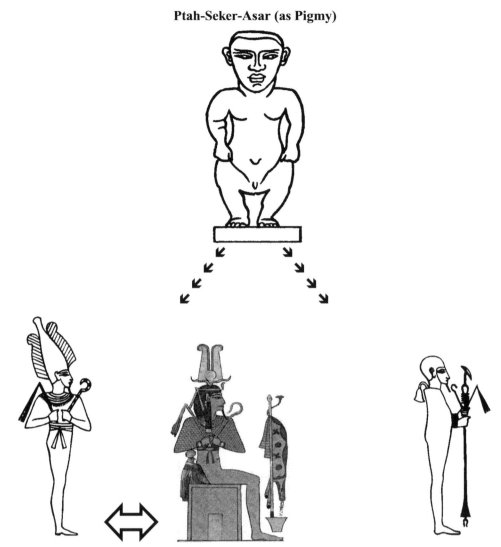

Figure 23: Above far-left The god Asar. Middle- is Ptah-Seker-Asar as an average sized man. Far right- The god Ptah of Memphis.

Ptah-Seker-Asar unites the three main spiritual traditions of the early Dynastic Period in ancient Kamit, that of Ra, Asar, and Ptah. Asar is part of Anunian theology, which is centered on the divinity Ra, and Ra is associated with the even earlier Heru as the all-encompassing Divinity. Also, Asar is associated with the divinity Heru, as Heru is Asar's son in the Asarian mystical tradition. Ptah is the central divinity in the theology of the Ancient Egyptian city of *Men-nefer* (also Het-Ka-Ptah), known as Memphis. He is associated, in his work of Creation, with the Divinity Tem, who is a form of Ra. Therefore, the dwarf figure of Ptah-Seker-Asar united the culture of Nubia with that of Kamit Also the religious iconography of Basu as the dwarf and the characteristic Nubian plumed headdress comes into the later Dynastic Period. Therefore, the impact of Nubian spirituality was felt all the way from the commencement of Kamitan religion through the late period.

Plate 2: (Below) In the upper right hand corner of the ceiling of the Peristyle Hall in the Temple of Aset a special image of the goddess Nut and the God Geb and the higher planes of existence can be seen. Nut and Geb. Below: -line drawing of the same scene. (Temple of Aset {Isis}).

The figure at left depicts another conceptualization of the Netherworld, which is at the same time the body of Nut in a forward bend posture.

The god Geb is on the ground practicing the Plough Yoga exercise posture. The goddess in the center symbolizes the lower heaven in which the moon traverses, the astral realm. The outermost goddess symbolizes the course of the sun in its astral journey and the causal plane.

Notice the characteristic Nubian headdress of Nut, which is also visible in the iconography of Bas. This iconography links the late Kamitan religion with that of the Pre-Dynastic era, and with the Nubian origins of Kamitan culture. Geb, who is in the plough posture, symbolizes the physical plane and all solid matter, while the goddesses represent the subtler levels of existence.

Figure 24: Goddess Mut, the Mother of Asar and Aset and Blackness as a Metaphor of Consciousness and as a Description of the gods and goddesses

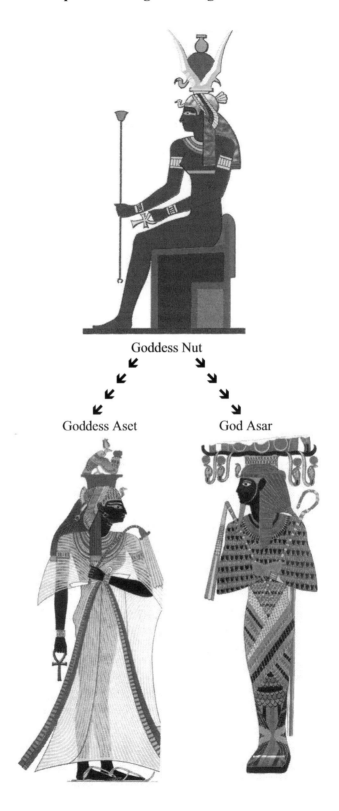

Goddess Nut

Goddess Aset   God Asar

In Kamitan philosophy, blackness is used as a descriptive nomenclature of the people, certain of the gods and goddesses as well as the concept of the transcendental.

In the Temple of Denderah in Kamit, it is inscribed that the goddess Nut gave birth to the goddess Aset there, and that upon her birth, Nut exclaimed: *"As"* (behold), *I have become thy mother."* This was the origin of the name "Ast," (Aset) later known as Isis to the Greeks and others. It further states that *"she was a dark-skinned child and was called Khnemet-ankhet"* or "the living lady of love". Thus, Aset also symbolizes the "blackness" of the vast un-manifest regions of existence. In this capacity she is also the ultimate expression of the African ideal prototype of the Christian Madonna, especially in statues where she is depicted holding the baby Heru in the same manner Mother Mary is portrayed holding baby Jesus. Her identification is also symbolized in her aspect as *Amentet,* the Duat, itself.

Ament means "hidden." It is a specific reference to the female form of the astral plane or Netherworld known as *Amenta* (Amentet, Amentat) or the Duat. Like her husband Asar, who was known as the "Lord of the Perfect Black," Aset was the Mistress of the Netherworld (Amentet, Amentat). Thus, Aset also symbolizes the "blackness" of the vast unmanifest regions of existence (the unmanifest). Upon further reflection into the mythology it becomes obvious that since Asar is the Duat, and since the goddess Amentet is also Amentat or the realm of Asar, they are in reality one and the same (both the realms and the deities). So Aset and Asar together form the hidden recesses of Creation. In essence they are the source of Creation, and are therefore both simultaneously considered to be the source of the Life Force which courses through Creation.

Table 9: Chronology of Nubian History

8,000 B.C.E.	**Pottery and community found at Karmah**
2,000 – 1550 B.C.E.	**Karmah Period**
1549 – 850 B.C.E.	**Unification with Kamit (Ancient Egypt) Period**
850 – 270 B.C.E.	**Napata Period**
716 B.C.E.	**25th Dynasty – beginning rulership of Egypt Period**
270 B.C.E. – 350 A.C.E.	**Meroe Period Independent Nation**
1st century B.C.E.– 1st century A.C.E.	**Judaism introduced– some Kushites adopt Judaism**
3rd –6th century A.C.E.	**Christianization Period – some Kushites adopt Christianity**
1000 A.C.E.	**Islamization Period, Axum city - Kushites and Arabs Merge**

Summary

Thus, it is clear that the Ancient Egyptians, while recognizing the geographical differences (Egypt is in the north and Kush is in the south) between their land and the land of the Nubians, also recognized the similitude of the lands. In effect the name of lands of Egypt and Nubia actually mean the same thing "black land" or "land of the blacks." The different words used to identify the two cultures (Kush and Kamit) simply denote the relative geographical locations and the ethnic (tribal) differentiation of inhabitants. The ethnic differences here do not relate to race or religion as these have been shown to be the same, but of customs and traditions that developed independently due to differences in distance from each other. This is done for the purpose of showing an underlying unity while at the same time denoting the practical differences of the two lands. This of course points to the underlying ethnic homogeneity between the two peoples, and at the same time acknowledges the cultural differences which developed due to the language changes and the accelerated development of the Ancient Egyptians.

Another force, which spurred the Ancient Egyptians to develop at a faster pace, was the interaction they had with the Asiatic peoples. Since the Ancient Egyptians were geographically located closer to Asia Minor, they encountered more Asiatics and Europeans than the Ethiopians, who were in an area that afforded them a relative form of seclusion. Some of the interactions were peaceful while others were hostile and this prompted (stimulated) the Ancient Egyptians to mature and advance in the areas of building technology, warfare and social as well as spiritual philosophy.

Recent archaeological finds have revealed that the region's people were producing sophisticated ceramics by 8000 B.C.E. Indeed, it seems likely that Nubia contributed as much to Ancient Egypt's development as Egypt did to Nubia's.[140] Nubian-Egyptian pottery from the Pre-Dynastic Period is the link between the Ancient Nubian (Ethiopians), the Ancient Egyptians and the Ancient Indus Valley culture.

Plate 7: Pre-Dynastic-Ancient Egyptian Neolithic Period Grave-including black and red pottery. (British Museum-Photo by M. Ashby)

The foundations of Egyptian religion were evident as far back as the Pre-Dynastic era as religious amulets from that era have been found spread throughout the region (Kamit-Kush). In the early period the dead were buried in cemeteries, along with pots and other domestic implements, from Badarian times. Many of these pots found in graves show a boat with a palm branch at the bow and two cabins, over one of which, at least, is the emblem of a divinity.[141] The distinctive pottery of this period has been compared and likened to that of the later finds in the Indus Valley. On some of the pottery designs were painted. Some were first in white with a dark red background, and later in red on a light background.

There were two periods of development in the Pharaonic system of rule in northeast Africa. The first developed prior to 10,000 B.C.E. as attested by the headdress of the Great Sphinx. The second period is the late Pre-Dynastic Period (prior to 5000 B.C.E.). There is evidence that the Pharaonic system of rule (kings and queens as spiritual leaders-head of religion) emerged in the Pre-Dynastic Period in Nubia (Kush) prior to its development in Kamit. The difference between the monarchy of Ancient Nubia and the Pharaonic system of Ancient Egypt may be seen in the domain of rulership. In Egypt the Pharaonic system developed into an empire when the "two lands" (Upper and Lower Egypt) were consolidated. Egypt had 42 monarchies (referred to as nomarchs since they ruled over nomes or municipalities), but what made the Pharaonic rule different is that it was rulership that united all of the separate nomes. So the Pharaoh was not just a king, but also an emperor. When we speak of a breakdown in the Pharaonic rule in the times when Egypt was not completely overpowered, we are only speaking of the loss of Pharaonic rule and not necessarily a total crash of the society. It would be as if the President of a country lost power temporarily but the governors of the cities or states remained in power, and later conspired to bring back order by pooling resources such as personnel and material in order to rebuild the government. This is what happened during the invasions of the Hyksos as well as the Assyrians. This was the state of affairs during the "intermediate" periods between the Old and Middle Kingdom Periods and between the Middle and New Kingdoms. The Ancient Egyptians were not strong enough to overcome the second Assyrian attack, and there was never a second opportunity to overthrow them since Alexander the Great defeated them and took their place. There was still not enough strength to overcome the Greeks, but also there was lesser need, since they upheld the Egyptian culture and religion. Thus the Egyptian culture remained relatively intact under the Greeks as compared to the conditions imposed by the Hyksos and Assyrians. These conditions would not remain the same under the control by the Roman-Christians and the later Arab-Muslims who actively sought to stamp out the old religion. Nubia was the last place to practice the Ancient Egyptian religion, and thus also the last to convert to Judaism, Christianity and Islam. Today, the Nubians living in southern Egypt consider themselves ethnically as Nubian, and at the same time nationally as Egyptian, and spiritually as Muslim.

Chapter 1 Section 3: History of Predynastic and Dynastic Egypt

Summary of Major Events in Ancient Egyptian History

As stated earlier, the origins of Ancient Egyptian civilization begin in the far reaches of pre-history. Ancient Egypt or Kamit had a civilization that flourished in Northeast Africa along the Nile River from before 10,000 B.C.E. (being conservative) until 30 B.C.E. In 30 B.C.E., Octavian, who was later known as the Roman Emperor Augustus, put the last Egyptian king, Ptolemy XIV, a Greek ruler, to death. After this Egypt was formally annexed to Rome. Traditional late 20th century Egyptologists normally divide Ancient Egyptian history into the following approximate periods. Of course, these dates need to be revised in light of the new evidences.

Table 10: Major Cultural-Theological Developments

Chronology of Ancient Egypt According to Confirmed Archeological Dating of artifacts and Monuments (Based on evidences presented in this book).[142]	The dates below are based on the opinions of orthodox Egyptologists[143]

38,000 B.C.E Beginning of the Great Year previous to the current one.
c. 10,500 B.C.E.-7,000 B.C.E. Creation of the Great Sphinx Modern archeological accepted dates – Sphinx means Hor-m-akhet or Heru (Horus) in the horizon. This means that the King is one with the Spirit, Ra as an enlightened person possessing an animal aspect (lion) and illuminated intellect. Anunian Theology – Ra
c. 10,000 B.C.E.-5,500 B.C.E. The Sky GOD- Realm of Light-Day – NETER Androgynous – All-encompassing –Absolute, Nameless Being, later identified with Ra-Herakhti (Sphinx)
>7,000 B.C.E. Kamitan Myth and Theology present in architecture
5,500-3,800 BCE EARLY DYNASTIC PERIOD – AND OLD KINGDOM PERIOD
5500+ B.C.E. to 600 A.C.E. Amun -Ra - Ptah (Horus) – Amenit - Rai – Sekhmet (male and female Trinity-Complementary Opposites)
5500+ B.C.E. Memphite Theology – Ptah
5500+ B.C.E. Hermopolitan Theology- Djehuti
5500+ B.C.E. The Asarian Resurrection Theology - Asar
5500+B.C.E. The Goddess Principle- Theology, Isis-Hathor-Net-Mut-Sekhmet-Buto
5500 B.C.E. (Dynasty 1) Beginning of the Dynastic Period (Unification of Upper and Lower Egypt)
5000 B.C.E. (5th Dynasty) Pyramid Texts - Egyptian Book of Coming Forth By Day - 42 Precepts of MAAT and codification of the Pre-Dynastic theologies (Pre-Dynastic Period: 10,000 B.C.E.-5,500 B.C.E.)
5000-4000 B.C.E. Construction of the Step Pyramid at Sakkara
4950 B.C.E. Neolithic – Fayum
4241 B.C.E. The Pharaonic (royal) calendar based on the Sothic system (star Sirius) was in use.
4000-3000 B.C.E CONSTRUCTION OF THE GREAT PYRAMIDS
3800-3500 B.C.E.- 1ST INTERMEDIATE PERIOD
3500-1730 B.C.E. MIDDLE KINGDOM
3000 B.C.E. WISDOM TEXTS-Precepts of Ptahotep, Instructions of Any, Instructions of Amenemope, Etc.
2040 B.C.E.-1786 B.C.E. COFFIN TEXTS
1730-1580 B.C.E. 2ND INTERMEDIATE PERIOD
1580-1075 B.C.E .NEW KINGDOM
1580 B.C.E.-Theban Theology - Amun
1570 B.C.E.-Books of Coming Forth By Day (Book of the Dead)
1353 B.C.E. Non-dualist Philosophy from the Pre-Dynastic Period was redefined by Akhnaton.
1075-656 BCE 3RD INTERMEDIATE
712-657 B.C.E. The Nubian Dynasty
664-332 BCE LATE PERIOD
	*See Appendix A
	
	The Late Pre-Dynastic (3000-2920 B.C.E.);[144]/[145]
	Early Dynastic Period (2920-2775 B.C.E.);
	    Dynasty 1-3
	
	The Old Kingdom or Old Empire (2575-234 B.C.E.);
	    Dynasty 4-8
	
	The First Intermediate Period (2134-2,040 B.C.E.);
	    Dynasty 9-11 (Theban)
	
	The Middle Kingdom or Middle Empire (2040-1640 B.C.E.);
	    Dynasty 11-14
	
	The Second Intermediate Period (1640-1532 B.C.E.);
	    Dynasty 15-17
	
	The New Kingdom or New Empire (1532-1070 B.C.E.);
	    Dynasty 18-20
	
	The third Intermediate Period (1070-712 B.C.E.);
	    Dynasty 21-25 (Nubia and Theban Area)
	
	The Late Period (712-332 B.C.E.).
	    Dynasty 25 (Nubia and All Egypt)-30
	
	In the Late Period of Ancient Egyptian history the following groups controlled Egypt.
	
	The Nubian Dynasty (712-657 B.C.E.);
	The Persian Dynasty (525-404 B.C.E.);
	The Native Revolt and re-establishment of Egyptian rule by Egyptians (404-343 B.C.E.);
	The Second Persian Period (343-332 B.C.E.);
	The Ptolemaic or Greek Period (Also known as the Hellenistic Period 332 B.C.E.- c. 30 B.C.E.);
	Roman Period (c.30 B.C.E.-395 A.C.E.);
	The Byzantine Period (395-642 A.C.E) and
	The Arab Conquest Period includes: the Caliphate and the Mamalukes Period (642-1517 A.C.E.);
	Ottoman Domination Period (1082-1882 A.C.E.);
	British colonialism Period (1882-1952 A.C.E.);
	Modern, Arab-Islamic Egypt (1952- present).

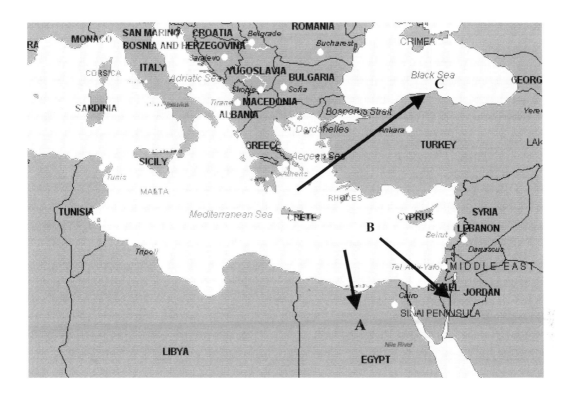

At about 2,890 B.C.E., the beginning of the IInd Dynasty, considerable trade was in progress between Egypt (A) and the Sinai (B). The Egyptians are believed to have traded as far to the north as the Black Sea (C). It is known that Pharaoh Pepi II of the VI Dynasty, ruler from c. 2,294 B.C.E.- c. 2,188 B.C.E., organized the caravan trade with Nubia, Punt and the Sudan. In the early New Kingdom period (1,580-1,075 B.C.E.), the famous Pharaoh, Queen Hatshepsut (1,473-1,458 B.C.E.) of Ancient Egypt, expanded maritime trade which is believed to have stretched as far as India[146] and the Far East.[147] It is believed that textiles, including cotton were brought back from India and used for mummy wrappings.

> In early times, the principal objects that were introduced to Egypt from Arabia and India were spices and various oriental productions. These were required either for the service of religion, or the purposes of luxury. A number of precious stones, such as lapis lazuli, and other items brought from those countries are frequently discovered in the tombs of Thebes, bearing the names of Pharaohs of the 18th[148] dynasty.[149]

-Sir Garner Wilkinson

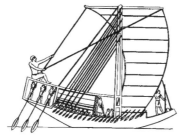

Figure 25: Trading Vessel in the 18th Dynasty (1580 B.C.E)[31]

The New Kingdom Period (1,580-1,075 B.C.E.) was a time wherein Ancient Egypt was at a peak in terms of art, philosophy, economic and political power as well as social prosperity. The period after the New Kingdom

---

[31] Revised dating based on correct evidence.

saw greatness in culture and architecture under the rulership of Rameses II. However, after his rule, Egypt saw a decline from which it would never recover. This is the period of the downfall of Ancient Egyptian culture in which the Libyans ruled after The Tanite (XXI) Dynasty. This was followed by the Nubian rulers who founded the XXII Dynasty and tried to restore Egypt to her past glory. However, having been weakened by the social and political turmoil of wars, Ancient Egypt fell to the Persians. The Persians conquered the country and were expelled briefly by native Egyptians, but they re-conquered the country until the Greeks, under Alexander, conquered them. The Romans followed the Greeks, and then the first Arab-Muslims conquered the land of Egypt in 640 A.C.E . The map below shows the areas of regular trade between the Ancient Egyptians and the other Africans living in the south. Queen Hatshepsut's trading parties and those of other Ancient Egyptian rulers commonly engaged in commerce with the land of "Punt."

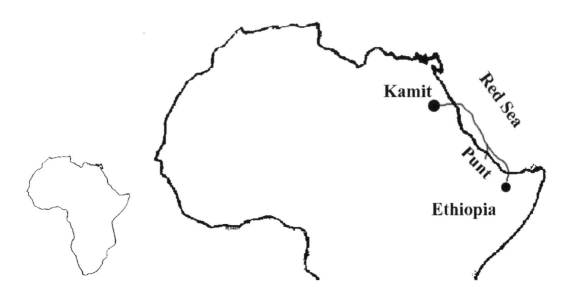

The Economy of Ancient Egypt

Ancient Egypt was a wealthy country due to its fertile lands, owing to the regular yearly Nile River deposits in the surrounding valley. It became the "grainstore" of the Roman Empire when the Romans conquered it. Corn, date-palms, vegetables and grapevines were grown, and beer and bread were the staple items of food and drink by the general population. Trade was through bartering since coinage did not exist. Royal expeditions were made to Syria, Punt, Sinai, India and other lands to obtain spices, timber, metals, and other materials through trade.

The Royal Graves and Ancient Scriptures

Much of the evidence of life in Ancient Egypt from the later periods of the 1st Dynasty derives from tombs, especially those that were found in the cemeteries at Sakkara, near Memphis, which dates up to the end of the first Dynasty. In addition, some large stone steles with the names of the Pharaohs on them survived at Abdu (Abydos). However, both sites (Abdu and Sakkara-Memphis) have suffered due to the effects of plundering in ancient and modern times, and deterioration due to the passage of time. At Sakkara, the actual burial was in a subterranean wood-lined chamber. At different periods, Mastabas and pyramids were used. These burial pyramids are not to be confused with the large Great Pyramids at Giza, Dahshur, Abusir, Maidum, the Step Pyramid at Sakkara, and other sites in which no texts or bodies or funerary implements were found. The burial pyramids contain scriptures related to the spiritual resurrection of the deceased, which were later converted to Coffin Texts, and subsequently to the Papyrus Texts. In later times these texts came to be known as "Book of the Dead" or "Book of Coming Forth by Day." The proper translation of the "Book of Coming Forth by Day," in the Kamitan language is "Rau Nu Prt M Hru," which literally translated means "Chapters of Going Into the Light," i.e. "Instructions on How to Attain Enlightenment." All of the spiritual scriptures of Ancient Egypt are based on the Pre-Dynastic myths related to the nature of the gods and goddesses. All of the scriptures are interrelated, presenting aspects of the mythic as well as mystical aspects of spirituality. The Wisdom Texts are philosophical expositions on the nature of right living, and the means to achieve harmony and spiritual enlightenment in life, which as the Kamitan sages defined it, is the only purpose and goal of life.

Phases of Ancient Egyptian Spiritual Literature

MYTHS AND BASIS OF ANCIENT EGYPTIAN RELIGION

SHEMSU HOR
The Myth of Heru and Hetheru
(Sky-Solar Theology incorporating male and female divinity) - Predynastic

SHETAUT ASAR-ASET-HERU
The Myth of Asar, Aset and Heru (Asarian Resurrection Theology) - Predynastic

SHETAUT ATUM-RA
The Myth of Creation (Anunian Theology) - Predynastic

SHETAUT PTAH
The Myth of Creation (Memphite Theology) - Predynastic and Early Dynastic

SHETAUT NET
The Myth of Creation (Saitian Theology – Goddess Spirituality) - Predynastic and Early Dynastic

PYRAMID TEXTS
(C. 5,000 B.C.E. OR PRIOR)

Pyramid of Unas
Pyramid of Teti,
Pyramid of Pepi I,
Pyramid of Mernere,
Pyramid of Pepi II

WISDOM TEXTS
(C. 3,000 B.C.E. – PTOLEMAIC PERIOD)
Precepts of Ptahotep
Instructions of Any
Instructions of Amenemope
Etc.

COFFIN TEXTS
(C. 2040 B.C.E.-1786 B.C.E.)

PAPYRUS TEXTS
(C. 1580 B.C.E.-Roman Period)[32]
Books of Coming Forth By Day
Example of famous papyruses:

Papyrus of Any
Papyrus of Hunefer
Papyrus of Kenna
Greenfield Papyrus, Etc.

Hieroglyphic Writing

Hieroglyphic Writing refers to a means "relating to, or being a system of writing, such as that of Ancient Egypt, in which pictorial symbols are used to represent meaning or sounds or a combination of meaning and sounds."[150] The term also means "carved in stone." So many cultures in history have created writings carved in stone. However, the hieroglyphs of Ancient Egypt are perhaps the most popular. Hieroglyphs have been discovered on labels and tablets from the Pre-Dynastic Period. These early hieroglyphics developed into the classical script of Egypt, however not enough have been found to render deciphering certain.[151] The decipherment of the Egyptian Hieroglyphs in the early 19th century has allowed the re-discovery of a wealth of spiritual literature and the basis for most of the modern day world religions. The *Pyramid Texts* and the *Book of Coming Forth By Day* are similar in scripture and purpose. It is correct to understand that the texts referred

---

[32] After 1570 BC they would evolve into a more unified text, the Egyptian Book of the Dead.

to as the *Book of Coming Forth By Day* evolved out of the *Pyramid Text* writings. This is because the *Pyramid Texts* are the early form of the well-known texts which have been called the *Book of Coming Forth By Day*. The *Pyramid Texts* are hieroglyphic writings contained in the pyramid tombs[33] of the kings of the early Dynastic Period. Both are collections of utterances, originally recorded in hieroglyphic, which lead the initiate (student of spiritual studies seeking to attain Enlightenment) to transform {his/her} consciousness from human to divine, by purifying the mind with wisdom about the neteru (gods and goddesses, divine forces in the universe), and through the practice of rituals which promote personality integration and thus, spiritual transformation. Each of these constitutes major treatises of Ancient Egyptian literature and philosophy, and together, as a collective, constitute an advanced, holistic system of spiritual development. All of these have, as the main purpose, to effect the union of the individual human being with the Transcendental Self. This philosophy of spiritual transcendence and enlightenment did not begin with the dawn of the Dynastic Period in Ancient Egypt.

The Writing systems used in Ancient Egypt

Hieroglyphic
(used through all periods by Priests and Priestesses)

Hieratic
(shorthand hieroglyphic, used by the Priests and Priestesses -
middle kingdom period to Coptic period)

Demotic
(used by the general population for non-secular purposes -
Late Period to Coptic period)

Coptic
(still presently used by the Coptic Priesthood)

First it must be understood that ancient hieroglyphic writing is not a system like any other writing. Unlike the English language, it is not just alphabetic and literal. Rather, there are several different levels of meaning. The glyphs can have a phonetic meaning, pun meaning, literal meaning, mythological meaning, mystical meaning, etc., because they use pictures and because they are essentially mystical writings. This means that learning the technical aspects of reading the glyphs is not enough to understand the true meaning of what is being said. Any person can learn to read the glyphs; this is the exoteric (outer) practice. However, not everyone can understand their deeper esoteric (inner) meaning. A true reader of the glyphs must be well versed in the mythology behind them as well as the mystical teachings behind them.

Becoming an expert on the glyphs is an added discipline because sometimes the meaning changes in different historical periods. Also, the Ancient Egyptians made use of several variations and spellings to write one word. This means that along with having knowledge of the main words that are used, it is necessary to have knowledge of the variations for the words that may appear in any text. Further, there are over 700 main glyphs, which are considered to be most common. However, there are several hundreds of glyphs, whose meaning are not known by Egyptologists. Thus, when working with texts, a reader may often encounter new words that may not occur again, and therefore, even adept Egyptologists resort to the use of dictionaries. Otherwise a person would be required to keep thousands of obscure terms in mind, which cover a vast period of Ancient Egyptian linguistic history. The period of history encompassed by the glyph ranges from before 5,000 B.C.E to 400 A.C.E. So this is a greater expense of time and linguistic change than the difference within the English language between Chaucer and Shakespeare and between Shakespeare and modern times. People in modern times cannot easily understand Shakespeare's English and can barely understand Chaucer's. And these are only time differentials of a few hundred years. What can then be said about expanses of thousands of years that are encountered between major periods of Ancient Egyptian history (PreDynastic Period, Old Kingdom period, Middle Kingdom period and New Kingdom period)? Along with the problem of not understanding many of the glyphs at all is the problem of interpretation. A survey of the translations of Egyptologists over the last 100 years reveals that often their interpretations are completely different even for

---

[33] Not to be confused with the Pyramids in Giza.

the same exact texts. This is due to their use of their own knowledge base (from western values, myth, religion and history) instead of applying the teachings within the confines of Ancient Egyptian culture, philosophy and mythology. Ancient Egypt cannot be completely understood from a perspective of twentieth century Western Culture any more than it can be understood from Greek culture in 500 B.C.E. It must be studied from within its own context and this means living and practicing the philosophy and mythology. This is the best way to gain insight into the true meanings of the Kamitan Heiroglyphs.

On The Meaning of The Hieroglyphs:

"We must now speak of the Ethiopian writing which is called hieroglyphic by the Egyptians, in order that we may omit nothing in our discussion of their antiquities. Now it is found that the forms of their letters take the shape of animals of every kind, and of the members of the human body, and of implements and especially carpenter's tools; for their writing does not express the intent concept by means of syllables joined one to another, but by its figurative meaning which has been impressed upon the memory by practice. For instance, they draw the picture of a hawk, a crocodile, a snake, and all of the members of the human body-an eye, a hand, a face, and the like. Now the hawk signifies to them everything which happens swiftly, since this animal is practically the swiftest of winged creatures...And the crocodile is a symbol of all that is evil, and the eye is the warder of justice and the guardian of the entire body. And as for the members of the body, the right hand with fingers extended signifies a procuring of livelihood, and the left with the fingers closed, a keeping and guarding of property. The same way of reasoning applies to the remaining characters, which represent parts of the body and implements and all other things; for by paying close attention to the significance which is inherent in each object and by training their minds through drills and exercise of the memory over a long period, they read from habit everything which has been written."

-Diodorus (Greek historian 100 B.C.)

While Diodorus speaks of *the Ethiopian writing which is called hieroglyphic,* we must remember that the Ethiopians used the same hieroglyphic writing up to the Meroitic period, when they were cut off from Egypt by the conquering forces of the Greeks. The Ancient Egyptian hieroglyphic language has many levels of complexity and therefore, the reader must be initiated into these in order to understand them. Otherwise, the understanding will remain at the superficial levels and the deeper philosophy and mysticism will be lost to the reader. The following are levels of reading in the Ancient Egyptian hieroglyphic language. Upon closer examination, the Ancient Egyptian system of writing is discovered to be an extremely sophisticated system of literature.

Phonetic (consonants and vowels) = sound of the word

Ideograms - Pictorial signs– picture of an object. Ex. Owl =

Determinatives (designate the relation of the phonetic parts to an object or concept)

Phonetic + Pictorial + Determinative = The mundane meaning of the word.

Symbolic (quality) aspect of the phonetics or determinatives (designates symbolic meaning of the word).

Mystical meaning = The Literal meaning + Symbolic aspect of the determinative or phonetic relationship + religious philosophy teachings related to the word sounds or pictures.

So in order to understanding a word of Ancient Egyptian hieroglyphic writing it is necessary to relate the words to the symbolic aspects of the images presented in the determinative and then also the mystical philosophy.

(Ex. Owl = 🦉) = (ability to see in the dark and get through the night) = (ability to get through in a

way or form.)

⇕   ⇕   ⇕
(mundane)   ⇔   (symbolic)   ⇔   (mystical)

There is a misconception about the Ancient Egyptian hieroglyphic language that it arrived with no development at all as if by magic to the African continent. This notion plays into the speculation that it was not produced and developed in Africa, by Africans. If the text itself is examined and if the writings from linguists who have studied it are examined, it becomes quickly obvious that there was a period of development of the language. Precisely, in relation to the developing a solution to the problem of confusion in the reading, the Ancient Egyptian scribes developed what are called determinatives, to be added to the word so as to make the meaning more accurate. However, there still remained some ambiguities, so then came the development of "alphabetic" signs. This development is recognized by linguists as being *"not derived from Mesopotamian writing, and demonstrates the total autonomy of the development of the hieroglyphic system."* The alphabetic signs are included below.

The Ancient Egyptian Hieroglyphic Alphabet:

a, A, b, a[34], d,   dj, f, g, h, k, m, n, p, q,   r,   s, sh, t, tj, w, y, ch, kh

The Pyramids and Other Temples

The massive pyramid complexes at Giza, Dahshur, Abusir, Maidum, the Step Pyramid at Sakkara, and other sites denote the high order of Ancient Egyptian Religion. These structures were not used as burial chambers for the kings, but rather as Temples. It has been shown that they were astronomically aligned and refer architecturally to aspects contained in the spiritual scriptures. For example, the pyramid complex at Giza, where the Great Sphinx is located, is referred to as the "Rastau" or passageway into the Orion Star Constellation, the abode of Asar (Osiris). This may be understood literally or it may be understood mystically as a passageway into the Netherworld, which is the scriptural abode of The Supreme Being, as Asar, and therefore the destination of all enlightened souls. As such, the Pyramids at Giza are a gigantic star-map of the stars on Orion's belt, which mystically serve to direct or guide the spiritual student (initiate) to the abode of Asar. Thus, it gives the initiate insight into the means and mechanisms (disciplines) by which {he/she} may attain spiritual enlightenment.[34]

Figure 26 PreDynastic Ancient Egyptian Temple

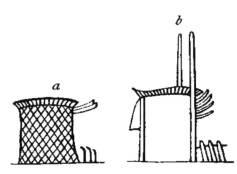

Archeological evidence has been discovered which shows that in the Pre-Dynastic era, the architecture already contained the basic elements that would be subsequently expressed in Kamitan history. The primary

---

[34] See the Kamitan book series by Muata Ashby

difference between the Pre-Dynastic architecture and the architecture in later times was that the later developments used stone instead of mud brick and wood. However in later times, houses and even royal palaces still continued to be made of mud brick and wood, a signal of the importance placed on spirituality as opposed to worldly life.

In Pre-Dynastic times, stone was mainly used for structures like the Sphinx complex in Giza, the Great Pyramids, Sun Temples, temples such as the so-called "Osirion" next to the temple of Asar (Osiris) in the Ancient Egyptian city of Abdu (Abydos), certain structures in the Saqqara (Sakkara) district, and a few other structures. Therefore, all of the elements that were present in the Pre-Dynastic architecture, including the wooden columns and palm tree elements, were faithfully reproduced in stone so that they might last "indefinitely." For example, the images above (a, b) are of the archaic temple. It shows a basic shrine with two posts (pillars) in front. The remains from such a temple have been discovered in the Ancient Egyptian city of Nekhen (Hierakonpolis), which in early Dynastic times was the capital in the south of the country.

The Anunian Temple: Cosmic Symbolism in the Solar Temple Architecture

The Benben, Tekhenu and Mer Temples

The pyramids (**Mer**) and obelisks (**Tekhenu**) are actually symbols of the primeval stone of creation upon which the spirit, in the form of the sun, first shone at the time of Creation. This stone is a metaphor of all that is solid, congealed and tangible upon which human life is based. In these sacred places, reenactments of the Mysteries of Creation that have been described in this volume were carried out.

Picture 27: Basic Ancient Egyptian Pyramid Temple Complex (Old Kingdom Period)

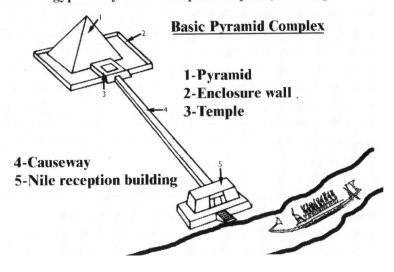

Basic Pyramid Complex

1-Pyramid
2-Enclosure wall
3-Temple

4-Causeway
5-Nile reception building

Picture 28: Basic Ancient Egyptian Obelisk Temple Complex (Old Kingdom Period)

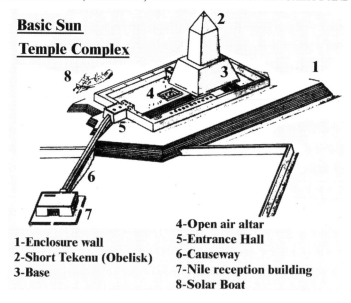

Basic Sun Temple Complex

1-Enclosure wall
2-Short Tekenu (Obelisk)
3-Base
4-Open air altar
5-Entrance Hall
6-Causeway
7-Nile reception building
8-Solar Boat

Plate 8: Late Middle Kingdom-Early New Kingdom Temple of Queen Hatshepsut

Figure 27: Ancient Egyptian New Kingdom Temple Design (Temple of Hatshepsut to Amun)

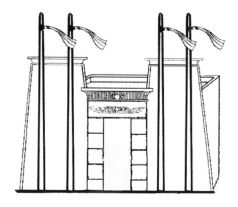

In the more ancient times (Old Kingdom and Middle-Kingdom), there were two principal temple forms, the Sun Temple (including the pyramid) and the Trinity Temple (with three main sections). There were two forms of the Sun Temples, the Ra and the Aton. In the New Kingdom period, the main Temple form used was the familiar three courts with pylon Temple design (above).

The reliefs, painted scenes and hieroglyphic texts carved on the temple complexes, tombs, and various shrines, as well as the papyrus scriptures which were buried with the deceased, give voluminous insights into the nature of the Ancient Egyptian views on life, death and the nature of the Divine. These teachings were avidly studied and recited by Priests and Priestesses of those times.

Even though, according to the mythology of the Kamitan system of the pantheon of gods and goddesses (neteru) of Ancient Egypt, the gods and goddesses are said to have come into being all at once, at various times in Kamitan history some divinities became more prominent. In the earliest periods, the mythology and mysticism of Heru and Hetheru were foremost. Next, the mythology and mysticism of Net and Ra became prominent. This was followed by the mythology and mysticism of Ptah, and subsequent to that, the mythology and mysticism of Amun became prominent. However, all throughout Ancient Egyptian history, the mythology and mysticism of the god Asar (Osiris), and the goddesses Aset (Isis), Net and Hetheru, maintained a consistent level of popularity and veneration throughout Kamit. Thus, it is clear that the Sphinx represents a high order of culture that existed prior to the Pre-Dynastic period. The pyramids represent a rejuvenation of culture, which gave rise to the Dynastic era, and this period first developed in the south, Upper Egypt, having its base in Hierakonpolis and Abdu. From there, the Per-aahs (Pharaohs) of Dynasty 1 annexed the north and established the new capital there, reestablishing Ancient Egyptian culture to its previous heights.

Egypt in the Pre-Dynastic Era: The Early History 10,000 B.C.E. (or earlier)-5,500 B.C.E.[35]

With the dating of the Sphinx we can ascertain that an advanced civilization requiring mathematics, organization of labor and religion in order to create the Sphinx complex, existed at least by 10,000 B.C.E. Remember that the Sphinx is the earliest evidence from Kamitan culture that is verifiable by archeological evidence. Using the evidences such as the Palermo Stone, the Turin Papyrus or the History of Manetho, we obtain far older dates. The oldest Egyptian paleoliths have been found in gravel sites around the river Nile. Important Mesolithic sites have been explored at Helwan, Kom Ombo, and Kharga. Neolithic sites have been studied at el-Omari, Merimda, and in the Fayum. There, barley and wheat similar to that grown today were cultivated, flax was woven into linen cloth and there is evidence of the domestication of animals, including cattle, sheep, goats, and pigs. Pottery, for the most part plain burnished, has been found, as well as stone implements, of which partly polished axes, adzes[153] (gouges) and winged arrowheads, were typical.[154] In ongoing excavations at Nekhen, Egypt (Hierakonpolis – Greek translation of the Egyptian name "city of the falcon god), several new Paleolithic sites have been discovered.

> Survey of the hill terrace on the western edge of the concession led to the discovery of at least 12 Middle Paleolithic sites, one of which was tested by limited excavation. The size and depth of deposit and the preservation and density of the artifacts at this site show it to be of immense importance for the study of this poorly understood period. Hierakonpolis just got older - by about 65,000 years![155]

The Fayum Neolithic site (of Ancient Egypt) has been dated by radiocarbon analysis to c. 4950 BC and although its age relative to the Badarian culture, the earliest prehistoric culture of Upper Egypt, has not been finally established, the Fayum appears to be earlier.[156]

Between 3800-3600 BC, black-topped polished bowls, referred to as Badarian ware and terra cotta figurines were produced in Egypt along with cosmetic articles and ivory combs. The terms Badarian, Amratian (Nagada I) and Gerzean (Nagada II) cultures are designations used to refer to the periods in the Ancient Egyptian Pre-Dynastic era. The Badarians made fine rippled pottery and used stone axes and arrowheads, which have been found to be similar to ones used in the Fayum area. While these cultures have, in the past, often been referred to as Pre-Dynastic cultures in Egypt, recent evidence has pointed to the understanding that these primitive cultures existed alongside the familiar high culture of Pharaonic Egypt. Perhaps this can be best understood by the example of differences in cultural development between people of the same culture who reside in a very isolated rural setting, as opposed to the city dwellers. In any case the evidences point to earlier human remains in the south of Egypt as opposed to the north.

---

[35] Revised dating based on most current correct evidence.

The Connections between the Pre-Dynastic and Dynastic culture of Ancient Egypt.

In Pre-Dynastic times (before 5,500 B.C.E.), Egyptian doctrine held that there is a realm of light (beyond our physical universe) where food, clothing and our bodies are of light, and further, that we will exist forever as beings of light along with other beings of light. This teaching is mystically related to the concept of the Pyramid texts related to "Akhus" – stars in the sky, that a human being becomes upon attaining divine status through living a life of virtue and attaining the status of divinity by reconstituting within oneself ones original cosmic forces..[36]

From the remotest times of Egypt, the Symbol of the Hawk was used to represent all-encompassing divinity (the Supreme Being, creator of all things): omnipotence, omnipresence, omniscience. The Hawk is also the symbol of the human soul. The implication is that the Supreme Being and the Human Soul are identical. Below Heru (the Hawk) is shown holding the Shen, the symbol of eternity, and the Ankh, the symbol of life. The Hawk is the symbol of Heru (Horus), the God of light, vision and speed. When looking at the Hawk symbol, we should be immediately drawn to those qualities (vision, tenacity and speed, freedom, Horus, etc.). When the hawk is enclosed within the "Het," Kamitan word for "house," it means that he is sheltered by his consort, Het-Heru. Together these two divinities compose the dynamic manifestation of the spirit in time and space, through the medium of male-female, i.e. the opposites. The universe is the Het and the spirit which inhabits it is Heru.

In Dynastic times, the doctrine of the realm of light and of a single God (Supreme Being) of whom creation is composed survived in the earliest religious texts. In chapter 64 of the *Egyptian Book of Coming Forth By Day,* the Supreme Being is referred to as *"The One Who Sees by His Own Light."* The main observable difference between the realm of light philosophy and the Pre-Dynastic and post-Dynastic philosophy of Egypt is that there were fewer deities in the Pre-Dynastic time, in the sense that the main divinity, Heru, and his counterpart, Hetheru, formed the essence of the spiritual teaching. The other divinities (beyond the central-high divinities) arise out of the central ones in the Late Pre-Dynastic and later Dynastic Periods.

Ra and Ra Herakti (Ra-Horus) are two of the symbolic forms that emerged to represent to *"Nameless One,"* the Supreme Being in later Egyptian times (Dynastic Period). In the hieroglyph to the left, below, Ra-Herakti (Ra-Horus) is shown holding the Ankh (symbol of life). The association with the sundisk gave a concrete, visual image for the purpose of public worship.

"NETER"; "Neters (Gods)"; "Ra"; "Ankh."

Before the beginning of the Dynastic Period (c 5,000 B.C.E.), the followers of Egyptian philosophy began to represent the divine forces of the Supreme Being, which operate through nature in zoomorphic forms. From the beginning of the first Dynasty until the end of Egyptian civilization (c. 600 A.C.E.), the followers of

---

[36] See also the section entitled **"The Consistent Pattern of Structure in African Religion" in Chapter 2.**

Egyptian religion that had worshipped the zoomorphic deities developed and incorporated new myths using anthropomorphic (human) forms.

One of the most popular Kamitan doctrines was that of Asar, Aset and Heru (Osiris, Isis and Horus, respectively). These Gods and Goddesses were mentioned in Pre-Dynastic times, however, the additional myths which were added to them such as the Asarian (Osirian) Resurrection myth resulted in increased popularity and gave the local priests the opportunity to add to the teachings handed down previously, and to cope with the new political and social changes throughout Egypt.

In some respects, however, the changes represented a downfall from the original teaching. For example the "realm of light" mentioned above came to be known by some as the "Land of Asar" (The West, i.e. the Netherworld) where after death, souls would go to work in the fields for Asar for all eternity. This "distasteful" prospect of working for all eternity caused some to fashion dolls (Ushabti) whose spirits would do the work for them. Some of these new doctrines and erroneous practices no doubt created new opportunities for unscrupulous priests and others with some degree of spiritual knowledge.

However, the mystical implications of the principals of the Asarian Resurrection myth and the mythology surrounding the various Gods of the Egyptian pantheon are still in accord with the Pre-Dynastic teachings. This is especially true when the teachings of the major theologies of Ancient Egypt are examined closely. For example, the Anunian Theology, Theban Theology, Memphite Theology, Zau[157] Theology (Goddess Net), Hetheru Theology, and of course Atonism and the Horemakhet (Ra-Harakti) teachings are directly related to each other, and to the solar principal, the source of all light. The realm of light theology is sometimes referred to by Western Egyptologists as the "Sky Religion."

The divinity of the realm of light was nameless and formless. Thus, a nameless "Supreme Being," *"Neter Neteru," "GOD of Gods,"* was referred to as *"The Hidden One"* until later times when myths were constructed for the understanding of the common people. *"PA NETER"*, or "THE GOD" was thought of as a FATHER-MOTHER CREATOR GOD and must not be confused with the *"Neters"* or "Gods and Goddesses," which represented the cosmic forces of the Universe. From an advanced point of view however, GOD is neither male nor female, but GOD is the source from which the Gods (gods and goddesses, Neters), humans and all creation comes. Therefore, the concept of *"NETER,"* encompasses a concept that goes beyond ordinary human - mental understanding. For the "common folk" (the uninitiated), *"NETER"* was referred to as *Nebertcher (Neberdjer)*, or *Amon - Ra - Ptah* (Holy Trinity), and was represented by a Sundisk or a single flag.

Plate 9: Left-Pre-Dynastic image of the Nile Goddess. Right- Dynastic Period image of goddess Aset.

The Pre-Dynastic symbol of the female - mother - Goddess (above left) is also represented in other parts of Africa and in the Dynastic Period of Egypt in the same pose. The wings are symbolic of the Egyptian Sky God Heru. The Goddesses Aset and Maat of Egypt are also represented with wings.

Figure 28: Below left - Image of the boat of Ptah-Sokar-Asar (Dynastic Periods)

Plate 10: Below right- Pre-Dynastic Pottery from Ancient Egypt

The two images above show the contiguity of the religious iconography used to depict the divine vehicle of the god "Ptah-Sokar-Asar." The image of the boat and the ritual related to its movement from one temple to another at festival times is one of the oldest and most popular rituals in Ancient Egyptian religion, so much so that it was incorporated into the religious life of the modern day Egyptians, who are Arabs, primarily practicing the religion of Islam[37]. The image includes two striking and characteristic forms, the bow shaped boat and the Ibex.

---

[37] This point will be elaborated on in more detail later in this text.

History of Dynastic Ancient Egypt

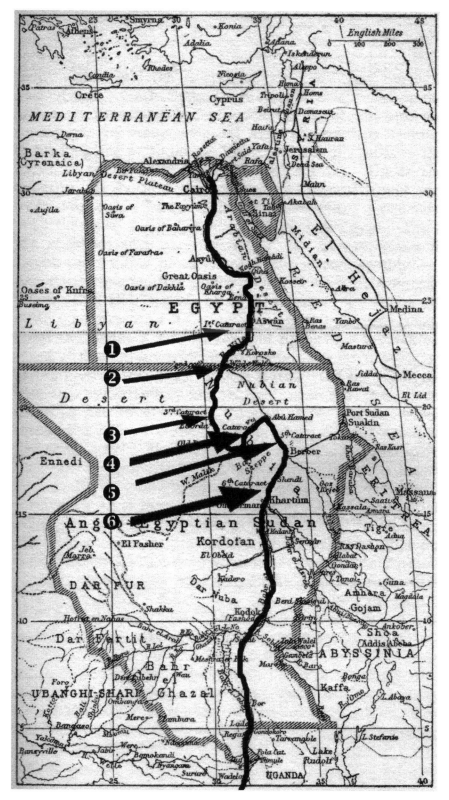

Figure 29 Above: **Map of Ancient Egypt (A) and Kush (B) showing the locations of the cataracts along the Nile River (numbers 1-6) from southern Egypt into northern Nubia (present day Sudan).**

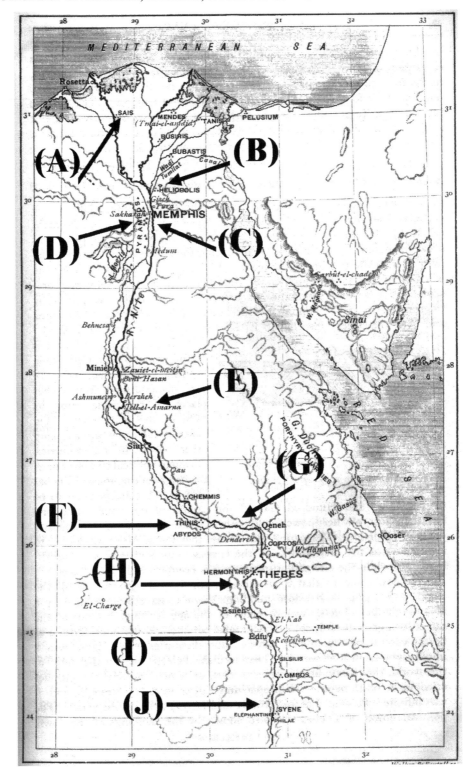

Figure 30: Above- The Land of Ancient Egypt-Nile Valley - The cities wherein the theology of the Trinity of Amun-Ra-Ptah was developed were: A- Sais (temple of Net), B- Anu (Heliopolis- temple of Ra), C-Men-nefer or Hetkaptah (Memphis, temple of Ptah), and D- Sakkara (Pyramid Texts), E- Akhet-Aton (City of Akhnaton, temple of Aton), F- Abdu (temple of Asar), G- Denderah (temple of Hetheru), H- Waset (Thebes, temple of Amun), I- Edfu (temple of Heru), J- Philae (temple of Aset). The cities wherein the theology of the Trinity of Asar-Aset-Heru was developed were Anu, Abydos, Philae, Edfu, Denderah and Edfu.

Old Kingdom Period 5,500-3,800 B.C.E.[38]

Prior to the Dynastic era, with which most people are familiar, Egypt had a long history of "nomes" (towns, governorship), ruled by kings and queens, referred to as "nomarchs" by Egyptologists and others. The Dynastic era history of Egypt begins with the unification of the two kingdoms of Upper and Lower Egypt. Actually, the unification was of several kingdoms into one Empire (one ruler over many kingdoms). This unification was achieved by king Mena (Menes) and the Shemsu Hor ("followers of Heru"). Religion began to take on the form that later became established. Evidence has been found of shrines to Heru and Hetheru, who protected the Pharaoh, and to the deities Net (Neith), Djehuti (Thoth), and Anpu (Anubis).[158] Recall that Heru is the falcon sky god, related to Ra, the Solar Divinity, whose worship is evident at the inception of the first Dynasty, but also in the Pre-Dynastic age. Mena unified the southern portion of Egypt from the base or capital at Abdu (Abydos), the ancient center of the worship of Asar (Osiris), and then the northern portion. Mena built a new capital at Men-nefer or Het-Ka-Ptah (Memphis), in the north, thereby consolidating and expanding the Ancient Egyptian religion and the foreign influence of Egyptian culture on the Asia Minor and India. With this unification, it meant that the nomes came under one ruler, the Per Aah (Pharaoh). So, in a sense Per Aah may be equated to the modern term "Emperor," however the Ancient Egyptian rulers had certain religious functions and social responsibilities that set them apart from emperors such as Alexander the Great, the Roman Emperors, the Persian Emperors, the Mesopotamian Emperors, etc.

The period of unification brought forth the first extensive books and spiritual writings in history, including the Pyramid Texts. The end of this period also elicited the greatest socio-philosophical writings from the Ancient Egyptians. These were the first "Wisdom Texts." The most famous of these was the Instructions of Ptahotep. These writings developed standards of righteous conduct much like the Confuciunist writings, and also taught about the glory of cosmic order, Maat, thereby infusing a spiritual consciousness into the social and political areas of society as they admonished rulers to rule with righteousness and by upholding truth in order to not suffer after death and to discover the Divine.

Government and Society in Ancient Egypt

The "Per-aah" or "Great House" is the institution of the seat of leadership in Ancient Egyptian civilization. The word Pharaoh is a corruption of the Ancient Egyptian word Per-Aah, and it is also erroneously translated as "king." It is more related to the status or position of being a caretaker, guardian and protector. The Per-Aah was also the High Priesthood of the country, the head of the religion and promoter and protector of the spiritual traditions, economy, safety and general welfare of the country. The Per-Aah was seen as an incarnation of Heru, the divinity of order, truth, righteousness, and redemption. Also, the Per-Aah could be a man or woman. As such the first duty of the Per-Aah was to maintain order and keep chaos (disorder, unrighteousness, famine, injustice, etc.) under control. The Per-Aah was assisted by high Priests and Priestesses (Kheri-Heb), and the day to day administration of the country was delegated to officials and educated nobility. In later times, the control of the priesthood was eroded, and the nobility as well as military leaders ruled with more autonomous control. This, along with invasions and internal corruption, weakened the Egyptian structure and led to Egypt being conquered in the Late Period by a sequence of various foreign groups (Persians, Assyrians, Libyans, Greeks, Romans and Arabs).

First intermediate Period 3,800-3,500 B.C.E.[39]

After the death of Pepi II, it is believed that Egypt was engulfed in a period of civil war and foreign infiltration, and the country began to degenerate. In Upper Egypt, the nomarchs (ruler of the individual nomes) were busy organizing their own minor kingdoms. The aristocracy was being dispossessed, cultivation of the land ceased, and famine became widespread. This period of disintegration lasted about 300 years. The kingdom was reunited when the kingdom of Thebes entered into a series of struggles due to internal instability and external pressure from attacking forces that ended with Egypt being reunited under Theban rule. The internal instability arose because Kamit reached a level of development in which the old ways and traditions which maintained order and stability were forgotten. The culture declined because of corruption and Maat

---

[38] Revised dating based on correct evidence.
[39] Revised dating based on correct evidence.

(righteousness) was not upheld. This situation is related in the didactic literature of the period which includes the writings known as the *Instructions of Merikara*. In that text and others of the period, a renewal of culture is promoted by a return to and an upholding of Maat. The next period of unification and reintegration of civilization is referred to as the *Middle Kingdom.*

The lack of strong government during this period led to an increase in tomb robbery. It is believed that the custom of burying small mummified figures with the corpse, which developed into the shabti figures and teaching of the Middle and New Kingdoms, began during this time. The shabti or ushabti is a miniature reproduction of the mummy which is supposed to serve in place of the mummified personality and endure hardships for that personality in the afterlife.

The important scripture known as the "Instruction of Merikara" emerges from this period. It details the instructions given by a king to his successor, and among the various wisdom teachings provided, it cautions against a lack of vigilance as concerns the Asiatic peoples. It gives particulars as to the psychology of the Asiatics that leads them to attack Egypt, and what must be done to uphold Egyptian culture and restore order to the land. This text shows that although Egypt was under pressure from the Asiatics, this intermediate period was not marked by total chaos.

Middle Kingdom Period 3,500-1,730 B.C.E.[40]

Plate 11: Left Per-aah (Pharaoh) Muntuhotep II (Muntuhotep)[159] – 11th Dynasty

Pharaoh Muntuhotep II completed the reunion of Egypt during the 11th Dynasty. The culture was revived, and the Pharaoh built a great temple consisting of two colonnaded terraces at Deir el-Bahri, opposite Waset (Luxor) . Pharaoh Hatshepsut had a copy of this temple made alongside it several hundred years later, at an even greater scale.

The Middle Kingdom saw a return to peace and order. Egypt's borders were again expanded to include Asia Minor, central and eastern Asia and northern Nubia. Under Senusert I (Sesostris), Ancient Egyptian culture extended over a vast region. There was trade and expedition to other countries in the Mediterranean, as well as along the East Coast of Africa. Security measures including fortresses were constructed to repel future attacks.

The literature of the period consists of instructions (Wisdom Texts), prophecies and tales, such as the advice of the aged Amenemhat I to his son, as well as wisdom texts. The tales of the Shipwrecked Sailor, Sinuhe, and the Eloquent Peasant all derive from this time.[160]

---

[40] Revised dating based on correct evidence.

Delta region

The Asiatics come into Kamit (Africa) through the Sinai Peninsula Asia Minor

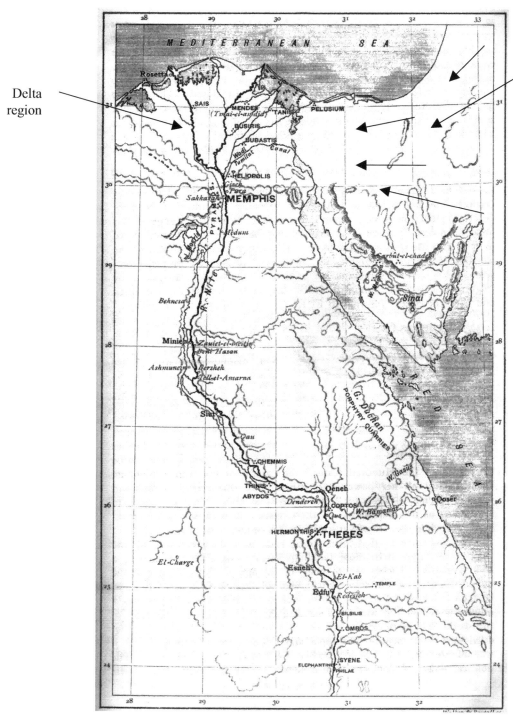

Second Intermediate Period 1,730-1,580 B.C.E.[41]

The era between the Middle Kingdom and the New Kingdom, starting with the 15th Dynasty was a degenerated age. The Hyksos were foreigners who achieved control of most of Egypt. They came into Egypt from Asia, subsequent to the emergence of the Aryans in the Near East. By the year 1730 B.C.E. they had established their capital at Avaris. In this manner they established themselves first as rulers in the Delta region, the northern part of the country. From here they easily extended their control over the chaotic and disunited parts of Egypt.

---

[41] Revised dating based on correct evidence.

The Hyksos rule was soon to end however. The 17th Dynasty was established at Waset (Thebes) at about the year 1650 B.C.E., and the Egyptians were able to gradually confine the Hyksos to north Egypt and south Palestine through a series of battles in which horse-drawn chariots were used.

New Kingdom Period 1,580 B.C.E[42]

By means of two inscriptions from the 18th Dynasty, it has been reliably established that the date for the commencement of the 18th Dynasty is 1580 B.C.E. The Pharaoh Ahmose eventually drove the Hyksos out of Egypt and pursued them into Palestine. He was the founder of the 18th Dynasty, with its capital at Thebes. Ahmose reoccupied Nubia, as far as the second cataract. His successor, Amunhotep I, extended Egyptian influence in Nubia and Syria. Thothmes I (1525–c. 1512 B.C.E.) extended the Egyptian borders even further, into Nubia, to far as Kurgus which is near the fifth cataract[43] (see map above). In Asia Minor he penetrated beyond the Euphrates river and contained a revolt in Naharein. Thothmes II, the son of Thothmes I, reigned briefly. His widow, Hatshepsut (1503–1482), became one of the most important rulers of the period.

Egypt Is The Supreme Power in Asia

Queen and Pharaoh Hatshepsut did not favor military undertakings. She instead emphasized peaceful projects such as an expedition to Punt, the construction Obelisks, and her funerary temple at Deir el-Bahri. She opened up new trade routs and bolstered the economy of Egypt.

After Hatshepsut's death, Thothmes III faced a serious threat from Asian powers, which had formed a coalition under the king of Kush. Thothmes III defeated them at Megiddo, and then mounted campaigns in Naharein and Syria. After the capture of Kush, Egypt was supreme in Asia, and there was also regular friendly contact with Crete (pre-classical Greece). During the reign of Thothmes IV, Egypt grew closer to the Mitanni (inhabitants of northern Mesopotamia-Persians) by forming an alliance with them against the Hittites. He cemented this alliance by marriage to a Mitanni princess. His successor, a weak ruler, Amunhotep III, neglected the empire in favor of lion hunts and other entertainments, even issuing large scarabs to commemorate his killing over 100 lions.[161]

The Akhnaton Period

The Hittites began expanding in Asia Minor, and won over several Asiatic princes in the reign of Amunhotep IV, later known as Akhnaton. Amunhotep IV ruled for approximately eighteen years. During his reign, he developed an overwhelming interest in religious matters, including the discipline of nonviolence, so much so that he became unwilling to issue military orders that he felt would result in the death of anyone. Thus, the Pharaoh failed to support those princes who remained loyal, and shortly thereafter Egyptian influence, even in Palestine and Syria, was diminished.

In the sixth year of his reign, Amunhotep IV proclaimed that the gods and goddesses of Egypt, including Amen-Ra, king of the gods, was at a culmination in Aton. The concept of Aton as a divinity existed as early as the concept of the other gods and goddesses (Neteru). He was born into the position as ruler under the name Amunhotep IV (peace in Amun), but he found greater fulfillment through the practices and disciplines of Aton worship, the tradition to which his mother, Queen Ti and her priest, Ai, already belonged. He changed his name to Akh-n-aton (Akhnaton, Akhenaton), which may be translated as "Spirit in the Sundisk." He simply wanted to affirm the ideal of Aton, which means face or mask of God. As Ancient Egyptian tradition always held, he affirmed that only one divinity existed, Aton, in the same manner as all the religious centers affirmed their main divinity (Amun in Thebes, Ra in Anu and Ptah in Memphis for example). In effect, Akhnaton wanted to return to a purer form of the religion, which actually leads back to Anunian theology, and the Horemakhet (Sphinx).[162]

---

[42] Revised dating based on correct evidence.
[43] Cataract: a section in a river where there are rapids, waterfalls.

Akhet-Aton: A New Capital City in The Center of the Country

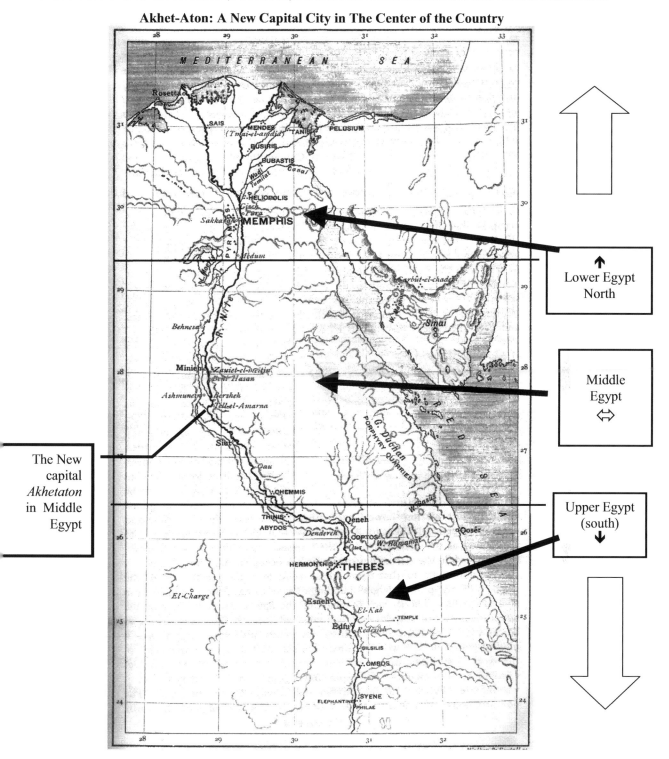

Akhnaton's move signaled a loss of power for Amun and his philosophy of the Aton was resisted, because at this time Egypt was a world Superpower and the priesthood under which this ascendancy occurred, the priests of Amun at Thebes, had become accustomed to the power and ritual of the current spiritual culture (centered around Amun), and resisted the change to Aton worship. Also, it must be noted that what Akhnaton was pushing for was a complete and utter turning away from the other symbols for the divine in favor of the Aton in the centers of Aton worship. This was perhaps an innovation not seen before in Kamitan spirituality. In previous cases where divinities rose to prominence, they did so by joining the ranks of the existing divinities, rather than by displacing them. However, Akhnaton saw that the way the other divinities were being worshipped was leading to an intensification of ritual practices as opposed to spiritual evolution. Therefore, he set out to reform Ancient Egyptian religion in the most effective manner possible. To complete the break, he founded a new capital at Akhnaton (translation "horizon of Aton" –Arab name-"Tell el-Amarna"), at a location that was exactly in the center between Upper Egypt and Lower Egypt. This signaled that he wanted to establish a tradition that was detached from the currently practicing sects. Animosity developed between Akhnaton and the Amun priesthood. Using his authority, Akhnaton had the property of Amun transferred to Aton. Akhnaton lived in a form of isolation with his court and family in the city he had created, and left control of the kingdom and preservation of the, at this time shrinking empire, to others. After his death, Tell el-Amarna was abandoned and the old religion restored by the priests of Amun.[163] Following the reign of Akhnaton came the reign of Tutankhamun. His period was short and the main interest he has drawn stems from the discovery of his tomb which was intact, and which gave much insight into the iconography and philosophy of the Ancient Egyptian religion. His name signaled the return of the dominance of religion of Amun (Tut-ankh-amun which means living image of Amun). Akhnaton was abandoned and its monuments were dismantled for constructions elsewhere.

The Akhnaton period proved to be very instructive of the extent to which the power of Waset (Thebes) and its preference for Amun (Supreme Being) and the traditional rituals of many gods and goddesses had been engrained. What Akhnaton did was not unique in Ancient Egyptian history. The elevation of Ra, Asar, Ptah and Net had all occurred in a similar way. They were all known since ancient times but were elevated by a group of Priests and Priestesses of a particular city. What Akhnaton did differently was that he tried to zealously force all the population to understand that all the gods and goddesses were "complete" in Aton, which was true in a mystical sense, but the tradition was to have a nome (city) dedicated to the newly elevated divinity and thereafter it would exist alongside the previous ones. This pragmatism that was lacking in Akhnaton's approach to elevating the Aton was not repeated in the later reign of Sage-king Seti I who elevated the god Set, while at the same time upholding the already elevated gods and goddesses by refurbishing and adding to their temples along with that of Set. So the conflict between Akhnaton and the Priests and Priestesses of Amun was not a theological one involving the rejection of a new divinity or the concept of Monotheism, but rather a rejection of what they perceived as the abandonment of thousands of years of the African religious tradition of worshipping a Supreme Being with its attendant lesser divinities, i.e. the gods and goddesses.[44]

The Ramesside Period

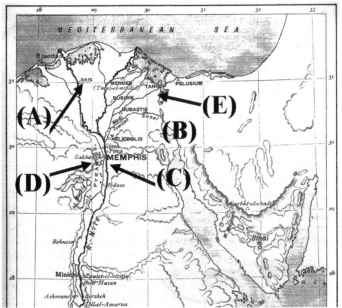

Above: Map of Lower Egypt with Djanet (Tanis) (E)

The 19th Dynasty (1290-1224 B.C.E.) was founded by Rameses I. His family came from the noble houses from the city of Tanis, which had been the seat of power of the foreign Hyksos rulers. In ancient times the worship of the god Set was popular. When the Hyksos established their capital at Tanis, they adopted Set as

---

[44] See the section entitled ***The Consistent Pattern of Structure in African Religion*** in Chapter 2

their tutelary symbol, and thus, the god Set became associated with invaders. During that time Set became associated with foreigners, evil, destruction and vice. Rameses' son was named Seti I (man of Set). Rameses II, who later become known as "the Great" continued on with Seti's struggle against the Hittites. This war was documented on the temple of Rameses, however other scenes proclaiming him victorious against other foes are symbolic of the king's duty to uphold righteousness (Maat) against *isfet* or n-Maat (unrighteousness), not just in war but by upholding the economy, courts, etc. In these duties Rameses proved to be most successful and his reign saw a great flowering of Kamitan culture, especially in the construction of temples. He augmented the Karnak Temple in Waset, finished his father's temple in Abdu, and built no less than three colossal temples for himself, and one for his wife, Queen Nefertari.

Rameses' 13th son, Merneptah, who by the time of Rameses' long reign was already old, succeeded him. Merneptah contended with a Palestinian revolt. The accounts of this conflict provide the first mention of Israel as one of the defeated peoples of Asia Minor under Egyptian rule. Merneptah also successfully dealt with invasions from the west of Egypt (modern day Libya). Merneptah's rule was followed by thirty years of confusion in which several Pharaohs reigned, most with uncertain claims to the throne.

The diminishing leadership of the government, as well as the increasing separation between the political leaders and the clergy and the minimization of the clergy, led to weakness in the social order of the country. In the 20th Dynasty, Rameses III was the last great Pharaoh of the New Kingdom. He reorganized the country's administration and the army, and began collecting tribute from Asia and Nubia again. His greatest victory was over the "peoples of the sea," Indo-Europeans, who, after sweeping over the Hittites, Cilicia, and Cyprus, were threatening Egypt. Advancing by land and sea along the coast of Palestine, Rameses III annihilated them and repulsed two Libyan attacks on the delta. The last 20 years of his reign were peaceful. There followed several unimportant Pharaohs, all named Rameses, most of whom were overshadowed by the High Priests of Amun. In the reign of Rameses XI, civil war broke out with Libyan involvement, and it was only suppressed due to the help of Nubian troops under the viceroy Pa-nehesi.[164] This event is one of several which show that the occasional animosity between the Nubians and Ancient Egyptians was not racially motivated, as some Western historians have suggested, but cultural and political. In the Late Period, the allegiance of the Nubians to the Ancient Egyptians would become more apparent.

In the city of Waset, during the 18th and 19th Dynasties, the Priests and Priestesses began to create a new version of *Prt M Hru*. These are usually referred to as the *Wasetian (Theban) recension* of the *Prt m Hru*. The *Wasetian Recension* adopted several texts from the older recension, but added many more new ones. This recension was produced on papyrus scrolls, and one of its principal features is the extensive use of vignettes.

Third Intermediate Period 1085 B.C.E.

The capital was moved to Tanis in 1085, signaling the end of the New Kingdom Dynastic Period. In the 21st Dynasty there were rival Pharaohs based at Tanis and at Thebes, but the two sets of rulers coexisted amicably, united by marriage ties, until the last high priest reunited Egypt as Pharaoh Psusennes II. When he died 945 B.C.E. the rule of Thebes came to an end—Sheshonq I (945–924), a member of a powerful family of Libyans based at Herakleopolis, took the throne founding the 22nd Dynasty. He asserted his authority in Upper Egypt, and it was probably then that some priests of Amun left Thebes for Napata, the future seat of the 25th Dynasty. Sheshonq (the Shishak of the Bible) attacked Palestine after the death of Solomon[45], and sacked Jerusalem, refilling his treasury and temporarily increasing the prestige of Egypt. Then followed 150 years of increasing anarchy, during which rival Libyan chieftains and the priests of Amun at Thebes vied for power.

---

[45] third king of Israel (c. 961-922 BC), son of David and Bathsheba.

Late Period

Nubian Restoration of African Rule by Africans in Egypt

Above left- The Nubian-Egyptian Pharaoh Shabaka
Above right- The Nubian-Egyptian Pharaoh Taharka

By the year 760 B.C.E. Egypt had been debilitated, and it is believed that the Egyptian Priests and Priestesses asked the Nubians for assistance in order to repel foreign invaders. They crowned the Nubian king Kashta as Pharaoh and his daughter Amenirdas I became the wife of Amun (High Priestess). This crowning caused would be attackers to desist in their efforts. However, later on Egypt was again threatened by the Libyans at around 730 B.C.E. From around 730 B.C.E., two rival movements to reunite Egypt emerged, one led by Tefnakht of the 24th Dynasty based at Sais, the city of goddess Net, and the other was led by Pi-ankhi (747–716 B.C.E.) of the Kushite (Cushite) kingdom based at Napata in Nubia. The Kushites gradually gained the control and transferred their capital from Napata to Thebes. Pi-ankhi defeated the Libyans and took control of the entire territory. Under the successor of Pi-ankhi, King Shabaka, (716-702 B.C.E.), there was a great resurgence in Egyptian art and philosophy. He was the patron of the restoration of the city of Memphis which was the seat of the worship of the god Ptah. So with this the Nubians made Egypt part of their empire which now stretched from Libya, down the Nile into Nubia.

A Return to the Old Ways

This was a unique period in Ancient Egyptian history, the Nubian rulers supported the renaissance of culture. Directed by the Temple System (Priests and Priestesses) the government was empowered to move society towards a positive and prosperous condition as it had been in the past. For this purpose the Priests and Priestesses supervised a return to the arts of the Old Kingdom Period which included the style of writing the hieroglyphic texts, Old Kingdom artistic forms in architecture and painting as well as Old Kingdom forms in government and social order. This is the period when texts of the Old Kingdom were rediscovered, transcribed anew and the old forms of worship were practiced. An example of such a text was the "Shabaka Inscription" detailing the teachings of Memphite Theology. The leaders of society saw the solution to the decline of Egyptian culture in returning to the older forms of social organization and regulation and turning away from the practices that were perceived as contradictory to the values of the older, stable and prosperous society. This renaissance was accepted and even welcomed by the people and supported by the Temple, and this shows the harmony that existed between the Nubians and the Egyptians since they already shared the same religion and cultural values. The renaissance progressed until the Assyrians successfully attacked the country and forced the Nubian leaders to leave the country. Foreigners then ruled Egypt. The Assyrians placed Psamtik I in power as a vassal Pharaoh until the power of the Assyrians waned. Psamtik I consolidated his power and then Egypt succeeded in throwing off the Assyrian rulers and he continued the renaissance that the Nubians had begun until new foreign attackers again captured Egypt.

Then the Kushite kings came under increasing pressure from the expanding Assyrian empire. The Assyrian king Sennacherib invaded Judah[165] at the end of the 8th century B.C.E., but was forced to retire 701 B.C.E. by plague. After continual encroachments over the next thirty years the Assyrian king Ashurbanipal occupied Thebes in 666 B.C.E.

Egyptians Regain Control of Egypt

Assyrian domination ended three years later when they were driven out of Thebes by Psamtik I (Psammetichus I) who had consolidated his power to throw off the Assyrian domination and reunited Egypt under the 26th (Saite - Greek) Dynasty. Initially, the Saite Dynasty faced challenges from the remnants of the Kushites who had been driven out by Assyria, but an expedition sent by Psamtik II c. 590 B.C.E. took Napata and defeated the Kushites. There was an attempt at expansion under Necho (610–595 B.C.E.) who destroyed Josiah of Judah[166] and invaded Syria, but he was defeated at Carchemish by the Babylonians in 605 B.C.E. and driven back to Egypt. After that Egypt enjoyed a brief period of independence before the Persian invasion 525 B.C.E.

Persian Conquest Period

Persia, already supreme in Asia, began to look toward Egypt as a valuable addition to their empire and Cambyses made Egypt a Persian province in 525 B.C.E. Darius I (called "the Great" (c.558-486 BC), Achamenid king of Persia.) restored order in the Persian empire by dividing it into provinces which allowed some degree of autonomy and tolerating religious diversity. He tried to codify Egyptian laws, built a temple at Kharga, and developed Egyptian trade, reopening the canal between the Mediterranean and the Red Sea first opened by Necho.

Egyptians Regain Control of Egypt

Greek successes in the Persian Wars encouraged the Egyptians to revolt. After several unsuccessful risings, a revolt under Inaros the Libyan and Amyrtaeus of Sais[46] with Athenian backing from 460 B.C.E. succeeded in driving the Persians into Memphis, but after an 18-month siege the rebels were defeated. The Athenians then became embroiled in half a century of struggles with Sparta and were not able to help Egypt against the Persians. Eventually Amyrtaeus succeeded in freeing Egypt from the Persians 405 B.C.E., becoming sole Pharaoh of the 28th Dynasty, 404–399 B.C.E.[167]

Second Persian Conquest Period

The Second Persian Conquest Period (343-332 B.C.E.) when the Persians marshaled their forces for another attack on Egypt, which was too weakened to repel the attacks. Though successful, the Persian conquest of Egypt was brief because the Persians fell before Alexander's Greek armies.

Greek Conquest Period - Very Late Period - Saite Dynasty (332 B.C.E.- 30 B.C.E.)

The 8th century B.C.E. saw the commencement of what would later become Greek Classical civilization. The earliest Greek philosophers, such as Thales (c. 634-546 B.C.E.), were known to have gone to Egypt for instruction. There is also evidence that Ancient Egypt took on the responsibility of helping the Greeks to construct temples in Greece itself, providing both instruction as well as assistance. This explains, in part, the assistance given by the Greeks to Egypt in her time of need. During this period the Greeks saw that the Persians were a threat to them as well. However, the Greeks were known, even in ancient times, to be confrontational and argumentative people. This led to innumerable conflicts with the Spartans and others, which distracted them from the higher goals of civilized living.

In 332 B.C.E. the general, Alexander, conquered all of Greece, Asia Minor, India and Northeast Africa (including Egypt). From that time on Egypt would not have an African king or queen again. This is known as the Ptolemaic or Greek Period (also known as the Hellenistic Period). It lasted from 332 B.C.E.- c. 30 B.C.E. This is the period wherein after Alexander's death, one of his generals by the name of Ptolemy took control of

---

[46] In ancient times Sais was considered as the sister city of the Greek Athens. In fact, the Greeks considered that the Greek goddess Athena was actually the Egyptian goddess Net, also known to the Greeks as Neith. So there was a close association between the two countries in the formative period of Greek culture (1000 B.C.E-500 B.C.E.)

Egypt. Ptolemy's family and army settled in Egypt and mixed with the local population, especially in the north. This family of rulers gave rise to the famous Cleopatra. She was the last Ptolemaic ruler until the Romans took control of Egypt under the rule of Caesar.

*For more details on Ancient Egypt and the origins of civilization in Ancient Greece see See African Origins Book II-Chapter 3 (See African Origins Book 2).

Early Christian, Roman Christian Conquest Periods and the Closing of Egyptian Temples

See African Origins Book II-Chapter 4 (See African Origins Book 2)

The Coptic Church Period (See African Origins Book 2)

The Coptic Church is the major Christian church in modern day Egypt. The name, Copt, was derived from the Greek word for "Egyptian" and the Arabic "qubt" which was westernized as "Copt." The origins of Egyptian Christianity can be found in the Gnostic mystery schools, which developed the Hermetic teachings (teachings of the Egyptian God Djehuti), in the period immediately preceding the Christian era. These schools were engendered by the early Greek philosophers who studied Egyptian philosophy and Alexander the Great who conquered Egypt and sought to establish a city of Enlightenment which would bridge the East and the West and spread the wisdom of Egypt to the world. Alexander knew, from his early instruction by Aristotle, that Egypt was the source of the most ancient knowledge and the repository of the world's greatest scholars and mystical philosophers. Thus, the Greeks under Alexander sought to appropriate and adopt the Ancient Egyptian traditions which they had been learning for the previous five centuries since the time of Thales, the first recognized Greek Philosopher (circa 700 B.C.E.), in order to carry on the mystical tradition of Egypt. These Gnostic Hellenists intermixed with the Jews living in Alexandria in northwest Lower Egypt. Four centuries after Alexander's conquest of Egypt, notable Christian philosophers would emerge out of Alexandria who would exert a strong influence on early Christianity and later cause the separation of the Egyptian Christians (Copts) from the Roman and Byzantine Christians. Some of the important Christian theologians who emerged from Alexandria included Clement of Alexandria, Origen and Arius.

The debates in the church over the true understanding of Christ (Christology) led to a separation between the Church in Egypt (Coptic Church) and the churches of Rome and Constantinople (which became the Western Empire and Eastern Empire). The majority of Egyptian Christians refused to go along with the decrees of the Council of Chalcedon in 451 A.C.E., that defined the person of Jesus the Christ as being "one in two natures." This doctrine of "two natures" seemed to imply the existence of two Christs, one being divine and the other human. These Egyptian Christians who refused the Council of Chalcedon faced charges of monophysitism. Monophysitism is the belief that Christ has only one nature rather than two. It is notable that the Council of Chalcedon was accepted both in Constantinople and in Rome, but not in Egypt. Thus, we see that the dualistic view of Christ was developed and promoted in Europe under the Roman church and in the Middle East under the church of Constantinople. It was Egypt, which sought to uphold the non-dualistic view of Christ, which viewed him as an all-encompassing Divine being. This was due to the tradition of non-dualism, which it assimilated from the Ancient Egyptian mystery schools. The Coptic Church of Egypt separated from Rome and Constantinople and set up its own Pope who is nominated by an Electoral College of clergy and laity. The Coptic Church has survived up to the present in Egypt. There are over seven million Coptic Christians there today and 22 million in total.

The sacred music of Ancient Egypt lives on in the Christian Coptic tradition of the Coptic Church mass. Anthropologists believe that the primary characteristics of modern Coptic music were adopted from the music of the Ancient Egyptians. These characteristics include the use of triangles and cymbals, and a strong vocal tradition. The Copts are regarded as the genetically purest direct descendents of the Ancient Egyptians due to their lack of intermarrying with the other Egyptians who are of Arab descent. The whole of the Coptic service is to be sung. The singing is alternated between the master chanter, the priest, and a choir of deacons. A technique of chanting and singing was also used in Ancient Egypt during the processions and recitals of the mystery rituals.

For more details on the Coptic Period See African Origins Book II- Chapter 4 (See African Origins Book 2)

Arab and Muslim Conquest Period

See Chapter 4 (See African Origins Book 2)

The Revised Chronology of Ancient Egypt Based On New Archeological Evidence and the Omitted Records

The history which has been presented in the previous section is only the history of the "Dynastic Period." It reflects the view of traditional Egyptologists who have refused to accept the evidence of a Pre-Dynastic Period in Ancient Egyptian history contained in Ancient Egyptian documents such as the *Palermo Stone, Royal Tablets at Abydos, Royal Papyrus of Turin,* and the *Dynastic List of Manetho* and also have not become aware of the new findings concerning recent excavations as well as the new dating of the Sphinx. The eye-witness accounts of Greek historians Herodotus (c. 484-425 B.C.E.) and Diodorus (Greek historian died about 20 B.C.E.) corroborate the status and makeup of Kamitan culture in the late Dynastic Period which support the earlier accounts. These sources speak clearly of a Pre-Dynastic society which stretched far into antiquity. The Dynastic Period is what most people think of whenever Ancient Egypt is mentioned. This period is when the Pharaohs (kings and queens) ruled. The latter part of the Dynastic Period is when the Biblical story of Moses, Joseph, Abraham, etc., occurs. Therefore, those with a Christian background generally only have an idea about Ancient Egypt as it is related in the Bible. Although this biblical notion is very limited in scope and portrayed in a negative light, the significant impact of Ancient Egypt on Hebrew and Christian culture is evident even from the biblical scriptures. Actually, Egypt existed much earlier than most traditional Egyptologists are prepared to admit. The new archeological evidence related to the great Sphinx monument on the Giza Plateau and the ancient writings by Manetho, one of the last High Priests of Ancient Egypt, show that Ancient Egyptian history begins earlier than 10,000 B.C.E. and dates back to as early as 30,000-50,000 B.C.E. The actual date for the construction of the great Sphinx is 10,000 B.C.E. – 15,000 B.C.E. because the erosion damage on it would have had to occur 2,000-3,000 years prior to the climate in Egypt becoming like the present desert-like conditions. This new dating should not come as a surprise in view of other new archeological evidence. The Ancient Egyptian scripture itself claims that the Ancient Egyptians originated from the south, the land of Nubia, Ta Seti, "the land of the bow," as Nubia is also referred to. A report by the Oriental Institute in Chicago, one of the important orthodox Egyptology schools, stated that Ta Seti is known to have developed a pre-Pharaonic kingdom 300 years earlier than the first Egyptian Dynasty. Thus, these and other finds show a continuous flow of culture arising from the southern portion of Africa at its heart, extending to Ethiopia and into Ancient Egypt. Therefore, the advanced Sothic calendar which has been identified as being in use at 4241 B.C.E. as well as the histories given by the Ancient Egyptian texts themselves, speaking of a history going back beyond 30,000 years are now being corroborated. Newly refined radio carbon tests on organic material found in recent years in the Great Pyramid have shown that it "was built at least 374 years earlier" than previously thought.[168] The oldest radiocarbon dating of the organic material in the Great Pyramid yielded a date of 3809 B.C.E. Further, there is evidence that the lower section of the Great Pyramid is older than the upper parts.

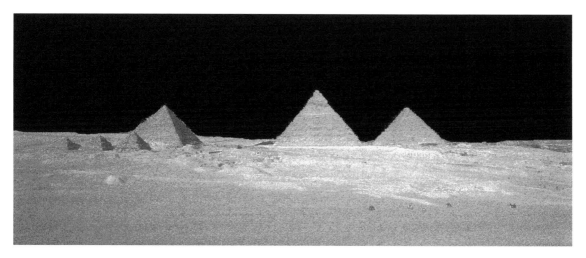

Plate 12: The Giza Pyramid Complex-Great Pyramid, far right.

While the date when the stone to create the Great Pyramid was originally cut apparently cannot as yet be dated with available instruments, tests performed on 16 samples of organic materials discovered in the Great Pyramid in Giza, Egypt, by a prominent orthodox Egyptologist (Mark Lehner) such as charcoal, showed that the pyramid was in use as early as 3809 B.C.E. So on this evidence alone the chronologies given for age of the Great Pyramid by traditional Egyptology as belonging to the reign of Pharaoh Khephren (Cheops) of 2551 B.C.E.- 2528 B.C.E. are simply untenable and must be revised forthwith. Therefore, while momentous, the evidence of the Sphinx fits into the larger scheme of scientific evidences which are unraveling the mysteries of history and leads us to the understanding of life in ancient Northeast Africa as a high point in human cultural achievement which was attained in Ancient Egypt and spread out to the rest of the world.

Plate 13: Great Pyramid Compared to the European Cathedrals[169]

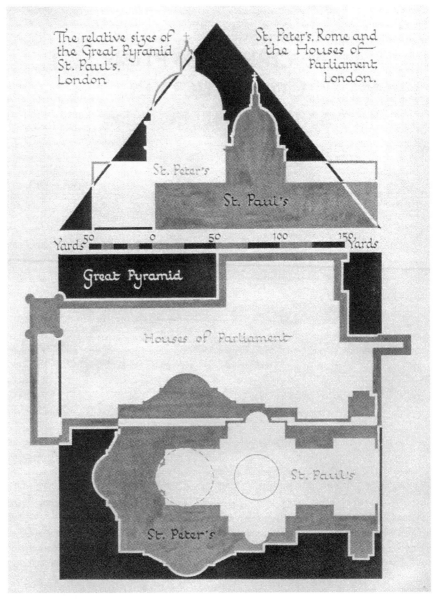

The massive size and majesty of the Great Pyramid can be discerned when compared to some of the European cathedrals, which took sometimes decades to construct. The picture above shows how these could easily fit within the volume of the pyramid with room to spear. This image also points to the organization, logistics and planning that went into the creation of the pyramids and partially explains the awe inspiring feeling that they evoke upon seeing them in person.

Also, new finds in northeastern Zaire by the Brooks and Yellen archeological team, in their dating of artifacts, arrived at refined and double-checked results confirming dates going back to 70,000 years. This means that a level of civilization had been attained in Africa 54,000 earlier than anywhere outside of Africa.[170] With this kind of evidence modern anthropology has accepted that human life began in Africa and then spread out to the rest of the world. This model has been supported by the advanced findings in the science of modern genetics, where it has been shown that all human beings have common ancestry in Africa and therefore, all humanity is of African descent. Still, the general public has received little notification except through periodic reports in journals or the occasional stories appearing in newsmagazines. Therefore, an entire reworking of the chronologies for the origins of humankind as well as the emergence of civilization must be revised. Further, the textbooks for elementary and high schools must be revised.

Many scholars have had difficulty in dating the events of Ancient Egypt. This is due to many reasons. One of these is that they have sought to date these events in terms which relate to other cultures and thereby extrapolate dates based on correlated factors which can be verified through the writings or records of other cultures. This is of course difficult because, as we will see, Ancient Egyptian history extends so far into the past that there is no other culture to compare it to except itself. Hence, the tendency has been the practice of compressing the timeline of events in Ancient Egypt so that they fit within the time frame of history that is known about other cultures. The surviving texts of Ancient Egypt have provided a chronology and timetable. The History of Manetho is only one source. However, in the last one hundred years, the traditional (orthodox) Egyptologists have rejected these records as "impossible" or "unbelievable." In the early years of Egyptology many scholars, such as Champollion, Sir Flinders Petrie and Brested gave dates of 5867 B.C.E., 5500 B.C.E. and 4241[171] respectively for the commencement of the Dynastic Period (unification of Upper and Lower Egypt under one ruler) which were more in line with the histories given by the Ancient Egyptians themselves and the revised perspective promoted by new archeological evidences. Note that the date of unification does not mean the inception of civilization or the beginning of culture, art, science, philosophy, etc., but rather the political consolidation of the country. Later Egyptologists reduced this number to 3400 B.C.E. and then 3200 B.C.E., and until recent excavations in Abydos and Hierakonpolis the consensus was c. 2900 B.C.E., which is below the date set for Mesopotamia, which was originally lower than that of the first dates set for Ancient Egypt by the early Egyptologists.

Moreover, Western renderings of the Ancient Egyptian hieroglyphic texts often promote the literal meanings of words even when there are different readings possible in accordance with the myths. The treatment is confined to the viewpoint of outsiders, looking at primitive religious superstitions. In this capacity oftentimes nonsensical translations are obtained and explained away as unintelligible or erroneous passages due to ancient scribal erratum. The inability to understand the hieroglyphic language is predicated upon the fallacy that it is a strictly literal form of language. In effect, while having performed a service to humanity by decoding the language for humanity, Western Egyptologists and linguists have *projected* their own understanding of philosophy, religion and language, and therefore cannot incorporate the mythic and mystic component of the language which constitutes its special form of *reasoning* alluded to in the following quotation. The Greek classic writer Diodorus introduces the multi-aspected nature of the hieroglyphic language.

"We must now speak of the Ethiopian writing which is called hieroglyphic by the Egyptians, in order that we may omit nothing in our discussion of their antiquities. Now it is found that the forms of their letters take the shape of animals of every kind, and of the members of the human body, and of implements and especially carpenter's tools; for their writing does not express the intent concept by means of syllables joined one to another, but by its figurative meaning which has been impressed upon the memory by practice. For instance, they draw the picture of a hawk, a crocodile, a snake, and all of the members of the human body-an eye, a hand, a face, and the like. Now the hawk signifies to them everything which happens swiftly, since this animal is practically the swiftest of winged creatures...And the crocodile is a symbol of all that is evil, and the eye is the warder of justice and the guardian of the entire body. And as for the members of the body, the right hand with fingers extended signifies a procuring of livelihood, and the left with the fingers closed, a keeping and guarding of property. The same way of reasoning applies to the remaining characters, which represent parts of the body and implements and all other things; for by paying close attention to the significance which is inherent in each object and by training their minds through drills and exercise of the memory over a long period, they read from habit everything which has been written."

-Recorded by Diodorus (Greek historian 100 B.C.)

Table 11: Chronology of Ancient Egypt according to Flinders Petrie[172]

Period.	Dynasty.	Names.	B.C.
Prehistoric.			8000–5500
Early kings.	I.	Narmer, Mena, Zer,	5500–5400
	II.	Khasekhem,	5000
	III.	Zeser, Senoferu,	4900–4700
Pyramid age : Old Kingdom.	IV.	Khufu, Khafra, Menkaura,	4700–4500
	V.	Noferarkara, Unas,	4400–4200
	VI.	Pepy II,	4100–4000
	IX.	Khety,	3800
	XI.	Antef V,	3500
Middle Kingdom.	XII.	Senusert I, Senusert II, Senusert III,	3400–3300
		Amenemhat III,	3300–3259
	XIII.	Hor,	3200
New Kingdom.	XVIII.	Aahmes, Queens Aah-hotep, Aahmes,	1587–1562
		Tahutmes I, Tahutmes II, Hatshepsut,	1541–1481
		Tahutmes III, Amenhotep II, Tahutmes IV,	1481–1414
		Amenhotep III, Akhenaten, Tutankhamen,	1414–1344
	XIX.	Sety I, Ramessu II, Merenptah,	1326–1214
		Sety II, Tausert,	1214–1203
	XX.	Ramessu III, IV, XII,	1202–1129
	XXI.	Isiemkheb,	1050
	XXII.	Shishak kings,	952–749
	XXIII.	Pedubast, Pefaabast,	755–725
Ethiopian.	XXV.	Amenardys, Taharqa, Tanutamen,	720–664
Saite.	XXVI.	Aahmes II,	570–526
	XXX.	Nekhthorheb (Nectanebo),	378–361
Ptolemies.		Cleopatra Cocce,	130–106
Romans.			30–A.D. 640

Ancient Egypt is in modern times populated by a culture which is classified as "Arab." The Arabs are members of an Asiatic[173] people inhabiting Arabia, whose language and Islamic religion spread widely throughout Asia Minor (the Middle East) and northern Africa from the seventh century. Having conquered Egypt since the 7th century A.C.E., the Arabs, who now refer to themselves as "Egyptians," have adopted the heritage, but not the legacy of Ancient Egypt. That is, the government and schools espouse the idea that Ancient Egyptian culture and civilization is part of the past history of the modern people. The modern Arabs admittedly care little about Ancient Egypt except to the extent that is a magnet for tourists and is therefore a tourism financial boon. The government trains "guides" to lead tourists around the temples and other sites of the country and they are taught to espouse the deficient chronology of Ancient Egypt and many distorted renditions of the myths. Further, one can hear in the speech of many guides a disdain and sometimes even disgust for the images presented in the iconography of the temples. Interviews[174] led to the discovery that the general view of those who are brought up in orthodox Islamic culture is that Ancient Egyptian religion was not religion at all, but rather feeble attempts at theorizing about spiritual matters. In fact, the underlying view, confirmed in many interviews of Arabs born in Egypt, is that they view "Islam as the only true" religion and religions such as Hinduism as "idolatry." Therefore, as Hinduism is essentially compatible with Neterianism (the religion of Shetaut Neter), one may expect the same treatment of the Ancient Egyptian religion. Consequently, the philosophy, art and spirituality of Ancient Egypt are perceived as nothing more than commodities to attract foreign dollars into the ailing economy and at another level, they are means by which some Arabs attain higher status in the society by becoming "Egyptologists." These "Egyptologists" constitute some of the most vehement opponents to any view which suggests an older chronology for Ancient Egypt and anything that might suggest that there is a form of spirituality as correct and or valid as Islam. Consequently, they are some of the most ardent supporters of the orthodox Egyptological views.

The Far Reaching Implications of the New Evidence Concerning the Sphinx and Other New Archeological Evidence in Egypt and the Rest of Africa

In the last 20 years traditional Egyptologists, archeologists and others have been taking note of recent studies performed on the Ancient Egyptian Sphinx which sits at Giza in Egypt. Beginning with such students of Ancient Egyptian culture and architecture as R. A. Schwaller de Lubicz in the 1950's, and most recently, John Anthony West, with his book *Serpent In the Sky*, many researchers have used modern technology to study the ancient monument and their discoveries have startled the world. They now understand that the erosion damage on the Sphinx could not have occurred after the period 10,000-7,000 B.C.E. because this was the last period in which there would have been enough rainfall in the area to cause such damage. This means that most of the damage which the Sphinx displays itself, which would have taken thousands of years to occur, would have happened prior to that time (10,000 B.C.E.).

Many scholars have downplayed or misunderstood the new geological evidences related to the Great Sphinx. One example are the authors of the book *In Search of the Cradle of Civilization,* Georg Feuerstein, David Frawley (prominent western Indologists), and Subhash Kak, in which the authors state the following: (highlighted text is by Ashby)

> In seeking to refute current archeological thinking about the Sphinx, West relies on a *single geological feature*. Understandably, most Egyptologists have been less than accepting of his redating of this monument, *hoping* that some other explanation can be found for the *strange* marks of erosion. P. 6

The characterization of the evidence as a "single geological feature" implies it stands alone as an anomaly that does not fit into the greater picture of Ancient Egyptian history and is completely without basis. In support of orthodox Egyptologists, the authors agree with them, stating that their attitude is understandable. Now, even if there were only a single form of evidence, does this mean that it is or should be considered suspect especially when considering the fact that Egyptology and archeology are not exact sciences and geology is an exact science? Further, the authors mention the wishful thinking of the orthodox Egyptologists as they search in vein (hoping) for some other way to explain the evidence. Yet, the authors seem to agree with the Egyptological view and thereby pass over this evidence as an inconsistency that need not be dealt with further.

> The following evidences must also be taken into account when examining the geology of the Sphinx and the Giza plateau.
>
> ➢ The surrounding Sphinx Temple architecture is similarly affected.
>
> ➢ Astronomical evidence agrees with the geological findings.
>
> ➢ Ancient Egyptian historical documents concur with the evidence.

It is important to understand that what we have in the Sphinx is not just a monument now dated as the earliest monument in history (based on irrefutable geological evidence). Its existence signifies the earliest practice not only of high-art and architecture, but it is also the first monumental statue in history dedicated to religion. This massive project including the Sphinx and its attendant Temple required intensive planning and engineering skill. Despite its deteriorated state, the Sphinx stands not only as the most ancient mystical symbol in this historical period, but also as the most ancient architectural monument, and a testament to the presence of Ancient African (Egyptian) culture in the earliest period of antiquity. Further, this means that while the two other emerging civilizations of antiquity (Sumer and Indus) were in their Neolithic period (characterized by the development of agriculture, pottery and the making of polished stone implements), Ancient Egypt had already achieved mastery over monumental art, architecture and religion as an adjunct to social order, as the Sphinx is a symbol of the Pharaoh (leader and upholder of Maat-order, justice and truth) as the god Heru. The iconography of the Sphinx is typical of that which is seen throughout Ancient Egyptian history and signals the achievement of the a culture of high morals which governs the entire civilization to the Persian and Greek conquest.

Plate 14: The Great Sphinx of Ancient Egypt-showing the classical Pharaonic headdress popularized in Dynastic times. Also, the water damage can be seen in the form of vertical indentations in the sides of the monument.

> The water erosion of the Sphinx is to history what the convertibility of matter into energy is to physics.

> -John Anthony West *Serpent In the Sky*

Many people have heard of the new evidence concerning the water damage on the Sphinx and how it has been shown to be much older than previously thought. However, as we saw earlier, detractors usually claim that this is only one piece of evidence that is inconclusive. This is the usual opinion of the uninformed. The findings have been confirmed by seismographic tests[175] as well as examination of the water damage on the structures related to the Sphinx and the Sphinx Temple, as compared to the rest of the structures surrounding it which display the typical decay due to wind and sand. It has been conclusively found that the Sphinx and its adjacent structures (Sphinx Temple) were built in a different era and that the surrounding structures do not display the water damage. Therefore, the wind and sand damaged structures belong to the Dynastic Era and the Sphinx belongs to the Pre-Dynastic Era. Therefore, the evidence supporting the older dating of the Sphinx is well founded and confirmed.

Plate 15: Sphinx rump and Sphinx enclosure show detail of the water damage (vertical damage).

The new evidence related to the Sphinx affects many other forms of evidence which traditional Egyptologists have also sought to dismiss. Therefore, it is a momentous discovery on the order the discernment of the Ancient Egyptian Hieroglyphic text. It requires an opening up of the closely held chronologies and timelines of ancient cultures for revision, thereby allowing the deeper study of the human experience on this earth and making the discovery of our collective past glory possible. Thus, it is clear to see that the problem in assigning dates to events in Ancient Egypt arises when there is an unwillingness to let go of closely held notions based on biased information that is accepted as truth and passed on from one generation of orthodox Egyptologists to the next generation, rather than on authentic scholarship (constant search for truth). This deficiency led to the exclusion of the ancient historical writings of Ancient Egypt (*Palermo Stone, Royal Tablets at Abydos, Royal Papyrus of Turin,* the *Dynastic List* of Manetho). However, now, with the irrefutable evidence of the antiquity of the Sphinx, and the excavations at Abydos and Hierakonpolis, the mounting archeological evidence and the loosening grip of Western scholars on the field of Egyptology, it is no longer possible to ignore the far reaching implications of the Ancient Egyptian historical documents.

The History of Manetho

The evidence concerning the new dating of the Sphinx affects the treatment of the History of Manetho. Manetho was one of the last Ancient Egyptian High Priests who retained the knowledge of the ancient history of Egypt. In 241 B.C.E. he was commissioned to compile a series of wisdom texts by King Ptolemy II, one of the Macedonian (Greek) rulers of Egypt after it was captured and controlled by the Greeks. One of Manetho's compositions included a history of Egypt. However, Manetho's original writings did not survive into the present. Therefore, the accounts of his writings by the Greeks who studied his work constitute the current remaining record of his work, and some of the accounts differ from each other in certain respects. His history has come down to us in the form of translation, part of which are missing certain portions. However, it has been ascertained that he grouped the Dynastic Rulers of Ancient Egypt into 30 Dynasties containing around 330 Pharaohs in a period of around 4,500 years (going back from his time-241 B.C.E.). According to Manetho Ancient Egyptian chronology included the following periods:

1- The Gods - This period was the genesis. It began with the emergence of the great Ennead or Company of gods and goddesses headed by Ra, the Supreme Being. According to the creation myth, the God, Ra himself, ruled over the earth.

2- The Demigods - After the Gods, the Demigods ruled the earth. Then came a descendent line of royal rulers followed by 30 rulers in the city of Memphis. These were followed by another set of royal rulers. The Heru Shemsu often mentioned in various texts referring to the ancient worship of Heru as the Supreme Spirit belong to this age. (Ra is an aspect of Heru).

3- The Spirits of the Dead - After the period of the Demigods came the Spirits of the Dead.

According to the Turin Papyrus (original Ancient Egyptian document dating to c.1440 B.C.E.), the dates of the periods are:

1- The Gods – 23,200

2- The Demigods – 13,420

3- The Spirits of the Dead – cannot be deciphered due to damage on the document.

Total: A minimum of 36,620 years before the unification (fist Dynasty).

According to Eusebius, the dates of the periods of Ancient Egypt *before* Menes, the uniter of the two lands into one empire, total: 28,927 years before the unification.

According to Diodorus of Sicily, the dates of the periods total 33,000 before the unification.

These periods were then followed by the Dynastic Period which is the only period of Ancient Egypt of which most people have knowledge (c. 5,000 B.C.E.-30 B.C.E.). Due to the deficiencies in the historical record, an exact dating for each period preceding the Dynastic is not available. However, it is reasonably certain that the total number of years outlined above goes back in history to at least 28,927 years from the time when Manetho was writing in 241 B.C.E. This gives a total of number of years around the beginning of the preceding Kamitan "Great Year" former to the commencement of our current one.

Support for this remote date comes from the writings of Herodotus. According to Herodotus, he was told by one of his Egyptian guides in 450 B.C.E. that "the sun had risen twice where it now set, and twice set where it now rises." This statement has been recognized by scholars as a reference to the processional cycles. This means that the Ancient Egyptians witnessed the beginning of the previous Great Year to our current one. Since the beginning of the current Great Year is reckoned at 10,858 B.C.E., this would mean that the beginning of Ancient Egyptian records goes back to 36,748 (10,858 + 25,890 the period of the previous great year =36,748).

> 4- Mortal Men – i.e. The Pre-Dynastic and Dynastic Periods- Rulership by Pharaohs (Kings and Queens).

This period must be divided into the Pre-Dynastic age and the Dynastic age, for the Dynastic age that is often used to represent the beginning of Ancient Egyptian civilization only refers to the time of the major unification of all the kingdoms (nomes) of the Southern ands Northern portions of the country into one single nation.

The Pharaonic (royal) calendar based on the Sothic system (star Sirius) containing cycles of 1,460 years, was in use by 4,241 B.C.E. This certainly required extensive astronomical skills and time for observation. The Sothic system is based on the *Heliacal* (i.e. appears in the sky just as the sun breaks through the eastern horizon) rising of the star Sirius in the eastern sky, signaling the New Year as well as the inundation season. Therefore, the history of Kamit (Egypt) must be reckoned to be extremely ancient. Thus, in order to grasp the antiquity of Ancient Egyptian culture, religion and philosophy, we will review the calendar systems used by the Ancient Egyptians.

The Stellar Symbolism related to the Pole Star and the Opening of the mouth and Eyes Ceremony in Ancient Egypt

As introduced earlier, Herodotus, in his book of history, quoted one of his guides as having told him that in Egyptian history had lasted for a period of time in which, "the sun had twice risen where it now set, and twice set where it now rises."[176]

> "This remark Schwaller de Lubicz interpreted as a description of the passage of one and a half precessional cycles. This would place the date of foundation around 36,000 BC, a date in broad agreement with the other sources."[177]

There are three constellations that circulate around the North Pole of the planet earth. These are Draco, Ursa Major and Ursa Minor. The Great Pyramid was discovered to have a shaft that points to the North Pole. Precession is the slow revolution of the Earth's axis of rotation (wobbling) about the poles of the ecliptic. The eclipticis a great circle inscribed on a terrestrial globe inclined at an approximate angle of 23°27' to the equator and representing the apparent motion of the sun in relation to the earth during a year. It is caused by lunar and solar perturbations acting on the Earth's equatorial bulge and causes a westward motion of the stars that takes around 25,868 years to complete.[178] During the past 5000 years the line of direction of the North Pole has moved from the star Thuban, or Alpha (a) Draconis, in the constellation Draco, to within one degree of the bright star Polaris, also known as Alpha (a) Ursae Minoris, in the constellation Ursa Minor (Little Dipper), which is now the North Star. Polaris is a binary star of second magnitude, and is located at a distance of about 300 light-years from the earth. It is easy to locate in the sky because the two stars opposite the handle in the bowl of the dipper in the constellation Ursa Major (Big Dipper), which are called the Pointers, point to the star Polaris.[179]

Figure 31: The Kamitan Zodiac and the Precession of the Equinoxes and the History of Ancient Egypt

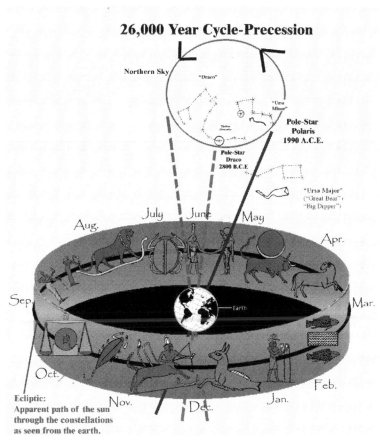

The Zodiac is an imaginary belt in the celestial sphere, extending about 8° on either side of the ecliptic. The ecliptic is a line that traces the apparent path of the Sun among the stars. It is believed that the width of the zodiac was originally determined so as to include the orbits of the Sun and Moon and of the five planets that were believed to have been known by people in ancient times (Mercury, Venus, Mars, Jupiter, and Saturn). The zodiac is divided into 12 sections of 30° each, which are called the signs of the zodiac. Because of the precession of the equinoxes about the ecliptic, a 25,920-year cycle or "Great Year" period, the first point of Aries retrogrades about 1° in 72 years, so that the sign Aries today lies in the constellation Pisces. In about 13,061 years, when the retrogression will have completed the entire circuit of 360°, the zodiacal signs and constellations will again coincide. It is believed that the zodiacal signs originated in Mesopotamia as early as 2000 B.C.E. and the Greeks adopted the symbols from the Babylonians and passed them on to the other ancient civilizations. The Chinese also adopted the 12-fold division, but called the signs rat, ox, tiger, hare, dragon, serpent, horse, sheep, monkey, hen, dog, and pig. Independently, the Aztec people devised a similar system.[180]

The calendar based on the Great Year was also used by the Ancient Egyptians. The Great Year is founded on the movement of the earth through the constellations known as the *Precession of the Equinoxes*. It is confirmed from the history given by the Ancient Egyptian Priest Manetho in the year 241 B.C.E. Each Great Year has 25,860 to 25,920 years and 12 arcs or constellations. Each passage through a constellation takes 2,155 – 2,160 years. These are known as the "Great Months" of the "Great Year." As explained earlier, the current cycle or year began at around 10,858 B.C.E. At about the year 36,766 B.C.E., according to Manetho, the Creator, Ra, ruled the earth in person from his throne in the Ancient Egyptian city of Anu (Greek-Heliopolis-city of the sun). By this reckoning our current year (2,002 A.C.E.) is actually the year 12,860 G.Y. based on the Great Year System of Ancient Egyptian reckoning.

The period of 36,525 years is also 25 times 1,460 which is the cycle of the helical rising of Sirius (when Sirius rises not only in the east but on the ecliptic, i.e. with the sun). The Sirian calendar was another time reckoning system based on the star Sirius and its relation with the sun of our solar system which contains a cycle of 1,460 years. An inscription by Censorinus informs us that the rising of Sirius occurred in 139 A.C.E. This means that the Sirian cycle also occurred in the years 1321 B.C.E, 2781 B.C.E, and 4241 B.C.E. By means of two inscriptions from the 18th Dynasty, it has been reliably established that the date for the 18th Dynasty is 1580 B.C.E.

According to the reckoning based on Manetho's history, if we take the average number of years in the Great Year and add it to the known year of the beginning of the current Great Year we get a total of 36,748 (25,890 + 10,858=36,748). If we compare this number with the history of Manetho we find a difference of 18 years, accountable by the deterioration in the translated records and the variance in the number of years in the Great Year cycle. Thus, we have match that supports the History and the practice of reckoning time by the Great Year. So we have reliable confirmations that the Sirian calendar was in use in Ancient Egypt at least as early as 4241 B.C.E.[181] and that a greater form of reckoning, the Great Year, corroborates the History of Manetho which takes Ancient Egyptian chronology and civilized use of mathematics, astronomy and time reckoning back to 36,748 B.C.E. This longer duration cycle system of time reckoning was supported by recent discoveries.

> "That the Egyptians handled astronomical cycles of even greater duration is indicated by inscriptions recently found by Soviet archeologists in newly opened graves during the period of their work on the Aswan Dam.[182] Here the cycles appear to cover periods of 35,525 years, which would be the equivalent of 25 cycles of 1461 years. The apparent discrepancy of one year in this recording of cycles is due to the sothic cycle of 1460 years being the equivalent of a civil cycle of 1461 years. According to Muck (researcher), there were three main cycles: one of 365 X 4 = 1460; another of 1460 X 25 = 36,500; and a third of 36,500 X 5 = 182,500 years."[183]

Let us recall the brilliant discovery by Joseph Campbell introduced earlier in relation to the same great age period being used in India, Iceland and Babylon and the unlikelihood of this arising by chance.

> "There are, however, instances that cannot be accounted for in this way, and then suggest the need for another interpretation: for example, in India the number of years assigned to an eon[184] is 4,320,000; whereas in the Icelandic *Poetic Edda* it is declared that in Othin's warrior hall, Valhall, there are 540 doors, through each of which, on the "day of the war of the wolf,"[185] 800 battle-ready warriors will pass to engage the antigods in combat.' But 540 times 800 equals 432,000!
>
> Moreover, a Chaldean priest, Berossos, writing in Greek ca. 289 B.C., reported that according to Mesopotamian belief 432,000 years elapsed between the crowning of the first earthly king and the coming of the deluge.
>
> No one, I should think, would wish to argue that these figures could have arisen independently in India, Iceland, and Babylon."[186]

When we compare the Indian, Icelandic and Babylonian system of Ages of time with that of Ancient Egypt some startling correlations can be observed; the same numbers appear.

Ancient Egyptian Age	Ancient Indian Age
25,920 Great Year	-----------------------------------
25,920 ÷ 6 = 4320	432,000 Kali Yuga – Iron Age 4,320,000 Maha Yuga – Great Age or Cycle
25,920 ÷ 4 = 8640	864,000 Dwapar Yuga – Copper Age
25,920 ÷ 2 = 1296	1,296,000 Treta Yuga – Silver Age
25,920 ÷ 15 = 1728	1,728,000 Satya Yuga – Golden or Truth Age

The *Royal Papyrus of Turin* gives a complete list of the kings who reigned over Upper and Lower Egypt from Menes to the New Empire, including mention of the duration of each reign. Before the list comes a section devoted to the Pre-Dynastic era. This section lists the kings who reigned before Menes, and the duration of each reign, establishing that there were nine Dynasties. According to Schwaller de Lubicz, some of these were called:

> ... the (venerables) of Memphis, the venerables of the North, and finally the *Shemsu-Hor*, usually translated as the 'Companions of Horus'.

> Fortunately, the last two lines have survived almost intact, as have indications regarding the number of years:

> venerables Shemsu-Hor, 13,429 years
> 'Reigns up to Shemsu-Hor, 23,200years (total 36,620)
> King Menes.[187]

The Turin Papyrus names the following neteru (gods and goddesses) as rulers in the Pre-Dynastic ages:
Ptah, Ra, Shu, Geb, Asar, Set, Heru, Djehuti, Maat

In support of the above, Diodorus of Sicily reports that several historians of his time reported Egypt was ruled by gods and heroes for a period of 18,000 years. After this Egypt was ruled by mortal kings for 15,000 years.[188] While it is true that this account differs with that of Manetho and the Turin Papyrus, the inescapable fact remains that every account refers to ages of rulers that go back beyond 30,000 B.C.E. as the earliest period of record keeping. The implications are far reaching. Consider that if we were to add the figure above for the period prior to the first king (King Menes) of our era and use the first confirmed date for the use of the calendar (4240 B.C.E.) we indeed would have a date over 40,000 B.C.E. for the beginnings of Ancient Egyptian history (36,620+4240).

Picture 26: Below right-The Great Heru m akhet (Sphinx) of Egypt-with the Panel of Djehutimes between its Paws. (19th century rendition of the Sphinx) [189]

Picture 23: Below left-The Great Heru m Akhet (Sphinx) of Ancient Egypt.

Plate 16: The Great Sphinx, covered in sand - Drawing by early Arab explorers[190]

The Sphinx is the oldest known monument and it relates to the solar mysticism of Anu as well as to the oldest form of spiritual practice known. From it we also derive certain important knowledge in reference to the antiquity of civilization in Ancient Egypt. The picture of the Great Sphinx above-right appeared in 1876. Notice the broad nose and thick lips with which it is endowed. Any visitor to Egypt who examines the Sphinx close up will see that even with the defacement of the nose, it is clearly an African face and not an Asiatic or European personality being depicted. Many other early Egyptologists concluded the same way upon gazing at the monument and this picture is but one example of their conviction on the subject.

Figure 32: The Per-Aah (Pharaoh) Djehutimes IIII (Thutmosis) makes offerings to the Great Heru m Akhet (Sphinx)

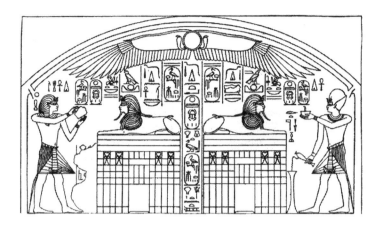

The Heru-em-akhet (Horemacket Ra-Herakhti (Herukhuti, Heruakhuti - Great Sphinx) Stele is a panel placed directly in front of the chest of the monument in between the two front paws. It recounts the story of how the prince Djehutimes IIII (Thutmosis IV- 18th Dynasty 1401-1391 B.C.E.) fell asleep at the base of the Sphinx on a hot day and the spirit of the Sphinx came to him. The inscription that survived with the Ancient Egyptian Sphinx also has serious implications for the revision of the dating of Ancient Egyptian history. The Sphinx came to him and offered him kingship and sovereignty over the world if Djehutimes would repair him and make devout offerings and worship. Having complied with the wishes of the Divine, to maintain the great monument and sustain the worship of Ra-Herakhti, Djehutimes became king and Egypt prospered under his reign with the favor of the Divine. According to Egyptologist Maspero, this was not the first time that the Sphinx was cleared:

> The stele of the Sphinx bears, on line 13, the cartouche of Khephren in the middle of a gap ....
> There, I believe, is the indication of an excavation of the Sphinx carried out under this prince,
> and consequently the more or less certain proof that the Sphinx was already covered with
> sand during the time of Cheops and his predecessors.[191]

R. A. Schwaller de Lubicz reports that legends support the contention that at a very early date in Ancient Egyptian history, the Old Kingdom fourth Dynasty (Cheops {Khufu} reigned 2551-2528 B.C.E., Khephren {Ra-ka-ef} reigned 2520-2494), the Sphinx was already considered ancient and as belonging to a remote past of Ancient Egyptian Culture.

> A legend affirms that even in Cheops' day, the age of the Sphinx was already so remote that it
> was impossible to situate it in time. This Sphinx is a human and colossal work. There is an
> enigma about it that is linked with the very enigma posed by the Sphinx itself.

It has been proposed, as a support of the use of the Great Year calendar, that the Ancient Egyptians instituted the use of different symbolisms in religion and government in accordance with the current symbolism of the particular age in question.[192] Thus, during the age (great month) of Leo, the lion symbolism would be used. What is compelling about this rationale is that the new evidence in reference to the age of the Sphinx coincides with the commencement of the New Great Year and the month of Leo, which began in 10,858 B.C.E. However, when it is understood that the damage on the Sphinx would have required thousands of years to produce, and when the history of Manetho as well as the conjunction of the Sphinx with the constellation Leo when it makes its heliacal rising at the beginning of each Great Year is taken into account, it becomes possible to understand that the Sphinx was already in existence at the commencement of our current Great Year, and to envision the possibility that the Sphinx was created at the beginning of the previous Great Year anniversary (36,748 B.C.E.).

The Great Sphinx and its attendant monuments as well as other structures throughout Egypt which appear to be compatible architecturally should therefore be considered as part of a pinnacle of high culture that was reached well before the Dynastic age, i.e. previous to 5,000 B.C.E. The form of the Sphinx itself, displaying the lion body with the human head, but also with the particularly "leonine" headdress including the lion's mane, was a legacy accepted by the Pharaohs of the Dynastic Period. In the Ancient Egyptian mythological system of government, the Pharaoh is considered as a living manifestation of Heru and he or she wields the leonine power which comes from the sun, Ra, in order to rule. Thus, the Pharaohs also wore and were depicted wearing the leonine headdress. The sundisk is the conduit through which the Spirit transmits Life Force energy to the world, i.e. the Lion Power, and this force is accessed by turning towards the Divine in the form of the sun. Hence, the orientation of the Sphinx towards the east, facing the rising sun. All of this mystical philosophy and more is contained in the symbolic-metaphorical form and teaching of the Sphinx. Thus, we have a link of Ancient Egyptian culture back to the Age of Leo and the commencement of the current cycle of the Great Year in remote antiquity.

Heru-m-akhet or "Heru in the Horizon" or "manifesting" in the horizon, the "Sphinx," actually represents an ancient conjunction formed by the great Sphinx in Giza, Egypt and the heavens. This conjunction signals the beginning of the "New Great Year." It has been noted by orthodox as well as nonconformist Egyptologists alike, that the main symbolisms used in Ancient Egypt vary over time Nonconformist Egyptilogists see this as a commemoration of the zodiacal symbol pertaining to the particular Great Month in question. What is controversial to the orthodox Egyptologists is the implication that the Ancient Egyptians marked time by the Great Year, and this would mean that Ancient Egyptian civilization goes back 12 millenniums, well beyond any other civilization in history. This further signifies that all of the history books and concepts related to history and the contributions of Africa to humanity would have to be rewritten. Also, since it has been shown that the Ancient Egyptians commemorated the Zodiacal sign of Leo at the commencement of the Great Year it means that the knowledge of the precession of the equinoxes, the Great Year and the signs of the Zodiac proceeded from Ancient Egypt to Babylon and Greece and not the other way around. The twelve zodiacal signs for these constellations were named by the 2nd-century astronomer Ptolemy, as follows: Aries (ram), Taurus (bull), Gemini (twins), Cancer (crab), Leo (lion), Virgo (virgin), Libra (balance), Scorpio (scorpion), Sagittarius (archer), Capricorn (goat), Aquarius (water-bearer), and Pisces (fishes).

> That is precisely what the records reveal. Mentu the bull disappears and is superceded by the ram of Amon. The character of the architecture loses its monolithic simplicity. While still within its recognizable tradition, there is no mistaking a change of 'character'. The Pharaohs incorporate Amon in the names they assume: Amenhotep, Amenophis, Tutankhamun.
>
> Egyptologists attribute the fall of Mentu and the rise of Amon to a hypothetical priestly feud, with the priests of Amon emerging victorious. There is nothing illogical or impossible about this hypothesis, but at the same time there is no evidence whatever to support it.
>
> The evidence shows a shift of symbolism, from duality under Gemini, to the bull, to the ram. These shifts coincide with the dates of the astronomical precession.
>
> Further corroboration of Egyptian knowledge and use of the precession of the equinoxes, and of the incredible coherence and deliberation of the Egyptian tradition, was deduced by Schwaller de Lubicz from a detailed study of the famous zodiac from the Temple of Denderah. This temple was constructed by the Ptolemies in the first century BC, upon the site of an earlier temple. The hieroglyphs declare that it was constructed according to the plan laid down in the time of the 'Companions of Horus' - that is to say, prior to the beginnings of Dynastic Egypt. Egyptologists regard this statement as a ritual figure of speech, intended to express regard for the tradition of the past.[193]

One striking form of symbolism that is seen from the beginning to the end of the Ancient Egyptian history is the Sphinx/Pharaonic Leonine headdress.

Figure 33: Above- The Heru-m-akhet (Sphinx) Pharaonic headdress.[194]

Figure 34: Below- Drawing of the Sphinx from a sculpture in Egypt

Picture 24: Constellation Leo-The Lion

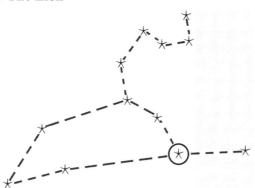

The Great Sphinx faces due east and in the year c. 10,800 B.C.E. a perfect conjunction is created as the Sphinx faces the rising sun and the constellation Leo, the lion.

Picture 25: The Sphinx faces due east at the beginning of the Great year and faces the Constellation Leo as it makes its Heliacal Rising.

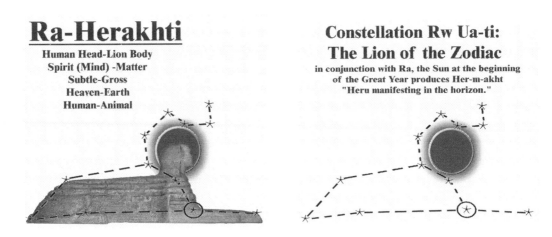

Ra-Herakhti

Human Head-Lion Body
Spirit (Mind) -Matter
Subtle-Gross
Heaven-Earth
Human-Animal

Constellation Rw Ua-ti:
The Lion of the Zodiac

in conjunction with Ra, the Sun at the beginning
of the Great Year produces Her-m-akht
"Heru manifesting in the horizon."

The Sphinx on Earth (Rw or Ru) as a Counterpart to the Sphinx in the Heavens.

The Sphinx on earth as a counterpart to the Sphinx in the heavens (Astral Plane), i.e. the horizon of the earth plane and the horizon of the astral plane. In this view, the Sphinx on earth and the Sphinx in heaven complement each other and form two halves of the akher-akhet symbol, but turned facing each other, looking at the sun which is between them, i.e. turning away from the earth plane and towards the Transcendental Spirit.

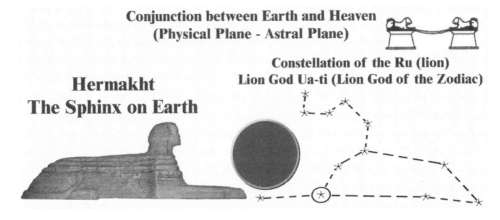

Conjunction between Earth and Heaven
(Physical Plane - Astral Plane)

Constellation of the Ru (lion)
Lion God Ua-ti (Lion God of the Zodiac)

Hermakht
The Sphinx on Earth

Figure 35: Below- The Ancient Egyptian zodiacal signs for the ages of the Ram, Bull and Lion

Opening of the Mouth with the Imperishable Stars

In the Hermetic Texts, which are the later development in Ancient Egyptian scripture, Hermes, the Greek name ascribed to the Ancient Egyptian god Djehuti, states to his pupil Asclepius (Egyptian Imhotep) that *"Did you know, O Asclepius, that Egypt is made in the image of heaven?"*[195] The Ancient Egyptian Pyramid Texts and the Pert M Heru (Book of Enlightenment) texts contain more references to stellar mysticism. The stellar symbolism of Ancient Egypt relates to the passage of time but also to mystical awakening and spiritual realization.

> As to these all, Maat and Djehuti, they are with Isdesba[47] Lord of Amentet. As to the divine beings behind Asar, they are again Mseti, Hapy, Duamutf, and Kebsenuf. They are behind the Chepesh[48] in the northern heavens.
>
> From Prt M Hru Chap. 4, V. 22

The Chepesh has important mystical symbolism. Mythically it represents the foreleg of the god Set which was torn out and thrown into the heavens by the god Heru during their epic battle. A similar teaching occurs in the Babylonian epic of Gilgemesh[196\197] when the "foreleg of the Bull of Heaven" is ripped out and thrown at the goddess Ishtar, who was the goddess or Queen of Heaven in Mesopotamia. It symbolizes the male generative capacity and is one of the offerings of Hetep given in Chapter 36 (usually referred to as #30B) of the Pert M Heru (Egyptian Book of the Dead). Its cosmic and mystical implications provides us with insight into Kamitan philosophy as well as ancient history.

Also, in ancient times the Chepesh symbol represented the "Northern path" of spiritual evolution. Since the constellation of the Ursa Major ("Great Bear" or "Big Dipper"), known to the Ancient Egyptians as "Meskhetiu," contains **seven** stars and occupied the location referred to as the "Pole Star." As it occupies the pole position it does not move, while all the other stars in the sky circle around it. This constellation, whose symbol is the foreleg, ⊶, was thus referred to as "the imperishables" in the earlier Pyramid Texts: "He (the king-enlightened initiate) climbs to the sky among the imperishable stars."[49]

Akhemu Seku - never setting stars – imperishable

Akhemu Urdu - never resting stars – setting

The Great Pyramid in Egypt, located in the area referred to as "The Giza Plateau" in modern times, incorporated this teaching. The main chamber in the Great Pyramid incorporates two shafts that pointed in ancient times to the Chepesh (Ursa {Bear} Major {Great} - the foreleg) in the north sky and to Orion (Sahu or Sah), the star system of Asar (Osiris) in the southern sky. The imperishable constellation refers to that which is unchanging, absolute, transcendental and perfect.

---

[47] A protector god in the Company of Gods and Goddesses of Djehuti.

[48] Big Dipper, common name applied to a conspicuous constellation in the northern celestial hemisphere, near the North Pole. It was known to the ancient Greeks as the Bear and the Wagon and to the Romans as Ursa Major (the Great Bear) and Septentriones (Seven Plowing Oxen). The seven brightest stars of the constellation form the easily identified outline of a giant dipper. To the Hindus, it represents the seven Rishis, or holy ancient Sages. "Big Dipper," Microsoft (R) Encarta. Copyright (c) 1994 Microsoft Corporation. Copyright (c) 1994 Funk & Wagnall's Corporation.

[49] Pyramid Texts 1120-23. *Egyptian Mysteries,* Lucie Lamy

Figure 36: The Great Pyramid of Egypt with the Mystical Constellations (view from the East) and the Perishable and Imperishable stars.

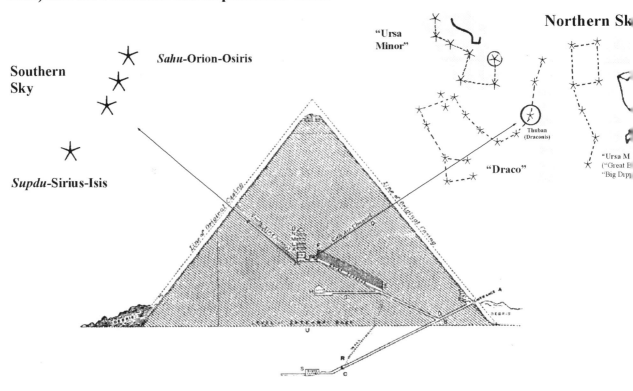

Figure 37: The Great Pyramid of Egypt with the Mystical Constellations (view from the South).

When the Great Pyramids are viewed over the course of one evening, from the south to north, the perishable stars (forming circles, moving below the horizon) can be seen moving around the the imperishable stars (those which do not set, that is go below the horizon) in the center. Time lapse photographs of this constellation **(Meskhetiu - Ursa Major ("Great Bear" or "Big Dipper"),** show it as remaining in the center and other stars moving around it. Also, it does not sink below the horizon and become "reborn" in the eastern horizon each day as do other stars. The Orion constellation refers to that which is changing, incarnating (rising in the east) and becoming. In this manner Asar is reborn through Sopdu (the star Sirius-Aset, Isis) in the form of Heru-Sopdu (Heru who is in Aset), also known as Sirius B. Therefore, mystically, the "Northern Path" is promoted as the path to immortality and enlightenment through the attainment of absolute consciousness which transcends the perishable and ever-changing nature of creation. The "Southern Path" is the process of

178

reincarnation, renewal and repeated embodiment (*uhem ankh* {Kamitan}), for the purpose of further spiritual evolution through self-discovery by means of human experiences. This teaching is also reflected in the zodiac inscription from the temple of Hetheru at Denderah and in the "Opening of the Mouth Ceremony" where a symbol of the imperishable constellation, ⌐, is carried by the priest. The mystical intent is to open the mind, through mystical wisdom and disciplines, so as to render it *uadjit*, ⬭⬭⬭ , (universal and infinite, all-encompassing, unlimited) and beyond the fluctuations of egoism, i.e. mortal consciousness.

Figure 38: Below left- Hieroglyph for the Chepesh (foreleg). Center-The Chepesh with constellation.[198] Right- The Chepesh as part of the Hetep offering in the *Pert M Heru* Texts and temple inscriptions.

Figure 39: The Hetep Offering Slab with the foreleg symbol.

Used in the Hetep (Hotep) offering table, the leg symbolizes the male gender. The goose symbolizes the female gender. Thus, the initiate offers duality in the form of sex awareness to the divinity in exchange for the realization of non-duality, or the transcendence of gender (dual) consciousness altogether, i.e. the "imperishable" or eternal realization of the Higher Self.

Figure 40: Vignettes from the Opening of the Mouth Ceremonies from the Ancient Egyptian texts. Left- with Chepesh (Chpsh-foreleg), Right with the Seba (Sba) ur instruments.

"O Initiate, I have come in search of you, for I am Horus; I have struck your mouth for you, for I am your beloved son; I have split open your mouth for you... I have split open your eyes for you... with the Chepch (Chpsh) of the Eye of Heru- Chepesh (Foreleg). I have split open your mouth for you... I have split open your eyes for you... with the adze of Upuaut..... with the adze of iron . . . [PT 11-13]

The opening of the mouth and eyes is a mystical teaching relating to expansion in expression (mouth) and awareness (open eyes). These factors (mouth and eyes) are the signs of the existence of consciousness or its absence. From the passages above we learn that the Priests and Priestesses "open" the mouth and eyes by touching them with the ritual instruments which symbolize the eternal, the absolute, i.e. the expansion of consciousness, immortality and spiritual enlightenment. Also, we learn that the adze instrument (Ursa minor) is actually also the Eye of Heru, which is the greatest offering-eucharist of the Egyptian mysteries. The Eye symbolizes divine consciousness as it is one and the same with Heru, Asar and Ra. Therefore, being touched with these instruments means attaining god-consciousness.

NOTES FOR CHAPTER 1

Commonly referred to as Chapter 17

Commonly referred to as Chapter 176

The Middle Passage: White Ships Black Cargo by Tom Feelings, John Henrik, Dr Clarke

Stolen Legacy, George James

Black Athena, The Afroasiatic Origins of Classical Civilization by Martin Bernal

Destruction of Black Civilization: *Great Issues of a Race from 4500bc to 2000ad* by Chancellor Williams

Stolen Legacy, George G.M. James

From Egypt to Greece, M. Ashby C. M. Books 1997

Manetho, W. G. Waddell

Encarta Encyclopedia, Copyright (c) 1994

Gen. 25:26

Gen. 47:9

60+130+430=620.

400-130-60=210.

Bible Myth: The African Origins of the Jewish People Gary Greenberg

The Power of Myth, Joseph Campbell

Traveler's Key to Ancient Egypt, John Anthony West

Black Man of The Nile and His Family by

The African Origin of Civilization, *Civilization or Barbarism,* Cheikh Anta Diop

Photo: From Cheikh Anta Diop's "Civilisation ou Barbarie", Courtesy of Présence Africaine.

Arts and Crafts of Ancient Egypt, Flinders Petrie

[4][14] Published in 1833 by the son of Champollion-Figeac, brother of Jean Fransçois Champollion.

[5] Ruins of Empires by Count Volney, (Diop, 1974, p. 28).

[6] The Zambesi and Its Tributaries, p. 526. N. Y., 1866.

[7] The Uganda Protectorate, Vol. II, p. 472. London, 1902.

[8] The Mediterranean Races, p. 243. N. Y., 1901.

[9] Royal Soc. of Arts Jour., Vol. XLIX, p. 594. 1901.

[0] *Egyptiene ancienne.*Paris: Collection l'Univers, 1839, pp 26-27

[1] Rawlinson, G. The Story of Egypt, p. 252. London. 1887.

[2] *Historie ancienne des peubles de l'Orient.*

[3] *Heresy in the University: The Black Athena Controversy and the Responsibilities of American Intellectuals* by Jacques Berlinerblan

[4] George, *Crimes of Perception,* xi (emphasis added); Peters, *Heresy and Authority,* 15, 17.

[5] P. L. Berger, Heretical Imperative, 28. Foucault, History *of* Sexuality, vol. 1, 93. On Foucault's use of this term, see James Miller, Passion *of* Michel Foucault, 108. Char, "Partage formel XXII," 0euvres completes, 160.

[6] Bernal, Black Athena 1: 2 (emphasis in original).

Metropolitan Museum New York

[8] *Compton's Interactive Encyclopedia.* Copyright (c) 1994, 1995

Copyright © 1995 Helicon Publishing Ltd Webster Encyclopedia

Gods and Symbols of Ancient Egypt by Manfred Lurker

Compton's Interactive Encyclopedia. Copyright (c) 1994, 1995

[2] *Compton's Interactive Encyclopedia.* Copyright (c) 1994, 1995

[3] *Feuerstein, Georg, The Shambhala Encyclopedia of Yoga* 1997

[4] *Aset (Isis) and Nebethet (Nephthys)* are ancient Egyptian goddesses who preside over the resurrection of Asar.

[5] See the book *Resurrecting Osiris* by Muata Ashby

[5] "Kush, Early Kingdom of," *Microsoft® Encarta® Africana.* ©&(p) 1999 Microsoft Corporation. All rights reserved.

Architecture - Medinet Habu temple -New Kingdom – Waset Egypt

American Heritage Dictionary

[9] Reproduced from an object in the Leyden Museum.

"Kush, Early Kingdom of," *Microsoft® Encarta® Africana.* ©&(p) 1999 Microsoft Corporation. All rights reserved.

Copyright © 1995 Helicon Publishing Ltd Encyclopedia

[2] Muata Ashby

[3] *Atlas of Ancient Egypt,* John Baines and Jaromir Malek, 1980

Atlas of Ancient Egypt, John Baines and Jaromir Malek, 1980

The Complete Temples of Ancient Egypt, Richard Wilkinson, 2000

Doshi, Saryu, Editor-Indian Council for Cultural Relations India and Egypt: Influences and Interactions 1993

Random House Encyclopedia.

1550 B.C.E.-1307 B.C.E. (conservative traditional Egyptology dating). 1580 B.C.E Based on 18th Dynasty inscriptions.

The Ancient Egyptians: Their Life and Customs, Sir Garner Wilkinson

[150] American Heritage Dictionary

[151] Copyright © 1995 Helicon Publishing Ltd Encyclopedia

[152] Architecture - Medinet Habu temple -New Kingdom – Waset Egypt

[153] **adz** or **adze** (ădz) *n.* An axlike tool with a curved blade at right angles to the handle, used for dressing wood.

[154] Copyright © 1995 Helicon Publishing Ltd Encyclopedia

[155] **Nekhen News,** Expedition reports, Hierakonpolis, Petrie Museum of Egyptian Archaeology University College, London

[156] *Egypt Uncovered,* Vivian Davies and Renée Friedman

[157] Greek name *Sais*

[158] Copyright © 1995 Helicon Publishing Ltd Encyclopedia

[159] Metropolitan Museum New York

[160] Encarta Encyclopedia, Copyright (c) 1994

[161] Copyright © 1995 Helicon Publishing Ltd Encyclopedia

[162] Anunian Theology by Muata Ashby

[163] Copyright © 1995 Helicon Publishing Ltd Encyclopedia

[164] Copyright © 1995 Helicon Publishing Ltd Encyclopedia

[165] The southern kingdom when, after Solomon's death, only the tribes of Judah and Benjamin followed the house of David. There were wars between the kings of Judah and Israel for 60 years. Random House Encyclopedia Copyright (C) 1983,1990 by Random House Inc.

[166] Josiah (c. 647-609 B.C.E.) King of Judah. Grandson of Manasseh and son of Amon, he succeeded to the throne at the age of eight. The discovery of a Book of Instruction (probably Deuteronomy, a book of the Old Testament) during repairs of the Temple 621 B.C.E. stimulated thorough reform, which included the removal of all sanctuaries except that of Jerusalem. He was killed in a clash at Megiddo with Pharaoh-nechoh, king of Egypt.
Copyright © 1995 Helicon Publishing Ltd Encyclopedia

[167] Copyright © 1995 Helicon Publishing Ltd Encyclopedia

[168] *Egypt: Child of Africa,* Ivan Van Sertima 1994

[169] *Ancient Egyptian Construction and Architecture* by Somers Clarke and R. Engelbach

[170] Ibid.

[171] This is the earliest confirmed date for the use of the advanced calendar in Ancient Egypt.

[172] *Arts and Crafts of Ancient Egypt,* Flinders Petrie

[173] A group of people who originally lived in Asia Minor (Middle East), especially Arabia with mixed North (Aryan?) and East (European) Asian and African ethnicity.

[174] Conducted by Muata Ashby while traveling throughout Egypt 2000 – speaking to northern Arab-Egyptians (in Cairo) and one Nubian-Egyptian in Aswan

[175] *Traveler's Key to Ancient Egypt,* John Anthony West

[176] *Histories,* Herodotus

[177] *Serpent in the Sky,* John Anthony West, p. 97

[178] Random House Encyclopedia Copyright (C) 1983,1990

[179] "North Star," Microsoft (R) Encarta. Copyright (c) 1994 Microsoft Corporation. Copyright (c) 1994 Funk & Wagnall's Corporation.

[180] "Zodiac," Microsoft (R) Encarta. Copyright (c) 1994 Microsoft Corporation. Copyright (c) 1994 Funk & Wagnall's Corporation.

[181] *Echoes of the Old Darkland,* Charles Finch

[182] Between the years 1960-1970

[183] *Secrets of the Great Pyramid,* Peter Tompkins

[184] A "Great Cycle" *(Mahayuga)* of cosmic time.

[185] I.e., at the ending of the cosmic eon, Wagner's *Götterdämmerung.*

[186] *The Mythic Image,* Joseph Campbell

[187] Sacred Science by Schwaller de Lubicz

[188] Diodorus Book 23

[189] This illustration appeared in the book *History of Egypt*-Samuel Sharp 1876 A.C.E.

[190] *Descriptions of Egypt*

[191] G. Maspero, *The Passing of the Empires* (New York, 1900).

[192] *Echoes of the Old Darkland,* Charles Finch

[193] *Serpent in the Sky,* John Anthony West, p. 100

[194] These illustrations appeared in the book *The Ancient Egyptians: Their Life and Customs*-Sir J. Garner Wilkinson 1854 A.C.E.

[195] *Hermetica,* Asclepius III, Solos Press ed., p. 136

[196] Col. V. l, 161

[197] **Gilgamesh,** legendary king of Babylonia, hero of an epic poem written on clay tablets, found in the ruins of Nineveh; epic has affinities with Old Testament, contains story of the flood. Excerpted from *Compton's Interactive Encyclopedia.* Copyright (c) 1994, 1995

[198] Sample from various Middle Kingdom Period coffin Lids.

Chapter 2: Religion and Culture in Ancient Egypt and Other African Nations

Gue Nyame
Ghananian Adinkira symbol meaning: "God is the Supreme power"

Overview of African Religions[199]\[200]\[201]\[202]\[203]

The term "African Religions" as used in our present context relates to the forms of religions that were developed on the continent of Africa by its indigenous or native peoples from ancient times. It will refer to those forms of religions which existed prior to the introduction of religions from outside of Africa and prior to influences from other societies outside of Africa. As of 1999, about half of the people in Africa consider themselves as adherents to Islam. A lesser number are adherents to Christianity and African Religions. A smaller number are adherents to Judaism or Hinduism.[50] So despite the work of Muslim and Christian missionaries, a substantial number of Africans still practice one of the African Religions. Also there are a substantial number of people of African descent who practice one of the African Religions outside of Africa as well.

Though the colonial period in Africa was short-lived when compared to the overall view of history, it had a profound effect on the culture and also never truly ended in many parts of the continent because of the imposition of *Neocolonialism* (control of individual countries by controlling the government that is run by locals.) and the new moves in the late 20th century to impose *Globalization* (control of the world economy by Western governments) on the world community. The following excerpt from Compton's Encyclopedia concisely sums up the colonial history of European nations in Africa.

"In what is called the "Scramble for Africa," European nations partitioned Africa at the Berlin West Africa Conference (1884-1885). The Germans got southwestern Africa, along with Tanganyika in East Africa. The Portuguese got Mozambique and Angola, in southern Africa. Belgium took the Congo, and France got Senegal, the Cameroons, and several other colonies in the western Sudan and Central Africa. The British got the rest, including Kenya and Uganda in East Africa, the Gold Coast (now Ghana) and the territory that became Nigeria in West Africa. The British already controlled Egypt, which they had occupied in 1882, as well as English-speaking Cape Colony and Natal on the southern tip of Africa. The British also dominated Southern Rhodesia (now Zimbabwe) and Northern Rhodesia (now Zambia) through the British South Africa Company under the leadership of Cecil Rhodes. The result was that almost every part of the African continent was a European colony."[204]

Another method to discern the essential elements of African religion is to study its most ancient forms, and then to correlate these with the aspects that persist into the present and compare these with the aspects that developed later. Thus, the study of Ancient Egyptian-Nubian (Cushite) religion is of extreme importance in reconstructing African religion and philosophy. As we have already seen, there are several areas of

---

[50]"African Religions: An Interpretation," *Microsoft® Encarta® Africana.* ©&(p) 1999 Microsoft Corporation. All rights reserved.

commonality between Ancient Egyptian-Nubian religion and other African religions. In this manner, Ancient Egyptian-Nubian spirituality may be seen as a centerpiece and perhaps even a pinnacle of African religious culture and philosophy.

The developments in Ancient Egypt are central to understanding African Religions and their history both before and after the rise of Kamitan civilization. This is because there was a close relationship between Neterian Religion and other African religions, as there was a relationship between Ancient Egypt and other African nations. The connection between Ancient Egypt and Nubia has been elaborated in previous chapters. Also, the fact that the Ancient Egyptians were "black" Africans and that the original Ancient Egyptians originated in the heart of Africa, the land now called Uganda, was also explained earlier. What is important to understand now is that the fundamental Ancient Egyptian Religious tenets can be found in other African religions. This means that the tenets were a common product of African spirituality. In this context, Ancient Egypt exemplified the concepts of African Spirituality in their most highly advanced form. This form, (Neterian Religion – Shetaut Neter) also led to the development of pre-Judaic and Islamic Arabian religions, Judaism, Christianity, as we will see throughout this book.

One of the problems in studying African religion is that the concepts, traditions and rituals of the varied religions were generally not committed to writing. The exception to this is the Neterian Religion, where there is extensive writing that has survived. Western researchers have tried to advance the idea that Northeast Africa and Ancient Egyptian culture and religion was part of Middle Eastern (Arabic) culture and religion, and that "Sub-Saharan Africa" is the land of "blacks" who do not have a refined notion of spirituality. From this, negative stereotyping led to the denigration of African culture and its people as backward savages who live in the jungle, ignorantly worshiping pagan gods. To those involved in initiating and perpetuation the salve trade, this made the enslavement of Africans[51] a more justifiable act during the period after the colonization of the New World (1492 A.C.E.-1800 A.C.E.) and then the colonization of Africa itself (1750 A.C.E.-1960 A.C.E.). The lack of scriptures or worship in western style churches or Mosques was used by Europeans and Arabs as an excuse to claim that they were bringing religion to Africans, and thus, according to the mandates of their scriptures (especially as will be discussed with respect to the Judeo-Christians and Muslims which sanctions the conquering of other peoples to "spread the word"), they were able to justify their actions to themselves as being Divine in nature. Another problem is that the African religious culture was and continues to be supported by language and shared history. The introduction of European languages, and the systematic prevention of the African people from speaking their own native languages or introducing tribal names has led to a situation of inter-tribal conflicts which were not previously present. This is due to the introduction of distorted *ethnonyms,* names given to the groups of villages or nations by the Europeans based on their anthropological studies and the pre-colonial African names of societies. This means that people who were at one time actually relatives might be caught in two different geographic areas, but due to colonial pressures their common language and common identity is suppressed until forgotten. Then the two begin to see one another as strangers, following the cause of the colonial ruler against the colonial ruler of the other territory. Thus, the modern interpretation for the word "tribe" as *"a group of people who are descended from common ancestors and ruled by a hereditary "chief," who share a single culture (including, in particular, language and religion), and live in a well-defined geographical region,*[52] is a misapplication as concerns many groups in present day Africa due to all of the distortion of African society in the past 200 years. In other words, people living in a present day "tribe" may not have a connection with common ancestors from other tribe members, or the tribe may have no such legacy because the disruption by colonists resulted in the tribal memory being lost or in other cases, the members of the tribe may be composed of people who lost their cultural identity (refugees, orphans, etc.) and were brought together for political or economic reasons and forced to speak a language, etc. This definition of the word "tribe" may be equated with or thought of interchangeably with the term "ethnic group."

African culture views religion as a living aspect of life which is passed on from parent to child and from elders and storytellers to the younger generations who grow up and continue the tradition by passing on the myths, culture and religious traditions to the next generation, and so on. This is called the *Sacred Oral*

---

[51] From the 1520s to the 1860s an estimated 11 to 12 million African men, women, and children were forcibly embarked on European vessels for a life of slavery in the Western Hemisphere. Many more Africans were captured or purchased in the interior of the continent but a large number died before reaching the coast. About 9 to 10 million Africans survived the Atlantic crossing to be purchased by planters and traders in the New World, where they worked principally as slave laborers in plantation economies requiring a large workforce. "Transatlantic Slave Trade," *Microsoft® Encarta® Africana.* © 1999 Microsoft Corporation. All rights reserved. Author's note: Other estimates run much higher but this one has been presented here to avoid needless arguments over the issue. Nevertheless this number pales in comparison to the deaths caused by the forced enslavement and kidnapping of Africans which estimates project at 100,000,000 (one hundred million) or more men, women and children.

[52] "Ethnicity and Identity in Africa: An Interpretation" *Microsoft® Encarta® Africana.* ©1999 Microsoft Corporation. All rights reserved.

Tradition in African religion. The *Sacred Oral Tradition* was passed on through mentorship, rituals, and intensive periods of education, including rites of passage.[53]

European travelers and missionaries later realized that the practice of religion did exist in Africa, but it was not consistent with their interpretation of what religion was supposed to be. Despite this realization, the invalidation of African spirituality continued and the missionary movements of Christianity and Islam continued, not in the spirit of sharing views on religion or having a meeting of minds on religious issues, but from a perspective of bringing a "superior" religion to people with inferior or no religion. This attitude also led to the denigration of African people as well.

Due to the transatlantic slave trade, colonization of Africa and the ensuing chaos which was perpetrated by European nations on African nations, with the special intent of preventing the continuation of the transmittance and practice of African religions and the promotion of Western religions and social concepts, the traditions of African religions have sometimes been altered, disrupted or completely lost. The lack of concrete writings prior to the time of the pre-African holocaust has led to a situation wherein much reconstruction of Ancient African traditions has been required. Some European scholars began this work, but many have been accused of distorting African religion, skewing it in light of Western cultural values and religious tenets, and in the context of European religion being superior by virtue of the fact that Europeans came to believe that monotheism is the advanced concept of religion. This means that some of the original wisdom of the practices, myths and systems of gods and goddesses has been misunderstood. The particular form of monotheism espoused by the three major Western religions (Judaism, Christianity, Islam) is actually a narrow concept which, when examined, is actually a form of intensified dogmatic idolatry. In contrast to African Religions, there are several examples of Western religions going to war against one another. The same is not the case with African religions originally. Conflicts between African groups did exist but not for the same reasons as between the Europeans; one such issue is ethnic differences as in the case of Rwanda. However, in modern times, Africans have fought each other over religion, especially those involved with Christianity and Islam. This is because the concept of African religion, while incorporating the teaching of monotheism, actually incorporates the pantheistic understanding as well. Pantheism relates to the understanding the God or the Divine, manifests as Creation and everything in it. So here we are confronted with the African concept of *Polytheistic Monotheism*, system of religion presenting a Supreme Being with many "lesser gods and goddesses" who serve the Supreme and sustain Creation and lead human beings to spiritual enlightenment and worldly prosperity. These religious principles will be discussed more in depth later on.

In this context the Western concept of monotheism has been degraded to a circumscribed idea that is expressed in a strict form of expression based on a "revelation." This is erroneous in view of the actions that Western Culture has perpetrated on other cultures and among themselves (wars, slavery, economic subjugation, etc.). The concept of revelation in the Western religions (Judaism, Christianity and Islam) holds that some absolute and perfect knowledge about the Supreme Being has been given. This is in stark contrast to the philosophy and tenet of African Religions (including Ancient Egyptian philosophy), Indian Vedanta philosophy, Buddhist philosophy, Chinese Taoism and other mystical traditions which holds that which is transcendental and unintelligible cannot be related in words, as the intellect cannot fathom the true nature of the Supreme Being. Thus, the Western religions and some orthodox religions that developed in Asia Minor such as the Zoroastrian religion, stand alone with the narrow concept of the Supreme Being that is touted as a high revelation that must be imposed on the rest of the world's societies.

As missionaries preached throughout Africa, they translated the European texts into the African languages. In the process of doing so, the missionaries realized that there was a term in African spirituality for "Supreme Being." But even then they attempted to characterize this African concept as a limited idea related to a Creator personality, and they viewed the rituals and propitiations to lesser divinities as proof of the inferiority of African religious concept. This European view of the African concept of the Supreme Being was called *deus otiotus* meaning "a remote god who is rarely invoked." The African concept of the Supreme is so lofty that it views a direct approach to the Supreme Being, an unintelligible existence, as presumptuous and irreverent. As expressed above, the African religious philosophical view is that the very naming of such a being constitutes the act of conditioning it, and this is contradictory to its essential nature. Further, the so-called reverence of Western religions which extol the glory of the Supreme Being does not cause the European practitioners of religion to be more faithful or peaceful, as history has shown. Rather, what develops is a form of lip service which denigrates the religious process since the words are expressed but the reverence, if any, does not translate to virtue or even tolerance of others. So the Western idea that reverencing a Supreme Being directly makes the people or the society more pious is unfounded. Within

---

[53] *Microsoft® Encarta® Africana.* ©1999 Microsoft Corporation. All rights reserved.

authentic Ancient African systems of Religion, the Supreme Being is to be approached not through intellectualizing (naming and classifying), but through ritual which facilitates the entering into transcendental consciousness wherein the being can be directly experienced without the encumbrances of illusory and limited mental concepts. Also, an approach through gods and goddesses was devised.

Further, Ancient African Religion does not therefore ascribe a gender to the Supreme Being. Thus it is less susceptible to male chauvinism (sexism, bigotry) unlike the patriarchal western religions. So there is more of a balance in African Religion between the roles played by men and women in the religious practices. Hence, philosophy and ritual in African Religion are highly advanced and integral aspects of religious practice and therefore, rituals are not primitive displays of superstition.

Some Western scholars have characterized African societies as resistant to change and this view has been accepted by some leading African scholars of religion such as John Mbiti. This in part explains the persistence of African religion despite the tumultuous history of Africa. In some parts of present day Africa, there is an upsurge in the revival of traditional African religion. Some Africans living in and outside of Africa feel that many social problems are due to interference from European governments, businesses and religions and a backlash of negative sentiment has begun to develop in recent years against the Western Culture and religion.

Table 12: List of African Religions

Kushite Religion	Bambara Religion	Igbo Religion
Kamitan (Ancient Egyptian) Religion	Bambuti Religion	Khol Religion
	Bandembu Religion	Langi Religion
	Banyakyusa Religion	Lovedu Religion
!Kung Religion	Banyakyusa Religion	Lugbara Religion
Acholi Religion	Banyamwezi Religion	Maasai Religion
Akamba Religion	Banyankore Religion	Mende Religion
Akhan Religion	Banyarwanda Religion	Nuer Religion
Akikuyu Religion	Banyoro Religion	Nupe Religion
Ashanti Religion	Barundi Religion	San Religion
Ateso Religion	Basukuma Religion	Shilluk Religion
Babemba Religion	Dinka Religion	Shona Religion
Bachagga Religion	Dogon Religion	Sotho Religion
Bacongo Religion	Edo Religion	Swazi Religion
Bafipa Religion	Ewe Religion	Tiv Religion
Baganda Religion	Fang Religion	Tswana Religion
Bagisu Religion	Fanti Religion	Western Africa
Bahaya Religion	Fon Religion	Xhosa Religion
Bahehe Religion	Ga Religion	Yoruba Religion
Baka Religion	Galla Religion	Zulu Religion
Baluba Religion		
Bamakonda Religion		Unknown Past Religions

Manifestations of African Religion in Latin America and the Caribbean

The religions of Latin America and the Caribbean are strongly rooted in African religion as a result of African peoples being brought to the Americas as slaves. These religions therefore reflect the slavery experiences (including but not limited to racism, exploitation and mistreatment) of the original African slaves and their descendants. They also reflect a mixture of traditions, including religious elements from the religions of the slave masters which were not in the original traditions brought from Africa. Some of the developments in the Americas included elements from Native American religions. One example of this is the spirituality of the African slaves who were brought to the Island of Puerto Rico in the Caribbean.

The first Africans actually arrived in Puerto Rico with Columbus in 1493 A.C.E as sailors. The African slave trade in Puerto Rico was not authorized by the Spanish government until 1510 A.C.E. The Taino Native American population were the native inhabitants of Puerto Rico and they were also enslaved by the Spaniards upon their arrival to the island. The enslavement and mistreatment of Taínos went on before and after slavery was permitted by the Spanish government. It was legally prohibited by a royal decree in 1542. However, the Spanish settlers (slave masters) continued to enslave them illegally. Since they were not physically suited for the heavy physical labor and violent clashes with European slavers as well as the rigors of European diseases, their numbers were reduced dramatically. The African slaves who were brought to the island of Puerto Rico, beginning in 1510 A.C.E., created a new culture as they mixed with the Taino Native American Population, creating an admixture of religious thought. The culture of Puerto Rico was further shaped by the amalgamation with the Spanish ruling class and the later Anglo-Americans. The Anglo-Americans who took control of the country imposed a form of racism that led to the development of a form of caste system. The almost extinct Native American population and those of (unmixed) African descent were segregated and discriminated against in favor of the mulatto population. However, even within this population, the darker skinned members were discriminated against in favor of lighter skinned members, who received the greater latitude of freedom in the general society. This policy of discrimination based on the shading of skin was instituted by the Europeans generally, but intensified when the USA took over Puerto Rico after the so called Spanish – American War.

In present day Puerto Rico, an independence movement has managed to prevent statehood. However, the majority of the population is pro-western. The society maintains an aspect of Creole[54] culture wherein the lighter skinned members of the population feel a superiority that is supported by preferential treatment from the Anglo society of the United States. It must be clear that in most, if not all of the groups brought over by slave masters, slavery destroyed traditional African secret societies and priesthoods.[205] Roman Catholicism was the only officially recognized religion in Puerto Rico as Puerto Rico was a colony of Spain and Roman Catholicism was the official religion of Spain also. However, most of the population practiced varied forms of religion which combined the African beliefs with Christian images and traditions. This situation was typical in other parts of the Caribbean and the Americas. Puerto Rico, like other Caribbean and American countries, has produced African scholars and African patriots.

Perhaps one of the best-known scholars in the field of African history and culture is Arturo Alfonso Schomburg. However, not many people know that he was born in Puerto Rico in 1874. He grew up in Puerto Rico and studied in the Dutch West Indies. When confronted by another student who challenged him by saying that peoples of African descent had not done anything significant in history, he countered with the achievements of those people of African descent on the island of Puerto Rico who had made such advances in the arts and writing that they had gained international recognition. This further spurred him on to travel the world seeking to document the achievements of Africans. He became a mentor to many 20th century Africentrists and is honored for amassing one of the largest and finest collections of books and evidences on the African contribution to humanity. By the time of his death in 1938, Arturo Alfonso Schomburg was recognized as a great scholar, humanist and African historian.

The African influence on Puerto Rican culture can be seen in such areas as the arts, food, music, dance, and language. For example, there is an African beat called *La Bomba,* that is still played especially within the circles of people of African descent and which has been recognized as an influence on latin music. The last enslaved Africans who came to the island were relatively young and came from Nigeria, Ghana, and Zaire.[206] Some African words that survive in the Puerto Rican language include:

- bembe – party
- bembas – lips
- guarapo – sugarcane juice
- mongo – limp

---

[54] **Creoles,** a name adopted by or applied to a number of ethnic groups in the New World who were descended from European colonists and/or African slaves. "Creole" can also refer to the language of such groups. Creoles," *Microsoft® Encarta® Africana.* ©&(p) 1999 Microsoft Corporation. All rights reserved.

The major African-derived religions of Latin American and Caribbean slaves include:

- Shango in Trinidad – Based on Yoruba Religion mixed with Christianity.

- Rastafarianism in Jamaica – based on Ethiopian Christianity and Judaism.

- Umbanda in Brazil – Based on Yoruba Religion mixed with Christianity

- Candomblé in Brazil – 3 Types all based on Yoruba Religion (Supreme Being with Orishas)

- Voodoo in Haiti – From Fon Vodun religion of Benin

- Santería in Cuba – Combination of Yoruba Religion and Christianity

The Common Fundamental Principles of African Religion

For many years, Westerners, specifically anthropologists, Christian missionaries and Muslims, did not regard African Religion as "true" religion. Muslims moving into Africa called the Africans *kaffirs*, or "unbelievers," which relates them as people who are atheistic, as opposed to having their own religion. Christians adopted the similar terms, and henceforth African religion came to be regarded as magic or superstition, fetishism or animism. If we look closely at the traditions of other African religions besides the Ancient Egyptian, we will discover that many, if not all, of the fundamental aspects of the highly evolved Kamitan religion that were later infused into the world religions can also be found in the African Religions of the past and present. Among the essential concepts common to all African religions are the following:

BLACK AFRICAN RELIGION (Sub-Saharan)	ANCIENT EGYPTIAN RELIGION (Corresponding name given to the same teaching in Kamit)
1. There is one God (Supreme Being)	1. Neter
2. That God expresses as Lesser divinities = gods and goddesses	2. Neteru
3. God and the universe are One =All objects in the universe are alive and divine	3. Neberdjer
4. Seek to discover the Menaing of Life.	4. Shetaut Neter
5. No separation between Sacred and Secular	5. Neter – Neterit, Heka - Hekat
6. Human beings have fallen from divinity due to vice	6. Isfet
7. Human beings can raise themselves up (discover the Divine) through virtue	7. Maakheru
8. Social order achieved through Ubuntu (African Spiritual Humanism)	8. Maat
9. Divine monarchy - King and Queen (A) administer secular (cultural) duties such as protecting the populace and administering equal justice for all and (B) (non-secular duties) officiate at spiritual ceremonies (as heads of the national religion)	9. Peraah (Pharaoh)
10. Men and Women can serve as priests and priestesses with equal rights and privilages.	10. Hm and Hmt
11. Highest Goal of Life = Mortal humans discover god and become godlike	11. Akhu

The Stages of African Religion

The Stages of African Religion		
Program of Religion (Universal Religion) 3-Stages	African Religion	Sema (Smai) Tawi (Egyptian Yoga) Based on the teachings of the Temple of Aset (Aswan, Egypt)
Myth	Storytelling (myths – proverbs)	Listening (to spiritual scriptures, teachings)
Ritual	Ritual (ceremony – Virtuous living)	Reflection (on & practice of the teachings)
Mysticism/Metaphysics	Ecstasy (Transcendental experience)	Meditation (on the teachings)

The complete program of religion has three steps which are necessary for the goal of religion, to discover and experience God, to be realized. Any spiritual movement that includes these steps can be called "religion" regardless of the name that it may be given by the culture that practices them. These steps include *Myth, Ritual* and *Mysticism* or *Metaphysics*. The table above shows how these three steps or stages manifest in African Religion (2nd column) and also how that same program is enjoined in the practice of Egyptian Yoga (3rd column). Egyptian Yoga (Sema Tawi)[207] may be thought of as the advanced disciplines to be practiced in order to promote the highest goal of the religious movement.

In African Religion, storytelling achieves the purpose of transmitting myths which contain the basic concepts of human identity as part of a culture, and offers insight into the nature of the universe. Myths also contain a special language of self-knowledge and also proverbs that provide moral education for an ethical society. Rituals are formal (ceremony) and informal (virtuous living) practices which allow a human being to come into harmony within themselves, the environment and the Spirit. This movement leads to an ecstatic experience which transcends time and space and allows a human being to discover and experience the Divine.

The African Definition for the Word "Religion"

Most African religions do not have a world that is correspondent to the western term *religion*. However, there are terms to describe the various activities, rituals, and traditions of the religious process. The African culture that developed in northeast Africa (Ancient Egyptian) did have a name for the practices and concepts of religion. In the Ancient Egyptian texts, a term appears which is used to describe the religious process as well as the disciplines to attain entry into knowledge of the higher aspects of spirituality, i.e. religion: *Shetaut Neter.*

Shetaut Neter
(Secrets about the Divine Self)

The term above is derived from ⬠𓅃 *Sheta* (Mystery), ⬠𓏏𓊵 *Sheta* (Hidden) and 𓏤 *Neter* (The Divinity). Thus we can now see why the Ancient Egyptian religion has come to be referred to as the "Egyptian Mysteries." Actually, this term is more closely approximated by the Chinese term "Tao." The term Tao in Taoism relates to the "Way of Nature." The Ancient Egyptian term relates to the quality of divinity which is "hidden." Thus, in Kamitan spirituality it means "the process of uncovering or discovering what is hidden or unknown about the Spirit - (Divine Self-Goddess-God)

The Concept of The Supreme Being and the Gods and Goddesses in African Religion

Pa Neter

In the Kamit religion, Pa-Neter means "The Supreme Being" and neteru, 𓏤𓏤𓏤, means "the gods and goddesses or cosmic forces in Creation." Also, the word "neteru" refers to creation itself. So, neter-u emanates from Neter. Creation is nothing but Supreme Being who has assumed various forms or neteru: trees, cake, bread, human beings, metal, air, fire, water, animals, planets, space, electricity, etc. The neteru are cosmic forces emanating from the Supreme Being. This is a profound teaching which should be reflected upon constantly so that the mind may become enlightened to its deeper meaning and thereby discover the Divinity in nature. The Divine Self is not only in Creation but is the very essence of every human being as well. Therefore, the substratum of every human being is in reality God as well. The task of authentic spiritual practice such as Yoga is to discover this essential nature within one's own heart. This can occur if one reflects upon this teaching and realizes its meaning by discovering its reality in the deepest recesses of one's own experience. When this occurs, the person who has attained this level of self-discovery is referred to as having become enlightened. They have discovered their true, divine nature. They have discovered their oneness with the Divine Self.

African religions recognize powers that emanate from the Supreme Being that circulate in the universe like a kind of *life force*. For example, the Dogon worship Amma, the Supreme Being, whose vital force, operates throughout the universe, and is called *Nyama*. The Igbo of southeastern Nigeria call the Supreme Being Chiukwu or Chineke, and the life force that operates in the universe is known as *Chi*[55]. Another example is to be found in Ancient Egyptian religion with the concept of Neberdjer, the Supreme Being, and Sekhem as the life force which operates throughout the universe. In this manner, the life force itself is to be understood as an intelligent cosmic energy which pervades all of Creation, sustaining it at all times and thereby also unifying it as well.

In African religion the Supreme Being is viewed as a transcendental essence which cannot be defined and therefore cannot be approached directly. One important reason given as to why the lesser spirit powers are invoked while the Supreme Being is seldom invoked or the recipient of offerings is that the Supreme Being, as the ultimate and all-pervasive power in the universe, already owns all and can therefore, receive nothing. For this reason representations of the Supreme Being do not occur in African religions, only the manifesting aspects are given form. These are used to promote the religious movement of the individual by allowing the individual to approach and understand a concrete aspect of the transcendental Spirit. This understanding of course relates to the higher, mystical aspect of religion. Thus, in African religion we see a consistent pattern of structure in the way in which the Spirit is presented across the panorama of African nations. This structure is simple, but extremely profound in conceptualization: The transcendental Supreme Being manifests as lesser or associated powers that emanate from the ultimate source (the same Supreme Being). There are also human beings that, through virtue, become higher powers, i.e. gods and goddesses. Thus, the higher concept behind the practice of ancestor worship in African religion is not of worshipping the souls of the departed relatives, but of propitiating the saints (deified forbears, i.e. canonized) and sages of the past who have elevated themselves and who have become part of the cosmic forces of the Supreme Being. This pattern holds true for African Religions including Ancient Egyptian religion. Again, this is the same course taken by the Western religions, although they do not admit nor profess to view the angels and saints in this way, in practice, many of the followers of those religions worship the angels and saints in the same fashion as within African Religion.

In most African religions, including the Ancient Egyptian, masks, headdress, costumes, the impersonation of lesser divinities are used as means to attract and propitiate the lesser spirits. Statues are also made of the

---

[55] Which is incidentally also the name for the life force in Chinese and Japanese spirituality.

lesser spirits as symbols (and not as idols in the Western sense of the concept). These are also used to attract and propitiate the lesser spirits. Again, these representations are not made of the Supreme Being.

Since the African Religious concept holds that God and the Universe are one, it follows thst there is no conflict between what is secular or sacred and the current, ongoing conflict in the West over Creation or Evolution as the cause behind the universe is inappropriate.

The Consistent Pattern of Structure in African Religion:

Supreme Being
⇕
Gods and Goddesses
↑
Deified Ancestors
↑
Mortal Human Beings

Human beings may attain the status of higher being through a life of virtue and or righteous leadership. This concept is accentuated in the religions of the peoples of East, Central, and Southern Africa, as well as the ancient Northeast (Nubia-Egypt) Africa. It is acknowledged within the philosophy that many of the lesser spirits in the religions of those areas once lived as human beings, often as kings. This is especially true of the Buganda of Uganda and the Shona in Zimbabwe.[56] Also, Ancient Egypt is to be included in this category, since there was a high teaching related to the Sheps and the Akhus. Shep means venerated ancestor and Akhu means enlightened ancestor, someone who has attained spiritual enlightenment. Also, the Pharaonic system of Ancient Egypt had as one of its main tenets that the kings and queens became divinities upon their death. So Ancient Egyptian religion and the religions of other African peoples appear to follow close parallels in many fundamental aspects of religious philosophy as well as the general program of religious movement.

Table 13: Examples of African Religions with the System of Supreme Being and Lesser Divinities[57]

African Religious System	Supreme Being	Lesser Spirits (Gods and Goddesses
Kamit (Ancient Egypt)	✓	✓
Nubia (Kush-Ethiopia)	✓	✓
Bakele	✓	✓
Bambara	✓	✓
Bantu	✓	✓
Buganda	✓	✓
Dahomey	✓	✓
Dinka	✓	✓
Dogon	✓	✓
Dokos	✓	✓
Edjou	✓	✓
Fon	✓	✓
Galla	✓	✓
Gugsa	✓	✓
Igbo	✓	✓
Jola	✓	✓
Makoosa	✓	✓
Masai	✓	✓
Nuer	✓	✓
Shekani	✓	✓
Yoruba	✓	✓

---

[56] *Microsoft® Encarta® Africana.* ©1999 Microsoft Corporation. All rights reserved.
[57] This is a partial list only since the list is quite extensive.

The "High God" and The Gods and Goddesses of Ancient Egypt

There were several "High God" systems in Ancient Egyptian religion as in other African religions. This is the next lowest position in the hierarchy of divinity after the Supreme Being. The term "High God (or Goddess)" means that the highest God or Goddess within that particular system of theology is considered to be the original deity from which all others emanated as cosmic forces. Thus, in the Asarian religion of Ancient Egypt, Asar is known as *Pa Neter* or *The God* (High God) and Creation is composed of the cosmic forces, *neters* or gods and goddesses, which originates from Asar. It is important to understand that the High Gods and Goddesses as well as the Egyptian Trinities originated from the same transcendental Supreme Being which was without name or form, but was referred to as *Neter Neteru* (Neter of Neters - Supreme Being above all gods and goddesses) and *Neb-er-tcher* (Neberdjer – All-encompassing Divinity).

In this manner, the initiate (in virtually all African religions) is to understand that all of the gods and goddesses are in reality symbols, with names and forms, which represent the Divine in the varied manifest forms of nature. This produces a two aspected format of religion in which there is a *personal* aspect and a *transpersonal* aspect of God. The personal aspect is fixed in time and space with a name and form. This form is readily understood by the masses of human beings with ordinary spiritual awareness and is used in myths and stories. The second aspect, the *transpersonal* side, points our interest towards that which lies beyond the symbolic form. This is the *unmanifest* form of the Divine as it is expressed in the mystical teachings of religious mythology. Thus, the High God is a personal symbol or representation, with a name and form, of the nameless, formless, unmanifest and transcendental Supreme Being. The High God or Goddess usually appears alone and gives rise to male and female gods and goddesses and human beings. One important reason given as to why the lesser spirit powers are invoked while the Supreme Being is seldom invoked or the recipient of offerings is that the Supreme Being, as the ultimate and all-pervasive power in the universe, already owns all and can therefore, receive nothing.

Single Supreme, Transcendental Being
(unmanifest realm beyond time and space - names and forms)
⇩
High God or Goddess
⇩
Lesser Gods and Goddesses

The Concept of God and Creation According to Ancient Egyptian Religion and Mystical Philosophy

The term *"Trinity"* was misunderstood by the Orthodox Catholic Christians and, because of this misunderstanding, some Gnostic groups even ridiculed them. However, upon closer examination it will be discovered that the Ancient Egyptian Trinity, which was later adopted by the Christians and Hindus, is nothing less than a development on the same system of polytheistic monotheism that characterizes African religion. The three in one metaphor was ancient by the time it was adopted by Catholicism. It was a term used to convey the idea of different aspects of the one reality. This same idea occurs in Egyptian as well as in Indian mythology. However, for deeper insights into the mystical meaning of the Trinity, we must look to Ancient Egypt. In Egyptian mythology, the Trinity was represented as three *metaphysical neters* or gods. They represent the manifestation of the unseen principles that support the universe and the visible aspects of God. The main Egyptian Trinity is composed of Amun, Ra and Ptah. Amun means that which is hidden and unintelligible, the underlying reality which sustains all things. Ra represents the subtle matter of creation as well as the mind. Ptah represents the visible aspect of Divinity, the phenomenal universe (gross physical matter). The Ancient Egyptian "Trinity" is also known as a manifestation of *Nebertcher* (Neberdjer*), the* "all encompassing" Divinity. Thus, the term Nebertcher is equivalent to the Vedantic Brahman, the Buddhist Dharmakaya and the Taoist Tao. The Ancient Egyptian text reads as follows:

"Nebertcher: Everything is Amun-Ra-Ptah, three in one."

The following passage from the *Hymns to Amun* (papyrus at Leyden) sums up the Ancient Egyptian understanding of the Trinity concept in creation, and that which transcends it.

He whose name is hidden is *AMUN*. *RA* belongeth to him as his face, and his body is *PTAH*.

Thus, within the mysticism of the Ancient Egyptian Trinity, the teaching of the triad of human consciousness (seer-seen-sight) is also found. Amun, the hidden aspect, is called the "eternal witness." This witness is one of the most important realizations in mystical philosophy, because it points to the existence of a transcendental awareness that lies beyond the conscious level of the mind. This mystical concept of the "witness" is also to be found in Indian philosophy under the Yoga teaching of *Sakshin* and the Buddhist teaching of *Mindfulness*. Sakshin is the "fourth" state of consciousness, beyond the waking, dream and dreamless sleep states. It is the goal of all mystics to achieve awareness with this state (Enlightenment).

The visible "gods" and "goddesses" with a name, form and other attributes are considered to be emanations of the one God, Nebertcher, meaning that which is without name, form or attributes (absolute). In the same way the Indian Trinity (Brahma, Shiva, and Vishnu) arises out of Brahman, the Absolute. They are responsible for the direction (management) of creation at every moment. In Indian mythology, each male aspect of the Trinity of Brahma - Shiva - Vishnu had his accompanying female aspect or manifesting energy: Saraswati - Kali - Lakshmi, respectively. Similarly, in the Egyptian system of gods and goddesses we have:

Male	Female
Amun	Amenit
Ra	Rai
Ptah	Sekhmet

Changes in the Way Lesser Beings (Spirits) are Viewed in African Religion Over Time

European and African historians have discovered many changes in the understanding and worship of lesser beings (gods and goddesses and deified human beings) in African Religion, over time. Some changes have been correlated to the emergence of agriculture, metal and even the slave trade. For example, the emergence of the earth goddess Ala religious sect among the Igbo people correlates to the increasing importance of agriculture. Among the Congo people of Central Africa and Jola people of Senegal, certain new religious sects related to lesser beings emerged in relation to the slave trade. They developed out of a need to explain the adversity that had befallen them, foreign conquest, enslavement, and the challenges of colonialism.[58]

Therefore, when studying specific African religions, the history of the peoples who developed the religion must be taken into account. Local variations should be evaluated as to their meaning for discerning the nature of African religion only in the context of general principles which are common to all the religions and exhibit the qualities that denote them as being ancient, preceding the historical influences from outside factors. The major outside factors influencing the development of African Religion include Judaism, Christianity, Islam, Arab slave trade, European slave trade, colonialism, and neocolonialism. So this means that when studying African culture and religion, caution must be exercised so as not to misinterpret the higher original aspects of African religion and culture with those that were engendered by disruptions, and then later on became assimilated into the culture. A superficial study would lead to the erroneous conclusion that all African Religion and its derivatives in the Diaspora are intact, correct or authentic forms of the practice of African Religion. Thus, careful studies, taking into account the disruptive factors above, must be undertaken.

It is also important to note that the practices of African religion, which constantly seek to bring a balance between the spirit and the material, seeing them as essentially the same, is still misunderstood by most Westerners. Many Africans who believe in the pantheistic view of African Religions have also accepted the Western religions, but this is not seen as a conflict since they inherently believe in one God. However, this belief of the Western traditions denies the divinity that is to be discovered in the realm of time and space, the realm of human events, due to the sharp demarcation between heaven and earth. In this philosophy there is a separation between God and humanity. So within the framework of orthodox Christianity, even if they see Jesus as an intermediary, a lesser spirit as the gods and goddesses of African religion, they do not see him as being able to fulfill all their needs in all situations. Thus, there is still a need for the variety of gods and goddesses in African religion. So while there is a commitment to God by many African converts to the Western religions, there remains a need to seek the assistance of minor deities to resolve concerns of a worldly nature. So there are many followers of religions like Islam, Christianity and Judaism who also continue to

---

[58] *Microsoft® Encarta® Africana.* ©1999 Microsoft Corporation. All rights reserved.

consult diviners and traditional healers, attend traditional rituals and participate in other aspects of African religion.

Manifestations of African Religious Expression and Transmission to the Next Generation

African religious thought expresses through oral traditions and the recitation of myth, and also through discussions between elders and the current generation. Rituals are a powerful means of transference of religious culture from generation to generation. They form an important part of African religion. Rituals are designed to attract and propitiate the spirit powers. Libations of millet beer, palm wine or water, and sometimes also foodstuffs are usually offered as part of a ritual. The libation is believed to augment the power of the spoken word. Less prevalent is the practice of animal sacrifice, which is believed to release the Life Force of the animal to augment the Life Force of the person promoting the ritual.

The concept of the divine word or *Hekau* is an extremely important part of Ancient Egyptian religion and is instructive in the study of all African religion. Some of the few differences between Ancient Egyptian religion and other African religions were the extensive development of the philosophy related to the "written word" in Ancient Egyptian religion and the expansive social infrastructure that allowed the development of advanced monumental architecture.

As explained earlier, the word religion is translated as Shetaut Neter in the Ancient African language of Kamit. These Shetaut (mysteries- rituals, wisdom, philosophy) about the Neter (Supreme Being) are related in the ⬚⬚ ııı *Shetit* or writings related to the hidden teaching. Those writings are referred to as 𓏞𓐰𓏤 *Medu Neter* or "Divine Speech," the writings of the god Djehuti (Ancient Egyptian god of the Hekau or divine word), and also refers to any hieroglyphic texts or inscriptions generally. The term Medu Neter makes use of a special hieroglyph, 𓌃 , which means "*medu*" or "staff - walking stick-words." This means that speech is the support for the Divine, 𓌙 . Thus, just as the staff supports an elderly person, the hieroglyphic writing (the word) is a prop (staff) which sustains the Divine in the realm of time and space. That is, the Divine writings contain the wisdom that enlightens us about the Divine, 𓊵𓏛𓄿𓂝𓏥𓌃 *Shetaut Neter.*

If Medu Neter is mastered, then the spiritual aspirant becomes 𓌳𓂝𓐰𓐰𓅱𓂋𓏤 Maakheru or true of thought, word and deed, that is, purified in body, mind and soul. The symbol Medu is static while the symbol of Kheru is dynamic.

This term (Maakheru or Maa kheru) uses the glyph 𓊪 kheru which is a rudder – oar (rowing), symbol of voice, meaning that purification occurs when the righteous movement of the word occurs, that is, when it is used (rowing-movement) to promote virtue, order, peace, harmony and truth. So Medu Neter is the potential word and Maa kheru is the perfected word.

The hieroglyphic texts (Medu Neter), which are the spiritual scriptures in general, become useful in the process of religion (Maakheru) when they are used as 𓎛𓂝𓅱𓏤𓀁 hekau - the Ancient Egyptian "Words of Power" when the word is 𓎛𓋴𓏤𓀁 Hesi, chanted and 𓈝𓂝𓏤 Shmai- sung and thereby one performs ★ 𓀀 **or** ★ 𓅓𓀢 Dua or worship of the Divine. The divine word allows the speaker to control the gods and goddesses, i.e. the cosmic forces. This concept is really based on the idea that human beings are in reality higher order beings (neteru-gods and goddesses), and this attainment becomes possible if they learn about the nature of the universe and elevate themselves through virtue and wisdom.

Rites of Passage

"Rites of Passage" or "transition rites" are important formalized means of transferring religious information and culture. Boys and girls are put through programs that lead them to understand and discover their place in life, society and their developing spiritual consciousness. The government or other such

194

institutions of the particular country do not charter most forms of religious instruction in traditional African religion. The rites of passage provide support for the initiates as they are socialized into the culture and at the same time are led to become productive members of the society. It engenders a sense of belonging, purpose and cultural identity to the initiate, all of which promote social harmony and a respect for tradition, as well as a reverence for the religion. Some societies remove the lower front incisors of the initiates during initiation rites. There is no evidence of this practice in Kamit. Removal of clothing and or ornaments may also be used to signify the loss or change of their previous status and the emergence into the new.

Male circumcision and female excision are also commonly practiced in some rites of passage. It should be noted that male circumcision and or female excision are not necessary or advisable practices, nor are they necessarily related to a spiritual perspective in life. Some societies engage in the practice as a ritual of practical necessity, for the purpose of hygiene, while others have attached to it, the concept of separating boys and girls from their childhood. In the case of the female, this practice has been used as a form of control over women by diminishing or eradicating their sexual capacity. This form of mutilation leaves not only emotional scars, but also a legacy that lasts for an entire lifetime including pain and sexual impotence (sexually unresponsiveness, frigidity). While it is true that the Ancient Egyptians circumcised the boys in the later period of the history, it is incorrect to say that this was an ancient tradition of Ancient Egypt. The existence of uncircumcised male mummies from the Old Kingdom proves that circumcision was not practiced generally in the early period of Ancient Egyptian history. When circumcision was performed, in some cases the procedure was merely cutting a slit on the foreskin of the penis enough to draw blood but not cutting it off completely. Also, there is no evidence of female circumcision, clitorectomy, or any excision at all in any Ancient Egyptian female mummies. Therefore, male circumcision and or female excision should not be considered as ancient or general practices of the African culture. So, male circumcision was used in Ancient Egypt at given periods, but not in the beginning, and even when it was performed, it was not generally throughout the entire society. At some points it did form part of a rites of passage, being performed close to the time of entering apprenticeship.

Rites of Passage in the Kamitan Society

In ancient Kamitan society, the formal Rites of Passage encompassed the movement from childhood into two main levels of social status leading to adulthood. These levels are related to the child's vocational training for later service to society. A child might be started in school sometime between the ages of 5 to 10 in accordance with his or her maturity. Thus, the first rite of passage is movement into primary school for 4 years. The child would learn to:
- read and write,
  - the exercises used to teach the reading and writing were the wisdom teachings of the great sages like Ptahotep, as well as the great stories with moral teachings.
- respect elders
- develop discipline in their actions (diligence was strictly imposed especially in the writing exercises that were used).

From here the child goes directly to an apprenticeship program. This might be in the Temple, the stables or other areas of society, to be trained in an occupation that would be useful to themselves and the nation. When the apprenticeship period is over, the student, now a teenager, moves into (graduates) to a full position that marks the passage from adolescence into adulthood. So the rites of passage was highly sophisticated and based on training to be a literate and productive member of society, having a valuable trade to offer by the age of 20. So clearly, in order to produce powerful young people who will some day rule the nation, it is important that the passages of early life be more than rituals or the child learning the ways of the elders. They should have moral and ethical training, as well as be taught reading, writing, and discipline and respect for righteous elders. The Temple and its ranks of clergy can be discerned from the following outline. The biography of the high priest Bekenchons, who served and died under Ramses II[208] provides an indication of the degrees as well as the years of training leading to the position of High Priest in his time.

1. 4 years in primary school
   a. beginning at age 5

2. 11 years education in one of the royal stables (apprenticeship period)

3. 4 Years as *Uab* priest of Amun,

4. 12 years as *divine father* priest.

5. 15 years served as *third* priest,

6. 12 years as *second* prophet.

7. Finally, in his fifty-ninth year, the king raised him to be "first prophet of Amun and chief of the prophets of all the gods."

General parameters of Rites of Passage

- Segregation from the ordinary events and duties of life for a period of time.
- Marks changes in stages of life (from the old to the new).
- Denotes new responsibilities in life.
- Initiates may be forcibly moved geographically, or made to strip themselves of clothing, hair, or other physical markings of their previous selves.
- Initiates may undergo physical trials.
- After the rites of passage program the initiates then reemerge, usually through formal ritual procedures, with a redefined identity and a changed social status (from death of the old to rebirth of the new) into the normal social fabric.
- The ritual of rites of passage should mark the culmination of the training of the initiate who will now assume a position of full participation in the social and economic activities of the community.

Religion and Dance

Dance was an important aspect of the religious festival-ritual in Ancient Egyptian religion and continues to be so in present day African religion. The dance may propitiate the spirits, and facilitate entry into an altered state of mind that is more sensitive to experiencing the spirit (higher consciousness). The !Kung of southern Africa use dance for prayer, healing and to elevate the inner Life Force, which is equivalent to the Ancient Egyptian practice of elevating the Arat Sekhem (Serpent Power, also known as Kundalini in India).

Evil, Suffering, Sin, and the Devil in African Religion

African religion (including Kamit) ascribes evil and suffering to disruptive spirits and unrighteous living. These are explained as beings called tricksters. In Kamit the disruptive spirits are referred to as *sebau*. Also, some humans who use special powers for harming others or to advance some personal gain are also blamed for maladies. Unrighteous conduct in life is a source for adversity, the experience of evil and suffering. Exú is a trickster of the Yoruba tradition and acts as the messenger god who causes strife by distorting messages between the human realm (prayers) and the Spirit realm, due to a dislike of a world that is too orderly. Exú was identified as the devil by missionaries. Actually, Exú, like the jackal character of Dogon religion, is actually a symbol of passion, desire, zest for life, curiosity and an adventurous nature. These qualities are not evil; they are expressions of a certain character. For the listener or observer, the dramatization of the consequences of the actions of such personalities through their myths develops the capacity of discernment between choices of righteousness and unrighteousness, and outcomes that lead to harmony and peace versus outcomes that lead to adversity and disturbance. The character Set in Ancient Egyptian religion, a symbol of the lower self, represents the energy of uncontrolled egoism and brute force. He was never considered as a devil, but many scholars and researchers of Ancient Egyptian mythology have made the error of considering him as the devil. Some even see him as the prototype for the devil in the Judeo-Christian and Islamic traditions. However, Set was never seen as the "source of evil itself" until the late Dynastic Period, which was when the Jewish people were living in Egypt. This notion of a personality who causes evil in human beings is extremely dangerous because it allows people with poor moral development to shirk responsibility for their actions. This is a fundamental difference between the African concept of evil and that of the orthodox Western religions. The African concept relates adversity to passion and a movement away from virtue while the Western religious traditions relate the problem of evil to a movement away from virtue under the influence of a demon (the devil). The African concept retains human responsibility while the Western model assigns the blame to an outside force.

In contrast to African religious belief, later Christian and Jewish theologians conceptualized the devil as being equated with "the supreme spirit of evil" who, for all time, has been ruling over a kingdom of all evil spirits, and is in constant opposition to God. The word "devil" is derived from the Latin *diabolus*, and from the Greek *diabolos,* which are adjectives that meaning *slanderous.* It is also used in ancient Greek as a noun to identify a specific person as being a slanderer. The term "diabolos" was used for the *Septuagint* or Greek translation of the Jewish Bible, not referring to human beings, but in order to translate the Hebrew word *ha-satan* (the satan). This expression was originally used as the title of one of the members of the divine court whose function was to act as a roving spy for God. Satan was supposed to have gathered intelligence about human beings during his travels on earth, much like the Hindu character Narada, a Sage who would relate information about the happenings on earth to Lord Vishnu (the Supreme Being).

At one point, Satan also meant "an opponent" and not a particular devil being with actual existence. At around the 6th century B.C.E., Satan appears in the Old Testament as an individual angel who is subordinate to God. Gradually, as Jewish and Christian tradition developed around this idea, Satan became known as a personality who was the source of all evil, and was responsible for leading human beings into sin. In later Jewish tradition, and therefore also in early Christian thought, this title became a proper name. Satan was then seen as a personified adversary, not only of human beings, but also primarily of God. The development of the devil as a personified evil adversary probably arose from the early Jewish and Christian association with the dualistic theologies of Persia as well as the dualistic philosophy of Zoroaster and the misunderstanding of the Egyptian character *Set*. In some segments of Jewish theology, the idea of Satan developed as an "evil impulse." Human beings are seen as susceptible to a force, which is outside of and separate from them. Therefore, with this view it is possible for a human being to become "possessed" by the evil force and coerced into wrongdoing. Jesus was seen as the savior who broke the power of the devil over human beings. As stated above, this view is dangerous because it negates the power of the human mind to control itself, the power of free will. It also opens the door to superstition and imagination about evil supernatural beings as being real and existing in fact, rather than understanding the symbolism behind these mythic portrayals.

It is important to note that in both the Christian and Jewish systems, the dualism concerning Satan, that is, of him being the antithesis of God, is without merit, since he is ultimately subject to God. This aspect is not emphasized in popular discourses. This view is more closely in tune with the original idea in the Ancient Egyptian teaching. Otherwise, if Satan were the true adversary of God, this would mean that God is not omnipotent, because there is a being who can limit his power. So the teaching related to Satan must be correctly understood in order to avoid error and misunderstanding in one's spiritual movement.

Evil must be understood as the actions of people who are ignorant of the higher spiritual reality within themselves. Such actions will be based on egoism, anger, hatred, greed, lust, jealousy, etc. Sin must therefore be understood as the idea of separation between one's self and God, the state of ignorance about one's own spiritual essence (egoism). Each person must take responsibility for their actions while striving to engender a sense of Divine Presence within themselves. When this occurs, the very basis of sin and ignorance is dispelled from the mind. At this stage of spiritual development there is transcendence of the notion of good and evil. Understanding all to be part of oneself, there is no need to debate about one's treatment of others. One's treatment of others becomes a spontaneous act based on love, compassion, forgiveness and magnanimity, much like there is instant forgiveness of one's teeth when they bite one's own tongue. This is the true goal of religion— to rise above ignorance (evil, egoism).

In Matthew Chapter 6, verses 9-13, Jesus instructs his followers as to how they should pray to God. The end of the prayer (verse 13) contains a peculiar statement, which seems, on the surface, to be very contradictory.

> 9. After this manner therefore pray ye: Our Father who art in heaven, Hallowed be thy name.
> 10 Thy kingdom come. Thy will be done on earth, as [it is] in heaven.
> 11 Give us this day our daily bread.
> 12 And forgive us our debts, as we forgive our debtors.
> 13 And lead us not into temptation, but deliver us from evil: For thine is the kingdom, and the
> power, and the glory, forever. Amen.

The ordinary Christian doctrine almost always presupposes the existence of an evil entity ordinarily referred to as the devil. However, verse 13 seems to refer to God as the source of temptation (evil). Thus, the prayer is implying that God has control over if whether or not one will fall into temptation (evil). Why should the asking of not being led into temptation be directed towards God and not the devil? The only answer, which is possible from a mystical point of view, is that God is the source of both evil and good. More accurately, God sustains Creation, and Creation is the venue where good and evil can exist. However, human beings always have a choice to follow the path of good or of evil. Then this understanding also leads to the conclusion that there is no devil as such, only evil or negative thoughts and actions. This teaching reflects the understanding and subtle exposition by the Christian Sages of the highly advanced teaching known as non-duality. This is an understanding that in reality the Supreme Being has no rivals or contenders. The Supreme Being is Absolute and Supreme, because {He/She} is the only reality behind good, as well as evil. In reality God transcends these two concepts which the mind has created for the purpose of understanding and explaining human activities. In the final analysis, an advanced spiritual aspirant must understand that there is no outside force that pushes an individual to evil actions. Evil is an expression of the level of the lack of understanding of one's true divine nature (God, Supreme Being), just as darkness is a manifestation of the degree to which the sun is absent.

A serious follower of the mystical teachings must develop a keen understanding of the true meaning of sin and its implications. Sinful acts are those acts *you* perform which carry you away from the discovery of your true being. They are characterized by pettiness, greed, anger, hard-heartedness, hatred, egoism, infatuation, etc. Virtuous acts are those acts *you* perform which move you forward towards integration of your personality and an eventual merging of your individual ego with the Cosmic Self, the Supreme Being. Virtue implies developing peace, contentment, selflessness, and finally, self-discovery. Virtuous acts are characterized by peacefulness, kindness, selflessness, sharing, giving, universal love, forgiveness, serenity and other lofty qualities.

From this mystical perspective, that which takes you away from Divine-realization is demoniac (sinful, satanic), while that which brings you closer to Divine-realization is divine. Hence, there is no Jesus-like "savior" outside of yourself, and likewise, there is no personality called *"the devil"* that exists in fact as a distinct personality outside of yourself. The thoughts and actions you choose are what you classify as either divine or demoniac. Therefore, your fate lies with the thoughts and actions by which you choose to live. Your present ego-personality is the creation of your past actions, feelings, thoughts and experiences.

Thus, the concept of the devil is not an indigenous African development. It is an infused notion that was brought in with Western religion, and which has been inherited by subsequent generations within those African communities practicing the Western religions in whole or in part. In this context, the Trickster spirit represents the forces of chaos that are unleashed by human ignorance and lack of mental discrimination between righteousness and unrighteousness. So the fate of every human being rests in their own hands and they must work to overcome the adversities and sufferings they themselves have engendered.

Ancestor Worship

Ancestor Worship may be defined as reverence that is granted to deceased relatives because they are believed to have influence on events in the world of the living or, less frequently, because they are believed to have attained the status of gods. In Kamitan Spirituality the correlate term is *uashu shepsu*. It means the honoring of venerated departed souls, souls who were virtuous. It is akin to the concept of saints such as those in the Christian tradition, who are prayed to for assistance in coping with worldly affairs. This concept is related to the cultural aspect of honoring elders and ancestors as a matter of respect. Further, it is a matter of promoting positive feeling towards the past through ritual and mental attitude, and making a bridge for prosperity in the future, for oneself in the hereafter as well as for the future on earth for the living descendants.

So there is a spiritual component, and also a cultural component, promoting harmony and continuity in society. The name of the deceased is remembered and food offerings are made to them at their tomb sites, which act as chapels. However, within the chapels, the ceremony becomes transformed into a worship of the Divine Self, since the divinity who presides over the chapel is understood to be the underlying essence of all souls, as well as the objective of all souls. Many examples of this can be seen all over Kamit, especially in the texts and images of worship of the tombs of the nobles and royalty.

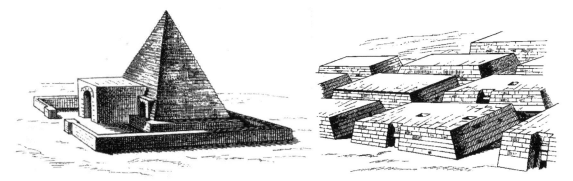

Figure 41: Above-left Pyramid tomb of the Old Kingdom Period.

Figure 42: Above-right Mastaba tomb of Giza area.

The term *Pyramid Text* is used because some of the kings from the Old Kingdom period inscribed *Prt m Hru* texts on the walls of their tombs. Mastabas (an Arab name for "low, long stone buildings") were used later, to the end of the 6th Dynasty. These structures were built to contain the body of the deceased, but also as places were friends and relatives could make offerings for the Ka (soul) of the deceased and utter Hekau (spiritual words of power) for the well being of the deceased and themselves. After the Pre-Dynastic graves, wooden coffins were used. These wooden coffins were followed by the use of sarcophagi (a stone coffin, often inscribed or decorated with sculpture.)

Possession by Spirits

Spirit possession is practiced by some African religions. The Fon people of Benin and the Yoruba of Nigeria believe that a spirit enters into the body of a devotee and uses the body, making it move, act and speak according to the spirit's influence. This allows the spirit to communicate with those gathered at the ritual through the possessed person. Possession by spirits is an idea often associated with ancestor worship. It is believed to be a form of intimate contact that can occur between human beings and a divinity during a ritual of trance. In its highest sense the communion is with a divine ancestor, someone who has become godlike. However, most practices in modern times involve the veneration of departed souls. During this time a divine spirit is believed to be able to take possession of the worshiper. The trance is often induced by rhythmic chanting, drumming, dance, and other techniques such as drugs, which are sometimes used to facilitate an altered state of consciousness.

In other religions of Africa, such as the Ancient Egyptian, lesser spirits converse with the devotee through visions and dreams, but do not possess the body of the devotees. In fact, the Kamitan concept of Words of Power allows the human being to actually control the supernatural (cosmic) forces instead of being controlled by them. "Controlling" the cosmic forces means realizing that one is in touch with the Supreme Being who is the source and ultimate abode of all powers. In the Kamitan concept of the Neteru there is no idea of allowing any spirits to take possession of the worshipper. Rather, it is incumbent upon the worshipper to take control of the discarnate forces and exert authority over them and thereby take the rightful place as master over them. The following Kamitan proverbs provide insight into the philosophy of spirits in relation to human beings.

"Salvation is the freeing of the soul from its bodily fetters; becoming a God through knowledge and wisdom; controlling the forces of the cosmos instead of being a slave to them;

subduing the lower nature and through awakening the higher self, ending the cycle of rebirth and dwelling with the Neteru who direct and control the Great Plan."

"Yield not to emotion, for there are discarnate forces around us who desire emotional existence. In the heat of passion one surrenders to the influence of these, ill health and unwise living results. Through firm instruction one can master one's emotions and these forces; in this, make them serve one. Thus the slave becomes the master."

The Pyramid texts, the oldest known extensive spiritual writings of Kamit and the world, speak of consuming the universal cosmic forces (neteru), literally consuming them. This is the concept of the Eucharist in which one is becoming the totality of what is consumed. In other words, the powers or energies of these lower beings (neteru) are to be assimilated and mastered by the worshipper (initiate). The initiate is thus transformed from the lower form of consciousness, whereby they exist as an ordinary mortal human being with disintegrated consciousness, in a state of weakness, to higher consciousness which is imbued with all the powers of the neteru. Thus, when all of these forces are brought together, they transform the initiate into a whole being, possessing all faculties, knowledge and capacity.

In modern times, these mystical practices and concepts have degraded in African religion due to many factors, namely slavery, colonization, disruption of African culture and tribal secret societies. Oftentimes, only the knowledge of the ritual remains and the original purpose, being forgotten, renders the ritual ineffective in its higher importance. In addition, they often become mixed with other elements and concepts which do not maintain the integrity and original intent of the practice. The practitioners often remain in a cycle of practicing the ritual for ritual sake and do not progress beyond that level, enjoying the emotional exuberance and tension relief that comes from physical exertion but gaining little higher consciousness integration. The temporary relief of tension causes many to imagine that they have discovered higher levels of consciousness, however, their personalities remain unchanged as they continue to live with the same foibles, fears, desires and faults. Authentic religion should improve life and lead human beings to empowerment both in the physical as well as the higher mental planes of existence, and not the reverse, to weakness, susceptibility and dependence.

Another problem that is prevalent in African religion is that many Priests and Priestesses within the African traditions have been accused of promoting rituals for profit, charging exorbitant fees for initiations and rituals. Priests and Priestesses are supposed to be facilitators for aspirants, to help them discover higher consciousness, and they should be compensated with a reasonable offering that will sustain their activities and service to the community. However, the usury fees charged by some practitioners approach the level of some Western Christian ministers who parade around in Cadillac's and Mercedes or even Rolls Royce cars, touting the benefits of being on the spiritual path, presenting themselves as success stories, having gained their wealth "through the grace of God," when actually they have duped the masses into believing fairy tales about what spirituality is and what the legitimate goal of Temple offerings is supposed to be. The offerings should benefit the community and not the egoistic designs of preachers, Western, Eastern or African. These misconceptions degrade the practice of religion and lead to frustration, dogmatism, ignorance and ultimately failure in the spiritual quest, both for the preachers and their followers.

Voodoo

Voodoo or vodun, is a religious and magical set of beliefs and practices of some Africans. It was originally brought over from Africa through the Africans who were taken as slaves to the Caribbean, the US South, and Brazil. Though originating in Benin, the practice of Voodoo outside Africa includes elements of West African cults and a supernatural pantheon of saints, borrowed largely from Catholicism. Magic, propitiatory rites and trance also play important roles in voodoo.[59] Some elements of the practice have been used by unscrupulous practitioners who wish harm on others. This has been popularized by the entertainment media of the West, and has maligned the practice of Voodoo. Voodoo is not a church but rather a cult or independent form of spiritual seeking. It has limited appeal and practice in the continent of Africa (restricted to Dahomey, now called Benin). It was popularized as its practice grew in the Caribbean.

---

[59] Random House Encyclopedia Copyright (C) 1983,1990 by Random House Inc.

MAAT-UBUNTU: Maat Philosophy of Ancient Africa and Humanism in Present Day African Religious Practice

After centuries of trying to stop the practice of African Religion and convert Africans to Christianity, the Catholic Church reversed itself and at the 1964 Vatican II conference of Bishops in Rome, officially accepted African Religion into the family of World religions as a full partner.[209] On a visit to Benin, Pope John Paul II apologized for centuries of denigration African religion by the Western Culture. African religion is universally accepted as a distinct and legitimate form of spirituality and continues to be practiced by a substantial number of people in and outside of Africa. It is practiced by many who on one hand profess to be converts to Western religions while at the same time retain the practice of some aspects of African religion in their life. One reason for its persistence is the quality of *Humanism* that characterizes it. The African term *Ubuntu* means humanism. Humanism is a fundamental concern for the human condition, a caring for fellow human beings with respect to their well being, but also it means a kind of openness, hospitality and compassion for those in need. The quality of Ubuntu has had the effect of tempering the harshness of other religions, as well as bringing to the forefront the sufferings and needs of others, and sometimes the inequities that are endured by others. Ubuntu is a kind of empathy and sympathy for others and a heartfelt desire to share with others. One important example of the effect of African religion and its quality of Ubuntu is the Aldura Church of Yoruba. In this church the Christian emphasis on salvation has given way to an approach that is more in line with the traditional needs of the people. The priests function as diviners, healers and ritual leaders. The concept of humanism may be best expressed in the following quotations:

> "African belief is basically the humanistic belief that doing good is good, while doing anything bad is bad. You are rewarded here on earth for your good deeds and punished for your iniquities. Indeed, many Africans believe that the ultimate punishment for bad or iniquitous behaviour is death."
>
> -N. Adu Kwabena-Essem is a freelance journalist,
based in Accra, Ghana

> "You know when it is there, and it is obvious when it is absent. It has to do with what it means to be truly human, it refers to gentleness, to compassion, to hospitality, to openness to others, to vulnerability, to being available for others and to know that you are bound up with them in the bundle of life, for a person is only a person through other persons."
>
> -South Africa's Archbishop Desmond Tutu,
winner of the Nobel Prize 1984

When compared to the concept of Ubuntu, the Kamitan concept of Ari Maat (Maatian Actions) is found to be in every way compatible with this concept of humanism or social awareness and caring. Maat is a philosophy, a spiritual symbol as well as a cosmic energy or force which pervades the entire universe. Maat is the path to promoting world order, justice, righteousness, correctness, harmony and peace. Maat is also the path that represents wisdom and spiritual awakening through balance and equanimity, as well as righteous living and selfless service to humanity. So Maat encompasses certain disciplines of right action which promote purity of heart and balance of mind. Maat is represented as a goddess with a feather held to the side of her head by a bandana and she is sometimes depicted with wings, a papyrus scepter in one hand and holding an ankh (symbol of life) in her other hand.

Forms of Goddess Maat

In Kamit, the judges were initiated into the teachings of MAAT, for only when there is justice and fairness in society can there be an abiding harmony and peace. Harmony and peace are necessary for the pursuit of true happiness and inner fulfillment in life. Thus, Kamitan spirituality includes a discipline for social order and harmony not unlike Confucianism of China or Dharma of India. Maat promotes social harmony and personal virtue which lead to spiritual enlightenment.

Many people are aware of the 42 Laws or Precepts of Maat. They are declarations of purity (also known as *negative confessions)*, found in the Kamitan Book of Enlightenment (Egyptian Book of the Dead), which a person who has lived a life of righteousness can utter at the time of the great judgment after death. All of the precepts concern moral rectitude in all aspects of life which leads to social order. Order leads to prosperity and harmony.

As an adjunct to the 42 precepts there are other injunctions given in the Wisdom Texts. These in turn are elaborated in the tomb inscriptions of Ancient Egypt. In Chapter 125 of the Book of the Dead, the person uttering the declarations states:

> "I have done God's will. I have given bread to the hungry, water to the thirsty, clothes to the clotheless and a boat to those who were shipwrecked. I made the prescribed offerings to the gods and goddesses and I also made offerings in the temple to the glorious spirits. Therefore, protect me when I go to face The God."[210]

The following tomb inscriptions were carved into the walls of those people who professed to have lived a righteous and orderly life. Central to this order and virtue are the acts of righteousness and the highest form of right action is selfless service. That is, all of the things a person can do to uphold truth, order and righteousness during their lives. The following is a summary of Ari Maat, which will be followed by a brief gloss on Maat Selfless Service.

The Actions of a Person Living by Maat Should Include:

❶

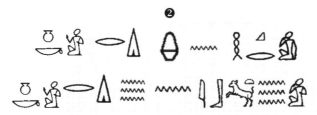

Nuk rdy maat - Give righteousness, order and truth to humanity

Maat is the ancient art of ethical conduct, righteous living (virtue) and truth. Aspirants learn to think and act with honesty, integrity, and truthfulness to promote positive self-development which will translate into the becoming reliable and responsible leaders and members of society.

❷

Nuk rdy ta n heker - Nuk rdy mu n abt
Give food to the hungry - Give water to the thirsty

Working to eradicate hunger and thirst in our community, and also world hunger, should be primary goals of a person living by Maat. Hunger prevents humanity from achieving its higher goals of peace and harmony. Hunger is a source of suffering and early death for millions of people around the world. Sharing food and drink are primary ways of showing compassion and promoting caring between human beings and societies. This promotes peace and prevents conflicts.

❸

Nuk rdy het n an het
Give shelter to the homeless

Working to provide homes for the homeless and alleviating the homeless situation in society should be a priority for a person living by Maat because all human beings require a proper place to dwell so that they can live well ordered and comfortable lives. Lack of shelter gives rise to discomfort and discomfort leads to strife.

❹

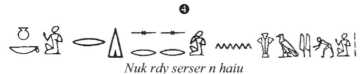

Nuk rdy serser n haiu
Give comfort to the weepers (suffering-disheartened)

Pain and suffering are all too prevalent in human life. One of the concerns of a person living by Maat should be to promote compassion and consolation to people who are suffering due to any reason and to promote immediate psychological support (refuge, moral support) for those in need.

❺

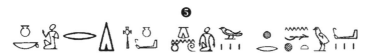

Nuk rdy netu genu kher nekhtu
Give protection to the weak from the strong

One of the main concerns of a person living by Maat should be social justice, the protection of the weaker members of society who are victims of crime or who are less able to help themselves when confronted with other members of society. The goal is to assist people by standing with them to provide moral, legal or other assistance.

❻

Nuk rdy rech n kheman
Give wisdom (counsel) to the ignorant

One of the main goals of a person living by Maat should be to train other human beings in the precepts of Maat and raise leaders who will study the ancient philosophy and be able to transmit it to others in society. This will promote the formation and growth of a well-informed segment of the population who will be able to promote peace, justice, understanding and spiritual enlightenment.

❼

Nuk rdy dept n an dept
Give opportunity to the discouraged

Having become wise and acting with virtue, teaching the ancient Maat Philosophy and assisting others in immediate and long-term need, a person living by Maat will thereby eventually assist them to become stronger and help themselves. Every human being needs to have the opportunity to develop and discover the meaning of life so as to grow and develop to their full potential. Therefore, justice and equal opportunity are essential human concerns for all people.

Maat Selfless Service is an important aspect of Chapter 33 (125) of the Book of the Dead. Here the initiate states {his/her} qualifications to be allowed into the inner shrine to see and become one with Asar (The Supreme Being). The initiate states that {he/she} helped those in need in various ways. This is one of the greatest and most secure methods of purifying the heart (becoming virtuous), because it makes one humble and it effaces the ego. Selfless Service is a vast area of spiritual practice and it forms the major part of the Yogic Path of Right Action. Every human being needs to understand the profound implications of selfless service and how to practice selfless service effectively in order to attain spiritual enlightenment, social order and harmony.

First it must be understood that according to Maat Philosophy, the Supreme Spirit (God, Goddess) manifests as all Creation, and is also present in all human beings. This being so, one must realize that one is interacting in, with and through the Supreme Spirit in all actions, speech and thought. Since human interrelations have a most profound influence on the human mind, they are the most powerful means of effecting a change in the personality. However, if mishandled, they can be a most effective method of leading a human being to psychological attachment and suffering as well. A person should understand that Maat comes to {him/her} in the form of human beings in need, so as to give the aspirant an opportunity to grow spiritually through selfless service. To be successful in selfless service, the aspirant must be able to sublimate the ego through developing patience, dealing with difficult personalities without developing resentment, not taking attacks personally, and developing a keen understanding of human nature and human needs. Selfless Service allows a human being to discover sentiments of caring for something greater than the little "me." This leads to purity of heart from the gross fetters of anger, hatred, greed, lust, jealousy, envy, etc., and also the attachments based on blood relations and other filial relationships, for in order to serve in the highest order, one must serve all equally, without favorites. As a servant of humanity, one's family becomes all human beings and nature itself. Therefore, the cause of environmental well being is also a high concern reflected in the following injunctions of the Maat philosophy. There are two injunctions that specifically address issues of public or selfless service to the community through service to nature and the preservation of natural resources.

(15) "I have not laid waste the ploughed lands."
(36) "I have never befouled the water." Variant: I have not held back the water from flowing in its season.
—From Chapter 33 of the Ancient Egyptian Pert M Heru

When asked how she could stand to serve such severely ill people and not feel disheartened, repulsed or depressed, Mother Teresa replied "I see only Jesus coming to me through people." This reply shows the saintly attitude towards humanity, and she also displayed the highest level of spiritual practice through the path of right action, which is known as Selfless Service. When Mother Teresa was asked how she is able to do all the work she has done, she would reply, "I do nothing…God does it all." Selfishness arises when a human being sees {him/her} self as separate from Creation and develops an egoistic selfishness, typified by the attitude of "I got mine you get yours." A mature and righteous person must develop sensitivity to the fact that all Creation is inexorably linked at all levels, the material and the spiritual, and therefore, a true aspirant feels empathy and compassion for all humanity and will not rest until all human beings have the essential needs of life, those being food, shelter and opportunity to grow and thrive. All problems of the world can be traced to the selfishness and hoarding of precious basic necessities by certain segments of the population, and the subsequent development of resentments, greed, hatred and violence which lead to untold social strife.

However, a person who lives by Maat does not pursue the betterment of the world in a sentimental manner, but with deep understanding of the fact that people's ignorance of their true divine essence is the root cause that has led them to their current condition of suffering, and therefore simply sending money or aid will not resolve the issue. Where food, clothing or funds are needed, they should be given, but in addition to these, one must undertake an effort to promote mystical spiritual wisdom (which includes the complete practice of religion: myth, ritual and mysticism) in humanity. Beyond the basic necessities of life, the world needs mystical spiritual wisdom most of all. Technology, comforts of life, entertainments and other conveniences should come later. This is how a well-ordered society is structured along Maatian-Ubuntu principles: Mystical spiritual foundation which provides basic necessities (food and shelter) for its members, from which all else (development of technology, entertainment, etc.) will follow. Only in this way will the technological developments, entertainment and other aspects of society develop in a righteous (ethical), balanced and harmonious way. This can be contrasted with the current predicament of most modern day societies where the emphasis is foremost on the development of technology and entertainment, without giving much thought to spirituality (ethics, balance, harmony, truth, righteousness). Consequently, there are many people currently existing in communities all over the world who are deprived of the basic needs of life (food and shelter).

Studying the teachings of yogic mysticism and their subsequent practice through selfless service will promote the enlightenment of humanity, which will end the cycle of egoism and disharmony between peoples of differing cultures. Therefore, the act of helping others is extremely important and should be pursued. Working in service of other human beings allows a person who lives by Maat to apply the teachings and experience the results. It allows the a person who lives by Maat to develop the capacity to adapt and adjust to changing conditions of life, and to other personalities, and still maintain the detachment and poise necessary to keep equal vision and awareness of the Divine, and thereby live by truth, and not by favoritism. All of this promotes integration of the personality of the person who lives by Maat. Therefore, the results of one's selfless service actions are immediate and always good, because no matter what the results of those actions are, the service itself is the goal of a person who lives by Maat.

What are the disciplines of Selfless Service?

Service is an important ingredient in the development of spiritual life. In selfless service one adopts the attitude of seeing and serving the Divine in everyone and every creature, and one is to feel as an instrument of the Divine, working to help the less able. The following are some important points to keep in mind when practicing selfless service.

First, having controlled the body, speech and thoughts, a person who lives by Maat should see {him/her} self as an instrument of the Divine, being used to bring harmony, peace, and help to the world. All human beings and nature are expressions of the Divine. Serving human beings and nature is serving the Supreme Divine Self (God).

In Chapter 34, Verse 10 of the Pert M Hru scripture, the initiate states that {he/she} has become a spiritual doctor: *There are sick, very ill people. I go to them, I spit on the arms, I set the shoulder, and I cleanse them.* As a servant of the Divine Self, a person who lives by Maat is also a healer. Just as it would be inappropriate for a medical doctor to lose {his/her} patience with {his/her} patient because the person is complaining due to their illness, so too it is inappropriate for an initiate to lose their patience when dealing with the masses of worldly-minded people, suffering from the illness of ignorance of their true essence. So, it must be clearly and profoundly understood that in serving, you are serving the true Self, not the ego.

Secondly, as discussed above, a person who lives by Maat should not expect a particular result from their actions. In other words one does not perform actions and wait for a reward or praises, and though working to achieve success in the project, one does not develop the expectation that one's efforts will succeed, because there may be failure in what one is trying to accomplish. If a person who lives by Maat focuses on the success of the project and failure occurs, the mind will become so imbalanced that it will negate the positive developments of personality integration, expansion and concentration which occurred as the project was pursued. Therefore, one's focus should be on doing one's part by performing the service, and letting the Divine handle the results. This provides a person who lives by Maat with peace and the ability to be more qualitative in the work being performed (without the egoistic content), and more harmonious, which will lead to being more sensitive to the needs of others and of the existence of the Spirit as the very essence of one's being.

Secular Maat Selfless Service Leads to Spiritual Maat Mysticism

The highly advanced and lofty teachings from Maat Philosophy of becoming one with the Supreme Being through righteous action is further augmented by the *Hymn to Maat* contained in the scripture now referred to as the Berlin papyrus below.

Maat Ankhu Maat
Maat is the source of life
Maat neb bu ten
Maat is in everywhere you are
Cha hena Maat
Rise in the morning with Maat
Ankh hena Maat
Live with Maat
Ha sema Maat
Let every limb join with Maat (i.e. let her guide your actions)
Maat her ten
Maat is who you are deep down (i.e. your true identity is one with the Divine)
Dua Maat neb bu ten
Adorations to goddess Maat, who is in everywhere you are!

For more extensive study of the Maat-Selfless Service teaching, see the books *Wisdom of Maati, 42 Precepts of Maat* and *Ancient Egyptian Book of the Dead* by Muata Ashby.

The Fundamental Principles of Neterian Religion

NETERIANISM
(The Oldest Known Religion in History)

The term "Neterianism" is derived from the name "Shetaut Neter." Shetaut Neter means the "Hidden Divinity." It is the ancient philosophy and mythic spiritual culture that gave rise to the Ancient Egyptian civilization. Those who follow the spiritual path of Shetaut Neter are therefore referred to as "Neterians." The fundamental principles common to all denominations of Neterian Religion may be summed up as follows.

Neterian Great Truths

1. *"Pa Neter ua ua Neberdjer m Neteru"* -"The Neter, the Supreme Being, is One and alone and as Neberdjer, manifesting everywhere and in all things in the form of Gods and Goddesses."

Neberdjer means "all-encompassing divinity," the all-inclusive, all-embracing Spirit which pervades all and who is the ultimate essence of all. This first truth unifies all the expressions of Kamitan religion.

2. *"an-Maat swy Saui Set s-Khemn"* – "Lack of righteousness brings fetters to the personality and these fetters lead to ignorance of the Divine."

When a human being acts in ways that contradict the natural order of nature, negative qualities of the mind will develop within that person's personality. These are the afflictions of Set. Set is the neteru of egoism and selfishness. The afflictions of Set include: anger, hatred, greed, lust, jealousy, envy, gluttony, dishonesty, hypocrisy, etc. So to be free from the fetters of set one must be free from the afflictions of Set.

3. *"s-Uashu s-Nafu n saiu Set"* -"Devotion to the Divine leads to freedom from the fetters of Set."

To be liberated (Nafu - freedom - to breath) from the afflictions of Set, one must be devoted to the Divine. Being devoted to the Divine means living by Maat. Maat is a way of life that is purifying to the heart and beneficial for society as it promotes virtue and order. Living by Maat means practicing Shedy (spiritual practices and disciplines).

Uashu means devotion and the classic pose of adoring the Divine is called "Dua," standing or sitting with upraised hands facing outwards towards the image of the divinity.

4. *"ari Shedy Rekh ab m Maakheru"* - "The practice of the Shedy disciplines leads to knowing oneself and the Divine. This is called being True of Speech."

Doing Shedy means to study profoundly, to penetrate the mysteries (Shetaut) and discover the nature of the Divine. There have been several practices designed by the sages of Ancient Kamit to facilitate the process of self-knowledge. These are the religious (Shetaut) traditions and the Sema (Smai) Tawi (yogic) disciplines related to them that augment the spiritual practices.

All the traditions relate the teachings of the sages by means of myths related to particular gods or goddesses. It is understood that all of these neteru are related, like brothers and sisters, having all emanated from the same source, the same Supremely Divine parent, who is neither male nor female, but encompasses the totality of the two.

The Great Truths of Neterianism are realized ḥ means of
Four Spiritual Disciplines in Three Steps

The four disciples are: Rekh Shedy (Wisdom), Ari Shedy (Righteous Action and Selfless Service), Uashu (Ushet) Shedy (Devotion) and Uaa Shedy (Meditation)

The Three Steps are: Listening, Ritual, and Meditation

SEDJM REKH SHEDY

L I S T E N

- ***Sedjm* REKH *Shedy* -Listening** to the WISDOM of the Neterian Traditions

  - Shetaut Asar — Teachings of the Asarian Tradition
  - Shetaut Anu — Teachings of the Ra Tradition
  - Shetaut Menefer — Teachings of the Ptah Tradition
  - Shetaut Waset — Teachings of the Amun Tradition
  - Shetaut Netrit — Teachings of the Goddess Tradition
  - Shetaut Aton — Teachings of the Aton Tradition

ARI SHEDY

R I T U A L

- ***Ari Maat Shedy* – Righteous Actions** – Purifies the GROSS impurities of the Heart

  - Maat Shedy — True Study of the Ways of hidden nature of Neter
  - Maat Aakhu — True Deeds that lead to glory
  - Maat Aru — True Ritual

UASHU (U SHET)S HEDY

- ***Ushet Shedy* – Devotion to the Divine** – Purifies the EMOTIONAL impurities of the Heart

  - Shmai — Divine Music
  - Sema Paut — Meditation in motion
  - Neter Arit — Divine Offerings – Selfless-Service – virtue -

UAA SHEDY

M E D I T A T E

- ***Uaa m Neter Shedy* -** 𓀢𓂝𓏏𓀢𓏏 **Meditation** Experience the Transcendental Supreme Self. The five forms of Neterian Meditation discipline include.

  - Arat Sekhem, - Meditation on the Subtle Life Force
  - Ari Sma Maat, - Meditation on the Righteous action
  - Nuk Pu-Ushet, - Meditation on the I am
  - Nuk Ra Akhu, - Meditation on the Glorious Light
  - Rekh – Khemn, -Meditation on the Wisdom Teaching

Summary of The Great Truths and the Shedy Paths to their Realization

Great Truths

Shedy Disciplines

I	I
God is One and in all things manifesting through the Neteru	Listen to the Wisdom Teachings (Become Wise) Learn the mysteries as taught by an authentic teacher which allows this profound statement to be understood.

I I	I I
Unrighteousness brings fetters and these cause ignorance of truth (#1)	Acting (Living) by Truth Apply the Philosophy of right action to become virtuous and purify the heart

I I I	I I I
Devotion to God allows the personality to free itself from the fetters	Devotion to the Divine Worship, ritual and divine love allows the personality purified by truth to eradicate the subtle ignorance that binds it to mortal existence.

I I I I	I I I I
The Shedy disciplines are the greatest form of worship of the Divine	Meditation Allows the whole person to go beyond the world of time and space and the gross and subtle ignorance of mortal human existence to discover that which transcends time and space.

Great Awakening
Occurs when all of the Great Truths have been realized by perfection of the Shedy disciplines to realize their true nature and actually experience oneness with the transcendental Supreme Being.

The Spiritual Culture and the Purpose of Life: Shetaut Neter

"Men and women are to become God-like through a life of virtue and the cultivation of the spirit through scientific knowledge, practice and bodily discipline."

-Ancient Egyptian Proverb

The highest forms of Joy, Peace and Contentment are obtained when the meaning of life is discovered. When the human being is in harmony with life, then it is possible to reflect and meditate upon the human condition and realize the limitations of worldly pursuits. When there is peace and harmony in life, a human being can practice any of the varied disciplines designated as Shetaut Neter to promote {his/her} evolution towards the ultimate goal of life, which Spiritual Enlightenment. Spiritual Enlightenment is the awakening of a human being to the awareness of the Transcendental essence which binds the universe and which is eternal and immutable. In this discovery is also the sobering and ecstatic realization that the human being is one with that Transcendental essence. With this realization comes great joy, peace and power to experience the fullness of life and to realize the purpose of life during the time on earth. The lotus is a symbol of Shetaut Neter, meaning the turning towards the light of truth, peace and transcendental harmony.

Shetaut Neter

We have established that the Ancient Egyptians were African peoples who lived in the north-eastern quadrant of the continent of Africa. They were descendants of the Nubians, who had themselves originated from farther south into the heart of Africa at the Great Lakes region, the sources of the Nile River. They created a vast civilization and culture earlier than any other society in known history and organized a nation that was based on the concepts of balance and order as well as spiritual enlightenment. These ancient African people called their land Kamit, and soon after developing a well-ordered society, they began to realize that the world is full of wonders, but also that life is fleeting, and that there must be something more to human existence. They developed spiritual systems that were designed to allow human beings to understand the nature of this secret being who is the essence of all Creation. They called this spiritual system "Shtaut Ntr (Shetaut Neter)."

Shetaut means secret.

Neter means Divinity.

Who is Neter in Kamitan Religion?

"**Ntr**

The symbol of Neter was described by an Ancient Kamitan priest as:
"That which is placed in the coffin"

The term Ntr ⌣, or Ntjr ⌣, comes from the Ancient Egyptian hieroglyphic language which did not record its vowels. However, the term survives in the Coptic language as *"Nutar."* The same Coptic meaning (divine force or sustaining power) applies in the present as it did in ancient times. It is a symbol composed of a wooden staff that was wrapped with strips of fabric, like a mummy. The strips alternate in color with yellow, green and blue. The mummy in Kamitan spirituality is understood to be the dead but resurrected Divinity. So the Nutar (Ntr) is actually every human being who does not really die, but goes to live on in a different form. Further, the resurrected spirit of every human being is that same Divinity. Phonetically, the term Nutar is related to other terms having the same meaning, such as the latin "Natura," the Spanish Naturalesa, the English "Nature" and "Nutriment", etc. In a real sense, as we will see, Natur means power manifesting as Neteru and the Neteru are the objects of creation, i.e. "nature."

Sacred Scriptures of Shetaut Neter

The following scriptures represent the foundational scriptures of Kamitan culture. They may be divided into three categories: *Mythic Scriptures*, *Mystical Philosophy* and *Ritual Scriptures*, and *Wisdom Scriptures* (Didactic Literature).

MYTHIC SCRIPTURES Literature	Mystical (Ritual) Philosophy Literature	Wisdom Texts Literature
SHETAUT ASAR-ASET-HERU The Myth of Asar, Aset and Heru (Asarian Resurrection Theology) - Predynastic **SHETAUT ATUM-RA** Anunian Theology Predynastic Shetaut Net/Aset/Hetheru Saitian Theology – Goddess Spirituality Predynastic **SHETAUT PTAH** Memphite Theology Predynastic Shetaut Amun Theban Theology Predynastic	**Pyramid Texts** (C. 5,500 B.C.E.-3,800 B.C.E.) **Coffin Texts** (C. 2040 B.C.E.-1786 B.C.E.) **Papyrus Texts** (C. 1580 B.C.E.-Roman Period)[60] Books of Coming Forth By Day Example of famous papyri: Papyrus of Any Papyrus of Hunefer Papyrus of Kenna Greenfield Papyrus, Etc.	**Wisdom Texts** (C. 3,000 B.C.E. – PTOLEMAIC PERIOD) Precepts of Ptahotep Instructions of Any Instructions of Amenemope Etc. Maat Declarations Literature (All Periods)

---

[60] After 1570 B.C.E they would evolve into a more unified text, the Egyptian Book of the Dead.

Neter and the Neteru

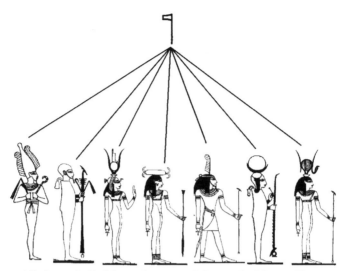

The Neteru (Gods and Goddesses) proceed from the Neter (Supreme Being)

As stated earlier, the concept of Neter and Neteru binds and ties all of the varied forms of Kamitan spirituality into one vision of the gods and goddesses all emerging from the same Supreme Being. Therefore, ultimately, Kamitan spirituality is not polytheistic, nor is it monotheistic, for it holds that the Supreme Being is more than a God or Goddess. The Supreme Being is an all-encompassing Absolute Divinity.

The Neteru

"Neteru"

The term "Neteru" means "gods and goddesses." This means that from the ultimate and transcendental Supreme Being, "Neter," come the Neteru. There are countless Neteru. So from the one come the many. These Neteru are cosmic forces that pervade the universe. They are the means by which Neter sustains Creation and manifests through it. So Neterianism is a monotheistic polytheism. The one Supreme Being expresses as many gods and goddesses. At the end of time, after their work of sustaining Creation is finished, these gods and goddesses are again absorbed back into the Supreme Being.

All of the spiritual systems of Ancient Egypt (Kamit) have one essential aspect that is common to all; they all hold that there is a Supreme Being (Neter) who manifests in a multiplicity of ways through nature, the Neteru. Like sunrays, the Neteru emanate from the Divine; they are its manifestations. So by studying the Neteru we learn about and are led to discover their source, the Neter, and with this discovery we are enlightened. The Neteru may be depicted anthropomorphically or zoomorphically in accordance with the teaching about Neter that is being conveyed through them.

The Neteru and Their Temples

Diagram 1: The Ancient Egyptian Temple Network

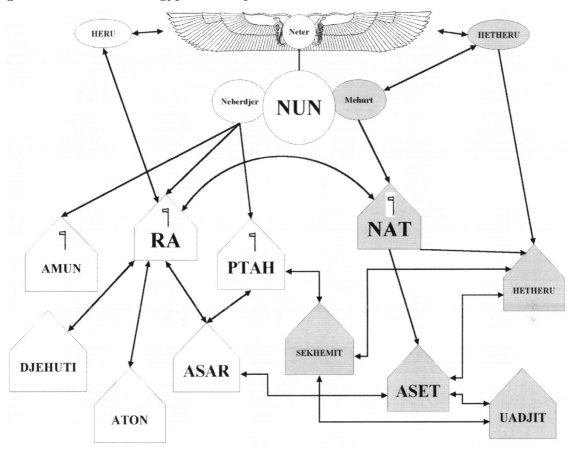

The sages of Kamit instituted a system by which the teachings of spirituality were espoused through a Temple organization. The major divinities were assigned to a particular city. That divinity or group of divinities became the "patron" divinity or divinities of that city. Also, the Priests and Priestesses of that Temple were in charge of seeing to the welfare of the people in that district as well as maintaining the traditions and disciplines of the traditions based on the particular divinity being worshipped. So the original concept of "Neter" became elaborated through the "theologies" of the various traditions. A dynamic expression of the teachings emerged, which though maintaining the integrity of the teachings, expressed nuances of variation in perspective on the teachings to suit the needs of varying kinds of personalities of the people of different locales.

In the diagram above, the primary or main divinities are denoted by the Neter symbol (⚑). The house structure represents the Temple for that particular divinity. The interconnections with the other Temples are based on original scriptural statements espoused by the Temples that linked the divinities of their Temple with the other divinities. So this means that the divinities should be viewed not as separate entities operating independently, but rather as family members who are in the same "business" together, i.e. the enlightenment of society, albeit through variations in form of worship, name, form (expression of the Divinity), etc. Ultimately, all the divinities are referred to as Neteru and they are all said to be emanations from the ultimate and Supreme Being. Thus, the teaching from any of the Temples leads to an understanding of the others, and these all lead back to the source, the highest Divinity. Thus, the teaching within any of the Temple systems would lead to the attainment of spiritual enlightenment, the Great Awakening.

The Neteru and Their Interrelationships

Diagram : The Primary Kamitan Neteru and their Interrelationships

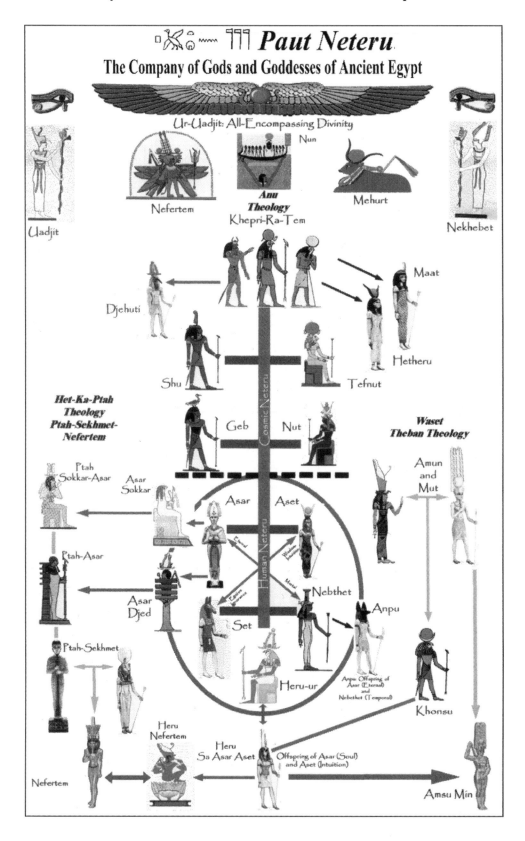

The same Supreme Being, Neter, is the winged all-encompassing transcendental Divinity, the Spirit who, in the early history, is called "Heru." The physical universe in which the Heru lives is called "Hetheru" or the "house of Heru." This divinity (Heru) is also the Nun or primeval substratum from which all matter is composed. The various divinities and the material universe are composed from this primeval substratum. Neter is actually androgynous and Heru, the Spirit, is related as a male aspect of that androgyny. However, Heru in the androgynous aspect, gives rise to the solar principle and this is seen in both the male and female divinities.

The image above provides an idea of the relationships between the divinities of the three main Neterian spiritual systems (traditions): Anunian Theology, Wasetian (Theban) Theology and Het-Ka-Ptah (Memphite) Theology. The traditions are composed of companies or groups of gods and goddesses. Their actions, teachings and interactions with each other and with human beings provide insight into their nature as well as that of human existence and Creation itself. The lines indicate direct scriptural relationships and the labels also indicate that some divinities from one system are the same in others, with only a name change. Again, this is attested to by the scriptures themselves in direct statements, like those found in the ***Prt m Hru*** text Chapter 4 (17).[61]

Listening to the Teachings

"Mestchert"

"Listening, to fill the ears, listen attentively-"

What should the ears be filled with?

The sages of Shetaut Neter enjoined that a Shemsu Neter (follower of Neter, an initiate or aspirant) should listen to the WISDOM of the Neterian Traditions. These are the myth related to the gods and goddesses containing the basic understanding of who they are, what they represent, how they relate human beings and to the Supreme Being. The myths allow us to be connected to the Divine.

An aspirant may choose any one of the 5 main Neterian Traditions.

- Shetaut Anu   – Teachings of the Ra Tradition
- Shetaut Menefer   – Teachings of the Ptah Tradition
- Shetaut Waset   – Teachings of the Amun Tradition
- Shetaut Netrit   – Teachings of the Goddess Tradition
- Shetaut Asar   – Teachings of the Asarian Tradition
- Shetaut Aton   – Teachings of the Aton Tradition

---

[61] See the book *The Egyptian Book of the Dead* by Muata Ashby

The Anunian Tradition

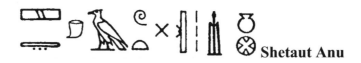 **Shetaut Anu**

The Mystery Teachings of the Anunian Tradition are related to the Divinity Ra and his company of Gods and Goddesses.[62] This Temple and its related Temples espouse the teachings of Creation, human origins and the path to spiritual enlightenment by means of the Supreme Being in the form of the god Ra. It tells of how Ra emerged from a primeval ocean and how human beings were created from his tears. The gods and goddesses, who are his children, go to form the elements of nature and the cosmic forces that maintain nature.

Below: The Heliopolitan Cosmogony.

The city of Anu (Amun-Ra)

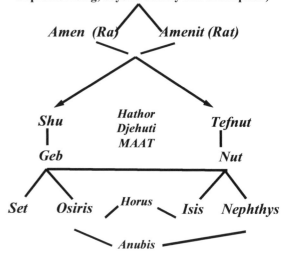

The Neters of Creation -
The Company of the Gods and Goddesses.
Neter Neteru
Nebertcher - Amun (unseen, hidden, ever present, Supreme Being, beyond duality and description)

Amen (Ra)   *Amenit (Rat)*

Shu   *Hathor*   *Tefnut*
              Djehuti
Geb   *MAAT*   *Nut*

Set   *Osiris*   *Horus*   *Isis*   *Nephthys*

Anubis

Top: Ra. From left to right, starting at the bottom level- The Gods and Goddesses of Anunian Theology: Shu, Tefnut, Nut, Geb, Aset, Asar, Set, Nebthet and Heru-Ur

---

[62] See the Book Anunian Theology by Muata Ashby

The Memphite Tradition

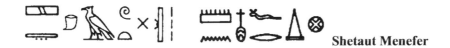 **Shetaut Menefer**

The Mystery Teachings of the Menefer (Memphite) Tradition are related to the Neterus known as Ptah, Sekhmit, Nefertem. The myths and philosophy of these divinities constitutes Memphite Theology.[63] This temple and its related temples espoused the teachings of Creation, human origins and the path to spiritual enlightenment by means of the Supreme Being in the form of the god Ptah and his family, who compose the Memphite Trinity. It tells of how Ptah emerged from a primeval ocean and how he created the universe by his will and the power of thought (mind). The gods and goddesses who are his thoughts, go to form the elements of nature and the cosmic forces that maintain nature. His spouse, Sekhmit has a powerful temple system of her own that is related to the Memphite teaching. The same is true for his son Nefertem.

Below: The Memphite Cosmogony.

The city of Hetkaptah (Ptah)

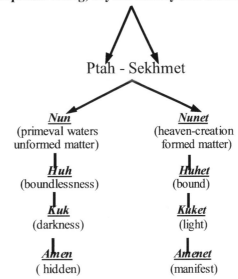

The Neters of Creation -
The Company of the Gods and Goddesses.
Neter Neteru
Nebertcher - Amun (unseen, hidden, ever present, Supreme Being, beyond duality and description)

Ptah - Sekhmet

Nun
(primeval waters
unformed matter)

Nunet
(heaven-creation
formed matter)

Huh
(boundlessness)

Huhet
(bound)

Kuk
(darkness)

Kuket
(light)

Amen
(hidden)

Amenet
(manifest)

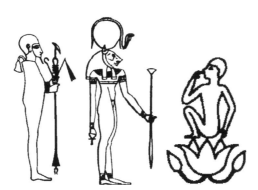

Ptah, Sekhmit and Nefertem

---

[63] See the Book Memphite Theology by Muata Ashby

The Theban Tradition

 Shetaut Amun

The Mystery Teachings of the Wasetian Tradition are related to the Neterus known as Amun, Mut Khonsu. This temple and its related temples espoused the teachings of Creation, human origins and the path to spiritual enlightenment by means of the Supreme Being in the form of the god Amun or Amun-Ra. It tells of how Amun and his family, the Trinity of Amun, Mut and Khonsu, manage the Universe along with his Company of Gods and Goddesses. This Temple became very important in the early part of the New Kingdom Era.

Below: The Trinity of Amun and the Company of Gods and Goddesses of Amun

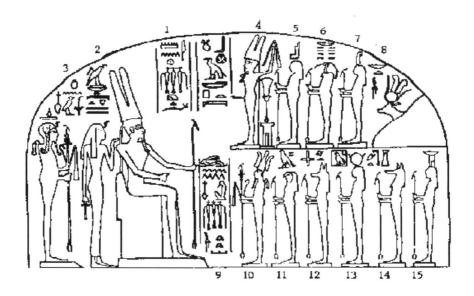

See the Book *Egyptian Yoga Vol. 2* for more on Amun, Mut and Khonsu by Muata Ashby

218

The Goddess Tradition

Shetaut Netrit

"Arat"

The hieroglyphic sign Arat means "Goddess." General, throughout ancient Kamit, the Mystery Teachings of the Goddess Tradition are related to the Divinity in the form of the Goddess. The Goddess was an integral part of all the Neterian traditions but special temples also developed around the worship of certain particular Goddesses who were also regarded as Supreme Beings in their own right. Thus as in other African religions, the goddess as well as the female gender were respected and elevated as the male divinities. The Goddess was also the author of Creation, giving birth to it as a great Cow. The following are the most important forms of the goddess.[64]

Aset, Net, Sekhmit, Mut, Hetheru

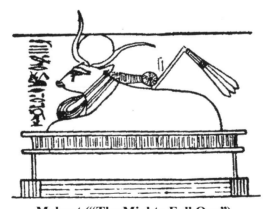

Mehurt ("The Mighty Full One")

---

[64] See the Books, *The Goddess Path, Mysteries of Isis, Glorious Light Meditation, Memphite Theology* and *Resurrecting Osiris* by Muata Ashby

The Asarian Tradition

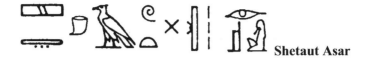 Shetaut Asar

This temple and its related temples espoused the teachings of Creation, human origins and the path to spiritual enlightenment by means of the Supreme Being in the form of the god Asar. It tells of how Asar and his family, the Trinity of Asar, Aset and Heru, manage the Universe and lead human beings to spiritual enlightenment and the resurrection of the soul. This Temple and its teaching were very important from the Pre-Dynastic era down to the Christian period. The Mystery Teachings of the Asarian Tradition are related to the Neterus known as: Asar, Aset, Heru (Osiris, Isis and Horus)

The tradition of Asar, Aset and Heru was practiced generally throughout the land of ancient Kamit. The centers of this tradition were the city of Abdu containing the Great Temple of Asar, the city of Pilak containing the Great Temple of Aset[65] and Edfu containing the Ggreat Temple of Heru.

---

[65] See the Book Resurrecting Osiris by Muata Ashby

The Aton Tradition

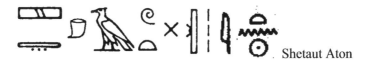 Shetaut Aton

This temple and its related temples espoused the teachings of Creation, human origins and the path to spiritual enlightenment by means of the Supreme Being in the form of the god Aton. It tells of how Aton with its dynamic life force created and sustains Creation. By recognizing Aton as the very substratum of all existence, human beings engage in devotional exercises and rituals and the study of the Hymns containing the wisdom teachings of Aton explaining that Aton manages the Universe and leads human beings to spiritual enlightenment and eternal life for the soul. This Temple and its teaching were very important in the middle New Kingdom Period. The Mystery Teachings of the Aton Tradition are related to the Neter Aton and its main exponent was the Sage King Akhnaton, who is depicted below with his family adoring the sundisk, symbol of the Aton.

Akhnaton, Nefertiti and Daughters

For more on Atonism and the Aton Theology see the Essence of Atonism Lecture Series by Sebai Muata Ashby ©2001

The General Principles of Shetaut Neter
(Teachings Presented in the Kamitan scriptures)

1. The Purpose of Life is to Attain the Great Awakening-Enlightenment-Know thyself.

2. SHETAUT NETER enjoins the Shedy (spiritual investigation) as the highest endeavor of life.

3. SHETAUT NETER enjoins that it is the responsibility of every human being to promote order and truth.

4. SHETAUT NETER enjoins the performance of Selfless Service to family, community and humanity.

5. SHETAUT NETER enjoins the Protection of nature.

6. SHETAUT NETER enjoins the Protection of the weak and oppressed.

7. SHETAUT NETER enjoins the Caring for hungry.

8. SHETAUT NETER enjoins the Caring for homeless.

9. SHETAUT NETER enjoins the equality for all people.

10. SHETAUT NETER enjoins the equality between men and women.

11. SHETAUT NETER enjoins the justice for all.

12. SHETAUT NETER enjoins the sharing of resources.

13. SHETAUT NETER enjoins the protection and proper raising of children.

14. SHETAUT NETER enjoins the movement towards balance and peace.

The Forces of Entropy

In Neterian religion, there is no concept of "evil" as is conceptualized in Western Culture. Rather, it is understood that the forces of entropy are constantly working in nature to bring that which has been constructed by human hands to their original natural state. The serpent Apep (Apophis), who daily tries to stop Ra's boat of creation, is the symbol of entropy. This concept of entropy has been referred to as "chaos" by Western Egyptologists.

Apep

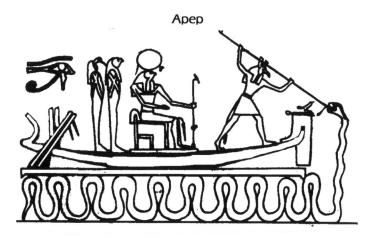

Above: Set protecting the boat of Ra from the forces of entropy (symbolized by the serpent Apep).

As expressed previously, in Neterian religion there is also no concept of a "devil" or "demon" as is conceived in the Judeo-Christian or Islamic traditions. Rather, it is understood that manifestations of detrimental situations and adversities arise as a result of unrighteous actions. These unrighteous actions are due to the "Setian" qualities in a human being. Set is the Neteru of egoism and the negative qualities which arise from egoism. Egoism is the idea of individuality based on identification with the body and mind only as being who one is. One has no deeper awareness of their deeper spiritual essence, and thus no understanding of their connectedness to all other objects (includes persons) in creation and the Divine Self. When the ego is under the control of the higher nature, it fights the forces of entropy (as above). However, when beset with ignorance, it leads to the degraded states of human existence. The vices (egoism, selfishness, extraverted ness, wonton sexuality (lust), jealousy, envy, greed, gluttony) are a result.

Set

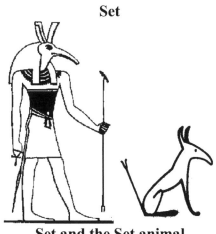

Set and the Set animal

The Great Awakening of Neterian Religion

"Nehast"

Nehast means to "wake up," to Awaken to the higher existence. In the Prt m Hru Text it is said:

Nuk pa Neter aah Neter Ujah asha ren[66]

"I am that same God, the Supreme One, who has myriad of mysterious names."

The goal of all the Neterian disciplines is to discover the meaning of "Who am I?," to unravel the mysteries of life and to fathom the depths of eternity and infinity. This is the task of all human beings and it is to be accomplished in this very lifetime.

This can be done by learning the ways of the Neteru, emulating them and finally becoming like them, Akhus, (enlightened beings), walking the earth as giants and accomplishing great deeds such as the creation of the universe!

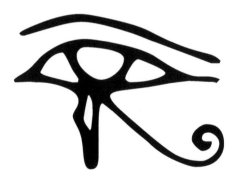

Udjat
The Eye of Heru is a quintessential symbol of awakening to Divine Consciousness, representing the concept of Nehast.

---

[66] (Prt M Hru 9:4)

Kamitan Religion as a Development of African Spirituality and the Influence of Kamitan Culture and Spirituality on African Cultures and World Cultures Over Time.

Figure 43: Human Origins- Modern Human Beings Originate in Africa – 150,000 – 100,000 B.C.E.

The history of modern humanity begins in Africa 150,000 years ago. All the human beings who are alive all over the earth today descend from an original group of human beings who lived 150,000 years ago in central-equatorial Africa. These human beings spread out from there and populated the rest of Africa over the next 50,000 years.

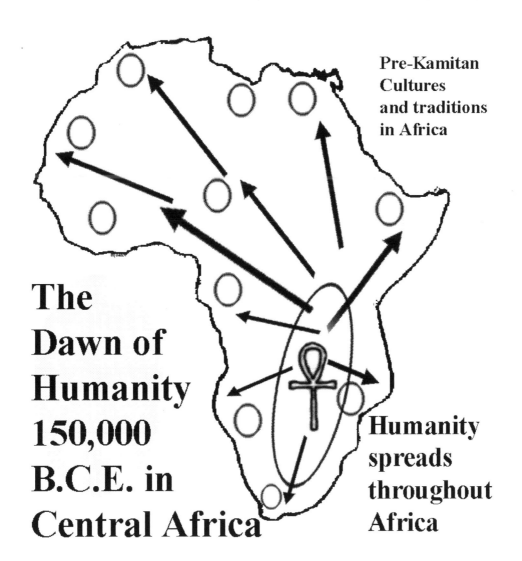

Pre-Kamitan Cultures and traditions in Africa

The Dawn of Humanity 150,000 B.C.E. in Central Africa

Humanity spreads throughout Africa

Figure 44: Human Cultural Development -Cultures develop throughout Africa – 36.000-10,000 B.C.E.

Over the next 50,000 years (150,000-100,000 B.C.E.) the people who populated Africa developed cultures that took on several unique aspects but at the same time manifested the principles that they had carried with them from the originating point to their new homes around the continent. These were a set of social (Maat-Ubuntu) and religious (Supreme Being served by lesser gods and goddesses) principles which became the basis of all African religions that would develop thereafter. Over time some of the groups lost contact and different languages developed, but the principles remained the same and became highly evolved in the Kush-Kamit region.

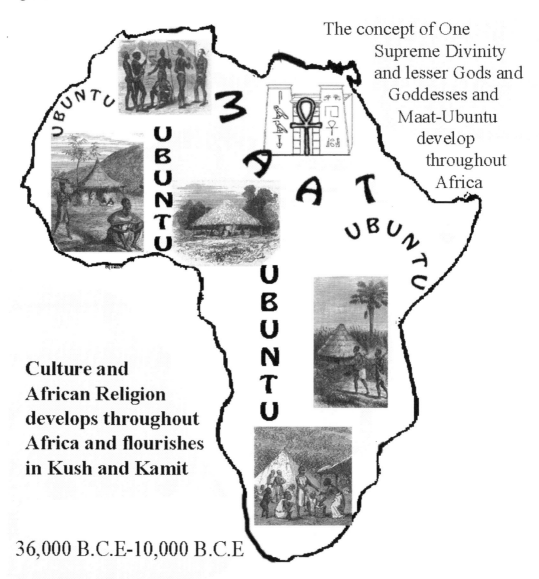

The concept of One Supreme Divinity and lesser Gods and Goddesses and Maat-Ubuntu develop throughout Africa

Culture and African Religion develops throughout Africa and flourishes in Kush and Kamit

36,000 B.C.E-10,000 B.C.E

Figure 5 African High Culture-Kamitan Culture Influences African Cultures

Between 36,000 B.C.E. and 10,000 B.C.E. the peoples of the northeastern quadrant of the continent were able to develop advanced culture and civilization. This became known as the Kush-Kamit Civilization. It was based on the same essential African spiritual and social principles as all other African cultures who originated in 150,000 B.C.E. in central-equatorial Africa. At about 4,000 B.C.E. the Kamitan culture began to influence other African nations with its highly evolved African philosophy which was actually an evolution of the same principles possessed by the other African cultures.

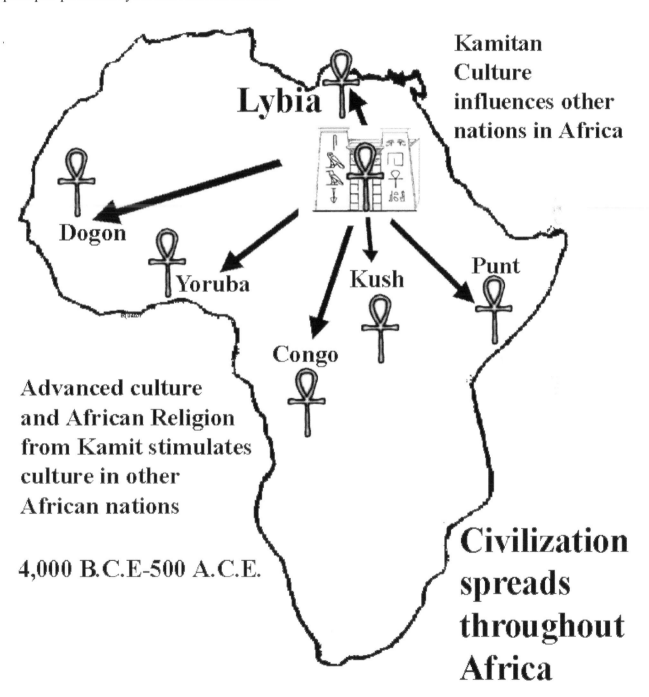

Kamitan Culture influences other nations in Africa

Lybia

Dogon

Yoruba

Kush

Punt

Congo

Advanced culture and African Religion from Kamit stimulates culture in other African nations

4,000 B.C.E-500 A.C.E.

Civilization spreads throughout Africa

Figure Kamitan Civilization Influences Cultures Outside of Africa 4BCE-9 ACE.

At about 3,500 B.C.E. or earlier, the Kamitan culture and civilization began to influence the peoples in Asia Minor (Mesopotamia) and South East Asia (India and China). At about 1,900-1,400 B.C.E. the Kamitan culture and civilization began to influence the archaic Greek culture (Minoans), thereby fomenting the development of culture and spirituality in those areas.

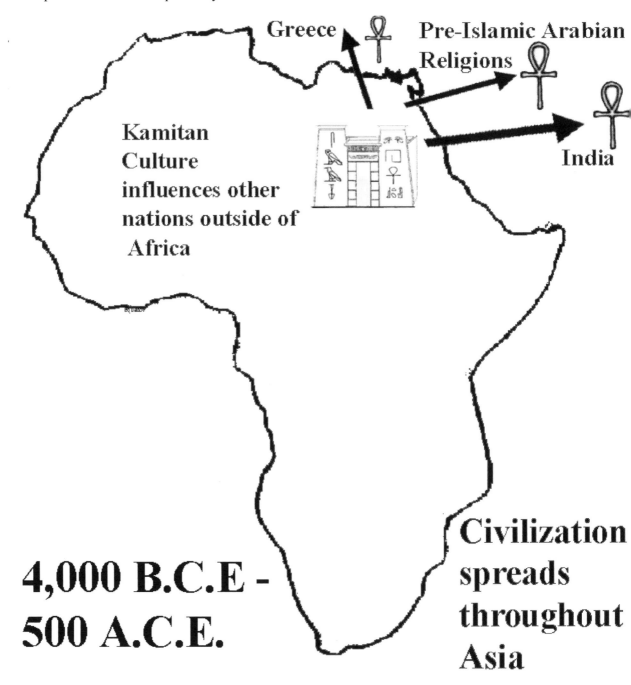

Greece

Pre-Islamic Arabian Religions

India

Kamitan Culture influences other nations outside of Africa

Civilization spreads throughout Asia

4,000 B.C.E - 500 A.C.E.

Ancient Egypt and Its Influence on Other African Religions

Plate: Picture of a display at the Brooklyn Museum (1998-2000) showing the similarity between the headrest of Ancient Egypt (foreground) and those used in other parts of Africa (background). (Photo by M. Ashby)

Foreground: Headrest and Mother nursing Child from Ancient Egypt Background: Headrest and Mother nursing Child from other parts of Africa

The display above shows the stark similarities noted widely in scholarly circles, between Ancient Egyptian artifacts and artifacts from other African nations. The headrest of Ancient Egypt in the foreground and the other African one in the background are alike in form, function, and color. The concept of the mother suckling the child depicted in the sculpture of Aset and Heru (foreground) and the West African sculpture in the background are also alike in concept, function and form. Also, Indian scholars have noted finding similar headrests in South India.[211]

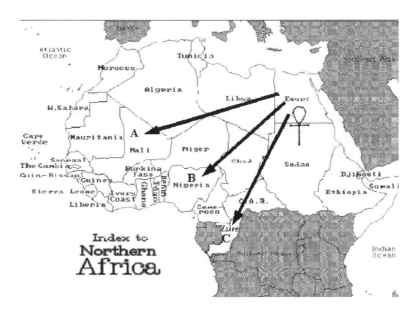

Figure-Above: A map of North-East Africa showing the location of *Ta-Meri* or *Kamit (Kamut)*, more commonly known as Ancient Egypt.

The arrows (in the map above) point to the geographical locations in Africa and Asia where the Ancient Egyptian influence spread during the height of Ancient Egyptian civilization, and also thereafter following the end of the Dynastic Period.

A- The Dogon of Mali.
B- The Yoruba of West Africa.
C- Zaire.
D- Greece and Rome.
E- India.

Ancient Egypt and the Dogon Nation

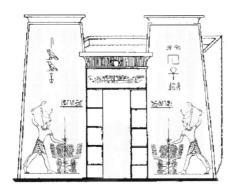 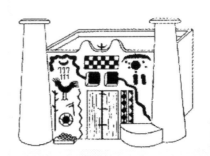

Figure 47: Above left- Kamitan Temple

The New Kingdom Period (1,900 B.C.E.-100 B.C.E.) Kamitan Temple

Figure 48: Above right- Dogon Temple

Late common era Dogon Temple (c. 1000 A.C.E.-2,000 A.C.E.)

The Dogon people of West Africa are perhaps known best for their extensive carvings of wooden figurative art and masks. The early history of the Dogon people is carried forth by oral traditions, and these claim that the Dogon came from the west bank of the Niger River during the period between the 10th to 13th centuries A.C.E. They emigrated west to northern Burkino Faso. The oral traditions also tell of their migration from north-east Africa. Thus, the Dogon claim themselves to be descendants of the Ancient Egyptians. The connection between Neterian Religion and Dogon religion is evident in several aspects of mythology including the name for the High God which is Amun in Shetaut Neter religion and Amma in Dogon religion. They share some of the Ancient Egyptian myths like the reverence for the star Sirius, but they have also incorporated elements from other religious systems over the years. In the scene above, notice the similarities of the Temples in the pylons and single entrance leading to a covered inner area of the Temples as well as the practice of placing inscriptions on the front of the Temple walls. These and other similarities, coupled with the ancestral legacy attested to by the Dogon themselves indicate that the Dogon and Kamitan cultures were at one time related, and that they have a common source in Kamit.

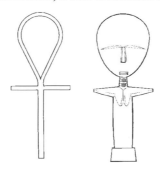

Figure 49: Above Left: Ankh-Ancient Egyptian Symbol and instrument of life. Right: Ahsanti Fertility doll from West African

Cultural Interactions Between the Ancient Egyptians and the Fon Nation

Above: From the tomb of Pharaoh Tutankhamun, a visual exposition of the idea expressed by the God Djehuti (Thoth)-Hermes: "As above, so below," as two serpents enclose the cosmic form of man (the universe). That which is above (spirit) is eternal, that which is below (matter) is also eternal. The serpent of the earth and the serpent of the sky encircle the lower as well as the higher self. The lower self and the higher self are complementary halves of the whole if brought into harmony.

The center area at the base of the spine is highlighted with a line and by the ram-headed hawk positioned with arms raised (in adoration "Ka") toward the sacral region of the spine - the root energy center (chakra).

The cosmic serpent went by many names in Ancient Egypt. There was the Kamutef serpent of Amun, and Mehen, the coiled serpent of the god Ra, known as the "coiled one." The Mehen serpent was known from the time of the coffin texts.[212] The serpent's body coils around the universe and stirs the primeval ocean into the varied forms of Creation as per the desire of God.

The Fon Nation of West Africa views the snake as the creator and sustainer of creation. Through its 3,500 "coils" above the earth, and 3,500 "coils" below the earth, the snake represents energy in perpetual motion, energy without which creation would immediately disintegrate. Note that the number 3,500 is a multiple of 3.5, the specific number ascribed in Kamit and India for the Serpent Power and Kundalini Yoga systems, respectively. This description recalls the Primeval Serpent of Ancient Egyptian mythology and Kundalini Yoga of India, with her "coiled up" cosmic energy which sustains all life. Another Fon story tells that a serpent carried GOD everywhere in its mouth in the making of creation. This is reminiscent of the Egyptian story of *"The Serpent in the Sky."* Also, the main character in Fon mythology, *Legba,* seeks to reconcile the rift between heaven and earth, which occurred in primeval times.

The Gods Murungu and Muntju (Monthu) of Kenya and Egypt in Africa

Murungu of Kenya

The Kikuyu people of Kenya, the tribes of Malawi, Zimbabwe, Zaire, Tanzania, Uganda and the Yao people of Mozambique worship the god Murungu (Mulungu)[213] as the supreme and transcendental divinity behind Creation. The Kikuyu's god is named "*Murungu.*" Kenya is an East-African republic in Africa, bounded on the north by Sudan and Ethiopia and on the east by Somalia and the Indian Ocean, on the south by Tanzania, and on the west by Lake Victoria and Uganda.[214] In ancient times Kenya was on the maritime trade route between Ethiopia and Egypt and India. Murungu cannot be seen, but is manifested in the sun, moon, thunder and lightning, stars, rain, the rainbow and in the great fig trees that serve as places of worship and sacrifice. These attributes of Murungu are closely related to the supreme divinity, Ra, in Ancient Kamit. Especially notable is the philosophy of understanding the Divine as supreme and transcendental and yet manifesting as Creation itself, but especially through the sun and moon. In Kamitan Anunian mysticism (based on the God Ra, whose main symbol is the sun) and Atonian (based on the divinity Aton, whose main symbol is the sundisk) mysticism, the Spirit is understood as manifesting through the sun and moon, not as being the object itself. This is an advanced understanding that there is a subtle essence beyond Creation and this conceptualization takes the religious philosophy outside the realm of idolatry.

Muntju of Ancient Egypt

In the aspect as the god of thunder and lightning, Murungu may be likened to Indra in the Vedic pantheon of Indian gods and goddesses. Indra was known to be the god of war among other attributes. Ra in Ancient Egypt has an aspect by the name of *Muntu (Montu, Monthu);* this aspect is the expression of war in Kamitan myth. The worship of Muntu was prominent in the 11th Dynasty Period. Muntu is related to Heru-Behded who is the warrior aspect of the god Heru, who is also an aspect of Ra.

Figure 50: Above-Left- The God Montju of Ancient Egypt. Above-Right Heru-Behded, The Warrior

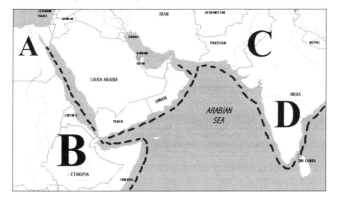

Figure 51: Above- (A-B) North-east Africa , Asia Minor, (C-D) South Asia (India) and the Egyptian-Indian trade routes in the Hellenistic (Greek) and Roman times.[215]

Evidence of Contact Between Ancient Egypt and other African Nations

Edward Wilmot Blyden (1832 - 1912) was one of the first African American theologian/scholars to recognize a connection between Ancient Egypt and the West African nations. He began to notice that the trade routs across the Sahara desert, which can be seen even today, transported goods and people, creating an inexorable connection between Northeast and West Africa. This contact existed since ancient times. The evidence of its existence can be found on the walls of the tombs of the nobles in Egypt. These are the same trade routs that were used by the Arabs to communicate, extend trade and spread the Islamic faith to West Africa, and they did so from their base in Egypt.

Ancient Traders: Painting from the "Tombs of the Nobles" in Egypt (New Kingdom) showing desert traders coming from other parts of Africa to Egypt. Note the hat of the first man from the right. This is the same type of hat used by traders in the present day region of West Sahara (Western Sudan) and it is also used by present day Dogons.

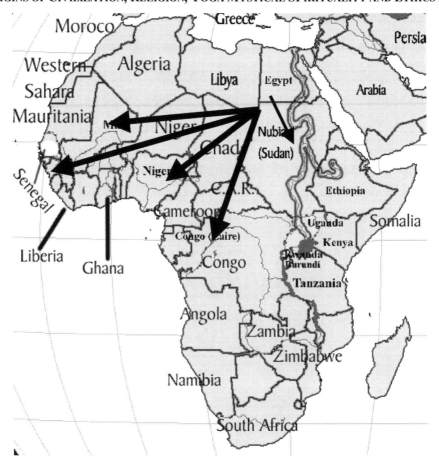

Above: The trade routs from Egypt to and from West Africa (Senegal, Mali, Nigeria, and Congo) and Kush (Nubia)

Cheikh Anta Diop presented compelling evidences to show that the Wolof language (Senegal) is derived from the Kamitan.[216] Since his time, other researchers have shown that evidences from linguistic correlations show a relationship. Also, J Olumide Lucas, in his book *The Religion of the Yorubas: Being an account of the religious beliefs and practices of the Yoruba peoples of southern Nigeria especially in relation to the religion of ancient Egypt,* presented evidences of linguistic nature as well as fundamental mythological nature to show the remnants of Ancient Egyptian religion and culture as surviving in Yoruba culture. While his work has been challenged as far as his method of classifying the evolution from the Kamitan to the Yoruba language, the mythological correlations are undeniable and powerful. What follows is a brief introduction to the mythological correlations between Kamitan and Yoruba religion. A more detailed discussion of this connection will be presented in a future volume.

Regional Correlations Between Kamitan Religion and other African Religions

Item of Correlation	Description	African Country or Culture where the Tradition was observed
Pigmies in the Royal Court	It was a tradition of the Pharaonic system in Kamit from the earliest period to have pigmies in the royal court.	Kamit, Kush, Unyoro, Mañbatto
The King Performs the ceremonial dance	The king performs a ceremonial dance for worship and renewal of the rulership and prosperity of the country.	Kamit, Unyoro, Mañbatto, Fon
Song of merriment and dispassion	At festivities the king and the people take part in a song whose statements are almost identical in two cultures.	Fon, Kamit (Song of the Harper)
Childbirth in the bush	The custom of women going into the bush to give birth.	Kamit, Kush (Sudan)
Injunctions of innocence	Statements proclaiming one's virtue, close similarity.	Kamit, Calabar

Interactions Between the Ancient Egyptians and the Yoruba Nation

Yoruba is a term that refers to a people (Oyo, Ife, Ilesha, Egbe, and Ijebu), a culture and a language originally based in Africa, as well as a religion. There are many parallels between Ancient Egyptian religion and the Yoruba religion. Both incorporate a system of divinities which represent cosmic forces, and many direct correlations can be observed between them. The Yoruba people reside in Western Africa (Nigeria). While many scholars of Yoruba openly state that there is little or no connection between these systems of spirituality, others have attempted to show linguistic correlations and contact in ancient times. As in the Dogon culture, some practitioners of Yoruba religion openly acknowledge their lineage to Ancient Egypt. The Asarian artifacts that have been discovered elsewhere in Africa[217] show that there was contact between Ancient Egypt and other countries in the interior of Africa. The Kamitan clergy carried with them certain aspects of spiritual knowledge which became incorporated in other cultures, through the influence of the clergy. Therefore, by looking at the mythology of Yoruba and Shetaut Neter, direct correlations in the fundamental theological principles of the religions are found which establish a relationship between the two.

The Yoruba religion has many similarities with the cosmogony, Gods and divination systems of Egypt. For example, one Yoruba creation story is almost identical to the Kamitan story described in the Shabaka Stone, later referred to as Memphite Theology. The Shabaka Stone describes the beginning as being a "watery and marshy place," and that the "Supreme Being" created the "Great God" whom he directed to create the world. The idea of a "Judgment after death" is also held by the Yorubas. It is similar to Kamitan idea of judgment as presented in the *Egyptian Book of the Dead* (*Egyptian Book of Coming Forth By Day*). In the Yoruba tradition, it is believed that after death, the spirit or soul of the person goes in front of God in order to give account of her or his life on earth. As in Ancient Kamit, the Yorubas believe that some will go to live with relatives in a good place, while others will end up in a bad place. Thus it is said in the Yoruba tradition:

> *All of the things we do when on earth,*
> *We will give account for in heaven.....*
> *We will state our case at the feet of GOD.*

The Yoruba and Kamitan System of Divinities

The next two images show the main divinities of Yoruba religion and those of Ancient Egyptian religion along with their mythological functions. Both systems have the same fundamental principles in relation to the nature of the Divine and the process in which that divine essence expresses in nature. From the Supreme and Transcendental Being (Olorun {Yoruba} or Neberdjer {Kamit}), the gods and goddesses emanate and thereby service Creation. Beyond matching in their manner of provenance, the correlations are homologous, matching even to the extent of the functions of the divinities. Both systems make use of an oracular scheme in which the Divinity communicates through the gods and goddesses, which represent natural (cosmic) forces in both systems, and also through direct means.

There have been many detractors within the ranks of followers of the Yoruba religion who have tried to assert that Yoruba spirituality is separate from other African religions, and some have alluded to the possibility that it emerged earlier than the Kamitan religion. While it is known and documented that Kamitan culture and spirituality go as far back as 10,000 B.C.E., Yoruba culture can only be documented to as far back as the 6th century A.C.E.[218] with the formation of Ife, the town in West Nigeria which is traditionally regarded as the oldest of the Yoruba kingdoms in the region. While Yoruba culture goes further back than the historical documentation suggests, the documentary evidences are used as a means to objectively compare historical relationships throughout history. The striking fact is that when the myths and philosophy of Yoruba spirituality are compared with the Kamitan, we begin to see a series of correlations that are inescapably well matched. Some of these include:

➤ Correlation of mythic characters and divinities in order and function.
➤ Correlation of cosmogony structure.
➤ Correlation of metaphysical intent of ritual.
➤ Correlation of oracular system.
➤ Correlation of metaphorical system of representing cosmic forces as divinities.
➤ Correlation of the function of the divinities in their mythic relationship to humanity and individual spiritual evolution.

There have been several scholars who have attempted to show a connection between Yoruba and Kamit based on linguistic correlations. However, this form of criteria is based on a mechanical interpretation of human interaction and evolutionary interaction. In other words, the idea that there needs to be a direct linguistic connection between two cultures in order to show a cultural, social or ethnic relationship is based on linear thinking rather than a scientific study of the manner in which human beings interact and influence each other. While a linguistic correlation (direct word borrowings or evolutions from one language to another) may be present, the absence of such factors should not preclude research into other forms of connection. For example, Dr. Cheikh Anta Diop discovered many connections between the Kamitan language and the Wolof language of West Africa.[219] As introduced earlier, while a linguistic correlations (direct word borrowings or evolutions from one language to another) may be present, the absence of such factors should not preclude research into other forms of connection. Therefore, phonetic connections may or be not present and in and of themselves offer only a superficial or theoretical basis to establish a connection, but if present along with correlations in other related factors (qualities-method of expression) such as meaning (definition), grammar, or etymology, then this kind of linguistic evidence carries more weight. This is what Diop has shown.

What is remarkable in these numerous cited examples is that we have not only grammatical and phonetic correlations, but also meaning (sense-connotation) correlations as well.

**Left: Goddess Aset of Kamit
suckling the child**

**Right: Goddess Oya of Yoruba,
suckling the child.**

Examples (partial list) of Some of the Correlations Presented by Cheikh Anta Diop[220]

Kamitan Words	Wolof Words
Ta = earth	*Ta* = inundated earth, the very image of Egypt, of the Nile Valley
Ta tenen = The earth that rises, the first mound that appeared within the *Nun,* from the primordial water, in order to serve as the place where the god Ra appeared in the sensible world.	*Ten* = *a* formed mound (in clay), as God made to create Adam; emergence, earth mound.
Kematef - mysterious initial snake that encircles the earth and eats its own tail (?)	*Kemtef, Kematef* = *the* limit of something, could apply to the mythical snake encircling the world and feeding each day off its own tail.
Elbo = *the* "floater" = the emergent mound where the sun appeared at the beginning of time = the town of Edfu.[221]	*Temb* = *to* float (a parasitic "m" before "b").
Erme = Ra's tears through which he created humanity, hence the name of the Egyptians. *Erme* = *men* par excellence	*Erem - ye*ram = mercy; the feeling of compassion often accompanied by tears.
Aar, aaru = *Paradise,* Elysian Fields	*Aar* =divine protection *Aaru* = protected by the divinity
Khem-min(t) = *the* god Min's sanctuary. = *kemmis* in Greek	*Ham "Min"* = *to* know Min; can also be applied to the prophet of Min, meaning, his first priest.
Anu = *Osiris's* ethnic group; word designated by a pillar	*Enou - ye*nou = to carry on the head *K-enou* = *pillar*

Thus, if we look at the myth and culture of the Yoruba nation, we can then go beyond the limited standards set by mainstream European scholarship in order to discover the connection between the Yoruba and the Kamitans.

The correlations between the Yoruba and Neterian Divinities may be viewed thusly:

Kamitan Divinities	Yoruba Divinities
Olorun	Neberdjer (Temu)
Elegba	Djehuti
Obatala	Asar
Ogun	Anpu
Shango	Set
Oya	Maat
Osun	Hetheru
Yemoja	Mehurt
Orunmilas	Apis
Odudua	Aset
Aganju (earth)	Geb

Plate: Yoruba System of Divinities

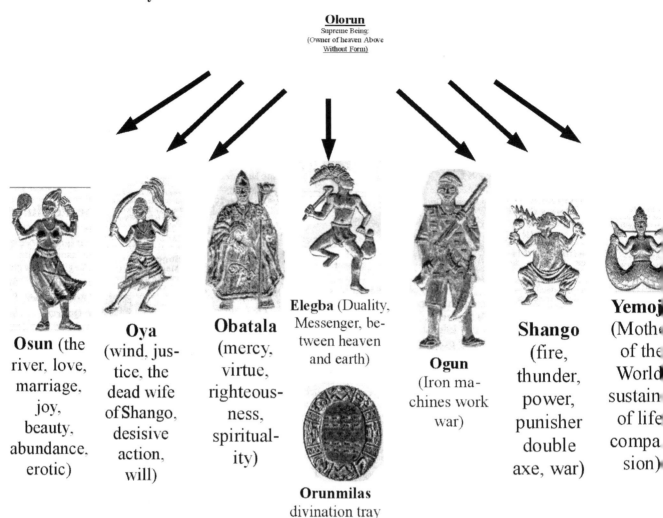

Olorun
Supreme Being
(Owner of heaven Above
Without Form)

Osun (the river, love, marriage, joy, beauty, abundance, erotic)

Oya (wind, justice, the dead wife of Shango, desisive action, will)

Obatala (mercy, virtue, righteousness, spirituality)

Elegba (Duality, Messenger, between heaven and earth)

Orunmilas divination tray

Ogun (Iron machines work war)

Shango (fire, thunder, power, punisher double axe, war)

Yemoj (Moth of the World sustain of life compa sion)

Yoruba religion holds that ***Olorun*** is the Supreme Divinity and that from here all other lesser divinities emanate. The lower order of divinities, the ***Orishas***, control and sustain creation and interact with human beings, visiting upon them either wisdom and prosperity or retribution and adversity. Also, there is a practice of ritual trance in which the divinity is allowed to "possess" the individual and thereby guide and cleanse the individual. For some the ritual of trance and possession has degraded into a search to become the divinity. This is in contrast to the Kamitan understanding of the idea which is to discover that one already has that divinity within, and only needs to discover and express that form of consciousness. The misunderstanding also sometimes holds that the divinities exist in fact, separate from human consciousness, whereas the Kamitan philosophy shows that the cosmic forces are innate. Further, the oracular system is sometimes relied upon in Yoruba as a substitute for common sense and responsibility. Kamitan spirituality prohibits the use of oracles in ordinary situations that human beings need to face in order to grow and evolve.

"Don't rely exclusively on the oracle for guidance; sometimes it is necessary for us to live our lives for ourselves and not to lean too heavily on other minds who, after all, have their own thing to do. If the Gods in their wisdom see fit to deny us access to outer time, then it is usually because of some decision made by our own free will or spirit, maybe even prior to entering the body."

-Ancient Egyptian Proverb

Figure: Kamitan System of Divinities

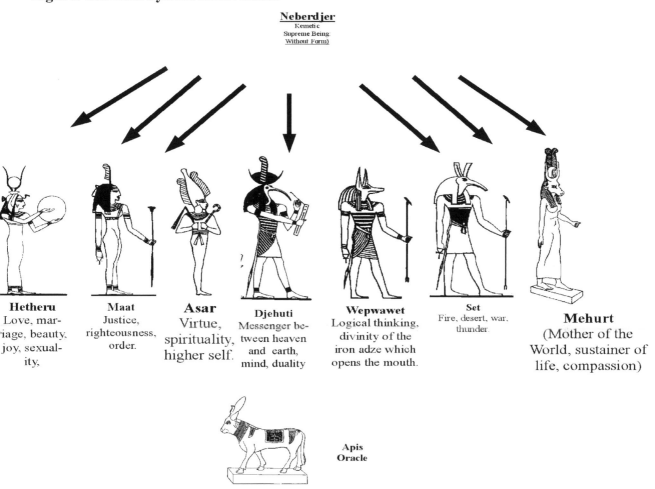

Neberdjer
Kemetic
Supreme Being:
Without Form)

Hetheru
Love, marriage, beauty, joy, sexuality,

Maat
Justice, righteousness, order.

Asar
Virtue, spirituality, higher self.

Djehuti
Messenger between heaven and earth, mind, duality

Wepwawet
Logical thinking, divinity of the iron adze which opens the mouth.

Set
Fire, desert, war, thunder.

Mehurt
(Mother of the World, sustainer of life, compassion)

Apis
Oracle

In the same manner that the Yoruba religion holds that **Olorun** is the Supreme Divinity and that from here all other lesser divinities emanate, Kamitan religion holds that **Neberdjer (Neter)** is the Supreme Divinity and that from here all other lesser divinities emanate. The lower order of divinities, the **neteru**, control and sustain creation and interact with human beings, visiting upon them either wisdom and prosperity or retribution and adversity. Further, the neteru are understood as aspects not only of Neberdjer, but also of the innermost human personality, which is essentially one with Neberdjer. Therefore, human beings are to discover their neteru nature by emulating the nature of the neteru, and opening up to the cosmic energy they represent, through ritual, but also through life discipline, i.e. living in accordance with the principles of Maat. Therefore, there is a deep mystic wisdom attached to the neteru, as they are understood to be a means by which a Kamitan initiate discovers their true nature as the Supreme Being.

The purpose of ritual identification with the neteru in Kamitan spirituality is to discover the aspects of one's innate essential nature and thereby become an enlightened being. As previously discussed, this idea is sometimes expressed as a "consumption" (eating) of the neteru since as we know, "you are what you eat."

"Whoever has eaten the knowledge of every god (neteru), their existence is for all eternity and everlasting in their spirit body; what they willeth they doeth."

-Ancient Egyptian Proverb

The tables which follow show more details as to the function and nature of the Yoruba gods and goddesses and the correlations with the Kamitan gods and goddesses.

Table A: General Gradations of the Main Yoruba Deities and their Mythological Significance

Spiritual Significance	YORUBA	*Spiritual Significance*
	Supreme Being: **Olorun** (Owner of Heaven Above) From this Divinity Emanates all existence (Creation, human beings and all deities -# unknown) ⬇	
	Major Orishas	
Negative Aspect (Destroyer)	← **Eshu (Elegba)** →	Positive Aspect (Creator-Sustainer)
	⬇ Male Aspect –Female Aspect ⬇	
	Orunmila (Deified Prophet) Creator of Ifa Divination System 16 Odus Deified Prophets or Cosmic Forces ⬇	
Creator God Presiding over Morality and Virtue and Purity	← **Obatala** Potter who Fashions men **Oduduwa** → Great Mother Nursing Child	Creator Goddess Mother of Yoruba people and Virtue
	Earth and Sky **Ogun** (Iron, War, Remover of Obstacles) **Sango** (Thunder, destruction, retribution, Anger) **Orisa Oko** (Farming, Agriculture, Harvest)	

Table B: General Gradations of the Main Kamitan Deities and their Mythological Significance

Spiritual Significance	KAMITAN	*Spiritual Significance*
	Supreme Being:	
	Neberdjer-Amun - Heru (Owner of Heaven Above) From this Divinity Emanates all existence (Creation, human beings and all deities -# unknown)	
	⬇	
	Major Neteru	
Negative Aspect (Destroyer)	⬅ **Heru (Heru-Set)** ➡	Positive Aspect (Creator-Sustainer)
	⬇	
Heru Male Aspect –Female Aspect **Hetheru**		
	⬇	
	Asar (as god of the Dead) (as **Apis**)	
	Deified Prophets or Cosmic Forces **Djehuti** **Imhotep**	
	⬇	
Creator God Presiding over Morality and Virtue and Purity	⬅ **Khnum** Potter who Fashions men **Aset and Maat** ➡ Great Mother Nursing Child	Creator Goddess Mother of Yoruba people and Virtue
	Earth and Sky	
	Wepwawet (Remover of Obstacles) **Set** (Thunder, destruction, retribution, Anger) **Asar (as man)** (Farming, Agriculture, Harvest)	

Other Correlations Between Kamitan and Yoruba Religion

Kamit	Yoruba
The Kamitans have called their temple *"Neter Het"* or "House (place) of the Divinity"	The Yoruba have called their temple *"Ile Orisha"* or "House (place) of the Divinity"
The Kamitans viewed the spirits as coming to inhabit the images upon being propitiated and the images themselves were not worshipped.	The Yoruba viewed the spirits as coming to inhabit the images upon being propitiated and the images themselves were not worshipped.
The Kamitan God Ptah Sokkar Asar is the potter who created human beings out of clay. Another potter divinity is Knum, who fashions the body out of clay (i.e. earth).	The Yoruba God Obatala created the first man and woman out of clay.
The Kamitan Goddess Aset the wife of Asar, is represented as a seated woman nursing a child.	The Yoruba Goddess Adudua, the wife of Obatala is represented as a seated woman nursing a child.
The priests in the Kamitan tradition were organized into grades.	The priests in the Yoruba tradition were organized into grades.

It should be borne in mind that prior to and during the move by European countries to colonize Africa itself (1750 A.C.E.-1960 A.C.E.), there were European explorers who visited African countries which were minimally or as yet entirely unaffected by Western Culture. Some of these travelers were Livingstone, Speke, Baker and Junker. Observations collected by researchers such as George Grenfell, Mr. Torday, Mr. Joyce of the British Museum, Sir Harry Johnston, Dr. Andrew Balfour of the Khartŭm and his colleagues, as well as the researches presented in the works of the Musée du Congo and varied other writers show the remnants of Ancient African customs and traditions prior to their disruption by the European colonization. So this form of study provides a certain perspective that may not be possible to achieve in the present day due to the social, political and economic devastations in Africa in the last 100 years.

The observations noted above have provided insights into several Kamitan rituals and traditions since the Ancient Kamitans were African, just as the study of Indian culture also provides insights, because the ancient Indians were part of the same Kushitic culture as were the Kamitans. Some examples of the traditions and rituals of other African cultures that provide insight into Kamitan traditions, have been given above. Some customs are found to have a direct correlation. On example is the Galla culture, who worship a Supreme Being which is associated with two other divinities, and so their system of religion, like the Kamitan, also contains a Trinity system. The Mpongwe believe in God who is named "Anyambia" who has both positive and negative qualities together. Anyambia is associated with two divinities, "Ombwiri" and "Onyambe," who represent good and evil, respectively, i.e. the forces of life, order, truth and righteousness (virtue) and the forces of entropy, that which is undesirable, disorder, etc. In the Ancient Egyptian Pyramid Texts and the Pert M Heru texts there are passages that speak of reestablishing the jaw bones. An ancient tradition of Uganda was to separate the jaw from the dead. A similar tradition was found among the Dahomey and Baganda. The symbolic rememberment of the body and the ability to speak again in the Netherworld is the important theme here. In Uganda, the ancient home of the Kamitans, a tradition of cutting and saving the umbilical cord and phallus of the kings were discovered.[222] These traditions can also be observed in Kamit.

These and other striking similarities between Ancient Egyptian (Kamitan) culture and traditions and those of other African cultures are not necessarily due to their having been given to African nations by the Kamitan culture. Rather, they should be thought of as indigenous developments by peoples in Africa, all of whom as we are now told by geneticist and archeologists, all emerged from the same place, the Great Lakes region and from South Africa at about 150,000 years ago. What happened in Kamit should be seen as a development from that same original common source which spread the cultural similarities throughout Africa from 150,000 B.C.E. to 100,000 B.C.E. The geography and agricultural conditions in Kamit allowed the Kamitans to develop a culture wherein the primordial customs and rituals were maintained in ritual and literary form, but not in actual literal practice. An example of this is the jaw tradition which is mentioned as an ancient tradition, but only the reconstitution part of the tradition is emphasized in Kamit and not the physical dismemberment of the king (of which there is no record or evidence of its being practiced in Kamit). This is why Kamit may be seen as the place where the flowering of African culture occurred as opposed to the sole source of culture and social advancement. However, in such cases as the correlations with the Yoruba, Nubian and Dogon cultures in Africa, Greece in Europe (western Asia), Cannanites in Asia Minor and Indians in east Asia, it is clear that there was contact and influence after the flowering in Kamit (15,000 B.C.E.-500 A.C.E.) which led to the adoption of traditions from Kamit to those other cultures. This is attested by the number and quality of correlations which rise above what could be expected as due to coincidence or simple chance. In this sense therefore, Kamitan culture can be seen as the epitome of African culture and since there are ample records to draw from, this record may be used effectively to reconstruct African culture and traditions.

African Masks

African masks are an integral part of African culture, art and spirituality. The mask tradition came to its height in Benin and Kamit. The following are examples of the Mask Art as it is used to related the earth realm to the spiritual realm through ritual.

Above left: Typical African Ritual Mask (Congo-Kinshasa) . Right Death of King Tutankhamun of Kamit

Above: Ancient Egyptian priest performs the rites of the dead while wearing a mask in the likeness of the god Anpu, the divinity of embalming.

Interactions Between the Ancient Egyptians and Cultures in the Americas

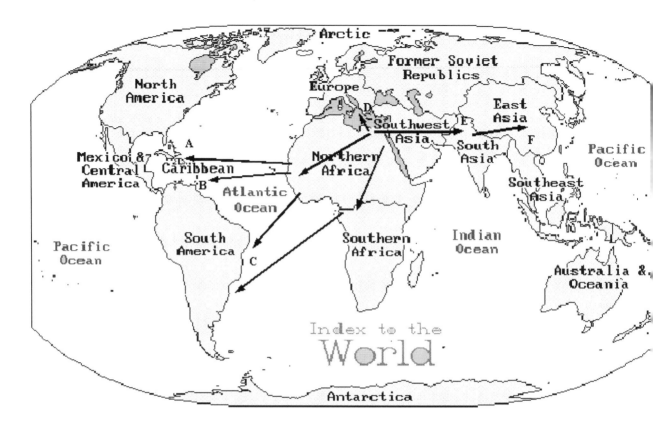

Figure 52: The map above shows the documented influence of Ancient Egyptian Culture on world religions.

A-B-C: Yoruba religion in the Caribbean was a result of the Yoruba followers in West Africa who were brought to the Western hemisphere as slaves. The influence is most visible in Cuba, Haiti and Brazil.

D-E-F: In Asia, the influence is most pronounced in Greek* mythology and philosophy, Sufism, Christian Gnosticism, Yoga and Vedanta philosophy in India, and from India, the influence was extended to Chinese Taoism.

*Here Greece is considered as part of Asia.

The map above illustrates that the traditions which passed from Ancient Egypt to other parts of Africa also influenced the Americans through the Africans who were brought there as slaves during the European slave trade period.

Brazil and the *Bumba Me Boi* – Rock the Bull

Figure 53: Priestesses in Ancient Egypt playing the Drum

There is a large population of people of African descent in South America who brought with them many of the customs and traditions of Africa as they were captured and enslaved by European peoples. Many have managed to preserve some of the traditions and at times even established cities of free people, sustaining the practice of some of their traditions without obstruction. An example of this is the culture of Bahia[67]. There is a festivity practiced by Brazilian tribes of mixed African and Native population called *Bumba Me Boi* – (Rock the Bull). It is a ritual that goes on for days in which drums (including hand drums like those played in Ancient Egypt) are used to "resurrect" a mythical bull. The hand drum is also used at births. This was also the case in Ancient Egypt; the inscriptions showing the priestesses playing the drums at the birthing houses are ample. Further, in Ancient Egypt when someone died, they were viewed as having become the god Asar, whose symbol is the bull, and the birth of a child was seen as the birth of the divinity Heru. The rituals of the *Prt M Hru* (*Ancient Egyptian Book of the Dead*) which were carried out for the deceased and the birthing house rituals were designed to effect a resurrection in consciousness of the participants. The mystic teaching is that when the drums are played a certain way, a particular tonal quality emerges that infuses the participants with life force and elevation of consciousness. In the *Bumba Me Boi* beats, this quality is called "the fifth." It is an interval of five notes played together. One drummer plays three beats and another plays two, and in so doing divide the same measure at once into three and two. After many hours and inducing a trance state, with the correct training and practice, the practitioner is supposed to be transported to higher realms of consciousness. The Brazilians practice this ritual even though it is mixed with the Christian tradition due to indoctrination during the slavery period. However, they have a tradition that their ancestors came from Egypt.[223]

Ancient Kamitans In Contact With the Americas

Another item of evidence proving the contact between Kamit and the Americas is Nicotine. Nicotine was discovered in the bowels of an Egyptian mummy. Nicotine comes from tobacco and this plant only grows in the Americas.[224]

Parapsychology and the Proofs of Ancient African Mysticism and Religion

Why should we follow or place so much importance on African religion? Why should we not consider it to be just so much superstition or primitive or childish attempts at religion, as some have called it? The basic tenets of mystical religion as put forth in such religious systems as Shetaut Neter, Yoruba, Dogon, etc. of Africa or the Hinduism, Taoism, of the East or the Native American Religions of the West cause much consternation for believers of the Western orthodox religions (Judaism, Christianity, and Islam). Yet, those Western religions believe in fantastic ideas, but these are not related as such. The idea that a man can throw a stick into a river and part the waters (Moses) is certainly supernatural. A man walking on water (Jesus) is

---

[67] **Bahia**, a state in northeastern Brazil that is considered as the cradle of Afro-Brazilian culture and is still in existence.

equally supernatural and some may even consider these ideas as superstitious or fantastic and even the rantings of a fanatic. However, since the Western Culture determines its paradigm of what is acceptable and this is reinforced through the media, these ideas are accepted and taken for granted while the beliefs of others are repudiated.

The basic tenets of mystical religions, such as reincarnation, telepathy, clairvoyance, clairaudience and premonition, which support the contention of ancient Sages that we exist in different planes and can access these to attain higher consciousness, are refuted by people without investigating deeper. Actually, experiments by Western scientists have shown these to be real and verifiable. Putting these parapsychological evidences together with the experiments of Quantum physicists takes us to another world paradigm. It takes us away from the paradigm based on an orthodox Western mentality which leads people to persist in denying the empirical evidences that have been produced to prove the existence of psychic phenomena, life after death, and the underlying unity of the material universe. It is a credit to the eminent late teacher Cheikh Anta Diop, who was an accomplished scientist, that upon examining the evidences conceded to these and included them in his book (*Civilization or Barbarism-Credit to Parapsychology*) as proofs of the validity and legitimacy of African religion and philosophy. The reader should review the following texts for more information on the proofs of psychic phenomena, reincarnation and life after death.

- ❑ *Many Lives Many Masters* – by Brian Weis
- ❑ *The Conscious Universe: The Scientific truth of Psychic Phenomena* by Dean Radin, Ph. D.
- ❑ *The Dao of Physics* by Fritjof Capra
- ❑ *Dancing Wu Li Masters* by Gary Zukav

African mystical philosophy is not merely a primitive superstition. It is based on the mystical experience of Sages and Saints throughout the history of Africa. These experiences were codified in the form of religious myths and shamanic (spiritualist) rituals that were designed to promote these experiences in others. This is the purpose for the Sema (yogic) disciplines that reached their height in Kamit. This high concept in spirituality formed the basis of the initiatic sciences of the Kamitan Temples. They constitute the highest expression of the African Spiritualist Consciousness that is common throughout the African Continent. This awareness of the underlying Supreme Being that pervades all is not a superstition, but rather an experience of the Divine and is therefore based on fact and not fiction. A religion that exhorts its followers to perpetually believe in concepts by faith alone without the prospect of attaining an actual experience of the Divine while the person is still alive is not promoting a full experience of religion and will therefore be limited, and consequently dogmatic. Therefore, faith is the beginning of religion and not its end. The end is to achieve a mystical experience of awareness and unity with the Divine, and not to simply implore the Divine or remain as an egoistic individual talking about religion and practicing its rituals, but attaining no higher experiences. That lower condition, due to the limited practice of religion, is what allows human beings to say they are practitioners of religion, while at the same time they promote war, greed and other detrimental aspects of society. That is not the advanced practice of religion. This is why it is so important to study African Religion and to bring it back to the forefront of human consciousness, so that the world will rediscover the ancient standard from which it has strayed and correct the imbalances that have characterized the practice of religion.

Challenges to African Religion in the 21st Century

Statistics:

❏ Currently, there are at least 730 million people in Africa, out of which 108 million practice Native African Religion.

❏ Most popular religion is Islam, mostly in Upper Sahara. Next is Native African Religion.

❏ There are fewer Christians than those practicing Native African Religion.

❏ There are only seven countries in Africa who have more than 50% of the population who practice Native African Religion[225]:

o Liberia	70%
o Togo	70%
o Benin	70%
o Burkina Faso	65%
o Guinea-Bissau	65%
o Madagascar	52%
o Cameroon	51%

Consider that Europe is a conglomerate of countries with different languages, customs, etc., like Africa, but they follow generally the same faith. In Europe, the main religion is Christianity. Imagine what the European population would do if they were actively forced by some other country outside Europe to change their languages and their religion. This is unthinkable, and yet if the peoples ability to speak their languages, practice their rituals and customs etc. were prevented, and they were forced to practice other customs over 2-3 generations, their spirituality and concepts of social organization would be disrupted. They would end up divided, some following the new religions and norms, while others try to recapture the old ways, and still, others being frustrated, would turn towards Marxist (there is no God) or secular (worldly – movement away from spirituality) philosophies. This is what has occurred to African countries at the hands of European colonial forces.

Above: The Challenges to African Religion: *Christianity, Islam, Marxism and Secularism*

Native African Religion has been challenged by Christianity and Islam for many years, but now also it is being challenged by at least two additional pressures, Marxism and secularism. The eminent Africologist Ali A. Mazrui noted, on a visit to Ethiopia in the mid 1980's, that the country had adopted Marxism,[226] a philosophy of socialism or collectivism that requires, like its opposite extreme, capitalism – globalism (*Globalization*), the dropping of traditional customs and the adoption of a way of life that excludes spirituality, and even denies any validity to religion. Marxism repudiates religion altogether. Secularity is the turning away from religion and living with the conviction that one can direct one's life without divine guidance. Secularity is a degrading force in society, turning it towards pleasure seeking, un-tempered by the moral restraints or ethics which comes from religion. Thus, in due course of time, corruption and greed degrades the moral structure of the population. Individualism, high-living and self-gratification are facilitated by the secular viewpoint. This seduces people into engaging in capitalistic or despotic forms of government that promote certain segments of the population to become wealthy, while others languish in abject poverty. Globalism, the new term referring to opening up trade worldwide, really means giving up traditional values as well as individual rights to property and resources to be controlled by the few who become wealthy.

India is an interesting example of the failure of Secularism. Thought of by many as an exotic land of yogis and saints, after independence from British colonial rule in the late 1940's A.C.E. took a path of establishing a secular government. The mostly Hindu population protested and accused the government of turning away from Dharma (philosophy of righteousness-moral values) and also a spiritual consciousness in the upbringing of the next generation, since the turn towards secularism required the banning of Hinduism from the educational system.[227] The problem continues to this day and more conflict has ensued within the different sects of Hinduism and between Hinduism and other religions in India such as Christianity and Buddhism. A better solution, which would also apply to Africa, is to create a government that upholds the common-fundamental-traditional spiritual values of all religious traditions, leaving the minor folk differences to the local populations.

Thus, there are many challenges to African Religion in the 21st Century. One possible solution is for Africa is to create a government that upholds the common-fundamental-traditional and moral values of all Native African religions, leaving the minor folk differences to the local population. In other words, Marxism and Secularism are unnecessary since there already is an African system of philosophy designed to take care of the population. Marxism and Secularism actually disrupt that already preexisting system and substitute it with a program that is anti-spiritual and is thus doomed to failure. Africans developed and instituted long ago a program of social order that came to its height of development in Kamit and lasted for THOUSANDS of years there and this program needs to be studied and adapted for use by present day Africans. Again, this points up the importance of learning about and rediscovering Ancient Kamit as Cheikh Anta Diop admonished.

> "Ancient Egypt was a Negro civilization. The history of Black Africa will remain suspended in air and cannot be written correct until African historians dare to connect it with the history of Egypt In particular, the study of languages, institutions, and so forth, cannot be treated properly; in a word, it will be impossible to build African humanities, a body of African human sciences, so long as that relationship does not appear legitimate."

> -Cheikh Anta Diop July 1973
> *African Origins of Civilization: Myth or Reality*

In this manner, the government and other social institutions could be based on ancient African principles of family, righteousness, order and justice (Maat-Ubuntu) and uphold the interests of all people equally and it would be based on moral values. In this respect, a federation of African countries could join and strengthen themselves to meet the *Challenges to African Religion in the 21st Century*. Such a program for the reorganization of African Religion and government will be the subject of an upcoming volume.

Conclusion

Given the persistence of African religion, even in the face of relentless pressure from Western religions, it is remarkable that its practice has continued to this day. It follows therefore that the practice of Western religions would not have attained their status if it were not due to the disruptions in African culture (Judaism, Christianity, Islam, Arab slave trade, European slave trade, colonialism, and neocolonialism). These disruptions were imposed on Africa through coercion (compulsion, duress) and not through natural adoption. Christianity was successfully spread throughout Africa because the first missionaries indoctrinated young children and the colonial governments suppressed the practice of African religion along with any indigenous practices that might promote the movement towards freedom from colonialism. The young generation passed on the new beliefs to their children as they grew up, and gradually the new beliefs gained more adherents. The spread of Islam was also by force, by punishing many who resisted its introduction, and also by allowing its practitioners, the Muslims, to become successful members of the society (government and commerce). In addition, in the beginning, it allowed the mixing of African religion with Islam. However, later on, the African religious aspects were suppressed, allowing only the practice of Islam.

So when we examine religion in Africa, especially the Western religions, we must look with caution when assessing the level of conversion to Western religion and the true nature of African spirituality. In one important sense the Western religions are unsuccessful because they deny the essential need of the African mind to seek harmony with the here and now while at the same time discovering a harmony with the Transcendental. Western religions are too focused (fanatically) with the hereafter, and this does not serve the greater need of African Spirituality. Thus, any religion developing in Africa must be able to meet the need of the African consciousness by:

- providing a humanistic approach to spirituality,

- providing a connection between the spirit realm and the practical reality that is pantheistic,

- being ritualistically fulfilling,

- being psychologically comforting and intellectually satisfying in its ability to explain life, and able to lead its practitioners to harmony and peace through virtue.

African Spirituality has much in common with Eastern religions such as Hinduism, in seeing the spirit in the mundane, i.e. pantheism. Given this similarity, the two forms of religion will be compatible, and thus many people of African descent seeking higher mystical philosophy, unfamiliar with their Kamitan spiritual heritage, have gravitated to the mystical Eastern traditions. But still, even here, under normal conditions, there would not be mass conversion of African peoples to the more orthodox Eastern traditions such as Hinduism, because the religions at this level of practice serve not only a spiritual purpose, but also a cultural purpose of identity and social stability. Thus, most Hindus in Africa are people of Indian descent who were brought there by the British and other colonial rulers as indentured servants (slaves). They have lived side by side with Africans practicing African religions, and have not had conflicts due to religious reasons, but rather due to reasons based on issues of cultural and racial discrimination.[68]

The Importance of Neterian Religion in the Study of African Religions

Above left: Adinkra symbol- *Adinkrahene, "chief of adinkra symbols"* **meaning charisma, greatness, leadership.**
Above right: The Kamitan symbol of "*Ra***" meaning light, glory, Supreme Being.**

---

[68] Due to the history of the caste system in India, suffering under British racism and colonialism, a developing self-centered national cultural ego, widespread ignorance in the Indian community about the origins of their own culture and lack of the authentic (complete) practice of their religion, there is a growing rift between Indians yand Africans.

Ancient Egyptian religion is an African religion. Ancient Egyptian religion has had a significant role to play in the development of African religions, holding the place as the first African nation to create a system of writing and to commit the tenets of the spiritual philosophy to writing for posterity. These features alone are remarkable aspects of African religion. However, the study of Ancient Egyptian religion also has the added important aspect of allowing us to clearly envision the fundamental and unifying principles of African religion, as it exemplifies and intellectually expounds on these as no other African religion does. Since Ancient Egyptian religion informs not only other African religions, but also the other world religions, this allows us to gain a deeper understanding of the practice, purpose and meaning of African religion and its place among the world community of world religions.

SANKOFA

Adinkra symbol- "return and get it" meaning: learn from the past!

NOTES FOR CHAPTER 2

"African Religions: An Interpretation," *Microsoft® Encarta® Africana.* © 1999 Microsoft Corporation. All rights reserved.

African Religion: World Religion by Aloysius M. Lugira

African Mythology by Geoffrey Parrinder

African Religions and Philosophy -- by John S. Mbiti

Civilization or Barbarism by Cheikh Anta Diop

Colonialism and Colonies," *Microsoft® Encarta® Encyclopedia 2000.* © 1993-1999 Microsoft Corporation. All rights reserved.

Religions, African, in Latin America and the Caribbean," *Microsoft® Encarta® Africana.* ©1999 Microsoft Corporation. All rights reserved.

[206] "African Religions," *Microsoft® Encarta® Encyclopedia 2000.* © 1993-1999 Microsoft Corporation. All rights reserved.

See the books *Egyptian Yoga Vol. 1* for more on the disciplines of Egyptian Yoga and *Mysteries of Isis* for more on the teachings of the Temple of Aset, by Muata Ashby

On his statue in the Glyptothek at Munich

[209] *African Religion: World Religion* by Aloysius M. Lugira

For the full text see the *Book of the Dead* by Muata Ashby

Pottery Headrests from Narsipur Sangam, F.R. Allchin, *Studies in Indian Prehistory*, D. Sen and A.K. Ghosh, eds., Calcutta, 1966, pp. 58-63

A Dictionary of Egyptian Gods and Goddesses, George Hart

Guide to the Gods, Marjorie Leach

"Kenya," Microsoft (R) Encarta. Copyright (c) 1994 Funk & Wagnall's Corporation.

Doshi, Saryu, Editor-Indian Council for Cultural Relations *India and Egypt: Influences and Interactions* 1993

The African Origin of Civilization, *Civilization or Barbarism,* Cheikh Anta Diop

The African Origin of Civilization, Cheikh Anta Diop – *Civilization or Barbarism*, Cheikh Anta Diop

Websters Encyclopedia.

Civilization or Barbarism

Civilization or Barbarism, Cheikh Anta Diop

Sauneron and Yoyotte, *La Naissance du Monde, op. cit., p. 35*

See journal Ins. Anthropological Society, Vol. XXXI, p. 1117 ff.; Vol. XXXII, P. 25 ff.; and *Kibuka, the War God of the Baganda*, in *Man*, No. 95, 1907, P- 161 ff.

Interview with Layne Redmond, prominent hand drummer, after attendance at a Brazilian festival.

Civilization or Barbarism, Cheikh Anta Diop

African Religion: World Religion by Aloysius M. Lugira

The Africans by Ali A. Mazrui

A Concise Encyclopedia of Hinduism, by Klaus K. Klostermaier

Bibliography

A Concise Encyclopedia of Hinduism, by Klaus K. Klostermaier

A Sanskrit-English Dictionary, Monier Williams, p. 528

A SON OF GOD: THE LIFE AND PHILOSOPHY OF AKHNATON, KING OF EGYPT, Savitri Devi, [1946]

African Presence in Early Asia edited by Ivan Van Sertima and Runoko Rashidi

Am I a Hindu?: the Hinduism Primer by Ed. Viswanathan

American Heritage Dictionary.

Ancient Architecture by S. Lloyd and H.W. Miller

Ancient Egypt the Light of the World by Gerald Massey

Ancient Egyptian Literature Volume I and II, by Miriam Lichtheim

Ancient, Medieval and Modern Christianity by Charles Guignebert

Anunian Theology by Muata Ashby

Art - Culture of India and Egypt, the author S. M El Mansouri

Arts and Crafts of Ancient Egypt, Flinders Petrie

Ashby, M. A., "Egyptian Yoga The Philosophy of Enlightenment Vol. 1, Sema Institute of Yoga-C.M. Book Publishing 1995

Atlas of Ancient Egypt, John Baines and Jaromir Malek, 1980

Barbara Adams (Petrie Museum of Egyptian Archaeology and Dr. Renée Friedman (University of California, Berkeley).

Based on the new discoveries at the city of Mehrgarh - Indus Valley

Better known as The Ancient Egyptian Book of the Dead by Dr. Muata Ashby 2000

Between the years 1960-1970

Bible Myth: The African Origins of the Jewish People Gary Greenberg

Black Athena, The Afroasiatic Origins of Classical Civilization by Martin Bernal

Black Man of The Nile and His Family by

Blackwell's book of Philosophy; Zeller's History of Philosophy; Diogenes Laertius; Kendrick's Ancient Egypt.

Buddha: the Intelligent Heart by Alistair Shearer

Cable News Network - world report

Cable News Network 1990-1991

Chanudaro Excavations, 1935-36 E.J.H. Mackay, American Oriental Society, New Heaven, 19443, pp. 25 and 22 pl. XCII, 38

Chanudaro Excavations, 1935-36 E.J.H. Mackay, American Oriental Society, New

Charles Elliot, Hinduism and Buddhism, vol. III, London, 1954, pp. 93-94

Christian and Islamic Spirituality by Maria Jaoudi

Christian Yoga by Muata Ashby for more details.

Christian Yoga: The Journey from Jesus to Christ, Muata Ashby

Civilisation ou Barbarie, Courtesy of Pr,sence Africaine. Cheikh Anta Diop's

Civilization or Barbarism by Cheikh Anta Diop

Civilizations of the Indus Valley and Beyond, Sir Mortimer Wheeler.

Comparative Mythology, Jaan Puhvel

Compton's Interactive Encyclopedia Copyright (c) 1994, 1995

Connection of Egypt with India, F.W.H. Migeod, Man, vol. 24, no. 118, London, 1924, p. 160

Dancing Wu Li Masters by Gary Zukov

Destruction of Black Civilization: Great Issues of a Race from 4500bc to 2000ad by Chancellor Williams

Diodorus Book 23

Doshi, Saryu, Editor-Indian Council for Cultural Relations India and Egypt: Influences and Interactions 1993

Dutta, P. C. 1984. Biological anthropology of Bronze Ace. Harappans: new perspectives. In The People of South Asia.

Echoes of the Old Darkland by Dr. Charles Finch

Egypt Uncovered, Vivian Davies and Ren,e Friedman

Egypt: Child of Africa, Ivan Van Sertima 1994

Egyptian Book of Coming forth by day of Anhai

Egyptian Book of Coming forth by day of Ani

Egyptian Book of Coming forth by day of Ankhwahibre

Egyptian Book of Coming forth by day of Kenna

Egyptian Book of the Dead by Gerald Massey

Egyptian Book of the Dead by Muata Ashby

Egyptian Coffin texts

Egyptian Magic by E.W. Budge

Egyptian Pyramid Texts

Egyptian Ru Pert Em Heru, Hymns of Amun and the Papyrus of Nesi-Khensu

Egyptian Tantra Yoga by Dr. Muata Ashby.

Egyptian Yoga: Volume I by Reginald Muata Ashby

Egyptian Yoga: Volume II by Reginald Muata Ashby

Eliade, Yoga: Immortality and Freedom, Bollingen Series LVI, 2nd edn. (Princeton: Princeton University Press, 1969), PP. 370-372 ("Patanjali and the Texts of Classic Yoga").

Encarta Encyclopedia. Copyright (c) 1994

Encyclopedia of Mysticism and Mystery Religions by John Ferguson

Encyclopedic Dictionary of Yoga by Georg Feurstein

Ferdmand's Handbook to the World's Religions

Feuerstein, Georg, The Shambhala Encyclopedia of Yoga 1997

Flinders Petrie, Memphis, vol. 1, London 1909, pp. 16-17 pl. XXXIX.

From an inscription in the temple of Denderah, Egypt.

From Egypt to Greece, M. Ashby C. M. Books 1997

From Fetish to God in Ancient Egypt by E.W. Budge

From the Turin Papyrus.

Funk and Wagnals New Encyclopedia

G. Lafaye. Historie des divinit,s d'Alexandrie hors de l' Egypte. Paris, 18984, p.259

G. Maspero, The Passing of the Empires (New York, 1900).

Gods of India, p. 35. Martin

Guide to the Gods, Marjorie Leach

H. G. Rawlinson, Intercourse between India and the Western World, Cambridge, 1916, p. 92.

H.G. Rawlinson, Intercourse Between India and the Western World, Cambridge, 1916, pp. 93-94

Hatha-Yoga-Pradipika, The Shambhala Encyclopedia of Yoga by Georg Feuerstein, Ph. D.

Hermetica, Asclepius III, Solos Press ed., p. 136

Hero of a Thousand Faces by Dr. Joseph Campbell

Herodotus Book III 124; Diogenes VIII 3; Pliny N. H., 36, 9; Antipho recorded by Porphyry.

Herodotus: The Histories

Hindu Myths by Wendy O'Flaherty

History and Geography of Human Genes Luigi Luca Cavaiii-Sforza, Paolo Menozzi, Alberto Piazza. Copyright @ 1994 by Princeton University Press

HOLY BIBLE- King James Version

HOLY BIBLE- New Revised Standard Version

In Search of the Cradle of Civilization, 1995, co-authored by Georg Feuerstein, David Frawley, and Subhash Kak.

Indian Myth and Legend, Donald A. Mckenzie

Indian Mythology, Veronica Ions

Initiation Into Egyptian Yoga by Dr. Muata Ashby.

Inscription at the Delphic Oracle. From Plutarch, Morals, Familiar Quotations, John Bartlett

Integral Yoga by Swami Jyotirmayananda

International Society for Krishna Consciousness

J. H. Breasted: Cambridge Ancient History (Edit. 1924), Vol. II, p. 120.

J. R. Lukacs, ed., pp. 59-75. New York: Plenum.

J.C.Harke, "The Indian Terracottas from Ancient Memphis: Are they really Indian?, Dr. Debala Mitra Volume, Delhi, 1991, pp. 55-61

Jnana Yoga by Swami Jyotirmayananda

John Marshal, Taxila, vols, II and III, London and New York, 1951, p. 605, pl. 186(e)

K. G. Krishnan, Uttankita Sanskrit Vidya Arangnya Epigraphs, vol. II, Mysore, 1989, pp 42 ff

Kosambi, D. D., Ancient India a History of its Culture and Civilisation, 1965.

Krishnan, op. cit., pp. 17-18

Kundalini by Gopi Krishna

Legends of the Egyptian Gods by E. Wallis Budge

Life in Ancient Egypt by Adolf Erman

Living Yoga, Georg Feuerstein, Stephan Bodian, with the staff of Yoga Journal

Love Lyrics of Ancient Egypt translated by Barbara Hughes Fowler

Love Songs of the New Kingdom, Translated from the Ancient Egyptian by John L. Foster.

Macdonell, A. A., Vedic Mythology, Delhi: Motilal Banarsidass, 1974.

Mackenzie, Donald A., Indian Myth and Legend, London 1913

Manetho, W. G. Waddell

Mansouri El S. M., Art - Culture of India and Egypt 1959

Meditation: The Ancient Egyptian Path to Enlightenment by Dr. Muata Ashby

Memphite Theology, Muata Ashby

Merriam-Webster Dictionary

Microsoft (R) Encarta Copyright (c) 1994 Funk & Wagnall's Corporation.

Middle Passage BET Television

Mircea Eliade, Yoga: Immortality and Freedom, Bollingen Series LVI, 2nd edn. (Princeton: Princeton University Press, 1969), PP. 370-372 (Patanjali and the Texts of Classic Yoga).

Monier-Williams, Indian Wisdom, p. 19.

Mysteries of the Creation Myth, Muata Ashby.

Mysteries of the Mexiacn Pyramids, Peter Tompkins, 1976

Mystical spirituality texts of India.

Mysticism of Hindu Gods and Goddesses by Swami Jyotirmayananda

Mysticism of the Mahabharata Swami Jyotirmayananda 1993

Mysticism of the Mahabharata by Swami Jyotirmayananda 1993

Mysticism of Ushet Reckat: Worship of the Goddess by Muata Ashby.

Myths and Symbol in Ancient Egypt by R.T. Rundle Clark

Nagaraja Rao, op. Cit., p. 144; also Allchin, op. Cit.

Nekhen News, Expedition reports, Hierakonpolis, Petrie Museum of Egyptian Archaeology

NEWSBRIEFS EARLIEST EGYPTIAN GLYPHS Volume 52 Number 2 March/April 1999

Nile Valley Contributions to Civilization and the video The Ancient Egyptian Origins of Yoga Philosophy and the book Egyptian Yoga Volume 1: The Philosophy of Enlightenment – by Dr. Muata Ashby

Of Ancient Egypt.

On the Mysteries, Iamblichus

Osiris, E. W. Budge

Pale Fox, by Marcel Griaule and Germaine Dieterlen

Petrie Museum in London (UC nos. 8816, 8931, 8788)

Porphyry, On Abstinence from Killing Animals, trans. Gillian Clark (Ithaak, 1999). (= De abstentia, Book IV, cha 6)

Pottery Headrests from Narsipur Sangam, F.R. Allchin, Studies in Indian Prehistory, D. Sen and A.K. Ghosh, eds Calcutta, 1966, pp. 58-63

Pottery Headrests from Narsipur Sangam, F.R. Allchin, Studies in Indian Prehistory, D. Sen and A.K. Ghosh, eds Calcutta, 1966, pp. 58-63

Prehistoric India and Ancient Egypt 1956 Ray, Kumar Sudhansu

Proof of Vedic Culture's Global Existence by Steven Knapp

Raja Yoga Sutras, Swami Jyotirmayananda

Random House Encyclopedia Copyright (C) 1983,1990

Rashidi, Runoko and Van Sertima, Ivan, Editors African Presence in Early Asia 1985-1995

Rawlinson, op. cit., p. 93

Ray, Kumar Sudhansu, Prehistoric India and Ancient Egypt 1956

Reading Egyptian Art, Richard H. Wilkinson

Resurrecting Osiris: The Path of Mystical Awakening and the Keys to Immortality by Muata Ashby

Rig Veda by Aryan and Indian Sages

Ruins of Empires by C.F. Volney

Sacred Science by Schwaller de Lubicz

SADHANA by Swami Sivananda

Sanskrit Keys to the Wisdom Religion, by Judith Tyberg

Secrets of the Great Pyramid, Peter Tompkins

Seidenberg (1978: 301)

Serpent in the Sky, John Anthony West,

Serpent Power by Muata Ashby.

Stele of Abu

Stele of Djehuti-nefer

Stolen Legacy" by George G. M. James

Tao Te Ching by Lao Tsu

TemTTchaas: Egyptian Proverbs by Muata Ashby

The Aeneid By Virgil, Translated by John Dryden

The African Origins of Civilization, Cheikh Anta Diop, 1974

The Ancient Egyptians: Their Life and Customs-Sir J. Garner Wilkinson 1854 A.C.E.

The Asarian Resurrection: The Ancient Egyptian Bible by Dr. Muata Ashby

The Bandlet of Righteousness: An Ethiopian Book of the Dead translated by E.A. Wallis Budge

The Bhagavad Gita translated by Antonio DE Nicolas

The Bhagavad Gita translated by Swami Jyotirmayananda

The Blooming Lotus of Divine Love by Dr. Muata Ashby

The Complete Temples of Ancient Egypt, Richard Wilkinson, (C) 2000

The Cycles of Time by Dr. Muata Ashby

The Ebers papyrus

The Egyptian Book of the Dead, Muata Ashby.

The Glorious Light Meditation System of Ancient Egypt by Dr. Muata Ashby.

The Gods of the Egyptians Vol. I, II by E. Wallis Budge

The Great Human Diasporas, Luigi Luca Cavalli-Sforza, Francesco Cavalli-Sforza. Cambridge Encyclopedia of Human Evolution, Editor, Steve Jones

The Greenfield papyrus

The Hero With A Thousand Faces, Joseph Campbell. The Power of Myth, Joseph Campbell

The Hidden Properties of Matter by Dr. Muata Ashby

The Hierakonpolis Expedition returned for its fourth season of renewed fieldwork under the direction of Barbara Adams (Petrie Museum of Egyptian Archaeology and Dr. Ren,e Friedman (University of California, Berkeley).

The Histories, Herodotus, Translated by Aubrey de Selincourt- The History of Herodotus By Herodotus, Translated by George Rawlinson

The Hymns of Amun by Dr. Muata Ashby

The Kybalion by Three Initiates (Hermes Trismegistos)

The Living Gita by Swami Satchidananda 3rd ed. 1997

The Meaning of the Dead Sea Scrolls by A. Powell Davies

The Middle Passage : White Ships Black Cargo by Tom Feelings, John Henrik, Dr Clarke

The Migration of Symbols, Count Goblet D' Alviella, 1894

The Mystery of the Sphinx on video by John Anthony West

The Mystical Teachings The Asarian Resurrection: Initiation Into The Third Level of Shetaut Asar, Muata Ashby

The Mythic Image, Joseph Campbell

The Nag Hammadi Library

The Opening of the Way by Isha Schwaller De Lubicz

The Origin of Mathematics,

The Origin of Western Barbarism by Michael Wood

The Passing of the Empires *by* G. Maspero (New York, 1900).

The Power of Myth, Bill Moyers and Joseph Campbell, 1989

The Priests of Ancient Egypt by Serge Sauneron, Grove p114

The RIG VEDA Ralph T.H. Griffith, translator 1889

The Shambhala Encyclopedia of Yoga, Feuerstein, Georg, 1997

The Sivananda Companion to Yoga, Lucy Lidell, Narayani, Giris Rabinovitch)

The Story of Islam

The Tantric Way by Ajit Mookerjee and Madhu Khanna

The Tao of Physics, Fritjof Capra

The Turin Papyrus

The Upanishads, Max Muller, translator

The Upanishads: Breath of the Eternal, Swami Prabhavananda and Frederick Manchester

The Wisdom of Isis by Dr. Muata Ashby

The Wisdom of Maati: Spiritual Enlightenment Through the Path of Righteous Action by Dr. Muata Ashby

The Yoga of Wisdom, Swami Jyotirmayananda

Thrice Greatest Hermes by G.R.S. Mead

Transformations of Myth Through Time by Joseph Campbell

Traveler's Key to Ancient Egypt, John Anthony West

Tutankhamen, Amenism, Atenism, and Egyptian Monotheism (Edit. 1923), p. 86. Sir Wallis Budge
Vedic Aryans and the Origins of Civilization by David Frawley
Video presentation -Nile Valley Contributions to Civilization and the video The
Websters Encyclopedia
Wilkins, Hindu Mythology, p. 33.
Yoga International, {The Flight of the Alone to the Alone}, November 2000
Yoga International, {The Flight of the Alone to the Alone}, November 2000
Yoga Journal, {The New Yoga} January/February 2000
Yoga Vasistha Ramayana translated by Swami Jyotirmayananda
Yoga Vasistha Vol. I by Sage Valmiki -Translation by Swami Jyotirmayananda
Yoga Vasistha, Nirvana Prakarana Swami Jyotirmayananda, 1998

Appendix A
Pre-history and Dynasties of Ancient Egypt

Listed here are the known kings of ancient Egypt and the approximate dates of their reigns as well as important personalities in world history and the approximate dates of their existence.

Ancient Egyptian Kings and Queens and the dates of their existence	Important Personalities in World cultures and the approximate dates of their existence
10,000-5000 BCE PREDYNASTIC AND PROTODYNASTIC PERIOD 10,000 King Horemakhet (Great Sphinx) **Neolithic settlements** **5000-4000 BCE Badarian** **Naqada III** King "Scorpion" King Narmer "Baleful Catfish" **5,500-3,800 BCE EARLY DYNASTIC PERIOD – AND OLD KINGDOM PERIOD** **Neolithic settlements** **4000-3500 BCE Naqada I (Amratian)** **3500-3100 BCE Naqada II (Gerzean)** **1st Dynasty** Aha "Fighter" (Menes) Djer "Stockade" Djet "Snake" Den Anedjib Semerkhet Qaa **2nd Dynasty** Hotepsekhemwy Raneb Nynetyer(Netjeren) Wadjnas Sened Peribsen Khasekhemwy (Khasekhem) **3rd Dynasty** Sanakht Djoser (Netjerkhet) Sekhemkhet Khaba Nebka Huni	

OLD KINGDOM

4th Dynasty
Sneferu
Khufu(Cheops)
Djedefre (Redjedef)
Khafre (Chephren)
Menkaure (Mycerinus)
Wehemka
Shepseskaf

Imhotep
(Kamitan (Ancient Egypt) Sage of the Old
Kingdom Period)

5th Dynasty
Userkaf
Sahure
Neferirkare Kakai
Shepseskare
Neferefre (Reneferef)
Nyuserre
Menkauhor
Djedkare Isesi
Unas

6th Dynasty
Teti
Meryre Pepy I
Merenre (Nemtyemzaf)
Neferkare Pepy II
Nitoqerty (Nitocris)

7th-8th Dynasties
Group of unknown rulers

**3800-3500 B.C.E.- 1ST INTERMEDIATE
PERIOD**
9th-10th (Herakleopolis) Dynasties
Akhtoy I (Achthoes)
Neferkare
Akhtoy II (Achthoes)
Akhtoy III (Achthoes)
Merykare

11th (Thebes) Dynasty
Mentuhotep I ("The Ancestor")
Inyotef I
Inyotef II
Inyotef III
Nebhepetre Mentuhotep II

3500-1730 BCE MIDDLE KINGDOM
11th (Thebes) Dynasty
Sankhkare Mentuhotep III
Nebtawyre Mentuhotep IV

12th (Itj-Tawy) Dynasty
Amenemhet I (Ammenemes)
Senwosret I (Sesostris)
Amenemhet II (Ammenemes)

Yogi Meditating with Serpents
(Indus Valley 2500 B.C.E.)

Senwosret II (Sesostris)
Senwosret III (Sesostris)
Amenemhet III
Amenemhet IV
Sobekneferu

13th (Itj-Tawy) Dynasties
Many unknown kings

14th (Western Delta) Dynasties
Group of unknown kings ruling at the
same time of the later part of the 13th Dynasty

**1730-1580 BCE 2ND INTERMEDIATE
PERIOD**

15th (Avaris)("Hyksos") Dynasty
*6 Unknown Asiatic rulers
Apopi (Apophis)
Khamudi

16th Dynasties
Group of 15 Dynasty's Hyksos vassals

17th (Thebes) Dynasties
Seqenenre Tao
Kamose

1580-1075 BCE NEW KINGDOM

1539-1292 18th (Thebes) Dynasty
1539-1514 Ahmose (Amosis)
1514-1493 Ahmenhotep I (Amenophis)
1493-1482 Thutmose I (Tuthmosis)
1482-1479 Thutmose II (Tuthmosis)
1479-1425 Thutmose III (Tuthmosis)
1473-1458 Hatshepsut
1426-1400 Ahmenhotep II (Amenophis)
1400-1390 Thutmose IV (Tuthmosis)
1390-1353 Ahmenhotep III (Amenophis)
1353-1336 Ahmenhotep
IV(Amenophis)/*Akhenaten*
1336-1332 Smenkhkare
1332-1322 Tutankhamun
1322-1319 Aya
1319-1292 Horemheb

1292-1190 19th (Thebes) Dynasty
1292-1290 Ramesses I (Ramses)
1290-1279 Sety I (Sethos)
1279-1213 Ramesses II (Ramses) "Ramses The
Great"
1213-1204 Merneptah
1204-1198 Sety II (Sethos)
1204-1200 Amenmesse
1198-1193 Siptah
1193-1190 Tewosret
1190-1075 20th (Thebes) Dynasty
1190-1187 Sethnakhte
1187-1156 Ramesses III(Ramses)
1156-1150 Ramesses IV(Ramses)
1150-1145 Ramesses V(Ramses)

Code of Hammurabi
(fl. 1792-1750 B.C.E.).

Aryan Culture in India Emerges
(2000-1500 B.C.E.)

Abraham ?
(c. 1900-1800 B.C.E.?)

Moses ?
(1200 B.C.E.?)

1150-1145 Ramesses V(Ramses)	
1145-1137 Ramesses VI(Ramses)	
1137-1129 Ramesses VII(Ramses)	
1128-1126 Ramesses VIII(Ramses)	
1126-1108 Ramesses IX(Ramses)	
1108-1104 Ramesses X(Ramses)	
1104-1075 Ramesses XI(Ramses)	
1075-656 BCE 3RD INTERMEDIATE	
1075-945 21st (Tanis) Dynasties	
1075-1049 Smendes	
1049-1045 Amenemnisu	
1045-997 Psusennes I	
999-990 Amenemope (Amenophthis)	
990-984 Osorkon the Elder (Osochor)	
984-959 Siamun	
959-945 Psusennes II	
945-712 22nd (Bubastis) Dynasties	
945-924 Shoshenq I	
924-889 Osorkon I	
889-874 Takelot I	
874-835 Osorkon II	
830-780 Shoshenq III	
780-736 Pemay	
763-725 Shoshenq V	
838-712 23rd Dynasties	
825-800 Takelot II	
796-768 Osorkon III	**Homer**
773-766 Takelot III	(Greek author of Iliad and the Odyssey – 800
766-747 Amunrud	B.C.E.)
727-712 24th (Sais) Dynasties	
727-719 Tefnakhte	
719-712 Bakenrenef (Bocchoris)	
760-656 25th ("Nubian" or "Kushite") Dynasties	
760-747 Kashta	
747-716 Piye (Piankhy)	
716-702 Shabaka	
702-690 Shebitku	
690-664 Taharqa	
664-656 Tantamani	
664-332 BCE LATE PERIOD	
664-525 26th (Sais) Dynasty	**Lao Tzu** (Taoism - China)
664-610 Psamtik I (Psammetichus)	(c. 604- c. 531 B.C.E.)
610-595 Necho II	
595-589 Psamtik II (Psammetichus)	**Zoroaster, or Zarathustra** (Zoroastrianism)
589-570 Apries	(c. 628- c. 551 B.C.E.)
570-526 Amasis	
525-405 27th Dynasty (Persian Conquest)	**Valmiki (Indian Sage)**
1st Persian occupation	(Author of the Ramayana)
521-486 Darius I	
486-466 Xerxes I	**Pythagoras** (Pythagoreanism)
409-399 28th (Sais) Dynasty	(c. 580- c. 500 B.C.E.).
409-399 Amyrtaeos	
399-380 29th (Mendes) Dynasty	**Buddha, name given to Siddhartha Gautama**
399-393 Nefaarud I (Nepherites)	(Buddhism- India)
393-381 Hakor (Achoris)	**(c. 563- c. 483 B.C.E.)**
381 Nefaarud II(Nepherites)	
	Vyasa (Indian Sage)
	(Author of the Mahabharata)
381-343 30th (Sebennytos) Dynasty	
381-362 Nakhtnebef (Nectanebo I)	**Mahavira (Jainism - India)**
365-362 Djedhor (Teos)	(c. 550 B.C.E.)
362-343 Nakhtnebef (Nectanebo II)	

343-332 31st Dynasty (Persian) 2nd Persian occupation **332 BCE-AD HELLENISTIC CONQUEST PERIOD** **332-305 32nd Dynasty (Alexandria)("Macedonian")** 332-323 Alexander III the Great 323-317 Philip III Arrhidaeus 323-310 Alexander IV 323-305 Ptolemy(Ptolemy I) **305-30 33rd Dynasty (Alexandria)("Ptolemaic")** 305-282 Ptolemy I Soter I 285-246 Ptolemy II Philadelphos 246-221 Ptolemy III Euergetes I 221-205 Ptolemy IV Philopator 205-180 Ptolemy V Epiphanes 180-164 Ptolemy VI Philopator 170-164 Ptolemy VIII Euergetes II 164 Ptolemy VII Neos Philopator 163-145 Ptolemy VI Philometor 145-116 Ptolemy VIII Euergetes II 116-110 Ptolemy IX Soter II 110-109 Ptolemy X Alexander I 109-107 Ptolemy IX Soter II 107-88 Ptolemy X Alexander I 88-80 Ptolemy IX Soter II 80 Ptolemy XI Alexander II 80-51 Ptolemy XII Neos Dionysos 51-30 Cleopatra VII 51-47 Ptolemy XIII 47-44 Ptolemy XIV 44-30 Ptolemy XV Caesarion **332 BCE-A.C.E. ROMAN CONQUEST PERIOD** 30 BCE-14 A.C.E. Augustus	**Socrates** (Greek Sage) (469-399 B.C.E.) **Plato** (Platonism) (427-347 B.C.E.) **Herodotus** (c. 484-425 B.C.E.) **Ashoka, emperor of India** (c. 274-136 B.C.E.) **Patanjali** –Raja Yoga Sutras (200 B.C.E.)
394 A.C.E. COPTIC CHRISTIAN CONQUEST PERIOD 394 A.C.E. Theodosius adopted Christianity as the state religion of Rome	**Apollonius (Greek Sage)** (50 B.C.E.-50 A.C.E.) **Jesus** (Christianity) (0 A.C.E.)
ARAB AND MUSLIM CONQUEST PERIOD (c. 700 A.C.E.)	**Roman Catholic Christian Emperor Justinian decrees that all Egyptian temples should be closed.** c. 550 century A.C.E. **Muhammad (Islam)** (c. 570-632 A.C.E.)

Appendix B

Basic Criteria of Civilization

In order to be considered a "Civilization," along with organized complex sociopolitical institutions, art, myt[h] agriculture, writing, and mathematics a culture must promote the following:

❶

A Civilization acknowledges the Philosophy of Universal Life

❷

A Civilization creates ethical institutions that support the Philosophy of Universal life
(Social, economic and political)

❸

A Civilization promotes transference of culture of Universal life
(traditions, rituals and ideals (ethics) in educational system (Free education-Literacy 100% Ex. Sweden)) and in government)

❹

A Civilization promotes Spiritual Conscience and Effective Spiritual Evolution
(Self-realization, spiritual evolution)

❺

A Civilization promotes health and well-being of ALL people, and nature:
protecting the rights of children, the poor, the infirm (Free healthcare), without cultural bias. Protecting animals and replenishes natural resources.

❻

A civilization manifests as
Well-ordered society with the majority of the population living in balance, truth, peace, contentment and non-violence.

Caring Culture in a Civilized Society

People (Caring) ↙ ↘ Young + Old	Nature (usage)	Government (social institutions)
<u>3 Basic Needs</u> Food Shelter Opportunity (Progeny, Career Advancement, Self-realization	Purity Replenishment	Ethics Justice (Social/Economic) Meritocracy Council of Elders Education (Writing, Math)

A "civilization" manifests a caring culture. A caring culture is a culture that provides for its people the three basic needs of life, protects the land and replenishes it while keeping it in trust for the future generations and its government institutions are created with a basis of ethics and spiritual consciousness.

General Index

Other Books From C M Books

P.O.Box 570459
Miami, Florida, 33257
(305) 378-6253 Fax: (305) 378-6253

This book is part of a series on the study and practice of Ancient Egyptian Yoga and Mystical Spirituality based on the writings of Dr. Muata Abhaya Ashby. They are also part of the Egyptian Yoga Course provided by the Sema Institute of Yoga. Below you will find a listing of the other books in this series. For more information send for the Egyptian Yoga Book-Audio-Video Catalog or the Egyptian Yoga Course Catalog.

Now you can study the teachings of Egyptian and Indian Yoga wisdom and Spirituality with the Egyptian Yoga Mystical Spirituality Series. The Egyptian Yoga Series takes you through the Initiation process and lead you to understand the mysteries of the soul and the Divine and to attain the highest goal of life: ENLIGHTENMENT. The *Egyptian Yoga Series*, takes you on an in depth study of Ancient Egyptian mythology and their inner mystical meaning. Each Book is prepared for the serious student of the mystical sciences and provides a study of the teachings along with exercises, assignments and projects to make the teachings understood and effective in real life. The Series is part of the Egyptian Yoga course but may be purchased even if you are not taking the course. The series is ideal for study groups.

Prices subject to change.

1. EGYPTIAN YOGA: THE PHILOSOPHY OF ENLIGHTENMENT An original, fully illustrated work, including hieroglyphs, detailing the meaning of the Egyptian mysteries, tantric yoga, psycho-spiritual and physical exercises. Egyptian Yoga is a guide to the practice of the highest spiritual philosophy which leads to absolute freedom from human misery and to immortality. It is well known by scholars that Egyptian philosophy is the basis of Western and Middle Eastern religious philosophies such as *Christianity, Islam, Judaism,* the *Kabala,* and Greek philosophy, but what about Indian philosophy, Yoga and Taoism? What were the original teachings? How can they be practiced today? What is the source of pain and suffering in the world and what is the solution? Discover the deepest mysteries of the mind and universe within and outside of your self. 8.5" X 11" ISBN: 1-884564-01-1 Soft $19.95

2. EGYPTIAN YOGA II: The Supreme Wisdom of Enlightenment by Dr. Muata Ashby ISBN 1-884564-39-9 $22.95 U.S. In this long awaited sequel to *Egyptian Yoga: The Philosophy of Enlightenment* you will take a fascinating and enlightening journey back in time and discover the teachings which constituted the epitome of Ancient Egyptian spiritual wisdom. What are the disciplines which lead to the fulfillment of all desires? Delve into the three states of consciousness (waking, dream and deep sleep) and the fourth state which transcends them all, Neberdjer, "The Absolute." These teachings of the city of Waset (Thebes) were the crowning achievement of the Sages of Ancient Egypt. They establish the standard mystical keys for understanding the profound mystical symbolism of the Triad of human consciousness.

3. THE KAMITAN DIET GUIDE TO HEALTH, DIET AND FASTING Health issues have always been important to human beings since the beginning of time. The earliest records of history show that the art of healing was held in high esteem since the time of Ancient Egypt. In the early 20th century, medical doctors had almost attained the status of sainthood by the promotion of the idea that they alone were "scientists" while other healing modalities and traditional healers who did not follow the "scientific method' were nothing but superstitious, ignorant charlatans who at best would take the money of their clients and at worst kill them with the unscientific "snake oils" and "irrational theories". In the late 20th century, the failure of the modern medical establishment's ability to lead the general public to good health, promoted the move by many in society towards "alternative medicine". Alternative medicine disciplines are those healing modalities which do not adhere to the philosophy of allopathic medicine. Allopathic medicine is what medical doctors practice by an large. It is the theory that disease is caused by agencies outside the body such as bacteria, viruses or physical means which affect the body. These can therefore be treated by medicines and therapies The natural healing method began in the absence of extensive technologies with the idea that all the answers for health may be found in nature or rather, the deviation from nature.

Therefore, the health of the body can be restored by correcting the aberration and thereby restoring balance. This is the area that will be covered in this volume. Allopathic techniques have their place in the art of healing. However, we should not forget that the body is a grand achievement of the spirit and built into it is the capacity to maintain itself and heal itself. Ashby, Muata ISBN: 1-884564-49-6 $24.95

4.   INITIATION INTO EGYPTIAN YOGA Shedy: Spiritual discipline or program, to go deeply into the mysteries, to study the mystery teachings and literature profoundly, to penetrate the mysteries. You will learn about the mysteries of initiation into the teachings and practice of Yoga and how to become an Initiate of the mystical sciences. This insightful manual is the first in a series which introduces you to the goals of daily spiritual and yoga practices: Meditation, Diet, Words of Power and the ancient wisdom teachings. 8.5" X 11" ISBN 1-884564-02-X   Soft Cover $24.95 U.S.

5.   *THE AFRICAN ORIGINS OF CIVILIZATION, MYSTICAL RELIGION AND YOGA PHILOSOPHY* HARD COVER EDITION ISBN: 1-884564-50-X $80.00 U.S.   81/2" X 11" Part 1, Part 2, Part 3 in one volume 683 Pages Hard Cover First Edition Three volumes in one. Over the past several years I have been asked to put together in one volume the most important evidences showing the correlations and common teachings between Kamitan (Ancient Egyptian) culture and religion and that of India. The questions of the history of Ancient Egypt, and the latest archeological evidences showing civilization and culture in Ancient Egypt and its spread to other countries, has intrigued many scholars as well as mystics over the years. Also, the possibility that Ancient Egyptian Priests and Priestesses migrated to Greece, India and other countries to carry on the traditions of the Ancient Egyptian Mysteries, has been speculated over the years as well. In chapter 1 of the book *Egyptian Yoga The Philosophy of Enlightenment,* 1995, I first introduced the deepest comparison between Ancient Egypt and India that had been brought forth up to that time. Now, in the year 2001 this new book, *THE AFRICAN ORIGINS OF CIVILIZATION, MYSTICAL RELIGION AND YOGA PHILOSOPHY,* more fully explores the motifs, symbols and philosophical correlations between Ancient Egyptian and Indian mysticism and clearly shows not only that Ancient Egypt and India were connected culturally but also spiritually. How does this knowledge help the spiritual aspirant? This discovery has great importance for the Yogis and mystics who follow the philosophy of Ancient Egypt and the mysticism of India. It means that India has a longer history and heritage than was previously understood. It shows that the mysteries of Ancient Egypt were essentially a yoga tradition which did not die but rather developed into the modern day systems of Yoga technology of India. It further shows that African culture developed Yoga Mysticism earlier than any other civilization in history. All of this expands our understanding of the unity of culture and the deep legacy of Yoga, which stretches into the distant past, beyond the Indus Valley civilization, the earliest known high culture in India as well as the Vedic tradition of Aryan culture. Therefore, Yoga culture and mysticism is the oldest known tradition of spiritual development and Indian mysticism is an extension of the Ancient Egyptian mysticism. By understanding the legacy which Ancient Egypt gave to India the mysticism of India is better understood and by comprehending the heritage of Indian Yoga, which is rooted in Ancient Egypt the Mysticism of Ancient Egypt is also better understood. This expanded understanding allows us to prove the underlying kinship of humanity, through the common symbols, motifs and philosophies which are not disparate and confusing teachings but in reality expressions of the same study of truth through metaphysics and mystical realization of Self. (HARD COVER)

6.   AFRICAN ORIGINS BOOK 1 PART 1 African Origins of African Civilization, Religion, Yoga Mysticism and Ethics Philosophy-Soft Cover $24.95 ISBN: 1-884564-55-0

7.   AFRICAN ORIGINS BOOK 2 PART 2 African Origins of Western Civilization, Religion and Philosophy(Soft) -Soft Cover $24.95 ISBN: 1-884564-56-9

8.   EGYPT AND INDIA (AFRICAN ORIGINS BOOK 3 PART 3) African Origins of Eastern Civilization, Religion, Yoga Mysticism and Philosophy-Soft Cover $29.95 (Soft) ISBN: 1-884564-57-7

9.   THE MYSTERIES OF ISIS: The Path of Wisdom, Immortality and Enlightenment   Through the study of ancient myth and the illumination of initiatic understanding the idea of God is expanded from the mythological comprehension to the metaphysical. Then this metaphysical understanding is related to you, the student, so as to begin understanding your true divine nature. ISBN 1-884564-24-0 $24.99

10. EGYPTIAN PROVERBS: TEMT TCHAAS *Temt Tchaas* means: collection of ——Ancient Egyptian Proverbs How to live according to MAAT Philosophy. Beginning Meditation. All proverbs are indexed for easy searches. For the first time in one volume, ——Ancient Egyptian Proverbs, wisdom teachings and meditations, fully illustrated with hieroglyphic text and symbols. EGYPTIAN PROVERBS is a unique collection of knowledge and wisdom which you can put into practice today and transform your life. 5.5"x 8.5" $14.95 U.S   ISBN: 1-884564-00-3

11. THE PATH OF DIVINE LOVE The Process of Mystical Transformation and The Path of Divine Love This Volume will focus on the ancient wisdom teachings and how to use them in a scientific process for self-transformation. Also, this volume will detail the process of transformation from ordinary consciousness to cosmic consciousness through the integrated practice of the teachings and the path of Devotional Love toward the Divine. 5.5"x 8.5" ISBN 1-884564-11-9 $22.99

12. INTRODUCTION TO MAAT PHILOSOPHY: Spiritual Enlightenment Through the Path of Virtue Known as Karma Yoga in India, the teachings of MAAT for living virtuously and with orderly wisdom are explained and the student is to begin practicing the precepts of Maat in daily life so as to promote the process of purification of the heart in preparation for the judgment of the soul. This judgment will be understood not as an event that will occur at the time of death but as an event that occurs continuously, at every moment in the life of the individual. The student will learn how to become allied with the forces of the Higher Self and to thereby begin cleansing the mind (heart) of impurities so as to attain a higher vision of reality. ISBN 1-884564-20-8 $22.99

13. MEDITATION The Ancient Egyptian Path to Enlightenment   Many people do not know about the rich history of meditation practice in Ancient Egypt. This volume outlines the theory of meditation and presents the Ancient Egyptian Hieroglyphic text which give instruction as to the nature of the mind and its three modes of expression. It also presents the texts which give instruction on the practice of meditation for spiritual Enlightenment and unity with the Divine. This volume allows the reader to begin practicing meditation by explaining, in easy to understand terms, the simplest form of meditation and working up to the most advanced form which was practiced in ancient times and which is still practiced by yogis around the world in modern times. ISBN 1-884564-27-7 $24.99

14. THE GLORIOUS LIGHT MEDITATION TECHNIQUE OF ANCIENT EGYPT ISBN: 1-884564-15-1$14.95 (PB) New for the year 2000. This volume is based on the earliest known instruction in history given for the practice of formal meditation. Discovered by Dr. Muata Ashby, it is inscribed on the walls of the Tomb of Seti I in Thebes Egypt. This volume details the philosophy and practice of this unique system of meditation originated in Ancient Egypt and the earliest practice of meditation known in the world which occurred in the most advanced African Culture.

15. THE SERPENT POWER: The Ancient Egyptian Mystical Wisdom of the Inner Life Force.   This Volume specifically deals with the latent life Force energy of the universe and in the human body, its control and sublimation. How to develop the Life Force energy of the subtle body. This Volume will introduce the esoteric wisdom of the science of how virtuous living acts in a subtle and mysterious way to cleanse the latent psychic energy conduits and vortices of the spiritual body. ISBN 1-884564-19-4 $22.95

16. EGYPTIAN YOGA MEDITATION IN MOTION Thef Neteru: *The Movement of The Gods and Goddesses* Discover the physical postures and exercises practiced thousands of years ago in Ancient Egypt which are today known as Yoga exercises. This work is based on the pictures and teachings from the Creation story of Ra, The Asarian Resurrection Myth and the carvings and reliefs from various Temples in Ancient Egypt 8.5" X 11" ISBN 1-884564-10-0 Soft Cover $18.99   Exercise video $21.99

17. EGYPTIAN TANTRA YOGA: The Art of Sex Sublimation and Universal Consciousness This Volume will expand on the male and female principles within the human body and in the universe and further detail the sublimation of sexual energy into spiritual energy. The student will study the deities Min and Hathor, Asar and Aset, Geb and Nut and discover the mystical implications for a practical spiritual discipline. This Volume will also focus on the Tantric aspects of Ancient Egyptian and Indian mysticism, the purpose of

sex and the mystical teachings of sexual sublimation which lead to self-knowledge and Enlightenment. 5.5"x 8.5" ISBN 1-884564-03-8 $24.95

18.   ASARIAN RELIGION: RESURRECTING OSIRIS The path of Mystical Awakening and the Keys to Immortality NEW REVISED AND EXPANDED EDITION!   The Ancient Sages created stories based on human and superhuman beings whose struggles, aspirations, needs and desires ultimately lead them to discover their true Self. The myth of Aset, Asar and Heru is no exception in this area. While there is no one source where the entire story may be found, pieces of it are inscribed in various ancient Temples walls, tombs, steles and papyri. For the first time available, the complete myth of Asar, Aset and Heru has been compiled from original Ancient Egyptian, Greek and Coptic Texts. This epic myth has been richly illustrated with reliefs from the Temple of Heru at Edfu, the Temple of Aset at Philae, the Temple of Asar at Abydos, the Temple of Hathor at Denderah and various papyri, inscriptions and reliefs.   Discover the myth which inspired the teachings of the *Shetaut Neter* (Egyptian Mystery System - Egyptian Yoga) and the Egyptian Book of Coming Forth By Day. Also, discover the three levels of Ancient Egyptian Religion, how to understand the mysteries of the Duat or Astral World and how to discover the abode of the Supreme in the Amenta, *The Other World*   The ancient religion of Asar, Aset and Heru, if properly understood, contains all of the elements necessary to lead the sincere aspirant to attain immortality through inner self-discovery.   This volume presents the entire myth and explores the main mystical themes and rituals associated with the myth for understating human existence, creation and the way to achieve spiritual emancipation - *Resurrection*. The Asarian myth is so powerful that it influenced and is still having an effect on the major world religions. Discover the origins and mystical meaning of the Christian Trinity, the Eucharist ritual and the ancient origin of the birthday of Jesus Christ. Soft Cover ISBN: 1-884564-27-5 $24.95

19.   THE EGYPTIAN BOOK OF THE DEAD MYSTICISM OF THE PERT EM HERU $26.95   ISBN# 1-884564-28-3 Size: 8½" X 11" I Know myself, I know myself, I am One With God!–From the Pert Em Heru "The Ru Pert em Heru" or "Ancient Egyptian Book of The Dead," or "Book of Coming Forth By Day" as it is more popularly known, has fascinated the world since the successful translation of Ancient Egyptian hieroglyphic scripture over 150 years ago. The astonishing writings in it reveal that the Ancient Egyptians believed in life after death and in an ultimate destiny to discover the Divine. The elegance and aesthetic beauty of the hieroglyphic text itself has inspired many see it as an art form in and of itself. But is there more to it than that? Did the Ancient Egyptian wisdom contain more than just aphorisms and hopes of eternal life beyond death? In this volume Dr. Muata Ashby, the author of over 25 books on Ancient Egyptian Yoga Philosophy has produced a new translation of the original texts which uncovers a mystical teaching underlying the sayings and rituals instituted by the Ancient Egyptian Sages and Saints. "Once the philosophy of Ancient Egypt is understood as a mystical tradition instead of as a religion or primitive mythology, it reveals its secrets which if practiced today will lead anyone to discover the glory of spiritual self-discovery. The Pert em Heru is in every way comparable to the Indian Upanishads or the Tibetan Book of the Dead." Muata Abhaya Ashby

20.   ANUNIAN THEOLOGY THE MYSTERIES OF RA The Philosophy of Anu and The Mystical Teachings of The Ancient Egyptian Creation Myth Discover the mystical teachings contained in the Creation Myth and the gods and goddesses who brought creation and human beings into existence. The Creation Myth holds the key to understanding the universe and for attaining spiritual Enlightenment. ISBN: 1-884564-38-0 40 pages $14.95

21.   MYSTERIES OF MIND AND MEMPHITE THEOLOGY Mysticism of Ptah, Egyptian Physics and Yoga Metaphysics and the Hidden properties of Matter   This Volume will go deeper into the philosophy of God as creation and will explore the concepts of modern science and how they correlate with ancient teachings. This Volume will lay the ground work for the understanding of the philosophy of universal consciousness and the initiatic/yogic insight into who or what is God? ISBN 1-884564-07-0 $21.95

22.   THE GODDESS AND THE EGYPTIAN MYSTERIESTHE PATH OF THE GODDESS THE GODDESS PATH The Secret Forms of the Goddess and the Rituals of Resurrection The Supreme Being may be worshipped as father or as mother. *Ushet Rekhat* or *Mother Worship*, is the spiritual process of worshipping the Divine in the form of the Divine Goddess. It celebrates the most important forms of the Goddess

including *Nathor, Maat, Aset, Arat, Amentet and Hathor* and explores their mystical meaning as well as the rising of *Sirius,* the star of Aset (Aset) and the new birth of Hor (Heru). The end of the year is a time of reckoning, reflection and engendering a new or renewed positive movement toward attaining spiritual Enlightenment. The Mother Worship devotional meditation ritual, performed on five days during the month of December and on New Year's Eve, is based on the Ushet Rekhit. During the ceremony, the cosmic forces, symbolized by Sirius - and the constellation of Orion ---, are harnessed through the understanding and devotional attitude of the participant. This propitiation draws the light of wisdom and health to all those who share in the ritual, leading to prosperity and wisdom. $14.95 ISBN 1-884564-18-6

23. *THE MYSTICAL JOURNEY FROM JESUS TO CHRIST* $24.95   ISBN# 1-884564-05-4 size: 8½" X 11" Discover the ancient Egyptian origins of Christianity before the Catholic Church and learn the mystical teachings given by Jesus to assist all humanity in becoming Christlike. Discover the secret meaning of the Gospels that were discovered in Egypt. Also discover how and why so many Christian churches came into being. Discover that the Bible still holds the keys to mystical realization even though its original writings were changed by the church. Discover how to practice the original teachings of Christianity which leads to the Kingdom of Heaven.

24. THE STORY OF ASAR, ASET AND HERU: An Ancient Egyptian Legend (For Children)   Now for the first time, the most ancient myth of Ancient Egypt comes alive for children. Inspired by the books *The Asarian Resurrection: The Ancient Egyptian Bible* and *The Mystical Teachings of The Asarian Resurrection, The Story of Asar, Aset and Heru* is an easy to understand and thrilling tale which inspired the children of Ancient Egypt to aspire to greatness and righteousness.   If you and your child have enjoyed stories like *The Lion King* and *Star Wars you* will love *The Story of Asar, Aset and Heru.* Also, if you know the story of Jesus and Krishna you will discover than Ancient Egypt had a similar myth and that this myth carries important spiritual teachings for living a fruitful and fulfilling life. This book may be used along with *The Parents Guide To The Asarian Resurrection Myth: How to Teach Yourself and Your Child the Principles of Universal Mystical Religion.* The guide provides some background to the Asarian Resurrection myth and it also gives insight into the mystical teachings contained in it which you may introduce to your child. It is designed for parents who wish to grow spiritually with their children and it serves as an introduction for those who would like to study the Asarian Resurrection Myth in depth and to practice its teachings. 41 pages 8.5" X 11"   ISBN: 1-884564-31-3 $12.95

25. THE PARENTS GUIDE TO THE AUSARIAN RESURRECTION MYTH: How to Teach Yourself and Your Child the Principles of Universal Mystical Religion.   This insightful manual brings for the timeless wisdom of the ancient through the Ancient Egyptian myth of Asar, Aset and Heru and the mystical teachings contained in it for parents who want to guide their children to understand and practice the teachings of mystical spirituality. This manual may be used with the children's storybook *The Story of Asar, Aset and Heru* by Dr. Muata Abhaya Ashby. 5.5"x 8.5"   ISBN: 1-884564-30-5 $14.95

26. HEALING THE CRIMINAL HEART BOOK 1 Introduction to Maat Philosophy, Yoga and Spiritual Redemption Through the Path of Virtue   Who is a criminal? Is there such a thing as a criminal heart? What is the source of evil and sinfulness and is there any way to rise above it? Is there redemption for those who have committed sins, even the worst crimes?   Ancient Egyptian mystical psychology holds important answers to these questions. Over ten thousand years ago mystical psychologists, the Sages of Ancient Egypt, studied and charted the human mind and spirit and laid out a path which will lead to spiritual redemption, prosperity and Enlightenment.   This introductory volume brings forth the teachings of the Asarian Resurrection, the most important myth of Ancient Egypt, with relation to the faults of human existence: anger, hatred, greed, lust, animosity, discontent, ignorance, egoism jealousy, bitterness, and a myriad of psycho-spiritual ailments which keep a human being in a state of negativity and adversity. 5.5"x 8.5"   ISBN: 1-884564-17-8 $15.95

27. THEATER & DRAMA OF THE ANCIENT EGYPTIAN MYSTERIES: Featuring the Ancient Egyptian stage play-"The Enlightenment of Hathor' Based on an Ancient Egyptian Drama, The original Theater - Mysticism of the Temple of Hetheru $14.95 By Dr. Muata Ashby

28. GUIDE TO PRINT ON DEMAND: SELF-PUBLISH FOR PROFIT, SPIRITUAL FULFILLMENT AND SERVICE TO HUMANITY Everyone asks us how we produced so many books in such a short time. Here are the secrets to writing and producing books that uplift humanity and how to get them printed for a fraction of the regular cost. Anyone can become an author even if they have limited funds. All that is necessary is the willingness to learn how the printing and book business work and the desire to follow the special instructions given here for preparing your manuscript format. Then you take your work directly to the non-traditional companies who can produce your books for less than the traditional book printer can. ISBN: 1-884564-40-2 $16.95 U. S.

29. Egyptian Mysteries: Vol. 1, Shetaut Neter ISBN: 1-884564-41-0 $19.99 What are the Mysteries? For thousands of years the spiritual tradition of Ancient Egypt, *Shetaut Neter,* "The Egyptian Mysteries," "The Secret Teachings," have fascinated, tantalized and amazed the world. At one time exalted and recognized as the highest culture of the world, by Africans, Europeans, Asiatics, Hindus, Buddhists and other cultures of the ancient world, in time it was shunned by the emerging orthodox world religions. Its temples desecrated, its philosophy maligned, its tradition spurned, its philosophy dormant in the mystical *Medu Neter,* the mysterious hieroglyphic texts which hold the secret symbolic meaning that has scarcely been discerned up to now. What are the secrets of *Nehast* {spiritual awakening and emancipation, resurrection}. More than just a literal translation, this volume is for awakening to the secret code *Shetitu* of the teaching which was not deciphered by Egyptologists, nor could be understood by ordinary spiritualists. This book is a reinstatement of the original science made available for our times, to the reincarnated followers of Ancient Egyptian culture and the prospect of spiritual freedom to break the bonds of *Khemn,* "ignorance," and slavery to evil forces: *Såaa* .

30. EGYPTIAN MYSTERIES VOL 2: Dictionary of Gods and Goddesses ISBN: 1-884564-23-2 $19.99 This book is about the mystery of neteru, the gods and goddesses of Ancient Egypt (Kamit, Kemet). Neteru means "Gods and Goddesses." But the Neterian teaching of Neteru represents more than the usual limited modern day concept of "divinities" or "spirits." The Neteru of Kamit are also metaphors, cosmic principles and vehicles for the enlightening teachings of Shetaut Neter (Ancient Egyptian-African Religion). Actually they are the elements for one of the most advanced systems of spirituality ever conceived in human history. Understanding the concept of neteru provides a firm basis for spiritual evolution and the pathway for viable culture, peace on earth and a healthy human society.   Why is it important to have gods and goddesses in our lives? In order for spiritual evolution to be possible, once a human being has accepted that there is existence after death and there is a transcendental being who exists beyond time and space knowledge, human beings need a connection to that which transcends the ordinary experience of human life in time and space and a means to understand the transcendental reality beyond the mundane reality.

31. EGYPTIAN MYSTERIES VOL. 3 The Priests and Priestesses of Ancient Egypt ISBN: 1-884564-53-4 $22.95 This volume details the path of Neterian priesthood, the joys, challenges and rewards of advanced Neterian life, the teachings that allowed the priests and priestesses to manage the most long lived civilization in human history and how that path can be adopted today; for those who want to tread the path of the Clergy of Shetaut Neter.

32. THE KING OF EGYPT: The Struggle of Good and Evil for Control of the World and The Human Soul ISBN 1-8840564-44-5 $18.95   Have you seen movies like The Lion King, Hamlet, The Odyssey, or The Little Buddha? These have been some of the most popular movies in modern times. The Sema Institute of Yoga is dedicated to researching and presenting the wisdom and culture of ancient Africa. The Script is designed to be produced as a motion picture but may be addapted for the theater as well. 160 pages bound or unbound (specify with your order) $19.95   copyright 1998 By Dr. Muata Ashby

33. FROM EGYPT TO GREECE: The Kamitan Origins of Greek Culture and Religion ISBN: 1-884564-47-X $22.95 U.S.   FROM EGYPT TO GREECE   This insightful manual is a quick reference to Ancient Egyptian mythology and philosophy and its correlation to what later became known as Greek and Rome mythology and philosophy. It outlines the basic tenets of the mythologies and shoes the ancient origins of Greek culture in Ancient Egypt. This volume also acts as a resource for Colleges students who would like to set

up fraternities and sororities based on the original Ancient Egyptian principles of Sheti and Maat philosophy. ISBN: 1-884564-47-X $22.95 U.S.

34. THE FORTY TWO PRECEPTS OF MAAT, THE PHILOSOPHY OF RIGHTEOUS ACTION AND THE ANCIENT EGYPTIAN WISDOM TEXTS <u>ADVANCED STUDIES</u> This manual is designed for use with the 1998 Maat Philosophy Class conducted by Dr. Muata Ashby. This is a detailed study of Maat Philosophy. It contains a compilation of the 42 laws or precepts of Maat and the corresponding principles which they represent along with the teachings of the ancient Egyptian Sages relating to each. Maat philosophy was the basis of Ancient Egyptian society and government as well as the heart of Ancient Egyptian myth and spirituality. Maat is at once a goddess, a cosmic force and a living social doctrine, which promotes social harmony and thereby paves the way for spiritual evolution in all levels of society. ISBN: 1-884564-48-8 $16.95 U.S.

Music Based on the Prt M Hru and other Kemetic Texts

Available on Compact Disc $14.99 and Audio Cassette $9.99

Adorations to the Goddess

Music for Worship of the Goddess

NEW Egyptian Yoga Music CD
by Sehu Maa
Ancient Egyptian Music CD
Instrumental Music played on reproductions of
Ancient Egyptian Instruments– Ideal for meditation
and
reflection on the Divine and for the practice of
spiritual programs and Yoga exercise sessions.

©1999 By Muata Ashby
CD $14.99 –

MERIT'S INSPIRATION
NEW Egyptian Yoga Music CD
by Sehu Maa
Ancient Egyptian Music CD
Instrumental Music played on
reproductions of Ancient Egyptian Instruments–
Ideal for meditation and
reflection on the Divine and for the practice of
spiritual programs and Yoga exercise sessions.
©1999 By

Muata Ashby
CD $14.99 –
UPC# 761527100429

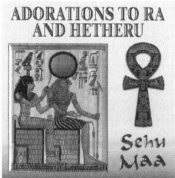

ANORATIONS TO RA AND HETHERU
NEW Egyptian Yoga Music CD
By Sehu Maa (Muata Ashby)
Based on the Words of Power of Ra and HetHeru
played on reproductions of Ancient Egyptian
Instruments **Ancient Egyptian Instruments used:**
Voice, Clapping, Nefer Lute, Tar Drum, Sistrums,
Cymbals – The Chants, Devotions, Rhythms and
Festive Songs Of the Neteru – Ideal for meditation,
and devotional singing and dancing.
©1999 By Muata Ashby
CD $14.99 –
UPC# 761527100221

SONGS TO ASAR ASET AND HERU
NEW
Egyptian Yoga Music CD
By Sehu Maa
played on reproductions of Ancient Egyptian
Instruments– The Chants, Devotions, Rhythms and

Festive Songs Of the Neteru - Ideal for meditation, and devotional singing and dancing.

Based on the Words of Power of Asar (Asar), Aset (Aset) and Heru (Heru) Om Asar Aset Heru is the third in a series of musical explorations of the Kemetic (Ancient Egyptian) tradition of music. Its ideas are based on the Ancient Egyptian Religion of Asar, Aset and Heru and it is designed for listening, meditation and worship. ©1999 By Muata Ashby

CD $14.99 –

UPC# 761527100122

HAARI OM: ANCIENT EGYPT MEETS INDIA IN MUSIC
NEW Music CD
By Sehu Maa

The Chants, Devotions, Rhythms and Festive Songs Of the Ancient Egypt and India, harmonized and played on reproductions of ancient instruments along with modern instruments and beats. Ideal for meditation, and devotional singing and dancing.

Haari Om is the fourth in a series of musical explorations of the Kemetic (Ancient Egyptian) and Indian traditions of music, chanting and devotional spiritual practice. Its ideas are based on the Ancient Egyptian Yoga spirituality and Indian Yoga spirituality.

©1999 By Muata Ashby
CD $14.99 –
UPC# 761527100528

RA AKHU: THE GLORIOUS LIGHT
NEW
Egyptian Yoga Music CD
By Sehu Maa

The fifth collection of original music compositions based on the Teachings and Words of The Trinity, the God Asar and the Goddess Nebethet, the Divinity Aten, the God Heru, and the Special Meditation Hekau or Words of Power of Ra from the Ancient Egyptian Tomb of Seti I and more...

played on reproductions of Ancient Egyptian Instruments and modern instruments - **Ancient Egyptian Instruments used: Voice, Clapping, Nefer Lute, Tar Drum, Sistrums, Cymbals**

– The Chants, Devotions, Rhythms and Festive Songs Of the Neteru – Ideal for meditation, and devotional singing and dancing.

©1999 By Muata Ashby
CD $14.99 –
UPC# 761527100825

GLORIES OF THE DIVINE MOTHER
Based on the hieroglyphic text of the worship of Goddess Net.
The Glories of The Great Mother
©2000 Muata Ashby
CD $14.99 UPC# 761527101129`

Order Form

Telephone orders: Call Toll Free: 1(305) 378-6253. Have your AMEX, Optima, Visa or MasterCard ready.

     Fax orders: 1-(305) 378-6253   E-MAIL ADDRESS: Semayoga@aol.com

Postal Orders: Sema Institute of Yoga, P.O. Box 570459, Miami, Fl. 33257. USA.

     Please send the following books and / or tapes.

ITEM

_____ Cost $_____

_____ Cost $_____

_____ Cost $_____

_____ Cost $_____

_____ Cost $_____

               Total $_____

Name:_____

Physical Address:_____

City:_____ State:_____ Zip:_____

Sales tax: Please add 6.5% for books shipped to Florida addresses

_____ Shipping: $6.50 for first book and .50¢ for each additional

_____ Shipping: Outside US $5.00 for first book and $3.00 for each additional

_____ Payment:_____

_____ Check -Include Driver License #:

     _____

_____ Credit card: _____ Visa, _____ MasterCard, _____ Optima, _____ AMEX.

Card number:_____

Name on card:_____ Exp. date:_____/_____

Copyright 1995-2002 Dr. R. Muata Abhaya Ashby

Sema Institute of Yoga

P.O.Box 570459, Miami, Florida, 33257

(305) 378-6253 Fax: (305) 378-6253

Printed in Great Britain
by Amazon